MOST SECRET AGENT OF EMPIRE

TALINE TER MINASSIAN

Most Secret Agent of Empire

Reginald Teague-Jones Master Spy of the Great Game

Translated by
Tom Rees

OXFORD
UNIVERSITY PRESS

OXFORD

UNIVERSITY PRESS

Oxford University Press, Inc., publishes works that further
Oxford University's objective of excellence
in research, scholarship, and education.

Oxford New York

Auckland   Cape Town   Dar es Salaam   Hong Kong   Karachi
Kuala Lumpur   Madrid   Melbourne   Mexico City   Nairobi
New Delhi   Shanghai   Taipei   Toronto

With offices in

Argentina   Austria   Brazil   Chile   Czech Republic   France   Greece
Guatemala   Hungary   Italy   Japan   Poland   Portugal   Singapore
South Korea   Switzerland   Thailand   Turkey   Ukraine   Vietnam

Published by Oxford University Press, Inc
198 Madison Avenue, New York, New York 10016

Published in the United Kingdom in 2014 by C. Hurst & Co. (Publishers) Ltd.

www.oup.com

Library of Congress Cataloging-in-Publication Data is available for this title
Minassian, Taline Ter
ISBN 9780190210762 (alk. paper)
Most Secret Agent of Empire: Reginald Teague-Jones Master Spy of the Great Game

Printed in India
on Acid-Free Paper

To the memory of Brian Pearce (1915–2008)

To the memory of my father, Levon Ter Minassian (1926–2009)

CONTENTS

CONTENTS

CONTENTS

CONTENTS

ACKNOWLEDGEMENTS

The first version of this, the first biography of Teague-Jones, was in French. The present account is offered to the English-reading public to whom in a sense it properly belongs. Tom Rees's elegant translation and Teague-Jones's own writings now presented in their original vigorous English make for a better book, not just a translation but in many respects a work of restoration. It will not, however, escape the reader that some of the details picked out here as examples of the exoticism of British culture derive from the French lens through which this historian has examined them. The product of a meeting beyond the grave between the descendant of a Dashnak revolutionary and a British agent pursued by a Bolshevik fatwa, the book owes a debt of gratitude to Brian Pearce for his assistance and to the historian Anahide Ter Minassian for her patient and painstaking scrutiny of the text. It would not have seen the light of day as an English version without the friendships I made during my adventures in pursuit of Reginald Teague-Jones. My translator Tom Rees, David Burnett, the publisher of Teague-Jones's Persian memoir and diary at Gollancz, Gill Boyes and Ann Randall who nursed him at Charlton House all provided invaluable help. I am grateful too to Antony Wynn, Matthew Lee, Christian Lequesne and Michael Dwyer, my editor at Hurst. And lastly my warm thanks go to Séverine Bézie for her vital contribution to the maps that feature in the book.

LIST OF ABBREVIATIONS

BSC	British Security Coordination
CIA	Central Intelligence Agency
DIB	Delhi Intelligence Bureau
GPU/KGB	Russian Secret Police; Intelligence Service of the USSR
IPI	Indian Political Intelligence; British intelligence agency in India
ISI	Inter-Services Intelligence; Pakistani intelligence agency
MI5	British domestic security service
NWFP	North West Frontier Province
OSS	Office of Strategic Services, United States intelligence agency formed during the Second World War and predecessor of the CIA
PWE	Political Warfare Executive
SIS, MI6	Secret Intelligence Service, British intelligence agency
SOE	Special Operations Executive

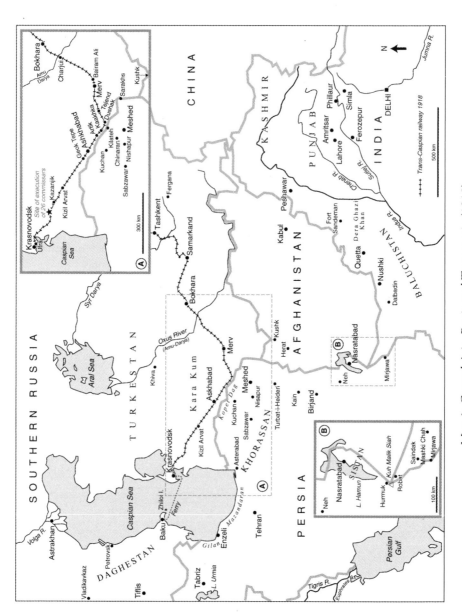

Map 1: Central Asia, Persia and Transcaspia (1918)

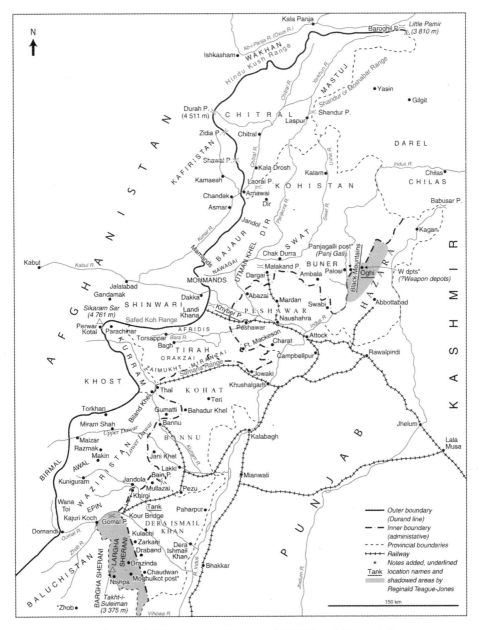

N

Kala Panja
Little Pamir
Baroghil P. ⚠ (3 810 m)
Ab-i-Panja R. (Oxus R.)
Ishkasham
WAKHAN
Hindu Kush Range
MASTUJ
Yakhun R.
Chitral R.
Yasin
Gilgit
Shandur or Moshabar Range
Durah P. (4 511 m)
CHITRAL
Shandur P.
Laspur
DAREL
Zidia P.
Chitral
Indus R.
Kala Drosh
Kalam
Chilas
Kamaesh
Laorái P.
KOHISTAN
CHILAS
Chandak
Arnawai
Asmar
Dir
Babusar P.
Jandol
Kagan
Chak Durra
Panjagalli post* (Panj Gali)
Malakand P.
BUNER
Palosi
Dargai
Ambala
Oghi
W dpts* (?Weapon depots)
Black Mountains
Abazai
Mardan
Swabi
Abbottabad
Khyber P.
PESHAWAR
Naushahra
Peshawar
Ft. Mackeson
Charat
Attock
Bagh
TIRAH
Campbellpur
Rawalpindi
ORAKZAI
Jowaki
Khushalgarh
Thal
KOHAT
Teri
Jhelum
Torkhan
Gumatti
Bahadur Khel
Lala Musa
Miram Shah
Bannu
Maizar
BANNU
Kalabagh
Razmak
Makin
Jani Khel
Kuniguram
Lakki
Bain P.
Mianwali
Jandola
Mullazai
Pezu
Khirgi
Wana
Tank
Toi
Paharpur
Kajuri Koch
Gomal P.
DERA ISMAIL KHAN
Dornandi
Kulachi
Zarkani
Draband
Dera Ismail Khan
Drazinda
Bhakkar
Nishpa
Chaudwan
Moghulkot post*
Takht-i-Suleiman (3 375 m)
*Zhob
Vihowa R.

PUNJAB
KASHMIR

Outer boundary (Durand line)
Inner boundary (administative)
Provincial boundaries
Railway
Notes added, underlined
Tank location names and shadowed areas by Reginald Teague-Jones
150 km

Map 2: The North West Frontier Province (NWFP) and Sherani Country

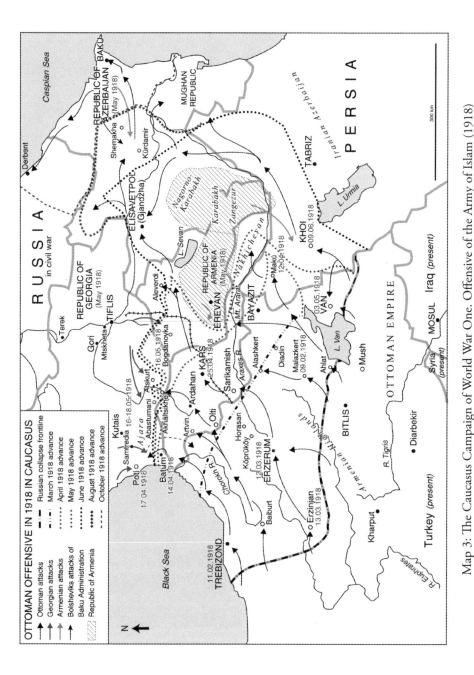

Map 3: The Caucasus Campaign of World War One. Offensive of the Army of Islam (1918)

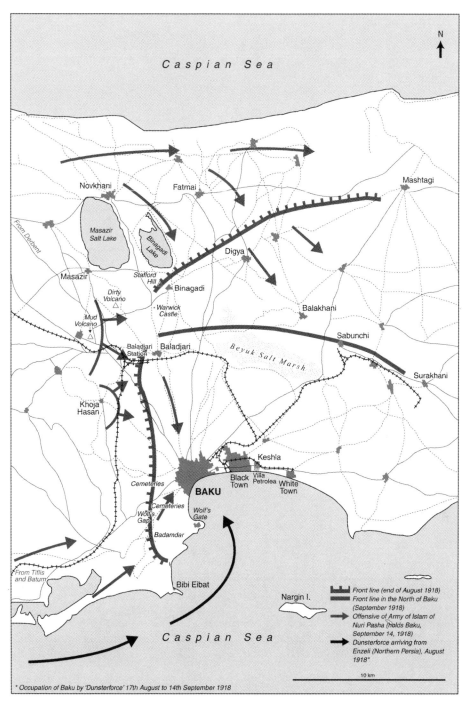

N

Caspian Sea

Mashtagi

Novkhani

Fatmai

Masazir
Salt Lake

From Derbent

Binagadi
Lake

Digya

Masazir

Stafford
Hill

Binagadi

Balakhani

Dirty
Volcano △

Warwick
Castle

Mud
Volcano △

Sabunchi

Baladjari
Station

Baladjari

Beyuk Salt Marsh

Surakhani

Khoja
Hasan

Keshla

Cemeteries

BAKU

Black Villa
Town Petrolea

White
Town

Cemeteries

Wolfi's
Gap

Wolf's
Gate

Badamdar

From Tiflis
and Batum

Bibi Eibat

Nargin I.

Front line (end of August 1918)

Front line in the North of Baku
(September 1918)

Offensive of Army of Islam of
Nuri Pasha (holds Baku,
September 14, 1918)

Dunsterforce arriving from
Enzeli (Northern Persia), August
1918*

Caspian Sea

10 km

* Occupation of Baku by 'Dunsterforce' 17th August to 14th September 1918

Map 4: The Battle of Baku (June–September 1918)

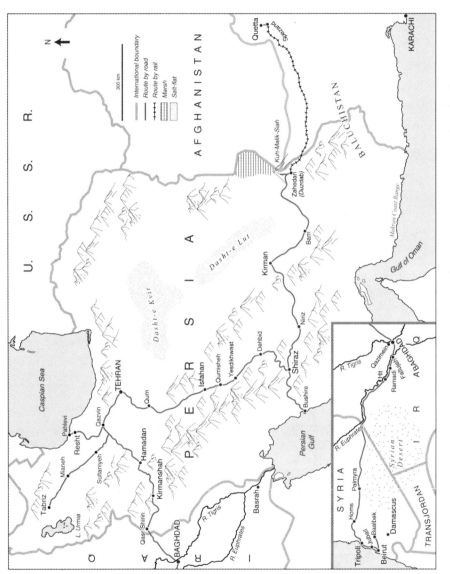

Map 5: From Beirut through Iran to India: Reginald Teague-Jones's journey with Zobeida (1926)

INTRODUCTION

An inscription on a tombstone can often serve as a useful starting point for a biography. But one would look in vain for an epitaph to Reginald Teague-Jones in Plymouth, where he died on 16 November 1988 at the age of ninety-nine. The 'spy who disappeared' had long since swapped his identity for that of Ronald Sinclair, yet there is no funerary monument with this name on it either. It is not that Reginald Teague-Jones, alias Ronald Sinclair, wished to depart this world without leaving any traces. On the contrary, he took care, within the authorised limits of a rigid professional code—that of a British secret service agent—to leave a profusion of clues behind, not for the descendants which his two marriages had failed to provide him with, but for 'some historian of the future'. When, like so many other servants of the British Empire, he presented his personal papers to the India Office in 1973, Reginald Teague-Jones consequently prepared the ground for the writing of this book. The letter which accompanied the deposit of his papers, to which access was only permitted after his death, even has the ring of a formal legacy: 'As regards the notes I sent you,' he wrote to a Foreign Office official, 'the India Office Library would seem to be the most fitting resting place for them. Perchance some historian of the future may dig them out and derive some interest from reading them. In the meantime, may they rest in peace!'[1] For despite the modest tone of the note enclosing this gift to his future biographer, Reginald Teague-Jones never had any doubt that his extraordinarily active and interesting life was worthy of a book about his exploits, even more so than any official recognition—though he had dreamed of a prestigious CMG as well as the OBE which he had been awarded. Indeed, as he wrote somewhat mischievously to his official correspondent, 'I cannot say more than wish you an equally interesting one', a phrase to which the latter added the slightly piqued marginal comment 'Yes, indeed.' Any reader of Teague-Jones's life will be driven to make a similar comparison and to suspect that his or her own life is grey, conventional and boring compared to his extraordinary youthful adventures on the fringes of a British Empire which still extended to the far reaches of the globe.

The writing of any biography rests on a losing bet. Even the most rigorous academic research into the archives cannot by itself reconstitute the full dimensions of someone's existence, or capture all the activities and psychological attributes of the personality that one is seeking to bring back to life. The portrait, never completely finished, is to an extent made up of the historian's subjective perspective. There is a mysterious personal pact between the subject of the book and his or her biographer, as though the latter was in some way predestined to write the biography, something that Walter Benjamin captured perfectly in one of his writings on history: 'It is therefore up to us to realise that the past is demanding restoration, of which perhaps a fragment happens to be within our power. There is a mysterious rendezvous between the departed generations and those to which we belong. Our presence on earth has been expected.'[2] My rendezvous with Reginald Teague-Jones took place in London in November 2003 on the top floor of the new British Library in the area of St Pancras station. On the third floor of this jewel of contemporary British architecture are now housed the printed works, the archives and the manuscripts of the India Office, the London headquarters of that part of the government of the British Empire. Like many former British agents, Reginald Teague-Jones had used the India Office library in its old premises in Blackfriars Road, where it was still to be found in the 1970s before the entire collection was transferred to the Asian and African sections of the new British Library. In this resolutely modern setting, there remain only a few items of furniture and some decor which recall the colonial origin of the collections in this holy of holies of international research. A magnificent East India Company chair by the entry door and some orientalist paintings in the reading room are discreet reminders of the British Raj in surroundings which have lost all other allusions to the old India Office.

It was through research on Baku at the end of the First World War that I first encountered Reginald Teague-Jones. He was an active agent in 1918 in the turbulent theatre of Central Asia and Transcaucasia, and it was some of the files from his personal collection that dealt with this subject and period that put me on his track. The papers, personal reminiscences, drawings, photographs and films kept in the British Library and Imperial War Museum struck me as being so interesting that, soon putting aside the original subject matter of my research, I began to forage through the entire collection, calling up one file after another. By this stage I had already fallen in love with the story of 'the spy who disappeared' four years after the execution of twenty-six commissars in Baku, only to reappear post-mortem in a *Times* obituary of 25 November 1988. The collection was so interesting, rich and well illustrated in relation to the key period for Teague-Jones's activities in Iran, Turkmenistan and the Caucasus that a biography simply demanded to be written. How could a historian of Russia and the Caucasus fail to be interested in an English agent of such wit and likeability, a man involved at the end of the First World War in the struggle against the Bolsheviks on the Transcaucasian and Transcaspian fronts? The idea seemed even more compelling because I had previously published work on the Soviet spy network in the Middle East during the same period. Furthermore, Teague-Jones's tracks in the Caucasus on the eve of its Sovietisation in 1920–1 crossed those of my paternal grandfather, Ruben Ter Minassian, known as Ruben, a revolutionary born under the

INTRODUCTION

Russian Empire, who had gone to the eastern vilayets of the Ottoman Empire to organise the Armenian self-defence effort before the First World War. He was a leader of the Dashnaks in the Armenian Revolutionary Federation and minister of defence in the short-lived independent Republic of Armenia from 1918 to 1920 before it was Sovietised like neighbouring Azerbaijan and Georgia. Although Teague-Jones may never have met him in person, he certainly noted information about him in one of his secret notebooks, and while in Georgia he met some of his close collaborators at a particularly critical period during the Sovietisation of Transcaucasia. The name of Ter Minassian appears several times in the travelling notebook which Teague-Jones brought back from Transcaucasia at the end of the First World War. These interlinked destinies formed the outline of a curiously foreordained project: it would fall to the granddaughter of a revolutionary Dashnak to undertake the biography of an English agent who was not particularly Armenophile—indeed, Teague-Jones was convinced that Great Britain needed to play the Muslim card if it was to continue to play a role as a great power on the Euro-Asiatic gaming table.

This biography would not have been feasible if Teague-Jones, who was in the habit of keeping a multitude of record-books recording his conversations and impressions and then destroying them from time to time, had not prepared his posterity by leaving an archive and even fragments of an autobiography composed at a later date on the basis of his travelling notebooks: notebooks which covered his experiences with a paramilitary force on the North West Frontier Province before 1914; memoirs of his solo mission in central Asia in 1918; an account of his adventures in Persia in 1926; and even a fictionalised story about the North West Frontier—everything which Teague-Jones left behind speaks of his intention to write an autobiography. Silence and secrecy being part of the fundamental discipline of the intelligence services, Reginald Teague-Jones was not to emerge from the shadows until after his death, a few months after the publication, under David Burnett's auspices, of his first book, *Adventures in Persia*. At the end of the 1980s, one of David Burnett's colleagues at the publishers Gollancz, who had been alerted by her mother while on holiday in Marbella, had drawn Burnett's attention to 'Ronald Sinclair'. He was living a sociable and studious life in retirement with his wife, Taddie, in an unremarkable modern block of flats called the Sirena Blanca of the kind one finds in seaside towns. The couple lived some distance from the sea in an ordinary three-room flat which at the rear looked out on the Andalusian mountains, the rocky aspect of which must have reminded Ronald Sinclair of the arid slopes of Waziristan which he had scaled in his youth. At the age of ninety-eight 'Ronald Sinclair' was looking for a good publisher for what was now a rather old-fashioned account of his adventures by car in Persia. The manuscript, like its author, immediately aroused David Burnett's enthusiasm. 'Ronald Sinclair' was attractive, witty, a man of irresistible charm, and before long the old couple, no longer capable of maintaining their independent existence, were to be repatriated by Gill Boyes, who had recently taken up a new career as director of a retirement home and who had been notified of the couple's existence by a doctor at San Pedro de Alcantara. It was at her suggestion that they moved back to Charlton

House in Mannamead Road, one of many similar residential homes in Plymouth, a town brimming with retirement homes and solicitors' offices, where David Burnett was to visit him on a number of occasions. Needless to say, for the twenty or so other residents of Charlton House at the time, 'Ronald Sinclair' came across as a colourful figure who fascinated those who talked to him with his conversation, upper-class accent and the general air of an old and eccentric British Army major.

Taddie, who was suffering from Parkinson's disease—and probably never knew about her husband's past—died shortly after the couple's arrival in Plymouth. Ann Randall, the nurse who was part of the social service team looking after 'Ronnie', was the other key figure in this period of his life. A genuine friendship sprang up between her and the elderly eccentric, a closeness which transcended the social gap between them to such an extent that the old soldier, who had no heir, went so far as to raise the possibility of leaving her his estate. Ann, who listened attentively to the story of his adventures, noted 'Ronnie's' terrified obsession that 'the Bolsheviks' might yet 'break down the garden door' to settle their scores with him. For Ann, who had never heard the word 'Bolshevik' before meeting 'Ronnie', this busy writer harnessed to his typewriter, teller of tall tales, keen gardener and animal lover, represented the quintessential English eccentric. Before long, one of Ann Randall's daughters was entrusted by 'Ronald Sinclair' with a personal mission to London: he asked her to find a copy of his films, which were held in an official library in Whitehall. It was to Gill Boyes that he confessed one day the secret of his first marriage to Valya Alexeieva, the love of his youth, whom he had met in the remotest part of the Caspian area somewhere between Baku and Krasnovodsk during the troubles of 1918. Now that Taddie was dead, could Gill Boyes help him to find Valya again? It was a surprising request from a man of his age, but that is how they came to make an expedition to London together to find Valya.

After many years working for MI5, Valya was now living in a state of extreme destitution in run-down housing in a poor part of the capital. Ronnie made it his job to bring her back and subsidise her living expenses by putting her up at his own expense in a separate room at Charlton House. How had he managed to find Valya after more than fifty years of separation? Was it through his friend Sonia Poliakoff? However it happened, the reunion came as something of a shock to Gill Boyes since, at the sight of 'Ronnie', Valya exclaimed 'Ah! Reggie.' This detail, added to the fact that the couple only spoke Russian to each other, introduced a certain piquancy to the situation even though 'Ronnie' continued to play his part to perfection, behaving as though there was nothing out of the ordinary, and attributing Valya's slip to her senility and poor mastery of English. Although he contributed to her keep, Reginald Teague-Jones took little interest in the practical details of the care that Valya's condition required, absorbed as he was in his daily writing work. Valya was soon to die in turn. But, still fit and lively thanks to Ann Randall's diligent care and rejuvenated by the expectation of the publication of his manuscript, 'Ronald Sinclair' declared to a young journalist who had come to interview him at the launch of his first book that he still enjoyed the pleasures of life to the full.

4

INTRODUCTION

His death came suddenly on 16 November 1988. The task of extracting the elements for an obituary from 'Ronald Sinclair's' papers fell to David Burnett. At this stage Burnett obviously suspected that 'Ronald Sinclair' had belonged to one or other of the British intelligence services. If he had any remaining doubts on the subject, while sorting out a quantity of personal papers he happened to find a large brown envelope—unfortunately empty—with the words 'MAJOR SINCLAIR, MI5' in capital letters. As for the manuscript based on the reports of his mission in Transcaucasia and Transcaspia, extracts of which Burnett would later publish under the title *The Spy Who Disappeared*, with a foreword and postscript by Peter Hopkirk, it confirmed that 'Ronald Sinclair' had been on a secret mission to Transcaspia in 1918. It was only three days after David Burnett's obituary, in a second obituary written by Peter Hopkirk, the famous specialist in the history of the Great Game, that the true identity of 'Ronald Sinclair' was revealed. He was none other than Reginald Teague-Jones, 'the spy who had disappeared' after the Soviet authorities had declared him guilty of the murder of twenty-six commissars in Baku. This public accusation, which was promulgated like an anathema, not only had the potential to disrupt the lives of Reginald Teague-Jones and his close colleagues, but also to prevent him from following a sufficiently discreet career in intelligence. Teague-Jones had thus disappeared in 1922 in order to pursue, under cover of various other jobs, a career in intelligence until his retirement at the beginning of the 1950s.

Despite the traces which Teague-Jones deliberately left in his voluminous personal files, this book would not have been possible without the help of a number of correspondents and informants, all of whom responded to my insistent requests for information. John le Carré, who had never heard of Teague-Jones before, advised me to get in touch with the chief historian at the Cabinet Office. There I was received by Mark Seaman, a specialist in intelligence and in the history of the Special Operations Executive (SOE). Although Teague-Jones's story meant nothing to him, he was able to explain the rules which govern the classification of archival material for the British secret services. In principle everything remains classified and therefore beyond the reach of the researcher. However, there is an exception in the case of the archives relating to the Indian Political Intelligence service (IPI), the very intelligence service for British India that Teague-Jones worked for at the outset of his career in India. This was a completely unexpected piece of luck, even though the declassified files, which have probably been expurgated and contain no signed reports, do not always enable the identity of a specific author to be established beyond doubt. While the research was slowly progressing, I finally managed to track down the last of Teague-Jones's close acquaintances, and to widen my English circle of 'the friends of Reggie'. David Burnett, the former editorial director at Gollancz, helped me to make considerable progress and to sharpen the outline of Teague-Jones's personality. Though I am unable to share his conviction, tinged with admiration, that Teague-Jones really was responsible for organising the shooting of the twenty-six commissars, I am grateful for his friendship and ready goodwill. Through David I was able to arrange a delightful, warm and friendly meeting with Ann Randall, the former nurse who had been part of 'Ronnie's' personal team at Charlton House. She had irreplaceable information for me about her patient's personality, and she also allowed me to consult documents and personal recollections of Teague-Jones which proved very useful.

This book retraces the exceptional story of a very loyal agent of the British Empire who was implicated in one of the most important events in the early history of the USSR: the affair of the twenty-six commissars. I was far from being the first in Britain to take an interest in the twenty-six commissars. Since the 1980s a historian of Soviet Russia, Brian Pearce, had devoted himself to the refutation of Soviet theses which attributed responsibility for the murder of the twenty-six Baku commissars to Teague-Jones—claims which had been regurgitated so often since the 1920s that Teague-Jones's guilt was now commonly acknowledged. A former member of the Communist Party of Great Britain, Brian Pearce had left the party in 1957, a year after Khrushchev's speech at the Twentieth Party Congress and the crushing of the uprising in Budapest. A talented French and Russian translator,[3] Pearce had had a double career as translator and historian. After a period of teaching English at the Soviet embassy in London, Pearce threw all of his intellectual energy and erudition—in every domain of Russian, Soviet and British history—into shedding some light on several fundamental episodes in the history of Anglo-Russian relations in the early years of the Soviet regime. It was through these endeavours that Pearce was to make an essential contribution to some misunderstood pieces of First World War historiography in *How Haig Saved Lenin* (1987) and *The Staroselsky Problem* (1994). In the first of these works, Pearce shows how the Allied victory in France in 1918 allowed Soviet Russia to survive in that crucial year without being overrun by Germany and the Central Powers. In the second, he describes Anglo-Russian relations in Persia through the medium of the fate of the Russian officers of the Cossack division in Persia from 1918 to 1920. In order to refute the legend of the twenty-six commissars, Pearce carried out a rigorous and intense enquiry, seeking out witnesses, pitilessly highlighting the contradictions and variants in the Soviet theses, and submitting the legend to a historical test based on empirical evidence. In so doing he attacked one of the founding myths of the Soviet regime which put a young British officer, Reginald Teague-Jones, in the dock, a man whom Soviet propaganda took pains to identify as the personification of British imperialism.

No doubt through the good offices of a former SIS officer, David Footman, or through some other agent using the India Office library at the time, Pearce managed to get in touch with Teague-Jones in 1979, proof that for those in inside circles his real identity was known. He was to receive a courteous but discouraging reply. Reginald Teague-Jones had no wish to stir up this old story, and warned him of the negative effects that his enquiry might have on the future development of Anglo-Soviet relations. Although Pearce did not carry out his project for a book on the twenty-six commissars, he did publish several important articles on the subject in the review *Sbornik*, a periodical publication issued by the Study Group on Revolutionary Russia, based in Leeds. It was through one of the correspondents of

INTRODUCTION

this group that I was finally able to contact Brian Pearce in the autumn of 2006 and form a firm friendship with him and his wife Margaret. It goes without saying that this book, particularly the chapter on the twenty-six commissars which he himself re-read a few months before his death, owes an enormous amount to our meetings, exchanges of letters, weekly telephone calls and to Brian's warm, outgoing and generous personality, thanks to which I was also able to consult the documents in his personal possession and the files that he had put together at the time he was carrying out his own research.

The scope of the present book is not confined to the scandal of the twenty-six commissars, but seeks to reconstitute what went before and what came after this defining moment, the main outlines of Reginald Teague-Jones's life, an agent who was born in an era when the Great Game was going full tilt and who died a few months before the Soviet withdrawal from Afghanistan and three years before the collapse of the USSR. With his much-travelled existence, passionate interest in the world, desire to understand, sharp eye for landscapes, faces and behaviour and, finally, his indispensable sense of humour brought to bear on the absurd aspects of missions which were sometimes far from exalted, Teague-Jones was an intelligence agent at the heart of the Great Game in both its old and new guises:

What was called 'the Great Game' was a very serious matter indeed. It was the struggle between Russia and Britain, starting in the middle of the nineteenth century, for domination of the vast region lying between the Caspian and Arabian Seas. As the Russians pressed down from Siberia and the Caucasus, the British thrust up from the Punjab and the Persian Gulf. By the beginning of the twentieth century a measure of stability had been reached in the eastern sector of the 'front'. Russia held West Turkestan while Britain held Kashmir, the Frontier Province and East Baluchistan. Afghanistan was left independent, a buffer state but with Britain acknowledged as the privileged neighbour, and with the Wakhan panhandle[4] preventing direct contact between Russians and British. In the western sector, however, the issue was still undecided. This western sector was Persia, and there the conflict for ascendancy went on until it was suspended in 1907 in face of the perceived threat from Germany to the interests of both contending parties.[5]

The subject of Harold Mackinder's theory at the beginning of the twentieth century, the Great Game for control of the Eurasian continent—the term which Arthur Conolly had popularised was later adopted by Rudyard Kipling—describes the strategic struggle between the British and Russian empires to establish the limits of their respective zones of influence in Persia, Afghanistan and Central Asia. As Brian Pearce has written, the first phase of the Great Game took place in the nineteenth century, and was brought to a close by the Anglo-Russian Convention of 1907. The great upheavals of the twentieth century—the constitutional revolution in Persia in 1905, the revolution of the Young Turks in the Ottoman Empire in 1908 and the Russian revolutions of 1905 and 1917—resulted in a constant reconfiguration of great power strategic rivalries in an arc stretching from the Balkans through the Caucasus and the Middle East to Central Asia. It is precisely on this terrain that one encounters Reginald Teague-Jones: in Russia in 1905, on the North West Frontier in 1914, in the Persian Gulf in 1917, in Central Asia in 1918, in the Caucasus and at Constantinople until the beginning of the 1920s, in Iraq and Persia in the middle of the 1920s. After the Second World War the development of strategic rivalries for control of the Eurasian area proved to be much more complex with the withdrawal of the British and the appearance of American power. Seen from the perspective of Central Asia, the cold war between the USSR and the West can be interpreted as a continuation of the Great Game. After all, did it not begin in 1946 with the Soviet refusal to evacuate northern Iran and end in 1989 with the Soviet withdrawal from Afghanistan? In the meantime, the assertion of American power in the Central Asian rimland, the decolonisation of the Indian subcontinent, the collapse of the Soviet Union and political emancipation on its Caucasian and Central Asian borders, and the 'balkanisation' of South East Europe were so many stages in the birth of a 'New Great Game'. From now on this played out in an area virtually identical to that of the end of the nineteenth century, from the Balkans through the Caucasus, extending to the 'Greater Middle East', a region defined by American diplomacy as including Afghanistan and Pakistan. Yet more complicated than the old version, this new Great Game involves a multitude of new actors, among them China, India, Pakistan, Russia and its former republics in Central Asia, Iran, Europe and the United States. Thus at the beginning of the twenty-first century the Great Game has become, in the words of the Tibetan specialist Alistair Lamb, a mass sport which has produced a quantity of players. There is no doubt that the explosive developments in 'Af-Pak', Central Asia and the Middle East would have been of enormous interest to Reginald Teague-Jones if he had lived to observe them. It is equally true that he had a premonition of the great geopolitical earthquake, the epicentre of which remains today, as yesterday, located in the tribal zones of the North West Frontier. Reginald Teague-Jones's exceptional destiny thus illuminates the origins of the chaos in which our planet finds itself today.

1

CHILDHOOD IN LIVERPOOL AND ST PETERSBURG

A young gentleman wearing a black *shapka* and a dark coat with a gleaming Astrakhan collar faces the photographer on the Nevsky Prospekt. With his fair skin, blonde hair and blue eyes, he could easily be mistaken for a young Russian from a prosperous St Petersburg family at the turn of the century. Outside, on the shores of the Gulf of Finland, the Russian winter lies deep. The boy has a slightly puzzled expression; he has one hand in his outer pocket, with the other slipped inside his new coat. His photograph will no doubt be sent to his mother and sisters who have stayed behind in England; his pose and Russian costume seem to make a kind of social statement. His gaze, which is not directed at anything in particular, hints at the innocence and pensiveness of a child. Although young Reginald does not know it, this time of his in Russia will determine the rest of his life. Like Rudyard Kipling's heroes—one is instantly reminded of Kim—Reginald Teague-Jones has been torn from his family circle under somewhat mysterious circumstances and is destined for an exceptional fate. Gifted with great intelligence and a variety of talents, he will travel through life like a free particle through space. Fatherless at an early age, childless, his family connections discreetly veiled, Teague-Jones's personal history is particularly hard to uncover; for although he is an assiduous diarist, it is rare that he refers to his childhood, his family and his friends. This omission can be attributed to social discomfort rather than to any difficulties in his personal life; his family origins, unlike those of the young Winston Churchill, give him no claim to belong to the British political elite. Reginald Jones's childhood—he would later hyphenate 'Teague', his middle name, to his surname—was full of travel and adventure from an early age. But his path also took him up the social ladder, thanks in particular to his education.

Liverpool: birthplace and departure point

Pendennis Street

Reginald Teague-Jones rarely referred to the details of his private and family life. The only clue he gave was a reference in his book, *Adventures in Persia*, published in 1988, the year of his death, to his birth almost a century earlier in Lancashire in 1889. This vague statement, taken with his change of identity in 1922, avoided the risk of his family being identified. In changing his name he was especially concerned to protect his mother and three sisters against any possible Bolshevik reprisals. There was probably a secondary reason too: in referring simply to Lancashire he could draw a veil over his place of birth—the outskirts of Liverpool—and his lower middle-class origins. Gill Boyce, the former manager of Charlton House, the retirement home in Plymouth where Teague-Jones ended his days, expressed great surprise that her former lodger was from Liverpool—nothing in his upper-class accent suggested such a background. The popular image of Liverpool is undoubtedly one of a tough place, but Teague-Jones did not actually come from the depths of the slums where immigrants, crammed together with working-class families, waited to take ship for some distant destination, or to try their luck in the great industrial port of Liverpool at the end of the nineteenth century.

It was at Walton-on-the-Hill, a parish on the north side of the Mersey less than 5 miles from Liverpool, that Reginald Teague-Jones first saw the light of day on 30 July 1889. The birth was at home, as was customary at the time, and was only registered eighteen days later, which again was not at all unusual. The child born at 55 Pendennis Street was the first-born of Frederick Jones and Elizabeth Deeley Smith, who had married the previous year on 14 July 1888 in the same parish of Walton-on-the-Hill in Holy Trinity Church in Breck Road, a short distance from Pendennis Street. Both were thirty-one years of age, but had rubbed shoulders with each other for some time since they lived a few doors away from each other in the same street.

It was doubtless his posting to a school in a rapidly expanding Liverpool that brought Frederick Jones to Walton. This was not his home city, since he was born in Worcester in the West Midlands, not very far away. Almost nothing is known of Reginald's father other than the fact that he taught foreign languages, which may help to explain Reginald's abilities in this field. He may have taught in a parish school, or in one of the schools financed by the industrialist and philanthropist, William Hartley, who had built a model village at Walton for the 1,200 workers in his jam factory where he provided them with houses to rent or to buy. Or he may have taught at home, as was often the case in England at that time. There is no clue to his reasons for moving from his hometown of Worcester to Liverpool other than the high degree of geographical mobility that was characteristic of British society of the day. Frederick's father, George Jones, who was not present at his son's marriage, is known to have been an agent for a manufacturer of organs. His firm on Commercial Road in East London produced harmoniums, American organs and concertinas, instruments for the church which had become an essential part of the Anglican rite.

The firm for which Reginald's grandfather worked remained in business from 1850 to 1906, and it seems to have been relatively prosperous. George Jones lived in Worcester. In 1891, a widower and already seventy years old, he had living with him a bachelor son Alfred who worked as a shop assistant in a grocery, and a daughter, Julia, who was single and a primary schoolteacher. It is possible that George Jones heard the performance of Elgar's organ sonata played on the organ of Worcester Cathedral on 8 July 1895; but there is no way of knowing whether the organ vendor, who offered a more modest range of products, went to concerts or even whether he was fond of music at all. Reginald's forebears on the side of his mother, Elizabeth Deeley Smith, provide some evidence of movement up the social scale to the levels of the middle class. Elizabeth's father George Smith, who was sixty-five at the time he attended his second daughter Elizabeth's wedding, simply described himself as a 'gentleman'. Born in Flintshire, in Wales, he had begun his working life as a drapery assistant, moving on to become a lick mercer, that is to say a dealer in fabrics made of silk or other expensive materials. Elizabeth Deeley—her mother's maiden name— was born on 23 November 1856 in Islington, North London. It must have been business reasons which led her father to set up in Liverpool in 1861, where the family settled in a house in Johnson Street in the Kirkdale district. It was a reasonably large household, made up, besides the parents, of Elizabeth's sisters Sarah and Mary, and mother-in-law, brother- and sister-in-law and a servant. The family moved house to Walton-on-the-Hill in Liverpool at some point in the following decade. This was a period in which the population of the district increased from 2,469 to 3,598, including 679 inmates of the new prison for the county of Liverpool.

Like many of the inhabitants of this neighbourhood on the outskirts of Liverpool, Reginald's parents lived in modest circumstances. With its straight lines and streets intersecting at right angles, the neighbourhood of Pendennis Street looks like a typical development of three-bedroom terrace-houses aimed at housing the lower middle classes. Although Reginald's parents did not live in one of the badly lit and ventilated slums built to house the working class, the succession of houses which they occupied together or separately, nos. 55, 73 and 75 Pendennis Street, must have been identical to each other owing to their uniform design. A more precise social picture of this neighbourhood, where the Jones family is known to have lived at least until 1894, can be gleamed from the 1891 Census.

When Frederick Jones arrived in Walton it appears that he rented a room in 55 Pendennis Street, where the only other occupants were two women of 'independent means', a widow, Jane New, aged fifty, and her sister Ellen, twenty years her senior. It may have been these two women who helped Reginald's mother at the birth of her first child, since the birth is registered to this address. Reginald's mother, who had previously lived at 73 Pendennis Street, must have found work in this neighbour-hood. She may have had a job as a servant in the household which appears in the 1891 Census. The family of the accountant who lived here, T. Simcock, included two young children whom she may well have looked after as nurse or housekeeper. The couple finally settled with Reginald in the adjoining house at no. 75, which had an extra room where Frederick Jones could give lessons. The Census also reveals the contrast in population densities even within the microcosm of this street. Pendennis Street was a world of employees with modest incomes who had come to Liverpool in search of decent jobs, but who were just as ready to leave the city to try their luck elsewhere, notably in the British colonies, and particularly in India.

Reginald stayed only briefly in Walton, spending his very early childhood in this small world where children played freely in the street. Perhaps his parents took him to visit the new Liverpool zoo, built in Walton in 1884, where the chief draw was Pongo the chimpanzee, the star attraction of the monkey house. Nothing but the old ticket-house now remains of the zoological gardens. The place was renowned not just as a zoo but also for the aesthetic success of its design. The monumental entry gates were crowned by a pair of Liver Birds in bronze, the mythical half-eagles, half-cormorants which symbolise the City of Liverpool. From 1911 onwards another pair took up their perch on the top of the two towers of the Royal Liver Building, looking down on the quays, the new icons of Liverpool.

Liverpool: 'Second City of the Empire'

Did Reginald Teague-Jones keep any memories of Liverpool? Were any images of the city imprinted on his young mind? It is tempting to think of Terence Davies's introspective and poetic film *Of Time and the City* (2008), a melancholy evocation of the disappearance of the Liverpool of his childhood after the Second World War. 'Liverpool is no longer the town I knew and loved as a child' he says of this work, which is a combination of autobiography, documentary and photographic archive. But the Liverpool of the 1950s to which Davies looks back longingly was already in economic decline, and quite unlike the extraordinarily active city of the end of the nineteenth century when it was a port serving the globe, at the height of its glory and claiming a place behind London as the 'second city of the Empire'. A slave-trading port from the seventeenth century onwards, then during the Industrial Revolution the great world port for cotton for the textile trade in Manchester and Lancashire, Liverpool had a period of fantastic growth in the nineteenth century. It was fed by a rapid rise in the population, nourished by the unceasing flow of immigrants from Ireland, where the potato blight spread rapidly between 1845 and 1849. In 1847, at the height of the Great Famine, some 300,000 Irish immigrants arrived in Liverpool. In many respects the place became an Irish city, to the point where it sent a member of the Irish Parliamentary Party as its MP to the Westminster Parliament.

Liverpool was at the peak of its power from the second half of the nineteenth and right up to the start of the twentieth century. There was frenetic and diverse growth in every sector, in the ports, the docks, trade, industry and insurance. The urban landscape combined notorious slums with triumphant modernity. For the new immigrants from nearby Wales on the other side of the Mersey Estuary, Liverpool offered the prospect of perpetual development. A total of 20,000 Welshmen settled there in the 1880s, looking for work in a town which incarnated the dynamism and modernity of the Victorian era. Liverpool became the informal capital of North Wales. In 1901 the city had 700,000 inhabitants. Archive footage from the turn of the new century shows the centre of Liverpool crowded with trams and businessmen in top-hats, and tall buildings whose facades reflect the power of money. The city which Teague-Jones knew was a 'world-city', which prefigures all the others he was to know during his lifetime, particularly New York.

As well as being a port of entry for the British Empire, Liverpool was also a port of departure for many young would-be emigrants. 'If Liverpool did not exist, it would have had to be invented' (Félicien de Myrbach, 1898) is the inscription at the entrance to St George's Hall, built in 1854. As a child Reginald was familiar with this landscape and absorbed the image of the fine colonnade of St George's Hall which he used to see through the tram window. He heard the hubbub of Lime Street Station and the noisy sirens of the steamships leaving for all the destinations of the world. In such surroundings how could one not long to travel? Like many young people in this generation who were encouraged to emigrate—particularly to Canada—Reginald was soon to slip his family moorings, apparently without much hesitation. He was thirteen when his father died in 1902, leaving his mother with four children and in some financial difficulty. It is unclear whether the family was still living in Liverpool at this time. However, some family friends offered to relieve Elizabeth of the care of her eldest son, to all appearances a very bright child, and to take the young Reginald to St Petersburg as a companion for their own son. This was a piece of luck for young Reginald, as it was common for a boy to start work at this age. And so, instead of crossing the Atlantic, Reginald Teague-Jones left London for Paris in 1902. There, the train which he caught at the Gare de l'Est would take him to Berlin, then on to Warsaw and Riga, and thence to his final destination, St Petersburg, capital of the Russian Empire.

An Englishman in Russia

It is discouraging for his biographer that Reginald Teague-Jones remained silent with regard to the circumstances of his voyage to Russia. Who were the friends who offered to look after Reginald during his stay in St Petersburg? What sort of affairs drew this well-off family to Russia? How did Reginald come to attend one of the best schools in St Petersburg? In the absence of hard facts, it is only possible to speculate on the basis of clues which surface here and there in the few fragmentary accounts which Teague-Jones devoted to this initiatory period in his life. It was an initiation into Russia, or more precisely St Petersburg, the window open on the Baltic, whose architectural splendours made a lasting impression on the young adolescent.

Dazzling St Petersburg

The horses on the Anichkov Bridge, St Michael's Castle, the Fontanka and Moika canals, the Nevsky Prospekt, the baroque gold and stucco of the Hermitage, the magnificent granite quaysides of the Neva, St Isaac's Cathedral, the Smolny Institute, the naval cathedral of St Nicholas, New Holland and Vassilievsky Islands—the fantastic topography of St Petersburg, a city built in nowhere land and from nothing, is above all else a feast of architecture marrying baroque with classicism. The young fourteen-year-old who had just arrived in the Russian capital was unlikely to have been interested in the imposing monuments designed by Rastrelli, Quarenghi or Vallin de la Mothe. But for three long years he lived in this city, absorbing its forms, its urban setting and layout. The friend who was looking after Reginald, perhaps a diplomat, or a language teacher like his father, or possibly a merchant, dealer or businessman, was a member of the small British community in St Petersburg. This community had been dominated since the nineteenth century by a small and very active nucleus of merchants, around whom gravitated diplomats, travellers, soldiers, sailors, engineers and craftsmen who constituted a 'communal-world'[1] in Marie-Louise Karttunen's phrase. This society of expatriates, which made a point of its distinctive social position and English identity, had much to offer by way of leisure pursuits and pleasures for members of the wealthy English middle class. In Russia they had freedoms which would have been denied to them by the Victorian codes of conduct which still prevailed in England. Given that he was not from the wealthy middle class, and had not hitherto lived in particularly comfortable circumstances, for Reginald the stay in St Petersburg was doubly exotic. It meant not only the journey to Russia, but also the crossing of a social frontier, which allowed him to mix with a section of English society that he would never have been able to meet on equal terms in England.

For an Englishman it was both agreeable and exciting to live in the capital of the Russian Empire at the beginning of the twentieth century. From the 1870s and especially the 1880s onwards, St Petersburg life had the seemingly justified reputation of providing the British colony with every conceivable kind of entertainment. It was reputed to be one of the gayest of the European capitals, at any rate for those living in the English community, which was large enough to make it possible to dine out every night without ever running the risk of meeting the same person twice. John Baddeley was the press correspondent for *The Standard* in St Petersburg for two decades. The picture he painted in 1921 of the English community in Russia was of a society entirely absorbed by the leisure pursuits and distractions which the imperial capital provided:

The British colony had passed through many vicissitudes to reach at the time of my arrival in Russia a stage that as far as regarded social amenity left really nothing to be desired. There were very few old people, the great majority of the leaders of the community being, by chance, young married couples, nearly all in receipt of good incomes and possessed of spacious apartments in St. Petersburg and pleasant country quarters at Ligovo, Murino, or elsewhere—with tennis lawns—where they spent the summer months and where they delighted to entertain their friends. There were pretty girls about, too, and altogether a more pleasant society, for a young man, it would have been difficult to find anywhere.[2]

Reginald, who was barely fourteen, was of course not old enough to take part in the social whirl and the dinners in town; but his easy acceptance of the new life, more glittering than his Pendennis Street beginnings, testifies to the freedom he felt. How could he not have been intoxicated by living in the heart of such a theatrical and spectacular capital city? It was an unforgettable experience. The magic of St Petersburg stimulated his adolescent imagination, as did his frequenting of smart English circles in the city, which gave him a chance of seeing or glimpsing imperial high society.

Like most of the English in the Russian capital, the family who had taken him in lived in the centre of St Petersburg. The British colony occupied an area that ran from Vassilievsky Island—where most of the British colony lived—to Anglisky Naberezhnaya (the English Quay) towards the south. It was one of the smartest quarters of the capital, and indeed both the Anglican Church and the British embassy lay within it. The richest of the English merchants lived alongside Russian aristocrats in mansions and splendid apartments on the English Quay. It is highly likely that Reginald lived there, near the Sheremetiev palace, the Naryshkin house and the mansions belonging to Baron Stiglitz and N. Rumantsiev where balls took place at the beginning of the twentieth century that were as brilliant as anything in Pushkin's time. The short article which Teague-Jones wrote about his memories of St Petersburg suggests that he lived in this prestigious quarter. He mentions the proximity of St Isaac's Cathedral whose brass bells woke him up in the small hours of the morning on the Sunday of 9 January 1905. He evokes the pale light of the winter sun shining through his double windows and the view which stretches before him. 'Across the neighbouring roofs, covered in a dazzling white blanket of fresh fallen snow, towered the great golden dome of the cathedral … and the magnificent granite quays of the Neva, while the other, three miles away, was lost in the haze of a distant sea of buildings.'[3] This description in fact corresponds with the view over the town from the English Quay.

St Petersburg was an opening into the Russian world he loved, but even more important for Reginald was the fact that it provided the means for climbing the social ladder within this England overseas, a real 'piece of England', according to the famous art critic Alexander Benois. For the time being he embraced its conventions, learning to speak English with the 'pure' accent and intonation used for generations by the English community of St Petersburg. Far from Liverpool and his dull suburb, he rubbed shoulders with the best society in town, and through the agency of his host family he took some steps outside the bounds of English society. Teague-Jones recalls having met a number of highly placed members of the Romanov Court, and even of having talked to Grand-Duke Nicholas. Was this Nicholas Konstantinovich (1850–1918) or Nicholas Nikolaievich (1856–1929), both of them Romanovs of elevated rank, and both equally fascinating personalities? Grand-Duke Nicholas Nikolaievich had led a tumultuous life. An orientalist with extravagant tastes, he had been despatched to Turkestan by Emperor Alexander III and had built a magnificent palace for himself at Tashkent. Or was it 'Nicolasha', Nicholas the Younger, a charismatic personality who was to be seen at military parades, and whose giant stature and strong, hoarse voice made a striking impression on those who encountered him? Some meeting of this kind certainly made a strong impression on the young adolescent who dreamed of adventures and military derring-do; even though the grand-duke's fate was not to be a great military leader. Popular with the troops in the imperial army, Nicholas Nikolaievich was commander of the 2nd Cavalry Division of the Guard from 1890 to 1905. He was then, in the middle of the revolutionary turmoil, appointed by Nicholas II to the command of the troops guarding St Petersburg, and made president of the State Defence Council. The same Grand-Duke Nicholas was to be given the job of supreme commander of the Imperial Russian Army—despite never having commanded troops in battle—a role in which he ultimately led the Russian forces to the crushing defeats at Tannenberg and the Mazury Lakes in 1915. But in 1904 these catastrophes were still far off in the future. 'Nicolasha' was one of the most influential people at Court, although hated by the empress, who could not forgive him for his hostility to Rasputin. To what extent did Reginald hear about the political tensions in the capital and the plots at Court? On this as on so many other points it is only possible to speculate. The only certainty is that these three years in Russia will have served as a veritable apprenticeship.

A German education at St Petersburg: the Annenschule

To be a pupil at the Annenschule in St Petersburg and to complete one's secondary schooling at this prestigious establishment were marks of belonging to the innermost circles of the St Petersburg elite. Nina Berberova refers to it in one of her novellas, and Igor Arkhangelski devotes an entire monograph to it. The 'Annenshulay', as it is pronounced in Russian, is unquestionably central to St Petersburg memories, as the crucible in which the political and cultural elites were formed at the beginning of the twentieth century and even on into the Soviet era. On the frontispiece of the great book about the establishment, the inscription reads: *Schola ad Santae Anna Petropoli MDCCCCII*, and there is an allegorical figure of the Empress Anna Ivanovna who bequeathed a substantial sum on her death for the construction of a church for the city's Germans. She is pictured as a helmeted war-goddess holding in her hand a great bronze shield while watching over the young dressed in antique loin-cloths who have come to drink at the various springs of knowledge. The school, which is situated near the church of St Anne, was founded in 1736 for the children of the German population of St Petersburg. It was in the heart of what was then the German quarter (*nemetskaya sloboda*) of the capital, near Liteiny Prospekt, where a Lutheran church, originally made of wood, had been built in 1720–2. The first pastor of the Lutheran community, Johan Leonard Shatner, began instructing his pupils in German, and he became so famous as a teacher that it became necessary to build a proper school, which first opened its doors in 1736. Such were the beginnings of that establishment of excellence, St Anne of St Petersburg, attached to the graceful church of St Anne, which had been designed by Yuri Felten (Georg Friedrich Veldten 1730–1801) the well-known architect in the Court of Catherine the Great.

The church in question, which was shut in 1935 before being transformed into a cinema in 1939, when it came to house the kino-teatr Spartak, is a marvel of neoclassical architecture. It stands in a district where the surrounding buildings, mostly built in the 1900s at the time that Reginald Teague-Jones used to frequent the area, are in northern—notably Finnish—style and taste, in the art nouveau manner. Felten, who had been Rastrelli's assistant during the building of the Winter Palace, designed the architecture of St Anne's in the purest St Petersburg style. The proportions and balance of the church, which faces the school, are the expression of a particular intellectual programme and worldview: it is more a temple of knowledge than a temple of faith. It left an abiding memory of grace and harmony for Reginald Teague-Jones, who regularly visited the church from 1903 onwards. With its half-scale rotunda surmounted by a pointed turret, its slender columns with Ionic capitals and its lightly garlanded oculi, the building achieved a perfect synthesis between baroque and classicism. Reginald was registered as a new pupil at St Anne's school in 1903, and was thus to receive a German education—rather unusual for a young Englishman living in Russia. This was to prove fundamentally important for his outlook, not only insofar as his subsequent education was concerned, but also in his private life, since his second wife, Elsa Danecker ('Taddie'), was herself German. By joining the Annenschule in 1903 with its 1,700 pupils Reginald would have been submitting himself to an unrelenting work-discipline and pace. Reginald no doubt joined the school at the same time as the son of the family whose companion he was expected to be. In any event, he succeeded in benefiting from an educational system where the pupils were made to work 'like oxen'.

At the beginning of the twentieth century the Annenschule, then at its apogee, was made up of two Gymnasia for girls and boys respectively, a Realschule, an elementary school and an orphanage. The school's growth justified an extension of the buildings in 1905–6 on the other side of St Anne's church. Reginald must have been one of only a few English children to attend the school, where German-sounding patronymics dominated the pupils' names. In the school register his name appears among the many boys and girls who joined the school in these years, with names such as Juta and Elsa Jurgenson, Vladimir Ilintovich, Alexei Ijenlew, Nikolai Jonas, Therese and Margerete Johannsen, Rudolf Jelinek, Sergei Jurgens or Woldmar Ievlev; their Germanic names, often Russified, recall the German community which had been settled at St Petersburg for generations. In the era of Catherine the Great, this community was far and away the biggest and most active of the foreign colonies in the imperial capital. Of the 667,207 inhabitants of St Petersburg at the mid-point of the nineteenth century, 46,498 declared their mother-tongue as German. The great majority of the German community was Lutheran, but it also included 10 per cent who were Catholics and 1 per cent who were Orthodox, as well as some Jews. The Germans had settled on Vassilievsky Island, in the Vyborgsky district, along Liteiny Prospekt and Millionnaia Street, and for the most part held prestigious positions in intellectual, artistic and scientific professions, some even as members of the Russian Academy of Sciences. Whether as doctors, scientists, artists, sculptors, writers, architects, teachers or soldiers, the Germans had become part of the high culture of St Petersburg society. The establishment on Kirochnaya Street—from the German *Kirche*, whence its post-revolutionary change of name to the Combatants for Atheism Street—was the breeding-ground for this elite; it was one of four German schools in St Petersburg before the First World War, through which passed some 80,000 pupils, Germans, Russians and expatriates of all origins, including young Reginald. In the middle of the nineteenth century, a third of all pupils were Orthodox, which is a sign of the school's appeal to Russians of good family. Its prestige is emphasised by Igor Arkhangelsky,[4] who records among its graduates the educationalist P.F. Lesgaft (1837–1909), the doctor E.E. Eikhvald (1839–89), the jurist A.F. Koni (1844–1927), the ethnographer N.N. Miklukho-Maklay (1846–88), the sculptor R.R. Bach (1859–1933), the famous jeweller Pierre-Carl Fabergé (1846–1920) and the orientalist and specialist in ancient history V.V. Struve (1889–1965). The Annenschule's reputation for excellence continued after the 1917 Revolution, when it educated a good number of artists, writers and philosophers, including the poet and Nobel Prize-winner Joseph Brodsky.

When Reginald joined the school it was at the peak of its expansion under the leadership of its director Josef Koenig, a talented pedagogue and energetic administrator, who directed it from 1884 to 1910. Austere, with piercing blue eyes in which one might catch a glimpse of humour, Josef Koenig ran his establishment in masterly fashion, with a combination of rigour, tradition, innovation and modernity. It was a Prussian education, and the basic values of the members of the Schulrat, its Council of Governors who regulated school life—imposing clergymen and German barons covered in medals and decorations—were obedience and discipline. Most of the teachers were male and German. They included a large number of laymen, but also Protestant pastors, priests of different ranks in the Orthodox hierarchy—looking like bearded popes straight out of a Repin painting—and a Catholic monk, father Hyacinth Kristinus. They make an impressive picture, these teachers of Reginald's, with their spectacles and monocles, beards and moustaches, bow-ties and stiff collars. The female teachers look less starchy; some of them must have been English or French, whose job was to teach languages to the girls.

In reality the teaching on offer was a good deal less traditional than the teachers' austere appearance suggests. The Annenschule had been declared a State Gymnasium by a ukase of Nicholas I in 1852. The school curriculum had traditionally been close to that of a Realschule, with the emphasis on modern knowledge. The education provided by the establishment prepared pupils for entry to university (Moscow, St Petersburg, Dorpat, Helsinki) and was a varied one. Reginald's subjects in the German language, for example, were religion, history, physical sciences, natural science, technology, calligraphy, arithmetic, mathematics and German; and he also studied Russian, French, English and Latin. The other subjects that were taught were singing, drawing and dance, and there were gymnastics in an ultra-modern gymnasium built by subscription in 1889. The school's emphasis on languages was slanted towards living languages: this had a clear effect on Reginald, who was to leave the Annenschule speaking four languages perfectly. The system of teaching favoured by Josef Koenig discouraged rote-learning and routine in favour of open enquiry, with a preference for education over instruction. Throughout his life Teague-Jones was to remain marked by this 'practical' teaching of languages, drawing and calligraphy, the last of which he made good use of when learning Persian. Not least of the Annenschule's achievements was to have fostered the success of two professional orientalists, V.V. Struve, who was to become director of the Oriental Institute at the Academy of Sciences, and Reginald Teague-Jones, a future orientalist practising on the ground, both of whom were members of the same leaving class in 1906.

Red Sunday: memories of the 1905 Revolution

On the eve of the great disturbances which would ultimately sweep away the Romanov dynasty, the young Teague-Jones was able to exercise his precocious powers of observation on events at St Petersburg which lay outside the boundaries of well-to-do society. In a period marked by the resurgence of terrorist attacks, defeat by Japan and the rising clamour of liberal demands from all quarters of the Russian Empire, political developments in Russia were to prove intellectually stimulating for a young man deeply interested in the country's past and present. Teague-Jones, who was able to 'objectify' historical events immediately, was a witness during his stay in Russia of an event which was to leave a permanent mark. He was among the idlers and strollers who were present on 'Red Sunday', the starting-point for the 1905 Revolution. He was witness to the ferocious repression handed out that day to the peaceful demonstrators who had come to beg Nicholas II to grant an amnesty, public liberties, compulsory free public education, equality of all before the law, the abolition of the factory inspectorate and the eight-hour day. He would recount his memories—which he described as his 'most impressive recollection'—of this terrible event thirty years later under the name of Ronald Sinclair in an article for *The Illustrated Weekly of India*.[5] In the absence of a psychoanalytic report, this is a precious source of information which makes it possible to assess the effect of this political event on his personal consciousness. Teague-Jones was present during the 1905 Revolution, a 'general rehearsal' for 1917, in Trotsky's words, the prelude for a series of events which were to seal Russia's destiny in the twentieth century. The highly impressionable sixteen-year-old schoolboy was to witness a massacre.

Warning bells and 'ice-hilling'

On that Sunday of 9 January 1905, Reginald Teague-Jones was getting ready to enjoy some winter sports, of which there was a great variety in St Petersburg, where one can ski in the Tauride gardens or skate on the Neva. It had snowed all night and the strange quiet of the early morning was suddenly broken by bells sounding the tocsin. Reginald had woken with a start: 'Boom! … With startling suddenness the brazen note of the giant bell of St Isaac's cathedral crashed out and reverberated far across the house-tops of the awakening city. Rubbing my eyes sleepily, I got out of bed and crossed to the window.' The bells were ringing, but Reginald was unaware that at day-break 150,000 demonstrators had come together from the different quarters of the city and assembled in the churches, to pray that the day would pass off peacefully. The demonstrators, led by Father Gapon, formed a procession which was more like a religious procession than a workers' demonstration. They sang hymns and carried crosses and icons: their plan was to go to the Winter Palace to make a very humble plea to the tsar. But during the night 12,000 men had been deployed around the city to prevent them from reaching the palace. Gapon, a preacher from the working-class quarters of St Petersburg, was the spokesman for the destitute who had been in revolt in recent days, during which 120,000 workers in the capital, notably employees of the Putilov factories, had been on strike. The crowd wanted to bring the tsar a petition in the form of a humble plea, the preamble to which reads as follows:

Sire! We, the workers and inhabitants of the city of St Petersburg, our wives, our children and our defenceless old parents, come to You, Sire, to seek justice and protection. Oppressed and reduced to destitution, we are treated like slaves who must bear their cruel lot in silence. Borne it we have, but we are always cast back into greater poverty, degradation and ignorance; despotism and arbitrary rule have us by the throat and we are suffocating. We have no strength left, Sire. Our patience is at an end. We have reached the terrible moment when it is better to die than to endure unbearable suffering any longer.[6]

Again the warning bell rang out, sinister, threatening, 'almost frightening', notes Teague-Jones, who had just finished reading a story about the night of the St Bartholomew's Day massacre[7] by G.A. Henty—a reporter and writer often described as 'imperialist', whose adventure stories were very popular at the end of the nineteenth century:

However, I was only an impressionable young schoolboy in St. Petersburg on a visit and by the time I had washed and dressed, my thoughts were centred on the much more interesting subject of breakfast. Meanwhile, the bells had finished ringing in the Sabbath, and were again silent. I forgot all about them and the sinister thoughts they had inspired, but before many hours were over I was to witness a drama the horror of which would remain in my memory the whole of my life.[8]

Like one of the heroes of Henty's many novels which, whether historical or contemporary, invariably featured a boy or a young man living in troubled times—from the Roman Conquest to British India via the struggle for Serbian independence—Reginald Teague-Jones set off unaware to meet revolutionary Russia.

On that day he had the pleasant prospect of passing his time having fun on the ice with a group of friends. The English in St Petersburg had quickly taken to the pleasures of winter sports—skiing, sledging, ice-skating, sleigh-racing—and were said to have invented some kinds of open-air games themselves, which no one else played. 'Ice-hilling', a new version of 'Russian Mountains', is the most interesting example because it was part of local social activity in English and German circles in St Petersburg, both of which Reginald was eligible to frequent. The 'ice-hill' played by the English in St Petersburg was an 'aristocratic' pursuit enjoyed by young men and women on one of the English ice-hills on Krestovsky Island, near Vassilievsky Island. Spending the day on the ice of one of the 'English hills' in St Petersburg promised a good day out: sliding in the biting cold, coffee, tea and steaming samovars, sometimes a dance, all of which were regular club entertainments. The ice-hill in question consisted of a heap of large slabs of ice taken from the Neva and piled against a wooden frame, 'standing about as high as an average house'.[9] The ice surface was polished until it was like a mirror, and the young who reached the top of the run by means of three flights of steps could push themselves off the top at their own risk. The setting in which this rather rough and dangerous sport was practised by the English was exclusively private, according to Marie-Louise Karttunen, although in the 1890s members of the German embassy were also invited to take part. In any event, on Sunday, 9 January 1905 Reginald went to one of the many skating-rinks in the city and was preparing to spend the day on the ice with a group of friends. 'On this particular occasion a number of us young people went off as usual. I had been skating some time when I suddenly remembered that I was invited to go to a birthday party that evening, and that I had to go into town to purchase a present.'[10]

The preludes to an expected drama

Reginald therefore left the rink, said goodbye to his friends and, after hailing the first *izvozchik* (coachman) to pass, asked to be driven to Gostinny Dvor, the famous department store in St Petersburg, which lies quite far up the Nevsky Prospekt at some distance from the Neva. The traffic that day was particularly slow-moving, so Reginald had plenty of time in which to contemplate the golden spire on the Admiralty, and to listen to the bell in the distance ringing to announce that the tsar of all the Russias, or some important member of the Court, was leaving the Winter Palace. Nicholas II was in fact leaving the capital for his residence at Tsarskoye Selo, where he was looking forward to a day of walks and games of dominoes:

For me, however, such occasions always provided a thrill, and while through the friends with whom I was staying I had met a number of highly placed personages, and had even spoken to the Grand Duke Nicholas, I had never had more than the most fleeting glimpses of the 'Little Father' himself. Save for one subsequent occasion when, as a privileged spectator, I watched him at very close quarters ride up on horseback and take the salute of the assembled Corps of Imperial Guards, my recollections of the ill-fated Tsar are those of a pale bearded face at the window of the state coach dashing past with its fast trotting horses, and vanishing in a blur of snow dust and a splash of bright yellow liveries spangled with miniature black eagles.[11]

The tsar, apparently unaware of any danger, left the town at the same time as the excited crowd was coming to him with a petition. The demonstration had been forbidden and the police were patrolling the city. But the demonstrators, led by women and children dressed in their finest array—in order to discourage the soldiers from shooting—were converging in long columns on the Winter Palace. To keep up the demonstrators' morale, a rumour had been spread that refreshments were waiting for them at the Winter Palace, and even that there was to be a parade to celebrate the great occasion.[12] Gapon, dressed in a white robe, bearded and carrying a crucifix, was at the head of one of the columns, exhorting the people not to weaken: 'Comrades, it is better to die for our demands than to live as we have lived until now!' In reply, the people shout: 'We will die!'[13]

Reginald was unaware of the crowd's movements, but before his cab could reach the Nevsky Prospekt, the traffic came to an abrupt halt. As they waited, his *izvozchik* exchanged a few words with another *izvozchik* coming from the other direction. It emerged from the exchange that traffic was at a complete standstill:

'We can't go on Baryn', he said finally, 'the police have closed the road.' Nor could we turn back, it appeared, for other traffic had piled up behind us. There was nothing for it but to pay my fare and get out and walk. Police and mounted gendarmerie were everywhere. I had never seen so many of them out before. Obviously there was something of unusual importance going on, and I was bitten with curiosity to find out what it might be.[14]

Reginald reached Nevsky Prospekt easily enough on foot, where things still seemed to be very quiet, and went up the street in the direction of Gostinny Dvor. As he crossed the majestic avenue by one of the tram stops, a squadron of Don Cossacks on horseback suddenly appeared:

A body-guard, I thought, going on escort duty to one of the palaces, but I noticed how grim they looked with slung carbines and the much dreaded *nagaiki* or loaded whips held loosely in their right hands. It occurred to me that they looked more like a patrol than an escort, and I was right. They were a patrol, and I was soon to have very good cause to remember them.[15]

Further up the Nevsky Prospekt the young man finally reached the arcades of Gostinny Dvor. The shop windows here—particularly those of the Court jewellers— were one of the major attractions of that period, but on this day there were more people about than usual. They had formed little groups, and Reginald, sensing something unusual about the atmosphere, listened to their conversations:

'Maria Ivanovna has gone also to the palace', I heard one woman say. By her looks the speaker was an ordinary working class woman, for she wore a simple shawl over her head instead of a hat, one of the marks of distinction, in that by-gone bourgeois age, between the lower classes and the *intelligentsia*. I remember thinking it curious at the time that a woman of her type should know someone who had gone to the Palace. Then I heard another person mention the Palace, and a man standing near me said with a curse 'They have let loose the Cossacks, damn them; it looks like trouble'.

— '*V tchom delyo?* What is the excitement about?', I asked him.

— 'A big crowd ... gone to the Winter Palace ... a *deputatsia* or a *demonstratsia* ... gone to see the Tsar.'

— 'What for? When?' I asked.

— '*Bog znaet*. God knows what for', he replied, and spat viciously. '*Dooraki*'. 'Silly fools, that's what they are. Asking for trouble. They will have the Cossacks after them if they are not careful'.

So that was all the excitement was about! A *demonstratsia*! My schoolboy mind became fired with imagination. Why not go along and see the show! After all, why not? The Winter Palace was not far away; it would not take long to get there. My shopping could wait till afterwards. There would probably be a big show at the Palace. I might even get a sight of the Tsar. And feeling thoroughly thrilled at the idea, I left the Gostinny Dvor, crossed the street again, and walked on up the Nevsky.[16]

All traffic movement had been stopped and the famous avenue was now patrolled by a large number of Cossack detachments and mounted police.

Caught in the crowd: Teague-Jones, witness to the massacre

Reginald went back down the Nevsky Prospekt to find the crowd which, lower down, was moving in a steady stream towards the Winter Palace. Here, on the right hand side, he reached a street leading to the Winter Palace, which was entirely occupied by a company of infantry. In front of him a dense crowd seemed to be moving forward. In fact the demonstrators had already been fired on for the first time and felt the sabres of the Cossack cavalry at Troitsky Bridge, near the Peter and Paul Fortress. The moving crowd in front of Reginald came to an abrupt halt. Behind him, demonstrators, strollers and gawpers were still arriving and he was suddenly caught in an indescribable crush. The tension went up a notch:

From somewhere ahead, behind the massive blocks of buildings which walled in the Palace Square, came a muffled roar—the voice of a distant crowd. I imagined I could hear the sound of singing, but could not be sure, because of the noise immediately around me. Suddenly a word of command rang out, followed by another. There was an unexpected backward movement of the crowd. The soldiers were clearing the roadway. The pavements were already crowded, but in a few moments they now became completely jammed with humanity. A boot scraped my shin and came down heavily on my toes. The pressure increased until the breath was almost crushed from my body. A woman near me cried out in pain.[17]

In fact a powerful body of cavalry and several cannons had been placed in front of the Winter Palace to prevent the demonstrators advancing on to the square. The initial order to the Cossacks and police was to bring the crowd—now numbering more than 60,000—to heel by using their whips and the flat of their sabres.[18] But instead of retreating, the demonstrators continued their forward march. When they saw the forces of order assume the firing position, they fell on their knees and made the sign of the cross in supplication. Then a bugle call, which Reginald heard, gave the signal for the massacre which was the first step in the irreparable rupture between people and tsar: the soldiers had begun to fire on the crowd.

Then from the direction of the Square behind the blocks of buildings there was suddenly heard the sound of shooting. It might have been rifle fire, or machine guns, or both. The effect on the crowd was instantaneous. They seemed to know by instinct what the firing meant. For a moment I caught my breath. So apparently did everyone else, for there was a momentary pause, and then the next instant … panic. Women screamed, men shouted, fought, cursed and struggled. It was 'Back to the Nevsky. Back out of this!'[19]

23

The crowd, in the grip of panic, was jammed in a cul-de-sac, while those in the square could hear the continuing fusillade. 'That death—sudden death—awaited us ahead, no one doubted. I experienced the feelings of a bullock that has just scented the slaughter house. The screams of the women frightened me almost more than anything else,' Teague-Jones recalls. He nonetheless succeeded in retreating with the crowd without being crushed or trampled underfoot, unlike several women near him. The impotent mass gradually managed to retrace its steps, and Reginald, after some seemingly interminable minutes, was able to get his breath back and regain the Nevsky Prospekt:

My overcoat was torn: I had lost my hat, and I was feeling very bruised and shaken. The shouting and screaming further back continued, but I was well out of it, or so I thought … It all happened in a moment. There was a sudden clatter of hoofs and savage yells, and, as if from nowhere, a party of Cossacks came charging at full gallop down the side of the street. There was no time to do anything. A number of people who had left the pavement and were trying to cross to the other side of the Nevsky were ridden down and trampled on. I saw a young girl, scarcely older than myself, flung screaming into the gutter. Her head struck the kerb with a terrible thud, and blood flowed from an open cut across her face. The Cossacks were using their *nagaiki*. A howl of fury went up from the crowd around me. How they hated these Cossacks. Some of these reined up and pulled their horses to their launches. One man near me, a workman, I think he was, flung himself with a curse at the nearest horseman and seized his arm. Another jumped and gripped the Cossack's leg. The horse plunged and trampled on the girl lying in the gutter. I think it killed her.[20]

The massacre, in the different parts of the city where confrontations took place, would end with 200 dead and 800 injured, a real massacre of the innocents in which neither women nor children were spared. Teague-Jones's testimony of this unfortunate girl's death is corroborated by others, in which another girl was literally crucified, her body riddled with bullets, on an iron grating on which she was perching to get a better view of the demonstration, and a little boy who had climbed on to an equestrian statue of Prince Przewalski was blown into the air by an artillery salvo.[21] The furious crowd roared its hatred of the Cossacks. The Cossack who had fallen from his horse when attacked by the demonstrators was quickly rescued by his comrades who lashed out on all sides with their whips:

Fortunately for me, I was knocked over by one of the horses before the whip could catch me, and I rolled down several steps into a sunken doorway. My head struck the stonework, but I fell on something soft. Beneath me a man lay very still with his bloodstained hands covering his face. I also lay still, afraid to move. Immediately above me the air was filled with shout and curses with the snorting of the horses and the groans of the wounded. Then the Cossacks rode off. Dazed and shaken, I crawled cautiously up the steps. On the pavement, about a dozen people were sprawling, some of them moaning, some quite still. Others were in the roadway. Among them, still lying in the gutter was the young girl. A man was just stooping to pull her on to the pavement, but she was evidently already dead. I felt very sick, and began to vomit. Then, under the impulse of a sudden fear, I turned and started to run for home. Other people also began to run, carefully hugging the inside of the pavement for fear of the mounted patrols. Breathless I reached a side street, and from there walked home in safety.[22]

The Red Sunday Massacre was a fundamental event, the starting point of the 1905 Revolution, which came to an end when the tsar conceded a representative assembly, the Duma, thus establishing a semi-constitutional regime in Russia. Whether it was a 'dress rehearsal', or a 'failed Revolution' in the course of which the first Soviets appeared, 1905 was an irreparable historical rupture. Reginald was to learn a little later, when the city had quietened down, what had really happened on the Palace square, across the way from the alley in which he had been trapped. The troops had intentionally allowed the demonstrators on to the square, and had then blocked all the exits. 'Without warning, a murderous fire had been opened on the helpless crowd, and the great majority of them—men, women and children—had been shot in cold blood.'[23] Treachery and deceit on the part of the forces of order had prevailed over the naivety and trust of the people, whose mood had immediately changed from disbelief to anger. Like many others trapped in the crowd, Teague-Jones was a witness to this crucial psychological turning-point. His memories of 1905, set down thirty years later, shine a light on the psychology and the physical characteristics of the crowd. He picks out, as it were in a painting, a few emblematic figures like that of the girl who fell into the gutter, less reminiscent of Gavroche than of a character in the St Bartholomew's Day Massacre of August 1572, to which he refers at the beginning of his account.

Red Sunday horrified educated St Petersburg society, particularly the young and very young who, like Reginald, were on the Nevsky Prospekt that day. Alexander Kerensky, then a 24-year-old student, was also present. Kerensky, a member of the Socialist Revolutionary (SR) party and the future head of the provisional government in 1917, wrote to his parents in Tashkent:

Oh! These 'awful days' in Peter will remain for ever in the memory of everybody who lived through them. Now there is silence, but the silence before the storm. Both sides are preparing and reviewing their own forces. Only one side can prevail. Either the demands of society will be satisfied (i.e. a freely elected legislature of people's representative) or there will be a bloody and terrible conflict, no doubt ending in the victory of reaction.[24]

A young boy, Alexander Pasternak, the brother of the writer, was so disturbed by the shooting that he declared his enthusiasm for the revolution. He is said to have run through the streets of one of St Petersburg's well-to-do quarters with a group of friends shouting: 'We are all Social–Democrats.'[25] It was not the same with Reginald Teague-Jones, who was certainly horrified by the massacre, but for whom it was not a political baptism. He was already sceptical about revolutionary ideas, and was not a committed witness in the manner of the American journalist John Reed during the October days of 1917. But although he was influenced by Russian social distinctions, which are fully recognised in his account—from the heights of imperial society to the women of the people and the coachmen—he still manifests genuine sympathy for the Russian people, who are the very embodiment of Russia.

On the evening of Red Sunday, after the final scuffles at the barricades which the demonstrators had erected along the Nevsky Prospekt, especially around Our Lady of Khazan, calm returned to St Petersburg. It is not known whether Reginald recovered his emotions sufficiently to go to the birthday party that evening after all. But either from the street or from his bedroom window there was a new and sinister sight for him to contemplate:

That Sunday evening the church bells again clanged out their call to prayer, while down certain side streets leading to the Neva, a long line of country carts, roughly covered with sacking, carried the slaughtered victims to the river. Holes were cut in the ice, and the bodies were thrown in, like so much carrion, to be carried away by the freezing torrent below.[26]

The ice sheets on the Neva, formerly a place for games and pleasure, had now become the symbol of the terrible tragedy of Russia. As in Alexander Sokurov's film, *The Russian Ark* (2002), which in the only sequence shot in the Hermitage Museum evokes in a single icy breath from the Neva three centuries of Russian history, Reginald Teague-Jones's account finishes with a meditation on the tragic course of Russian history. The overthrow of the Romanovs, the arrival of the Soviet regime in 1917 and all the massacres to come in the Stalinist era flow from the 1905 Revolution. Teague-Jones's Red Sunday is an emblematic sequence of events in Russian history which in a way prefigures everything that is to follow. For young Reginald the terrible and traumatising events of 1905 serve as an initiation into Russia and its history. It is quite evident that this early acquaintance with Russia, linguistic, historical and political, had a role to play in his future career, even though he would never again have the chance to return to St Petersburg.

2

FROM THE PUNJAB TO THE NORTH WEST FRONTIER

THE MAKING OF A GENTLEMAN OF THE RAJ

Little is known of the latter part of Reginald Teague-Jones's youth or how the time spent on his education and training was spread between St Petersburg, London and New Delhi. He probably returned from Russia in 1906, when he was barely seventeen, armed with a good knowledge of Russian, French and German. He found his family living in a precarious financial state. Although the precise details are unclear, it was likely to be his family's situation which explains his departure to India, where before the First World War a middle-class family could hope for an improvement in social status and better living conditions. The informed advice of an uncle who was a career officer in India no doubt played a part in this decision. So too the opportunity for young Reginald to have a less constrained professional career than would have been the case in England, where he had in any event not lived for long. After his return from Russia, Reginald does not seem to have settled on a satisfactory direction to follow in London. He entered King's College at London University but left without taking the exams, and he failed, or failed to show up for, the entrance exam for the Foreign Office, a setback which may be explained by his modest social background and the fact that he did not belong to the Oxbridge caste. The setback proved providential since it closed the door to a conventional diplomatic career and determined his future vocation working in intelligence for other organisations like the police and the army, who were in closer touch with the real world. His training took place at the high watermark of the British Empire in the Punjab, and would turn Teague-Jones, like many British men of his generation, into a natural defender of the imperial mission, which began at the forward posts of the famous North West Frontier.

MOST SECRET AGENT OF EMPIRE

An ambition: joining the Indian Political Service

In the period since the terrorist attacks of 11 September 2001, the tribal zones of Pakistan—before Partition, India's North West Frontier—have become the centre of the fight against 'Global Jihad'. To those unfamiliar with the subject, these acts of 'terrorism' and the area's chronic instability might look like a new phenomenon. But when one looks closely at the British archives and at Teague-Jones's personal notes, one is on the contrary struck by the similarity between the problems posed by the Frontier in British India at the beginning of the twentieth century, and those of the frontier between Afghanistan and Pakistan at the beginning of the twenty-first.

A foretaste of the Frontier: the Punjab

Although his family had settled in Delhi, between 1911 and 1913 young Reginald himself lived in two remote parts of South West Punjab, Phillaur and Ferozepur. *Thacker's Indian Directory* lists him as assistant superintendent of police in the region, a job which provided him with a living but for which he felt no particular vocation. Indeed, he admitted as much several decades later: 'I was never in my element during my short service as a Policeman, and I would have given anything to have continued in the Political Department.'[1] Although these brief remarks hint at some dissatisfaction with his career beginnings in a relatively low-prestige job in the police, the post itself had a decisive effect on his future trajectory, and was evidence of the changes which had taken place in internal British policy in India. The creation in Britain in 1887 of a special police force for tackling political crime was a response to Irish terrorism, and gave birth to a special branch concerned with intelligence. This 'Irish model' lay behind the creation of the Frontier Constabulary—a paramilitary force— in the turbulent North West Frontier region. The latter had been 'governed' from 1849 on by the newly conquered Punjab, a strategic forward post for the Frontier. From it, the British attempted to maintain control over the Khyber Pass and what are now the tribal areas of Pakistan. Control was only relative, the product of the close-border system operated during the second half of the nineteenth century. The system combined a policy of non-intervention, based on routine surveillance by garrisons, with punitive expeditions or specially formed 'columns' to put a stop to tribal raids, such as 'Tip and Run', 'Butcher and Bolt' or 'Harry and Hurry'. The thirty years which followed the Indian Mutiny of 1857/8 were relatively quiet—only eleven punitive expeditions—compared with the period of the second Afghan War (1878–80) and its aftermath, which required no fewer than twelve expeditions between 1877 and 1881.[2] The 1897 campaign which Winston Churchill chronicled in *The Story of the Malakand Field Force* was almost a full-blown tribal revolt, but the changeable Mahsuds stood aside this time, allowing the British to retake control of the tribal areas just to the north of the Tochi Valley. Our hero approached the 'turbulent frontier',[3] which was a factor in British expansion and part of the imperial territorial mission, after stages spent in the plains of the Punjab and on the banks of the Sutlej, a tributary of the Indus.

When he arrived at Phillaur to join the Punjab Police Academy in 1911 as a young trainee assistant superintendent of police, Teague-Jones was joining an institution created relatively recently, with responsibility for rationalising the maintenance of order on the outer limits of the British Empire. The police training centre was set up in September 1891 in the fort at Phillaur, 350 kilometres to the north of Delhi on the Great Trunk Road. Phillaur, which lies on the banks of the Sutlej and was founded by Mogul Emperor Shah Jehan (1628–58), had a strategic function from the outset. The strengthening of the fortifications in 1809 was a response to the British capture of the neighbouring fort of Ludhiana. It was only after the death of Maharajah Ranjit Singh (1839), the decline of the Kingdom of Lahore (the Sikh kingdom of the Punjab, which extended from the banks of the Sutlej in the south-east to Afghanistan in the west and Kashmir in the north) and the subsequent defeat of the Sikhs at the Battle of Aliwal in 1846 that the British succeeded in taking the fort of Phillaur, as a preliminary to their assertion of complete control over the rest of the Punjab (1849). The fortress is a military construction with two monumental entry gates—the Lahore Gate and the Delhi Gate—and a system of curtain-walls. The vast complex currently houses not only the resources necessary for police training (horses, dogs, weapons store and a finger-print department) but also a library, a hospital, a museum and even, built into the walls, the mausoleum of a saint, Pir Baba Abdullah Shah Ji. The fort is self-contained, housing all the essential activities of the little town of Phillaur, where the population in Teague-Jones's time totalled no more than 7,000.

The Police Training School was in 1911 a relatively new institution, with a precise mission: training police officers for the North West Frontier province. The fort, origi-nally used by the British as cantonments, was under army control until 1890, when it was transferred to the civil authorities. The Police Training School, founded on 9 September 1891, and the finger-print bureau, established in August 1894, were intended to train modern police who would be more effective on the ground. Directed by J.M. Bishop, assistant district superintendent and first principal of the new institution, the Punjab Police Academy had close links to the Indian Political Service. Its mission was complex: to teach the art of crime prevention and detection in a traditionally troublesome region where unwritten law took precedence over official law. One of the establishment's jobs was to teach and put into practice some of the rudiments of political intelligence.[4] There is no reference in Teague-Jones's writings to this period of gloomy garrison life, set against an exotic natural backdrop, even though he must have already been keeping a diary. It was a part of his youth that evokes the world of Rudyard Kipling and the very essence of a British India confronted by the banditry of the Thugs and Dacoits.[5] Burglars, counterfeiters, illicit distillers, opium smugglers, cattle-poisoners, it is the deviants in native society who provided Teague-Jones with some of his first experiences in this region. It was also in the Punjab, where Hindus, Muslims and Sikhs co-habit, where he first encountered the religious complexity of India and, since he learned several vernacular languages during this period, its linguistic diversity. Furthermore, his stay in the Punjab, with its high density of Muslims, led him to become acquainted with some of the major political issues of the day, characterised by the rise of the Indian national movement. Hindu patriotic fervour, which had been stoked, according to the viceroy, Lord Dufferin (1884–8), by a 'microscopic minority', led to violent clashes with the Muslim community; there was a crisis of confidence in Congress on the part of the Muslim elite, and in consequence Muslims opted for loyal support of British rule. It was in the Punjab that Teague-Jones began to take the measure of 'the Muslim question' and its potential value for British policy.

The probationary period of classes and instruction at the police academy in Phillaur was followed by his first duties on the ground, again in the Punjab. It was at Ferozepur in the south-west Punjab, now in India, a stone's throw away from the Frontier, where Teague-Jones served as assistant police superintendent in 1912 and 1913. Ferozepur, which had been founded in the fourteenth century by Feroz Shah Tugalq and bore his name, had been occupied by the British since 1838. Sir Henry Lawrence, the assistant political agent, built cantonments there, and the fort which lay within the cantonments became a military garrison in 1839. Teague-Jones would undoubtedly have taken up residence in the cantonments, 3 kilometres from the centre of the town,[6] which was laid out in colonial style with houses, bungalows, lawns, gardens and exotic birds. Residence is perhaps not the right word, since British civil administration at the lower level of the districts rested on the shoulders of a handful of men and barely a dozen police officers. Given the strategic nature of the region and its inherent instability, a posting to Ferozepur, the bastion from which the first Anglo-Afghan War was launched in 1838, and then the Sikh War in 1845–6, was far from being a routine job. The young man enjoyed crossing his district on horseback and settling local disputes, and in particular displayed his qualities by establishing direct contact with a local—almost entirely rural—population which 'only understands power when incarnated in a particular man'.[7]

Ferozepur lies in the heart of a rich alluvial plain which floods during the rainy season. Before the Partition of India it was a flourishing and populous city living essentially off the surrounding agricultural economy, which was based on wheat, cotton, chick-peas and millet. It is situated on one of the main invasion routes from Baluchistan or the Khyber Pass to the subcontinent—the mainland—and as a critical strategic staging-post it brought Teague-Jones progressively closer to the more exciting North West Frontier territory. Teague-Jones was not comfortable in the job; he would have liked to escape the everyday conformity that a career as a colonial administrator entailed, a post that was likely to have been particularly frustrating since he did not come from the exalted ranks of the Indian Civil Service (ICS). With the exception of travels off the beaten track in his district and some short visits as a tourist to Lahore and Amritsar, his leisure time was limited to reading and, no doubt, shooting. The banks of the Sutlej teemed with game and Teague-Jones was one of those hard-riding officers depicted by Rudyard Kipling: black partridge and grey partridge, all kinds of wild geese and ducks, great Indian bustards, green pigeons; he would have indulged in his passion for shooting[8] in the neighbourhood of Ferozepur.

The shotgun and the rifle were pleasures in what is likely to have been a rather austere life, serving as an outlet for the boredom of a colonial society ruled by Victorian values—even if the extremely select Ferozepur Club was not founded until 1925. Were there any amorous intrigues, or friendships made, during this period? Teague-Jones left no recollections of this time in his youth, perhaps because it was too dreary, or, on the contrary, perhaps because it was too full of contacts and networks. We do know, however, that he maintained a long-lasting friendship from the time of his stay in Peshawar, probably at the beginning of the First World War, with Dorothy Kate Fox-Strangways, who had been born into a family with links to the aristocracy. She married Major Ernest Gardiner Collings whom she had to follow to Peshawar after her marriage at the age of twenty-two in 1914. Teague-Jones, who also knew Kate's sister, Marjorie Fox-Strangways, kept in touch with this family throughout his life. Geoffrey Stephen d'Auvergne Collings, born in 1924, was godson to Reginald Teague-Jones, who had become Ronald Sinclair in 1922.

The experience of living in British colonial society, with a class system no less highly stratified than the Indian caste system, must have given Teague-Jones something of a complex about his status, coupled with a wish to move up the social ladder, as is suggested by his decision to hyphenate his two names so as to make them more distinguished. At the start of his career he would undoubtedly have encountered members of the prestigious Indian Civil Service, recruitment to which was very selective and largely restricted to the well-to-do middle class and gentry of the mother country. Young Reginald did not come from such a background, which tended to arouse in him a mixture of fascination and repulsion which he was to feel for the rest of his life. On becoming an officer in the Indian Army Reserve during the First World War he increasingly rubbed shoulders with the aristocracy and landed gentry, who accounted for a progressively larger proportion of officers in the Indian Army[9] during the course of the nineteenth century. Without being a proper member of this gentlemanly elite within the British Empire, Teague-Jones embraced its codes of behaviour, while distancing himself from the sort of official imperialism formulated in the 1920s by Sir Arthur Hirtzel.[10] For if 'the ICS ideal is that of the public schools of the day, who value character, sincerity and physical fitness above intellectual subtlety',[11] Teague-Jones himself lacked neither subtlety nor humour. But he did not belong to the gentlemanly diaspora, for whom the door was open to networks and influence throughout the immense British Empire. He would nonetheless succeed in becoming part of it as much for his abilities on the ground as for his talents as an observer, entering by the side-door of the Indian Political Service at the start of the First World War.

The Indian Political Service: a caste within the colonial administration

The circumstances in which Teague Jones made contact with the Indian Political Service before the First World War are unclear. His movement from a civilian job as a police superintendent to a military role—he was probably transferred to the Indian Army Reserve in 1916, first with the rank of lieutenant and then as captain—is no easier to trace. There is evidence in the archives of his being awarded a military MBE on 3 June 1919 for services in connection with military operations in Persia, while Ronald Sinclair was awarded a civil OBE on 30 December 1922 for his services in the Punjab police.[12] Even though it will never be possible to document this transition on the basis of the archives, it was during the immediate pre-war period that Teague-Jones, who was recruited for his brains, his linguistic abilities and his liking for adventure, entered the world of political intelligence. This was the beginning of a career which would see him carry out a variety of functions in the three branches of intelligence, diplomatic, police and military. The first stages of his career in India were thus radically different from those of members of the ICS, even though he was in constant contact with them. They came from the upper echelons of society, Oxford- and Cambridge-educated—even though the ICS lost some of its appeal after the First World War. Teague-Jones remained understandably silent about his colleagues, his friends and the networks with whose help he took his first steps in the world of intelligence. Indeed, almost nothing is known of this period other than the fact that he belonged to a specific branch of the British intelligence system that answered directly to the government of India rather than London. One possibility, although there is no concrete evidence to support it, is that Sir Vivian Gabriel (1875–1950), with whom Teague-Jones had connections, was involved in his appointment in some way.

Sir Edmund Vivian Gabriel, a member of the Indian Political Service, was fifteen years older than Teague-Jones and their professional paths intersected. The career of this British officer, who held a high-ranking protocol position at Buckingham Palace as a gentleman usher in ordinary, was the archetype of the senior British civil servant in India.[13] As a connoisseur of the North West Frontier, Colonel Gabriel—in white helmet, fitted waistcoat, with a monocle on a ribbon and sitting ramrod straight on his black pony—was given the task of welcoming and guiding the 'Croisière Jaune'—a much–publicised crossing of Asia by car sponsored by Citroën—through the Khyber Pass in 1931. So far as the members of the Citroën team were concerned, there was not the slightest shadow of a doubt that he belonged to the British intelligence service. Once again the North West Frontier was the stage for this meeting. Le Fèvre noted in his journal:

We are in English territory. On the 'Anglo-Afghan Frontier'. Two signposts and an unguarded barrier with red and white stripes. In the distance a sort of cottage, and, in front of us, a notice-board: 'Frontier of India. Travellers are not permitted to pass this notice-board unless they have complied with the passport regulations.' The place is deserted, a passage between two hills. Fortunately Colonel Vivian Gabriel was waiting for us. He has had instructions from his government to facilitate the mission's passage in Kashmir, through the Himalayas and up to the high passes in the Pamirs. He is an extremely distinguished man, who appears to have a surprisingly realistic view of matters. He didn't conceal what he thought: crossing this gigantic mountain-range by car is inconceivable.[14]

FROM THE PUNJAB TO THE NORTH WEST FRONTIER

In his private diary Audouin-Dubreuil wrote of Vivian Gabriel:

It seemed to me that the Colonel had received another telegram in cipher requesting him to exert pressure on us not to attempt the Pamirs. In any case, Vivian Gabriel, who has been going up and down the only track in these mountains on horse-back for a year, reckons that two-thirds of the route will be impossible for the cars to manage. He is a sensible, clear-headed man. What if he were right? We would be stuck.[15]

If Teague-Jones wished to show the existence of his friendship with Gabriel without revealing its extent—which was usual for him—it may have been for reasons to do with professional advantage and personal prestige. Vivian Gabriel, who was knighted in 1937, was to cross Teague-Jones's (now Ronald Sinclair's) path again in the United States during the Second World War. From 1940 to 1946, when Sir Vivian Gabriel was a member of the British Air Commission in the United States, Ronald Sinclair was working at the British consulate on harmonising the British and American intelligence systems. Leaving aside his possible involvement in Teague-Jones's early career, which cannot be verified one way or another, Gabriel is a prime example of the British elite in India; his high reputation and extensive social reach epitomise success in the Indian Political Service. Although Teague-Jones may not have been a member of the service proper, all his postings, from Aden to Persia and from the North West Frontier to Baluchistan, are signs that he belonged to one of the branches of British intelligence. Around 1913 he was involved in the fight against smuggling and slavery in Aden, Muscat and the Makran Coast to the south of Baluchistan. This temporary mission arose out of British policy in the area, which made Aden into an important staging-post on the maritime route to India. Originally a coaling-station, latterly a petroleum supply-depot, in the nineteenth century Aden was a base from which the British sought to extend their influence, particularly in trade, into the mountains of Yemen. To bolster its alliances in the Arabian Peninsula, the government of British India supplied arms to allies such as the Sabahs of Kuwait or the Imam Yahya who had rebelled against Ottoman power[16] in the mountains of Yemen. The region of the three Gulfs—the Gulf of Aden, the Gulf of Oman and the Persian Gulf—presented a number of challenges to British power: piracy, the traffic in slaves bought in East Africa by merchants from Muscat and the Trucial Coast and sold in the Gulf, the Arabian Peninsula or Persia, and the arms trade. The fight against the trafficking of arms from the Persian Gulf into the North West Frontier of India, via Persia and Baluchistan, was certainly an essential aspect of Teague-Jones's mission—whether police or political—in this region just before 1914.

The Indian Political Service, which was known as the 'Foreign and Political Department of the Government of India' until 1937, was no more of a 'service', properly speaking, than it was 'Indian' in its make-up, or 'political' in its concerns.[17] It was a body whose members had been seconded from other services, the majority from the Indian Army (70 per cent) and the Indian Civil Service (30 per cent); only a few officers were seconded from the Indian police or other services. The Political Service numbered 170 officers at the time of Partition in 1947, and comprised the 'diplomatic' representatives of British India in the Indian States, and also the administrators from the geostrategic zones that called for tighter surveillance, like the North West Frontier or Baluchistan. The secretariat of the central government of India was also staffed by officials from the Indian Political Service. Teague-Jones would have been in close liaison with the Indian Political Service when, at the beginning of the First World War, he joined an intelligence service, Indian Political Intelligence, which was answerable to the government of India. The history of this shadowy organisation, to which Teague-Jones probably belonged until its dissolution in 1947, is particularly interesting because its archives, which were opened in 1947, remain the only source of information from a British intelligence service that researchers are able to access.

A shadow organisation: the Indian Political Intelligence Service

There seems to be no doubt that Teague-Jones belonged to Indian Political Intelligence, even though he painstakingly expurgated his personal papers by removing most of his original reports, especially his manuscript notes. He left the historian some obvious clues, including a mention of a report to the DIB (director of the Intelligence Bureau), known at the end of the colonial period as the secret service of the government of British India, and an empty manila envelope addressed to Ronald Sinclair MI5. It is relatively easy to trace the sources for reports held in the archives of the War Office, the Foreign Office, the government of India and Indian Political Intelligence, as will become clear in reading this work. But there is no organisational chart or official description of the service which makes it possible to determine confidently and precisely the circumstances and nature of Teague-Jones's place in the service, which some in India[18] today claim as one of the first intelligence services in the world, and which is certainly one of the least well known. There is no doubt that Teague-Jones attracted the attention of one or more of his superiors as early as 1912–13. It would have been extraordinary if he had not. A young officer who could speak Russian, German and French, who was diligently learning Indian languages and Persian, and had considerable gifts for observation and analysis and was reliably level-headed, could not fail to be recruited, beginning with a CID mission in the Punjab.

Teague-Jones's entry into the world of shadows coincided with the beginnings of the IPI, whose origins date to 1910, when Major John Wallinger, a senior officer in the Indian police, was appointed by London to carry out surveillance on Indian revolutionary agitation. In 1915, after the outbreak of the First World War and with a rise in nationalist agitation, Wallinger obtained an assistant, Philip C. Vickery, born in 1890, 'an Indian Police Officer whose duty is to keep a watch on Indian revolutionaries and on criminals connected with India of all nationalities, in the UK and on the Continent of Europe'.[19] Teague-Jones was bound to cross Vickery's path at this point; the latter, after working in intelligence for the Punjab CID, became Wallinger's assistant at the IPI, a post which entailed travelling between India and the United States between 1915 and 1922. Upon returning to the Punjab CID in 1923, he was to succeed Wallinger as the head of the IPI in 1926, a post in which he remained until Indian independence. Vickery, who was renowned for his tact and great discretion, had the delicate task of transferring responsibility for police and intelligence to the Indian authorities, among a number of other jobs. According to a note in the IPI archives:

it was with some hesitation that he has been allowed to serve in this country for so long, but it is generally recognised that it would be some time before a successor could prove himself as efficient and it has been felt that the maximum efficiency is required while constitutional changes are taking place in India. It has also been felt that with the transfer of police matters to Indian control there may be some reluctance on the part of outside organisations to give secret information to Indian Intelligence and that it is therefore desirable to have as an intermediary a person who has already obtained the complete confidence of those organisations.[20]

In August 1947, therefore, Philip Vickery presided over the transfer of the service to T.G. Sanjevi Pillai, director of the Intelligence Bureau, the intelligence service of independent India. On the British side, in 1950 the remaining staff of IPI were transferred to SO4, a branch of MI5. A shadowy organisation, IPI had a distinctive identity as a branch of the British intelligence system. Although in practice it functioned as though it was autonomous, IPI had in fact been affiliated to the DIB since the time of the Government of India Act (1935). As a principally colonial intelligence service, IPI was responsible to two British authorities, the India Office in London and the government of India in Delhi. Within India, there was an IPI network in each province, with a central intelligence officer, usually backed by local police forces, collecting information. As an 'Indian' intelligence organisation during the colonial period, IPI reported simultaneously in India to the India Office (Public and Judicial Department) and to the DIB, while maintaining links and close contact with Scotland Yard, and especially MI5, with which it shared offices in London from 1924 onwards.

Nothing more definite can be said about Teague-Jones's first steps in the world of intelligence. Of course Teague-Jones never revealed the circumstances under which he took a secret job, any more than Ronald Sinclair did later. But the manuscript of his adventure story, *Khyber Blood-Feud*, which was largely inspired by his own experiences of the Afghan frontier, introduces a young hero, Jim, with whom the author must have identified even though the action has been transposed to the Second World War. The scene of the action is the Khyber Pass; *Khyber Blood-Feud* is the story of a blood-debt, an authentic autobiographical experience which supports the hypothesis that it is a *roman à clef*. How can there be any doubt that when our hero is recruited for a secret mission to the Pathan tribes, Jim is a double for the young Reginald?

For reasons which you will easily understand, it won't be possible for you to maintain direct personal contact with me, for it's essential that nobody should suspect that you're working with us.

— You mean that I'll be working … under cover?

— I mean, explained the General, watching Jim's face closely as he spoke, that you would have to lose your present identity for a time. In fact, you'd have to become a Pathan.

— A Pathan?

Jim was silent for a few moments. He was thinking hard.

— Does the thought of that worry you, Jim? I wouldn't want …

— Not really Sir. The only thing is that … well you [know] that I've been away from all this … atmosphere … for so long that … well, my Pashtu for instance, is very rusty …

— Of course, my boy, I realize all that, and I'd never dream of asking you to undertake something for which I didn't feel you were completely competent and fully equipped.

Jim breathed a little more freely. He had not been prepared for this eventuality.

— Look here Jim, the General noted his hesitation, my idea is for Mahboob Ali to take you in hand and put you through a complete course, until you can mix with Pathans and Afghans as one of them. Now, I wouldn't think of asking this to any of my own officers because I know of no other officer who would be suitable to undertake it. But for you I'm sure it'll present very little difficulty, and it shouldn't take you very long for you already have it in your blood. Why, I remember you, Jim, when you were a kid, and how you used to run around the bazaars just like any other little Pathan youngster …

— But the language … Remember I haven't heard Pashtu spoken in years … not until the other day …

— As for the language, the General laughed, why Mahboob Ali used to tell me that he'd heard you come out with some of the spiciest terms of bazaar abuse, and wondered where you'd picked them up. No, I really don't think the dialect will give you much trouble once you begin to hear it spoken all around you again.

— No, I don't think so either, really, Jim agreed. The General's words had reassured him and his self-confidence was restored. He knew now that this was no dream. The thing was a reality; a thrilling reality. And he was ready for anything.[21]

The training-ground: the North West Frontier Province

Control of territory and the political stakes connected with it can be observed both in detail and at a more general level in the North West Frontier Province, on the outer limits of British India and Afghanistan. One of the most remote and potentially most dangerous areas on the planet, the 'frontier' or more precisely 'the frontier territory' could serve as an academic case study in geopolitics, a discipline which indeed emerged at the end of the nineteenth century. The Frontier, which lies in one of the contact zones that Halford Mackinder[22] and subsequently Nicholas Spykman[23] characterised as the zone between 'heartland' and 'rimland', controls the invasion routes to the subcontinent. It has been a prize since the time of Alexander the Great and Tamerlane—and it remains one today, as the 1979 Soviet invasion of Afghanistan demonstrates. More recently still, it has proved impossible to bring stability to 'Talibanistan', the quasi-autonomous tribal areas which have become impregnable retreats seething with jihadists and terrorists. On the eve of the First World War, the North West Frontier Province defined the limits between the area under British domination in India, and Afghanistan: a buffer state against the southward pressure of the 'benevolent Northern Power', as Rudyard Kipling described the Russian Empire in his novel *Kim*. These were the basic components of the Great Game, the term popularised by Kipling as a description of the strategic conflict between the British and Russian empires for supremacy in Central Asia. From 1813 up to the Anglo-Russian Convention of 1907 which settled the respective spheres of influence of the two empires, the Great Game was characterised by indirect confrontation and localised conflicts, such as the two Anglo-Afghan Wars of 1838 and 1878; the outcome of the latter, which was catastrophic for the English, made it impossible to rectify the state of permanent instability prevailing in the region. Thus Afghanistan remained a buffer state for the battle between shadow forces, a place where international tensions on its borders gave rise to proxy warfare within. The border areas were the territory of cross-border tribes, whose raids perpetually threatened English positions. Against this backdrop, Teague-Jones's unpublished journals evoke his experience on the ground in Frontier tribal territory at the beginning of the First World War, and enable one to grasp, thanks to their author's skills as observer and writer, the concrete rewards for territorial control. The unpublished journals belong to a rich tradition of accounts of the Frontier given by many other officers, both British and Indian. Dated to 1914 and 1915, they describe the early career of their author as a young English officer posted to India to a new force, the Frontier Constabulary, charged with responsibility for maintaining law and order in the tribal territories of the North West Frontier. What form did British control over power and territory take in 1914 in the wild mountains of this region, where control was difficult to exercise and tribal tensions held sway?

Administrative and political frontiers: controlling the hinterland

The North West Frontier Province (see Map 2), lying between the giants of the Hindu Kush, whose peaks run from Pakistan as far as Tajikistan, reaching as high as 7,000 metres, and the Indus plain, overlooks one of the main invasion routes into India. Used by Alexander the Great in 326, and then by all subsequent conquerors—from the White Huns in the fifth century to the campaigns of Babur, founder of the Moghul Empire in the sixteenth century—this mountainous territory is a stony, hard, warlike world, dominated by clans and tribes. Combining a harsh mountain climate with that of a sub-desert, the high valleys are locked in a series of mountain-chains crossed by cols and passes, of which the most famous is the Khyber Pass, the communication channel for caravans from Peshawar to Kabul. Mountains, warfare and a strict honour code set the rules for this world of clans and tribes, dominated by men whose authority, rank and honour are signified by weapons, the turban and the blood-debt. The predominant culture is Pashto or Pathan, but Baluchis are equally numerous in some districts of the North West Frontier Province.

These tribes, whose territory—the well-known tribal areas—stretches all along the frontier between India and Pakistan, had differing reputations with the British military and colonial administration. For both Baluchis and Pathans, Sunnite Muslims, hospitality is a sacred duty, and the blood-debt is the price of the honour code—the notorious Pushtunwali. But the stereotypes held by the occupying English contrasted the trustworthiness and honesty of the Baluchi with the treacherous, yet free, virile and wild Pathan, just as they set the ignorance and laxity in religious observance of the Baluchi against the fanaticism and strict observance of the Pathan.[24] Since ancient times the roads and valleys used by the caravans had been furnished with watchtowers for the protection of the convoys, but only a kilometre away from the road the interior was beyond all control; this was the domain where tribal law prevailed. As General George MacMunn suggests:

there is the great tangled mass that lies between the Indus, and let us say the Kabul–Kandahar Road, and also across the Indus in the valleys of the Swat river. They lie as an island, or assemblage of islands, among which the channels of the passes from the uplands and from the Oxus lead down to the Indus, and through which they wind and emerge.[25]

The Durand Line, drawn in 1893 through a jagged and hostile mountain region in the middle of tribal territory, marks the border between India and Afghanistan, and is the product of an agreement which also moved the frontier between Russia and Afghanistan to the north of the Amu Darya. In exchange for settling the respective spheres of influence of Great Britain and Russia, the British agreed to make no further attempts to interfere in the internal affairs of Afghanistan beyond the outer boundary; this line, determined by military considerations, runs through Pashto tribal territory.[26] It is to be distinguished from the administrative frontier, or internal frontier, known as the administrative boundary, which runs partly along the foot of the mountains and partly deeper into them, in order to ensure control over the passes (the Gomal Pass, the Khyber Pass etc.). The Frontier is therefore not a line, but rather the hinterland territory lying between the Durand Line and the administrative frontier, with a width varying between 30 and 150 kilometres. It encompasses the tribal areas which the British government had no means of occupying systematically through the installation of a regular administration. Finally, the limits of the North West Frontier Province, the proper provincial administrative boundary, constituted a third line, a distance away from the internal frontier. These three successive lines defined the variable geometry of the border line, which was more a front than a frontier, even though the Indian border was clearly defined and watched. There were six administrative districts, created in 1901, running from north to south: Hazara, Peshawar, Kohat, Bannu, Dera Ismail Khan and Dera Ghazi Khan, the last of which belonged administratively to Punjab province. They bordered the hinterland in this zone of foot-hills, plains and mountains—the word 'hill' in this context denotes an ordinary rocky, arid mountain, but 'in India even the highest ranges of the Himalayas are only "hills"'. Within the hinterland, that is to say beyond the administrative frontier, the mountains are distinctly more jagged and wild, an arid labyrinth slashed by deep gorges and passes which lend themselves to ambushes. It is from here, in particular from Waziristan, that the formidable Mahsud tribes launched their raids.

In this setting territorial control was not simply a matter of controlling a boundary line. The special technique of 'frontier warfare' called for incursions and patrols in the hinterland, based on British outposts scattered all along the administrative frontier; here, in order to repel raids, one must first avoid ambushes. This band of territory, which lacked the rigidity of other international frontiers, may therefore be thought of as a buffer zone—a buffer to a buffer—wedged between India and Afghanistan. What forms did the military defence of the North West Frontier take successively from 1892 onwards? At first entrusted, except for the Peshawar district, to a force of irregulars—the Punjab Frontier Force—from 1903 onwards the military defence of the Frontier was the responsibility of the Border Military Police, an authentic Frontier militia composed of divisions from Peshawar and Quetta. Due to a shortage of recruits and permanent officers in consequence of the unattractive pay on offer, it became necessary to reorganise military control of the Frontier in 1913. The new body, the Frontier Constabulary, with only a dozen British officers, was a paramilitary police force comparable to the one the English had recently organised for Ireland, the Royal Irish Constabulary. The Frontier Constabulary, which Teague-Jones joined in 1914, had duties which went beyond those of an ordinary police force and made it possible to do without the slow and heavy intervention of regular troops. The Frontier Constabulary was expected to perform an effective preventive role in the hinterland, an exciting mission which was likely to attract young officers who did not fear the formidable mountains and the perils they concealed. This role became especially important, and dangerous, as a result of the Ottoman sultan's decision, as an ally of the Central Powers, to summon all believers to jihad in his capacity as caliph in 1914, thereby ensuring that the effects of the First World War were immediately felt in these highly remote regions. In this context, the North West Frontier, the bastion of the British Empire in India, seemed threatened by the tribes of the hinterland, who were capable of mobilising several hundred thousand armed fighters. It is true that Afghanistan maintained a position of strict neutrality during the First World War, but the power of the mullahs in Kabul naturally led the British to increase surveillance on the Frontier. The daring activities of the tribes grew on the news of the departure of British troops for Europe, with the Mahsuds based in Waziristan redoubling their raids. With the assistance of half a dozen English regiments, the Frontier Constabulary was relatively effective in containing these attempts, thanks to a genuine understanding of territorial control; the different forms this took are described with precision in Teague-Jones's journals,[27] particularly those which deal with the Sherani country, on the borders of Waziristan, to which he was posted as a young officer from August 1914 to February 1916.

Sherani country

'The main function of the Frontier Constabulary was to hold outposts at strategic points along the Border, and in particular to patrol and guard the innumerable gorges and ravines and vulnerable areas where a tribal incursion or bodies of armed raiders might attempt to erupt or infiltrate into British territory.'[28] Teague-Jones's journals, those of a young district officer at the head of a Frontier regiment composed essentially of members of cross-frontier Pathan tribes, concern the Sherani country in 1914 and 1915. Sherani country lies in the southern sector of the Frontier, immediately adjacent to Baluchistan. The region was of high strategic importance to the British, who were trying to stabilise Baluchistan, the linking territory between India and Persia. It is a region which Teague-Jones, under a different name, was to explore again in the inter-war years. Although personal recollections of this type are not uncommon among the sources relating to the North West Frontier Province, the interest of these journals lies above all in the exceptional qualities of their author's observation and analysis, those of an intelligence officer gifted with unusual linguistic gifts, a taste for adventure and for writing, humour and human understanding. It lies also in the fact that they provide a precise account of experiences on the ground, which through observation of the Sherani country at local level reveals a much vaster set of territorial stakes at issue, the mastery of the whole Central Asian chessboard. Here the historian is in the position of a seismologist who sees a geological fault which is actually the manifestation of clashing tectonic plates. And Teague-Jones's observations are all the more interesting given that this particular geopolitical fault is still active today.

After his arrival at Tank, a base with cantonments in the Dera Ismail Khan District, and headquarters of the Frontier Constabulary, Teague-Jones, who was appointed assistant district officer in August 1914, moved next to the outpost of Draband, closer to the administrative frontier. As the name of the place, which derives from the word for col or pass, suggests, the outpost controlled the three principal passes which allow access to Sherani territory. The most important of these was Zam Chaudwan, through which passed the only caravan route from the Indus Valley to Baluchistan, and which in consequence served as a commercial artery. Further north the two other passes—Drazinda and Sheikh Haidar—had no commercial value at all, but were the entry and escape routes for Mahsud tribal raids. Half-ruined, the Draband fort seemed to dissolve into the desolate surrounding country. 'I suppose it might be called a post, but really, from its appearance, with the exception of the guard presenting arms at the entrance gate, one would at first sight have supposed it to some very dilapidated caravanserai …'[29] With its walls of dried mud, the Draband fort was literally falling into ruins. The recent rains had caused the watchtower to crumble, leading to the death of a sergeant (*Havildar*). 'Any enemy with any guts could get in unperceived any night he chose, yet this is a Frontier outpost in a particularly wild and dangerous locality!'[30] Similarly, on the other side of the administrative frontier, the forts on Sherani territory had been left—despite their great strategic value—in a shocking state of decay. Zarkani, with its walls built of mud bricks and its stone watchtowers, was a typical frontier fort designed to maintain continuous surveillance against snipers or surprise attacks. Nishpa, lying at the foot of Takht-i-Suleiman[31] (3,375 metres) at the western end of Sherani territory, had been wrecked by the torrential rains of the last few years:

The post is in a remarkably picturesque situation for this part of the world, more picturesque, indeed, than strategically sound. Down five hundred feet immediately below is the stream, and purer water never flowed, issuing a quarter of a mile above us from a magnificent gorge and passing through a second one just below us on its journeys to the foothills and the plains. The view of Nishpa as one approaches through the lower gorge is a striking one. The entrance of the gorge is as it were a gateway in the forbidding iron-bound wall of mountains. There, water has fought and vanquished solid rock … Turning in at the Pass, one stands amazed at the panorama which unfolds before and around one. Mountains tower above on every side, mountains whose very existence one never suspected despite their immediate proximity. To the south runs a razorback ridge, at present to a large extent covered with snow. To the north, a continuation of the same range is interrupted only by the Nishpa gorge. Above and beyond it the famous Takht-i-Suleiman towers up to nearly 12,000 feet, with its higher crags and chasms likewise covered with snow.[32]

The notoriously limited funding for the frontier forts, and more generally the meagre budget for surveillance efforts in the North West Frontier, were subjects to which Teague-Jones regularly devoted his pen:

It is always the old old question, the refusal of the Government to sanction sufficient money to do anything properly. One tithe of the vast sums spent on the futile Delhi Durbar would have built a chain of modern outposts right down the Frontier which would not have required repairs for years. Yet no, because it is possible to form mud into the shape and semblance of buildings, the Baboos in Government prefer to make do with jerry patchwork, mending, rebuilding and supporting structures which the government of a third rate South American state would scorn to house their mules in.[33]

With its complement of ten officers and derisory resources, membership of the Frontier Constabulary demanded that one have no fear of hikes, field-sports or adventures within the tribal areas on both sides of the Frontier. The line in this labyrinth of stony gullies was invisible and dangerous, whether or not one was apprehensive about crossing it, like the young officer who accompanied Teague-Jones on an excursion into the hills to the north of the Bain Pass, who kept asking him: 'We are over the Border now, aren't we?'

Teague-Jones provides a local ethnography of the peoples and tribes of the Frontier—a classic colonial practice—but his journals and photographs, among which are some remarkable portraits, testify to the fascination which the men of the Frontier exercised. Recruitment into the Frontier Constabulary, which was basically an infantry force made up of companies and half-companies, followed standard British colonial logic in the recruitment of natives. Although belonging to different tribes and clans, the men were strictly observant Muslims who kept the fast of Ramadan even during the most difficult and testing patrols. Compared with the army regiments which were transferred from the south of India to the Tank cantonments in 1914 so as to replace the British and Indian troops despatched for duties in Mesopotamia, the companies within the Frontier Constabulary were better suited to the difficulties of life on the Frontier. In 1914–15 they were locally recruited from the tribes in the Khyber region on much the same principle as for the regular army in that, among the Pathan tribes, the Afridis, the Khattaks and the Yusufzais, who had the reputation of 'martial races', constituted the majority of the combat troops. The Frontier Constabulary brought locals to join these warriors from neighbouring regions like the Marwats from Derajat, 'excellent soldiers', whose knowledge of the country was evidently deemed to be essential:

The Marwats are not generally recruited into the regular Indian Army, and are regarded as being of inferior fighting material to the better known tribes of Afridis, Khattacks, Yussufzais, and other Pathans. But for the constabulary they are essential for their knowledge of the country. This was my first meeting with them, and I must say they turned out very smartly for my inspection. As I got to know them better, for toughness and discipline, I could not have wished for finer soldiers.[34]

In contrast, the half-company of Sheranis was not formed for the purpose of recruiting and training soldiers. The Sheranis, from cross-frontier tribes, were considered indispensable in establishing relations between men of the Frontier Constabulary and the local population. They compensated for the total ignorance of the Khattaks, whose garrison had been established at Nishpa in the middle of the Sherani highlands. The Khattaks, who came from a more distant district in the north and did not know the region or speak the language, were for example incapable of telling the Sheranis from the Mahsuds, whose raids out of Waziristan were on the rise again in 1914, and particularly in 1915. The recruitment of a handful of local Sheranis was the only way of ensuring that the Frontier Constabulary had the means of communicating necessary to ensure the relative control of the territory:

When therefore a pursuit or picketing party goes out, it is advisable to have one of two of these Sheranis with them to act as guides, and, if occasion arose, to prevent them from firing on peaceful 'Miranais', as the Sheranis are popularly called, in mistake for Mahsuds. Moreover, they are most useful for sending out with messages and communications from post to post. On such occasions, they go alone and unarmed [as a weapon was such a desirable trophy that it would almost always cost its owner his life].[35]

Thus control over the Frontier and the hinterland could not be maintained without the collaboration of some elements from the local tribes. And it was their local knowledge as much as their bravery which made these Pathan recruits so essential a resource for the Frontier Constabulary.

The special character of this Frontier warfare is a feature that most witnesses from this era constantly emphasise, which is hardly surprising given that the war on the borders of Afghanistan and Pakistan continues to pose an enduring challenge to the most sophisticated military technologies:

At the time of the outbreak of war in 1914, the Frontier Constabulary had for sole armament the old Martini-Henry single shot rifle, taking a heavy black powder cartridge with solid lead bullet. For a long time this had been the favourite weapon on the Frontier, but the regular army had long since been armed with modern magazine rifles. The tribesmen, too, were discarding their ancient jezails and flintlocks and acquiring more modern weapons. Also, more significant, by 1915 the Mahsud and Waziri raiding parties were not only increasing their activities, but were coming down in much larger parties. Instead of five or six, they were now operating in bands of upwards of 20 men.[36]

The first requirement of the war on the Frontier was relative control over the territory, which entailed constant trekking activity on the part of the Frontier Constabulary. Long foot-patrols through the mountains demanded camps, bivouacs and searches for sources of water. But the central character of Frontier warfare was its landscape—mountainous, though not as high as the highest mountains—a rocky labyrinth which lent itself to ambushes. Teague-Jones both wrote about and photographed the main features of the Frontier landscape. The border territory of the hinterland is made up of a tangled network of *nullahs*, narrow valleys characteristic of this arid mountain country, which have been dug out by the torrents which roar down them during the infrequent rains, but the bed of which is dry most of the time. The *nullahs* provide a means of penetrating the country and have obvious strategic value, just as the narrow gorges (*tangi*) and the ravines (*darra*) are features favouring Mahsud ambushes. The ambush (*chapao*), a favourite tactic of the Frontier tribes, followed an often-repeated scenario featuring a band of Mahsud attackers (*ghadi*) and a pursuing group[37] (*chigga*): the attack was generally launched by raiders lying in ambush behind large boulders in the *nullah*. Knowing the names of these topological features and understanding Pashto was fundamental to control of the territory. These ordinary raids on Frontier territory had become so common in 1914–15 that Teague-Jones no longer bothered to enumerate them, and simply recorded the more picturesque details. Attack by a *lashkar*, a real battle group, was much more to be feared and could pose a threat to the headquarters stationed at Tank. In this case it was the intelligence officers who evaluated the reality of the threat. In the example described by Teague-Jones, the British intelligence officer based in Waziristan estimated the numbers of the *lashkar* to be 1,500 men, a figure which could be increased if the Mahsud Shabikhel clan were to join them. A close and detailed knowledge of the political chessboard occupied by the Frontier tribes was also one of the necessary conditions for control of the territory. Finally, the arms traffic in the Frontier had enabled the local tribes to acquire a museum-worthy collection of almost every type and generation of fire-arm:[38] Teague-Jones encountered two unhappy Powindahs from the Suleiman Khal tribe looking for their camels which the Mahsuds had stolen, who were carrying a rifle made in Saint-Etienne in 1874.

The Frontier Constabulary's mission also extended to control of the flows passing through this remote country from time to time, such as the migrating herds at the time of the *tirni*—a tax on cattle and sheep levied by the tribesmen—or supervising caravans such as those of the cross-border Powindah nomads, leaving their pastures for Khorasan or Afghanistan. On the second Sunday of every month one of the Frontier Constabulary's duties was to check the caravan leaving Draband. Led by Powindahs mounted on camels, the monthly convoy of travellers who had gathered at the Draband fort climbed in stages through the Sherani country as far as Moghulkot—the last of the Frontier Constabulary forts—and crossed the gorges of the Katau Drabar on its way to Fort Sandeman in Baluchistan. The watch kept on the caravan was a sign at local level of the geostrategic importance which the British authorities attached to Baluchistan.

The Frontier: a territory for elites?

Did this remote country, which brought the English into contact with brave mountain warriors, play a role in the making of the political and military British elite? The North West Frontier did not call for the same kind of personnel as in the rest of India, as is clear from the comment of Sir Harcourt Butler, foreign secretary for the government of India, in 1910: 'We want lean and keen men on the Frontier, and fat and good-natured men in the States.'[39] Warfare in the Frontier, with its mountainous topography and the adventures to be found there, heroic, dangerous or sometimes comical, thus made an ideal training ground for a military and political elite,[40] which was fascinated and challenged by tribal society with its honour code, but able to counter the warriors of the Frontier with the British virtues of courage and virility. From the time of its creation in 1913, the Frontier Constabulary, when recruiting officers, had stressed the 'opportunities for distinction' which an adventurous life on the Frontier would offer in abundance. While manpower rose as high as 4,000 men in the 1930s, there were continuing losses in the 1920s, with several hundred dead or wounded each year.[41] Frontier warfare was a schooling in endurance and bravery, which demanded a great deal of patrolling, and numerous trekking expeditions during which death was a constant threat. It also involved schooling in survival: when on patrol rations were very tight, with just a little flour for chapattis, and a handful of chick-peas. In this wild country, then, hunting was still of great importance, and here the English reverted to aristocratic sporting habits. Like Churchill before him,[42] Teague-Jones was no exception, recounting stories of his hunts for brown bear or for *markhor*, the large wild goat of northern India. In the spectacular Frontier country with its warlike inhabitants, man regressed to the primitive state characteristic of a masculine society, which had a fascination for Teague-Jones. The North West Frontier was a decisive stage in the training of an intelligence officer who, in the remote corners of Sherani territory, read Turgenev's *Annals of a Sportsman* in Russian and *Campaigns on the North-West Frontier* in English, while perfecting his Persian grammar. To get an idea of the everyday reality of a Frontier officer, here for example are Teague-Jones's notes dated 5 October 1914, in which one can perceive the humour and imperturbable phlegm brought to bear on the events of the day:

Spent the best part of the day on the road to Nishpa and exploring various nullahs on the way, and noting the location of any springs or water-holes. There is no telegraph anywhere nearer than Moghulkot, which is full fifteen miles away, so looked forward to having a nice quiet time and proposed to spend a week exploring the surrounding area. In the middle of the night I was awakened by a telegram brought all the way from Moghulkot by a Sherani sowar. The telegram was a long one from the Assistant Commissioner in Tank warning me that a party of four Mahsuds dressed in uniforms of the South Waziristan Militia were out with the declared object of capturing and carrying off a British Officer alive.

Next morning I took my gun out and accompanied by a small escort I climbed about in the neighbouring gorge in the hopes of bagging an elusive chicken for the pot. After a good deal of exercise I managed to bag one, which furnished me with a tasty breakfast.

Life in an outpost tends to become very monotonous after a time. There are days when one does not feel inclined to go toiling through ravines and water-courses, exploring nullahs and climbing summits. Nor does one as a rule, on the other hand, get many quiet moments to oneself. Life in a post is very condensed in the matter of room, and the constant babel of voices, the crowing of roosters, the horrid noise made by the Indian fowl when she has just laid an egg, and, worst of all, the braying of the post donkey, all these sounds combine to render peace impossible. The quietest time is in the afternoon; the donkey for some reason does not bray so much, and most of the sepoys are asleep on their charpais.

The evening is the worst time. It is quite impossible for one sepoy to converse with another in measured tones, he bawls at the top of his voice. This goes on incessantly from sundown until around ten p.m. Then someone will produce an 'ardab' (a native string instrument) and a 'sing-song' is proposed. For this, however, the Sahib's permission is required, and the Jemadar comes gliding into the room with a grave salute and asks if there is any objection to a little 'tamasha'.

The wretched Sahib, who has just settled down to a little quiet reading, has not the heart to refuse. He really has a great affection for his men, whom he works very hard when on duty, but at other times treats as a lot of boisterous schoolboys, resignedly gives his consent, but on the understanding that the 'tamasha' must stop promptly at eleven p.m. To do them justice, this order is invariably strictly obeyed.[43]

A place of solitude and endurance, part Boy Scout territory and part colony, the Frontier was an unforgettable place of apprenticeship for this young man, barely twenty-five years old, who was behaving towards his men with the paternalism of an officer at the head of a native regiment. In 1914 the empire rested on the shoulders of people like this.

The complexity of Frontier politics, the rivalries of clans and tribes, their relevance to the much wider context of the problems of the age—the defence of the subcontinent, the hypothetical Russian threat, the stabilisation of Afghanistan—where events and reactions to them were incomprehensible to an uninstructed foreigner, made for an exceptional training ground. Besides the learning of languages—Pashto, Persian and no doubt some other local languages—which would have a decisive effect on the formation of this intelligence officer, Teague-Jones's grasp of the political ethnography of the Frontier made it possible for him to understand almost any other kind of territory. Teague-Jones was to become an 'expert' on the regions of Central Asia, sent on a solo mission to Turkmenistan in 1918, pondering the role that Muslims might play in British strategy against the Bolsheviks in Central Asia[44] and later, towards the end of the 1920s, wandering on the roads of Baluchistan in the guise of a solitary eccentric British traveller, not far from the North West Frontier. And then there was the Frontier itself, a land where vengeance was more terrible than in old Spain or Corsica, and where, according to Winston Churchill:

except at the times of sowing and harvest, a continual state of feud and strife prevails through-out the land. Tribe wars with tribe. The people of one valley fight with those of the next. To the quarrels of communities are added the combats of individuals. Khan assails khan, each supported by his retainers. Every tribesman has a blood feud with his neighbour. Every man's hand is against the other, and all against the stranger.[45]

It is a viewpoint which is tempered in Teague-Jones's experience, as his journals relate. He appears to have formed genuine friendships through his participation in the settling of one of the notorious blood-feuds. At Bain, after a day on horseback in wild Frontier country, he notes on 16 March 1915:

Here at Bain, I made a cup of tea for myself and Jemadar Zaman Shah, a Zakkakhel Afridi. We talked of his home in the Khyber, we have a number of mutual friends up there. He knows Mandezai, the Kukkikhel, whom I once helped to settle a blood-feud. We talked till nightfall, leaning over the breastwork of the bastion. Our conversation was abruptly inter-rupted by a message from Mullazai that three separate raiding parties of Mahsuds are known to be out in this general area, and to warn Faqir Chowki. Damn the Mahsuds. Save for the cup of tea, I have had no food all day, I am going to eat my evening meal now, for I may get no opportunity later on.[46]

Teague-Jones provides us with hardly any more details about the conversation in his diary, which mentions his own involvement in this debt of honour. Many years later he would write *Khyber Blood-Feud*, a highly autobiographical novel whose char-acters and situations recall this tragedy on the Frontier. While European minds may look condescendingly on the patriarchal customs of the Frontier, blood justice and the honour code of tribal societies, it remains the case that they fascinated and helped to shape a special British Frontier elite.

The numerous photographs taken by Teague-Jones show how his way of looking at things evolved. The author—except when he is photographed among his men—never betrays any purpose other than that of a recorder exploring the otherness of the Frontier world through its landscapes and portraits of its inhabitants. Teague-Jones, who was incidentally a good draughtsman, was equipping himself with the weapons of the photographer. His viewpoint was taking shape. He aims and he shoots, intend-ing a comprehensiveness which gives his work—probably without him being aware of it—an 'anthropographic' quality. On the eve of the First World War the camera was a colonialist instrument: it was used to explore the multiple facets of the exotic, and shaped the way the West at any given moment looked at the colonised world. That an intelligence officer should have a gift for seeing is not without significance: in their admiration of the physical nobility of the men of the Frontier, his photo-graphs seem to have the same aim as his diary. Photographs fix memories in place, and although none of the photographs in Teague-Jones's collection is a bearer of secret intelligence, the collection reveals a capacity for looking at the world, country-side, men—and animals too—with the sympathy and curiosity which characterise the good intelligence agent and the good ethnographer. Teague-Jones's talent is evi-dent in his ability to conjure up the strangeness of the Frontier, and in the precision of his writing:

FROM THE PUNJAB TO THE NORTH WEST FRONTIER

It is night in Luni post. The day has been hot for the time of year, and one is grateful for darkness. Outside the post all is silent save for the incessant chirping of the crickets in the scrub, and the occasional chatter-chatter of an owl. Inside the post all is stir and bustle, for the present garrison consists chiefly of Khattaks, the finest dancers on the Frontier, and tonight they are going to have a dance.

Above us is the cloudless sky bright with stars and a silvery crescent but a few days old. Around us, the bare loop-holed walls of the post loom up against the star lit sky. The flickering light of a lantern falls on numbers of wooden charpais and dark figures flitting hither and thither. Up above can be heard the tramping of the sentry on the roof, and in the opposite corner of the post, the champing of the horses in the stables. One or two glimmering fires by the barracks denote a belated diner cooking his chapatties.

Suddenly, the loud thumping of a native drum drowns out all other sounds. The beds are pushed away to one side, and the sepoys flock together. The drumming is very irregular, this is the tuning-up, or rather the warming up of the drummer. Then a number of sepoys break into a wild chorus. They are selecting the tune. Several different choruses are tried, and finally one meets with general approval. The drummer now gets to work again. Slow and irregular, at first, the uneducated ear detects no rhythm in it. Gradually it quickens, and in the darkness one sees a cluster of human forms performing a slow kind of step dance, more or less in time with the drum. As the drumming quickens, the timing and the symmetry of the step become more apparent until the spectator himself feels carried away by the desire to move to the same rhythm.

In his ensuing description of the wild and mesmerising sabre dance, Teague-Jones takes on the mantle of a real ethnographer, recording the exact rhythms and movements of the dance:

Now the circle of dancers opens out, now draws together again, meanwhile the whole ring gradually moves round and round in a circle. Next, the lantern is placed in the centre of the circle, and the light flashes on weird figures, swinging arms, shaking heads and flowing baggy trousers. The beating of the drum grows still louder, the dancers redouble their efforts and to the beating of the drum is now added their wild chorus, culminating each time in a single clap of the hands ... This chorus when shouted with vigour, as it always is on these occasions, has a most weird effect. The drummer has now apparently reached his highest speed. Blood-curdling yells arise from the onlookers, mingled with frantic shouts of Allah! Suddenly, the drummer, dancers and shouting stop in a breath. The dance is ended.

After a brief pause, the drum again beats an introductory measure. The crowd of dim figures separate; a couple of lanterns are placed in the centre of the ring. Now the light falls on quivering sword blades, and, to the slow irregular beating of the drum, a single shadowy form steps into the circle. Pacing with curious, exaggerated strides backwards and forwards, now to one side, now to the other, he never ceases to perform rapid passes in the air, thrust and parry, guard and recover. The drum quickens its beat, and with it quicken also the movements of the dancer. Faster and faster, swaying one moment this way and then that, the glitter of the sword blade is like a live thing also dancing in the lamp light ... Suddenly again the rhythm switches ... the dancer flings out both arms straight from the shoulders and continuous twirling on his toes at a giddy rate until completely exhausted, he falls on his knees midst wild yells of applause from the throng.

Again there is brief pause, broken by the opening beats of the drum. The rhythm has now changed … This dance is also performed with swords, but instead of a single dancer, there are now two. The swordsman begins the same grotesque steps and arm-swinging as before, but this time the effect is enhanced by the chorus of onlookers and supporters. The pace grows terrific and now includes leaping and circling and rapid whirls as well as arm-swinging and foot-play. It is always a marvel to me that nobody ever seems to get injured at these shows, for as the pace becomes more furious, the audience in its excitement and enthusiasm edges right in, until the whirling swords in the centre have perilously little room in which to play.

To observe without being seen. One can sense in this discretion and reserve the talent for observation which is necessary for an intelligence officer:

These Khattak dances have a great fascination for me, and I generally like to watch them from a dark corner and, if possible, unperceived by the participants. One then feels that one is not watching a tamasha specially arranged for one's personal entertainment. They are certainly one of the wildest and weirdest sights on the Frontier.[47]

The visual qualities of the writing in this passage are no less evocative of its author's personality than of the rhythms of the traditional dance of the Frontier Khattaks, one of the best-known Indian dances. It is less the religious and narrative function of the dance than the limb-shaking rhythm which fascinates the observer; in a colonial setting it is a fresh expression of the 'primitive'. By watching the dance through the author's eyes, we are present at a scene which shapes his outlook: the Frontier territory is exerting a power of its own. If in 1892 Salisbury could assimilate the Frontier wars to 'the surf that marks the edge and the advance of the wave of civilisation',[48] Teague-Jones's observations from life in 1914 reflect a less dismissive approach.

The relationship between power and territory in the North West Frontier was one of variable geometry at local level, even though at continental level there were recurrent bursts of pressure. The outbreak of the First World War in 1914 marked a period of calm in the Great Game between Britain and Russia, now allies within the framework of the Entente. It was a very different picture in 1919 when the British system on the Frontier, under which, following Curzon's vision, the tribal areas had been organised as a 'marcher' territory, was brutally derailed by the outbreak of the third Anglo-Afghan War. With encouragement from the Bolshevik government, Amanullah, the new king of Afghanistan, had declared war in 1919 and crossed the frontier of British India, provoking an immediate revolt by the Frontier tribes. A single RAF bomb on Kabul put an end to what appeared to be the last phase of the Great Game, which was concluded by the Treaty of Rawalpindi on 8 August 1919. The British were then obliged to rebuild their entire system of control over the tribal territory of the Frontier. But was this really the last phase of the Great Game? In 1939 a report by Teague-Jones warned that the development of Soviet policy in Afghanistan was based on 'ethnological progression', that is to say on a strategy which made use of the tribes and minorities. Here we can spot the signs of the future expert, who at this early date had discerned the beginnings of a Soviet policy of influence in Afghanistan.

3

THE PERSIAN GULF AND THE HUNT FOR 'MR WASSMUSS'

Reginald Teague-Jones kept one trophy from the intelligence wars that fed imperial rivalries in the First World War. Its significance is strongly linked to the geopolitical issues of the day: it is the dust-jacket of an atlas published by Justus Perthes in 1912, and registered to the library of the German consulate in Bushire (Bushehr) in December 1913. German cartography,[1] generally known for its somewhat tendentious precision and authority, is not however on view here, for the good reason that only the fly-leaf[2] has been preserved, the atlas itself having been presented by Teague-Jones (alias Ronald Sinclair) to the Miami Public Library in 1960. The fly-leaf, which bears the colophon of the prestigious publishers of the Almanach de Gotha, has two manuscript inscriptions: one, which is dated with the Bushire consulate's imperial stamp to December 1913 and June 1914, is in German Gothic script, and the other is in English and in Ronald Sinclair's hand. A photograph pinned to the page bears the heading 'Kaiserlich Deutsches Konsulat' in Gothic letters and is of a man wearing a kind of cocked hat, and a uniform with gold braid and buttons, striking a pose. He has a large decoration round his neck and holds a sword in his left hand and, in his right, a cigar which he is smoking. The setting is the foot of a staircase leading up to the patio of an oriental building which houses the German consulate in Bushire. The master of the house who is wearing this official dress has an expression which seems somewhat incongruous for an imperial consul in circumstances like these. The cigar suggests a certain relaxation of mood, and the dreamy, almost naïve look on his face, and his slight smile, suggest a likeable and original sort of personality. According to the note in manuscript on the back of the photograph, this man is Wilhelm Wassmuss, the famous and charismatic German agent who rallied the tribes of southern Persia to the anti-British struggle during the First World War.

The photograph, which probably formed part of the information given to Teague-Jones for his mission to the Persian Gulf in 1917, is that of a human target. And the

49

page from the magnificent atlas is a war prize, the relic of a conflict between two agents of rival empires in Persia, itself the focal point of Euro-Asiatic rivalry. This was an inaugural mission to Persia for Teague-Jones; his knowledge of Persian and his taste for adventure would often bring him back again. In 1917, transferred to the Indian Army Reserve as a 2nd lieutenant, Teague-Jones was posted to military intelligence and assigned to duties in the Persian Gulf. One of the mission's objectives was the capture of Wilhelm Wassmuss, the imperial consul and agent of subversion who had been encouraging the cross-frontier tribes in Persia, Afghanistan and India, particularly the tribes of Fars in the south of Iran, to revolt against the British. Wassmuss's activities were threatening British supply lines on the Mesopotamian front, and there was therefore very good reason why the British should have ordered a number of agents and officers to hunt him down. Teague-Jones, who had started learning Urdu and Persian some years ago, and who spoke fluent German, was to be one of them. Though the only contact between 'the German Lawrence' and Teague-Jones was to be at second-hand, through the medium of an atlas which passed from one to the other, lovingly studied by both, there is no doubt that Wassmuss, an intrepid and inventive operator, inspired Teague-Jones's methods as an agent, notably in Transcaspia. In this first Persian adventure, Wassmuss was a kind of alter ego for Teague-Jones, with whom he shared a distinct liking for field-work and adventure, and an ability for melting into the background using 'ethnic' disguises.

The Great War and Persia

On the eve of the First World War the Persian state (see Map 1) was disintegrating. In the absence of political stability and financial and military resources, the constitutional revolution had come to an end: it had begun in December 1905, when the shah was obliged to grant a constitution and the creation of a parliament (Majlis). But in 1912 the constitution had been suspended for a second time, and the territory of Persia was under foreign control in consequence of its economic and financial obligations. After the Russian defeat in the 1904–5 Russo-Japanese War, imperial rivalries gave way to negotiations, which led to the signing of the Anglo-Russian Convention of 1907. Without formally infringing Persian independence and integrity, the Convention divided the country into three distinct zones. The western regions of the country that made up the Russian sphere of influence included Tehran, Iranian Azerbaijan, Asterabad and Khorasan (on the Russian border) and the shore of the Caspian with Gilan and Mazandaran. Britain secured a sphere of influence in the south-east quarter of the country, following a line connecting Birjand and Bandar Abbas by way of Kerman. By extending their sphere to Baluchistan the British secured the immediate approaches to India and Afghanistan, and controlled the Straits of Ormuz, the gateway to the Persian Gulf. The vast intermediate area between the Russian and British zones was defined as a 'neutral zone' in the 1907 agreement. In 1915, however, new agreements characteristic of the secret diplomacy practised by the Entente Powers provided for the extension of the British zone to the territory declared neutral in the 1907 Convention, in return for British acceptance of Russian territorial ambitions in Anatolia. The agreement allowed the British to consolidate their grip on the whole of Persia, except for the zone of Russian influence in the north. They were also able to exercise better control over the south-west zone, which contained the oilfields exploited by the Anglo-Persian Oil Company (APOC) since the sale of the concession rights by Knox d'Arcy in 1909, and large towns like Shiraz and Isfahan. The 1915 agreement was a further step in turning the Persian Gulf into an 'English Lake'.

Iran during the First World War: the theory and practice of 'neutrality'

Torn by great power rivalries, the consequences of the constitutionalist revolution, and a rise in dissidence among the leaders of Shia Islam, Persia held fresh geostrategic importance for Great Britain from 1912 onwards due to the British Navy's decision to change the fuel used in its ships from coal to oil. From that day on, Persia's oil was all the more desirable because it was a source of direct refuelling which was independent of the other Entente Powers. Against a backdrop of Anglo-Russian rivalry which persisted, despite the Entente which brought Russia and Britain together in 1914 as co-belligerents, the decay of the Persian state proceeded inexorably. The last monarch in the Qajar dynasty, Ahmad Shah, who acceded to the throne on his sixteenth birthday on 21 July 1914, was to be the final ruler of this state, which had already virtually ceased to exist.[3] Despite pressure from the British and the Russians to join the Entente camp, and though it had been had been transformed into a Russian protectorate in the north and a British one in the south, Persia ultimately declared neutrality in the First World War. A wise decision, which appeared to free Persia from its tutelary powers, Persian neutrality also demonstrated the hostility of most Persians to the Entente. How indeed could it be otherwise when Britain and Russia were occupying the country, and the Ottoman Empire, a hereditary enemy but nonetheless a Muslim state, had joined the war on the side of the Central Powers? Whether the question was Islamic solidarity, which soon resulted in a proclamation of jihad against the Entente, or an upsurge in nationalism resulting from the perpetual inroads on Persian sovereignty, every factor—leaving aside the divergences between Sunni and Shia—contributed to making Persia's neutrality one that was favourable to the Triple Alliance. The British, who were aware of being universally detested in Persia—subsequent Russian propaganda would consistently exploit this theme, as one may see in Bek-Nazarev's film *Khaspiuch*, made at Yerevan in 1927, whose subject matter is Anglo-Russian rivalry in Persia and the 1891 tobacco monopoly—tolerated this kind of neutrality for one major strategic reason: the possibility of preserving an independent oil supply in times of war which was independent of the United States.

The turn of events in Europe in 1915, which appeared to tilt the outcome of the war in favour of the Central Powers, encouraged Persia to engage in secret talks with Germany with the aim of forming an alliance. But this proved to be difficult inasmuch as demands for guarantees of sovereignty and territorial integrity were hard to reconcile with the conquering ambitions of the Ottoman Empire. Moreover, an agreement would require Germany's consent to a major financial commitment in order to break Persia's debt dependency on Russia and Great Britain. In this context, Persia's internal politics became completely subordinated to the clash between the belligerent powers. Under the pretext of guarding against a possible pro-German coup d'état in Tehran, a Russian army corps of 8,000 cavalry and 6,000 infantry under General Baratov marched on Qazvin in November 1915. In a highly confused situation, the Entente Allies managed to obtain the renewal of Persian pledges of neutrality, notably by securing the nomination of pro-British ministers to the government. The Iranian patriots, for their part, exasperated by the ever more intrusive supervision of the Russians and the British, left Tehran for Qom accompanied by the German ambassador, where they formed a national Defence Committee under Soleyman Mirza. Despite support from the gendarmerie and the presence of reinforcements from the Ottoman Army, the Committee was unable to resist General Baratov's advance, and he entered Isfahan on 16 March 1916. Having taken refuge at Kermanshah in the west of the country near Ottoman Mesopotamia, the National Defence Committee, which claimed the status of government in exile, henceforth enjoyed German protection. Led by the regional governor, Nezam-os-Saltana, and endowed with a poorly equipped army of 8,000 men whose command structure, made up of Ottoman officers and tribal chiefs, was reminiscent of the Mexican army, the national government, whose continued existence depended on support from the Triple Alliance, would not survive beyond 1917.

Jihad and pointed helmets

There were, similarly, precise limits in space and time to German dreams of expansion in the East,[4] dreams shared by the leadership of the Young Turks in the Ottoman Empire: these aspirations concerned the lands of Afghanistan and Persia from which, until 1917, the Germans would try to open a breach into the Indian subcontinent. A newcomer among the imperialist powers in the Middle East, Germany had been investing in the Ottoman Empire financially since the end of the nineteenth century. The famous Bagdadbahn, the Baghdad railway, born of a marriage between Deutsche Bank and the technological prowess of German industry—principally Siemens—created a direct link between Berlin and Baghdad on 2 June 1914. That was the completion date of the 1,600-kilometre section linking Konya in Anatolia to Baghdad in the heart of Mesopotamia, via Adana, Aleppo and Mosul. An engineering masterpiece, the Bagdadbahn satisfied commercial and strategic aims by making a land link to the East and beyond to India without any need for recourse to the Suez Canal in the event of a conflict blocking access to the canal for German shipping. The original plan, which was never realised, envisaged the extension of the line as far as Basra, and the creation of a port at the bottom of the Persian Gulf on the empty beaches of the emirate of Kuwait.[5] The project aroused British opposition: Lord Curzon applied pressure to the Sublime Porte, and a political agent, Colonel Malcolm Meade, was sent to Kuwait in order to overturn the German plan. In fact, the Germans had been installing a network of consuls and agents throughout the Persian Gulf from the beginning of the twentieth century onwards, and in addition to those of the railway engineers, the activities of a small import–export firm, Robert Wonckhaus, had also aroused British concerns. Between 1899 and 1906 the firm, which was probably underwritten by funds from Wilhelmstrasse, had opened offices in short order at Bahrain, Bushire, Basra, Mohammera and Bandar Abbas. From 1906 onwards a German shipping company had been running a regular freight and passenger service between Germany and the Gulf. A young English officer, Major Percy Cox, was despatched to the Gulf region in 1904 to counter the menace of German intrusion.

The German embassy in Constantinople, which stood in a dominating position on the Bosphorus, was the nerve centre of an oriental policy sustained by intense German/Ottoman diplomatic activity and by ties of friendship with members of the Young Turk Government. Enver Pasha had been the military attaché in Berlin, and the German ambassador in Constantinople, Baron Hans Freiherr von Wangenheim, was on intimate terms with the kaiser. A few influential figures, such as von Moltke and Thyssen, were to give a definite shape to William II's imperial dreams of raising the tribes and peoples of the East against Germany's rivals, starting with Great Britain. Persia was to be the hub for the Germanic jihad, both as an objective in itself, but also as a base for access to Afghanistan and to India beyond. On 23 November, shortly after the Ottoman Empire's entry into the war alongside Germany (2 November 1914), the caliph/sultan proclaimed a holy war against the Entente Powers to the entire Muslim world. The possibility of using Ottoman territory to organise anti-British subversion everywhere in the East was now open for the German authorities. William II was enthusiastic about the idea. On 30 July 1914 he wrote in a manuscript marginal note that 'we must tear off England's pacific and Christian mask … Our Consuls in Turkey and India must raise the whole Muslim world against this crafty and deceitful nation of shopkeepers; England must at least lose India, even if it costs us all our blood.' To the emir of Afghanistan he writes:

I wish to see the independence of the Muslim peoples and to ensure their freedom of action. It is not just for the present but also for the future that I wish with all my heart to assist these peoples in their struggle for independence, and my Government will support them.[6]

From the outset of the war German propaganda aimed at Persia developed the theme of a historical connection between Emperor William II and Cyrus the Great: was not the oldest name for Germany 'Cyrmanie', directly derived from Cyrus? Opinion in the bazaars nonetheless remained sceptical in the face of propaganda which went as far as intimating that William II, 'Haji Vilem', had converted to Islam. In addition to the propaganda effort, the German political and military authorities[7] fostered the creation of a Persian Committee chaired by Taqizada, one of the personalities in the constitutionalist revolution. They planned to launch various expeditions, some with the aim of stimulating anti-British and anti-Russian risings in Persia, others designed to penetrate English lines around Afghanistan so as to incite the emir and the cross-border tribes of the North West Province to lead a rebellion against British domination in India. The first concrete steps in realising the plan, which the Ottoman authorities had helped to prepare, were soon taken, with the departure of a German expedition to Baghdad on 6 September 1914. From there three German adventurers, a geographer—Captain Oskar Ritter von Niedermayer—a zoologist— Erich Zugmayer—and the former imperial consul at Bushire—Wilhelm Wassmuss— set up ambitious operations throughout Persian territory. The special mandate of a second mission was to destroy the oilfield installations in the south and to attempt to raise the Shiites of the Mesopotamian south against the British. Disagreements between the Germans and the Turks soon wrecked any semblance of coherence in these grandiose political projects, but in return left an astonishing freedom of action to the men at the head of the missions. Niedermayer, who arrived at Kermanshah in April 1915 and was joined at Isfahan by von Hentig, was to succeed in persuading the local clergy to preach jihad against the Russians and the British, before continuing on his path to Kabul. In the meantime Zugmayer penetrated into the country between Kerman and Yezd, taking over control of the telegraph and raiding the branches of the Imperial Bank of Persia in the process. Wilhelm Wassmuss for his part took the regions of the south and the hinterland of Bushire, the region of Tangistan, where he had already established a network of friendships with the local tribes. By the end of 1915, with a strong position in Shiraz, in Kermanshah, and in most of the cities except Tehran, the Germans had accordingly managed to establish control over almost the entire territory of Persia. In the same year Teague-Jones was still in the North West Frontier Province. But British efforts at reconquering lost territory, particularly in the south, would take him to Persia in 1917.

A police force in the South: the South Persia Rifles (SPR)

Alongside its efforts to undermine governments in Tehran and to place individuals susceptible to British influence in ministerial positions, from 1916 onwards the British followed a strategy of reconquering the southern and eastern regions of Persia. The strategy was hostile to Germany, but its objective was also to neutralise the influence of Russia, an ally until 1917, but in fact a formidable rival of British power in Persia. This power had been much reduced in any case, for since the beginning of 1916 most British and Russian consuls had been obliged to leave the cities of central and southern Persia; the British had only managed to protect their essential interests, to wit the oil region of Ahvaz and Abadan, thanks to support from most of the Bakhtiaris and the Arabic-speaking tribes of the Banu Ka'b. Yet this solid tribal block did not stop the elusive Wassmuss from orchestrating sabotage attacks such as the dynamiting of a pipeline in 1915 which stopped production for several months.[8] Among other actions carried out by the German 'privateers' were the assassinations of the Russian vice-consul at Isfahan and the British vice-consul at Shiraz, and the seizure of seven branches of the Imperial Bank of Persia in Kermanshah, Hamadan,

Sultanabad, Isfahan, Shiraz, Yezd and Kerman; all of which undermined the British presence in their zone of influence, except in the ports guarded by troops and warships. On the pretext of restoring the authority of the central government, re-establishing British control in Persia now became a fundamental objective. The strategy for the re-conquest, which was launched by the government of India and orchestrated on the spot by the British ambassador in Tehran, Marling, could not depend either on Persian forces or on the Russian forces now in action in the north with a Cossack brigade. The protection of Persia's eastern flank by a Russo-British force deployed in the east, the East Persia Cordon, certainly showed that cooperation between the English and the Russians was possible; but this force, whose aim was to prevent German agents infiltrating Afghan territory, only really started to be effective after Zugmayer[9] had already left.

Why was the East Persia Cordon so slow in getting off the ground? Christopher Sykes[10] had this to say:

Why the Russians and the English had till July 1915 made no preparation for the closing of the Afghan frontier remains one of the mysteries of that time. But they had not, and now they had to act with precipitation. There had been, of course, much fear of exciting Persian anger by the introduction of troops, but now there was no alternative. After a feverish correspondence with India and conferences with the Russians it was decided that the latter should make safe the northern and we the southern half of the frontier. The Russians were to guard a line running from Sarakhs, the meeting-place of their country, Persia and Afghanistan, continuing through Mashad, Turbat, Kain, and Birjand—we Birjand, Neh, Sistan and Kuh i Malik i Siah in Baluchistan. And now there began a race for the frontier which lasted the whole of July.

The northern half of the line lay in a bitter country but there is in that province just sufficient to make a rapid organization possible. The task of the Russians was not so appalling as that of the English.

The south-eastern provinces of Persia are perhaps the most dismal of all places emptied by a scorching sun. There was then no road and the troops could only labour to the occupation of their posts on camels. The hurry and desperation of the English involved them in comedies: it was first proposed that single individuals should be sent to the different oases as consuls, and when established should agitate the tribes into an excitement favouring the Allies, but this was abandoned upon the violent protests of the Persian governors. Eventually, after a complex history of tedium and heroism the cordon was formed all along the line. Niedermayer had not yet passed through. To the circumstance of scarcity was added the dreadful phenomenon of Sistan: the wind of hundred and twenty days. With a terrible regularity a hot dust-laden wind blows at this season about South-East Persia. It is a sandstorm which lasts four months.

The need to create a British army corps which would be recognised as legitimate by the central government in Tehran led to the organisation of a police force in southern Persia, the South Persia Rifles (the SPR, known by the Persians as the Espiâr), largely drawn from an Anglo-Indian expeditionary force. The organisation of this force was entrusted to Sir Percy Sykes (1867–1945). After distinguishing himself during the war in South Africa, Sykes had become an expert on eastern

Persia, familiar with both the southern section—he had been consul at Kerman and Sistan—and the northern section, having been consul at Meshed for eight years. Sykes had initially been posted to Chinese Turkestan in the First World War, but was recalled urgently to Delhi in January 1916, where he was informed that he had been appointed inspector general of the South Persia Rifles, and that his initial mission was to raise, train and maintain a locally recruited armed force. 'He was despatched from India on this apparently forlorn hope with two muzzle-loaders, no single machine-gun, three British and three Indian officers, and an escort of twenty-five Indian sowars. He reached Bandar Abbas on the Gulf in March, recruited fifty-three men within twenty-four hours and hoisted the flag.'[11] Like Wassmuss, Sykes was able to draw on existing networks and old friendships. During a talk he gave in April 1921 in front of an invited audience at the Royal Geographical Society, which included General Edmund Barrow and Sir Arthur Hirtzel, he recalled:

Upon landing at Bandar Abbas in March 1916 I was greeted by many old friends, and, thanks to their help, the energy of my officers was amply rewarded by the enlistment of as many recruits as could be managed, although at Delhi my chances of success were considered to be slight. Twelve days after landing the Persian flag was hoisted over the camp of the South Persia Rifles. The force never looked back, and in a comparatively short time was able to guard Bandar Abbas and an important section of the caravan route.[12]

Despite being deployed in difficult terrain and extremely testing heat, the SPR expeditionary force managed to regain control of southern Persia by means of a looping movement that finished in Shiraz. In July 1916 the English took back control of Kerman, a strategic point controlling the routes to Afghanistan and Baluchistan, which enabled them to raise a new SPR brigade in the area. In August they were at Yezd after a march of 220 miles down a wild valley, every nook and cranny of which was familiar to Sykes. On 11 September the SPR succeeded in joining up with Russian forces at Isfahan, and finally, on 11 November, Sykes entered Shiraz in the company of Farman Farma, a prince of the blood and heir to the Qajar throne. After receiving official recognition from the Persian government in March 1917, the SPR, which had been left to rely entirely on Sykes's skills in improvising recruitment, was finally reinforced by troops from the British Army in India.[13] Reginald Teague-Jones's posting to the Persian Gulf in 1917 is thus to be understood in the context of a British re-conquest of southern Persia. Upon arriving in Bandar Abbas, henceforth the base for an SPR regiment, he stayed in the Naiband camp on the immediate outskirts of the town, before setting off deep into the interior of the Persian Gulf in pursuit of Wilhelm Wassmuss.

The tribulations of the 'German Lawrence' in the Persian Gulf

I have reports from agents everywhere—pedlars in South Russia, Afghan horse dealers, Turcoman merchants, pilgrims on the road to Mecca, sheikhs in North Africa, sailors on the Black Sea coasters, sheep-skinned Mongols, Hindu fakirs, Greek traders in the Gulf, as well as respectable Consuls who use ciphers. They tell the same story. The East is waiting for a revelation. It has been promised one. Some star—man, prophecy, or trinket—is coming out of the West. The Germans know, and that is the card with which they are going to astonish the world.[14]

The British intelligence 'system' in Persia made it possible to inform London and Delhi of German policy in action, if not to prevent it. The latter had its ups and downs during the First World War, and Wilhelm Wassmuss's subversive activities belong both within the framework of organised German policy and that of a personal adventure story. Wassmuss, as a quintessential field agent, exemplified for Teague-Jones what to do and what not to do, and he would have no hesitation in later using some of his methods, such as ethnic disguise and tribal 'micro-diplomacy'. Wassmuss's operations, which began at the favourable moment of the German offensive from early 1915 to the spring of 1916, were to continue beyond the resumption of German activities in Persia which were made possible by Turkish troop advances between the summer of 1916 and February 1917. Thus in the spring of 1916 Raymond Lecomte, the French minister plenipotentiary at Tehran, noted that: 'Persia today has very nearly recovered its health, the German virus is no longer raging in the region which stretches from the mountains of Shiraz to the shores of the Persian Gulf. That is where Wassmuss is.'[15] So who exactly was Wassmuss, the adventurer, now to be found on the shores of the Gulf? How did he manage to give the British authorities the slip right until the very end? What was there about his mission to Persia, despite its failure, that served as a useful learning experience for Teague-Jones?

Wassmuss, a model field-agent

Bearing himself with dignity Wassmuss rode about the Tangistan from village to village. He was an impressive man to look at. He always wore his hair long and this showed to much advantage his fine forehead. His eyes were very penetrating but he generally looked upwards as though lost in thought. His features were regular and they had in them an expression of great power. Although he was short, broad and heavy, yet he had a certain elegance in his gait and he was a remarkable horseman. He pleased the tribesmen.[16]

This physical and psychological portrait of 'Wassmuss of Persia' summarises the few known biographical details of this influential agent. Wilhelm Wassmuss was born in 1880, in Ohlendorf, at the bottom of the Gopslau Valley in the Harz Mountains south-east of Hanover. He entered the Foreign Office (Auswärtiges Amt) in 1906, and was first posted as a junior officer to Madagascar, before being promoted to vice-consul, and then consul, at Bushire in the Persian Gulf. At the time, Wassmuss's mission, closely scrutinised by Major Percy Cox, was to procure the same advantages for the German Navy in the Gulf as those possessed by the British. Wassmuss did not, however, stay long in Bushire, and returned to Madagascar in 1910 where he led a secluded life, almost entirely devoted from then on to an obsessive study of the desert country of Iran and its peoples. These efforts were crowned with apparent success, since in 1913 Wassmuss was once again posted to the small town of Bushire, which occupied an important geostrategic position.

Bushire (see Map 5), which was one of Persia's principal naval ports, lies on the Persian Gulf more than 700 kilometres to the south of Tehran. It was founded by Nadir Shah in 1736, and was rapidly annexed to the British sphere of interest, as from 1763 the East India Company had secured the right to establish a commercial base there, to which the Royal Navy was able to add a naval base at the end of the eighteenth century. In the nineteenth century, the town's functions as a trading centre and port continued to develop in tandem with British importance in the region. Bushire was occupied by the British in 1856 as it was to be again in 1915, at the point where Wassmuss's intrigues had reached their height. Bushire is in fact one in a chain of ports along the Persian Gulf, 'wretched towns of 10,000 to 15,000 inhabitants, through which English influence has its hooks into Persia'.[17] The climate was truly hellish. Torrid summers, with hot winds carrying the dust of Arabia, drove away most of the inhabitants, whereas the winter was made slightly more bearable by the north-west wind, the *chemal*, which brought a little rain. The houses of Bushire then became habitable in low rooms aired by the *badgir*, or wind-towers, that rise above roof-top level. The local population was not, properly speaking, Persian, but rather Arab and African. The Persian coast, formed out of enormous banks of gravel, sheets of sand and soil stinking of oil and sulphur, has a desolate look, and Bushire was a modest harbour with a few date palms, sheltered within a coastal depression. There were few Europeans, and in the languishing British colony at Bushire, Wassmuss's entertainments struck a flamboyant note on the eve of the First World War. According to Christopher Sykes, the Germans and the British were on visiting terms at the time. 'The depressed colony of our countrymen were often invited to Wassmuss's garden and entertained with huge potations of beer.'[18] In a mildly intoxicated haze, Wassmuss dreamt of the wild and phantasmagorical hinterland north and north-west of Bushire, the notorious land of the Deshistan defiles and Tangistan. He explored the back-country tirelessly, beginning with the town of Ahram, and built a solid network of friendships among the Tangistani nomads, in whom he was passionately interested. Wassmuss spoke classical Persian and also the Tangistani dialect, and numbered among his main friends Hussain, the sheikh of Kutar, Ghazanfar-es-Saltaneh, the sheikh of Borazjan, as well as Zar Khidair, the sheikh of Ahram, who was considered to be an important man in Tangistan. Fired by genuine enthusiasm, Wassmuss was on intimate terms with the tribes, whose dress he soon adopted: a heavy camel-hair coat and a small round hat.

When war broke out in Europe in July 1914, the British, who had helped the government of Fars to get a temporary grip on brigandage, were still masters of the region. On the surface, events elsewhere not affecting the small European colony at Bushire, and on 4 August 1914 Wassmuss was even invited to dine at the British legation. He politely declined the invitation and left Bushire for Constantinople, leaving the German consulate in Bushire to a Dr Listermann. At the embassy in Constantinople there was a meeting arranged by Ambassador Wangenheim, during which a practical plan was decided upon which went far beyond what Wassmuss was hoping for. Within the framework of the new German policy, he was directed to organise a guerrilla war in southern Persia against the British. In order to carry out this mission, which William II had personally ordered, Wassmuss was given the gold he needed to buy weapons and consciences, but no preparatory training.

As one of the first field-agents in the Great War, before Lawrence of Arabia, Wassmuss literally improvised his mission of subversion on the terrain of Tangistan. Wassmuss and his companions took the steamer *Pioneer*, which was used by both the Ottomans and the British during the war, and descended the Tigris to a point south of Kut-el-Amara, where the British had just been defeated by the Ottomans, about 160 kilometres south-east of Baghdad. From here, Wassmuss crossed the Turco-Persian border on 1 February 1915 and reached Shiraz, where he had been appointed consul. Although Wassmuss was captured on 5 March 1915 by tribesmen loyal to a local pro-British tribal chief, he contrived to escape and to reach Borazjan, not far from Bushire, which was under the control of a pro-German governor. By way of reprisal, the British at Bushire proceeded to arrest Listermann, who was then deported to India, and to take possession of the consular archives, which contained the details of Niedermayer's mission. Wassmuss of Persia was a strange character; with a square build, blue eyes and a look that combined melancholy with inspiration, he had real charisma. A German patriot, mystic, megalomaniac, fanatically attached to Germany's mission in the East, Wassmuss was an actor who loved disguise, who was capable of falsehood and duplicity, and he was a true believer in the principle of Germanic domination. His effective actions among the tribes of Tangistan and his ability to thwart the English were what lay behind Teague-Jones's mission in 1917. Due to his strong convictions, Wassmuss was singularly lacking in caution and professionalism; among the personal effects abandoned on the occasion of his first escape was the key to the cipher used by Germany during the war. Once in the hands of the British, the copy which Wassmuss had left behind made it possible to decode the famous Zimmermann telegram (16 January 1917) which was to play such a decisive role in the US entry into the war on 2 April 1917. Wassmuss's blunder consequently affected the outcome of the First World War. But the British, who had offered a reward of £15,000 for his capture, would not succeed in catching him before the war's end.

Once well away from Shiraz, the fugitive Wassmuss abandoned his Persian clothes and resumed European dress, the only kind which he thought to be safe now that he was on the run. He assumed the identity of a 'Mr Witt', a so-called prospector for the Anglo-Persian Oil Company, and made an effort to speak Persian with an English accent. He managed to follow the road from the oil-wells across the Bakhtiari Hills as far as Isfahan without being unmasked, with such success that in March 1919 the British had completely lost track of him. Wassmuss continued on his northward path, and even showed himself in public at Kashan during the festival of Nowruz, the Persian New Year. Yet Wassmuss was finally arrested by the British after being spotted by an Armenian telegraph operator, who foiled his plan to get to Kum. After a period of imprisonment, Wassmuss was released in the autumn of 1919 and returned to Berlin via Alexandria, Marseilles and Cologne. As the promoter of the plan for the 'liberation' of the tribes of southern Persia, he laid siege to the Auswärtiges Amt, demanding that the Weimar Republic honour the promises of support that had been made during the war. Although his efforts were fruitless, they highlight his obvious sincerity. He returned to Bushire in 1924 on his honeymoon, where his unobtrusive arrival was tolerated by the British. Impatient to return to Tangistan, he was recognised and feted at the very first village he came to on the road. In Bushire he made the acquaintance of Herr Wilhelm Mayer, a farmer who had tried his luck raising sheep in Australia. The two men set up an agricultural enterprise, and Wassmuss had hopes of being appointed consul again, but these were ultimately denied. In December 1924 he tried to farm on his own account at Shahgudak, near Bushire. With his wife, he planned to live off the produce of his own land and to make some restitution to the tribesmen who had offered their support during the war. He was not allowing, however, for the fickleness of the local tribes, which had renewed their allegiance to the British. Despite the excellent soil, Wassmuss's date-palms failed to grow—a local sheikh, Sheikh Nasser, rubbed the growth off the young trees behind his back—and Wassmuss, husband and wife, soon fell into poverty. Faced with the treachery of the sheikhs, Wassmuss and his wife were then obliged to leave Shahgudak. Back in Berlin, Wilhelm died wretched and almost completely forgotten in November 1931.

Reginald Teague-Jones on Wassmuss's track

Apart from the brief manuscript note on the page of the atlas taken from Wilhelm Wassmuss, there are no written sources to flesh out the details of Teague-Jones's mission. The note in question, written in Miami in 1960, recalls in a few lines and many years afterwards the purpose of his mission in the Persian Gulf:

In 1917 I was posted to the Persian Gulf and in my capacity of Intelligence Officer Persian Gulf, one of my prime objectives was the capture of Wassmuss. Indeed, so imperative had his 'liquidation' been that in June 1917 I received a personal letter from the Chief of the General Staff in Simla—General Kirkpatrick—ordering me to do every thing possible to effect the capture of Wassmuss 'dead or alive'. NB. I did capture his right hand man Bruggmann but all I ever had of Wassmuss was this Atlas. I have kept it all these years but now, on leaving the United States, I have presented it to the Public Library in Miami retaining only this front page with Wassmuss's signature.[19]

Photographs from Ronald Sinclair's collection held by the Imperial War Museum add a few items to the souvenirs of this mission to the Gulf. One of the photos, which shows a peaceful scene at Naib in the Persian Gulf near Bandar Abbas, may have been taken by Teague-Jones in an SPR camp overlooking the Straits of Ormuz where he disembarked on his arrival from India in 1917. The scene is an odd one; three British officers, hatless under a straw awning, have taken off their pith helmets and are absorbed in doing some 'embroidery', under the amused eye of a native and a donkey. Bent over their work, the three men are plying their needles in the top left corner of the borders of three carpets. While the black-and-white photographs do not

reveal their colours, the patterns of the three carpets are those of the tribes of southern Persia. Are they embroidering their names, a date or a place-name in the carpet-
borders, which are traditionally the place for a range of inscriptions, such as verses
from the Koran, lines of poetry or dedications, date of manufacture or place of production? It is important to note that the carpet industry played a part in German
strategy. PETAG (Persische Teppich-Gesellschaft AG) was founded before the war at
Tabriz, with the aim not only of opening up new markets, but also of establishing
German political influence in Iranian Azerbaijan. Was it purely coincidental that
Schünemann, who helped set up a base for Niedermayer's expedition at the end of
February 1915, had been the director of PETAG at Tabriz in 1911? During the war
PETAG's factory, which had extraterritorial status, had undoubtedly played an
important political role in northern Persia. Finally, carpets have a role of some impor-
tance in intelligence: in Persia, they offer the most natural pretext for going into the
bazaar, which serves as a barometer of political and social tensions.

Teague-Jones's journey from India was probably by ship to the Persian Gulf via the
Gulf of Oman. On his way to Naiband near Bandar Abbas, a key control post for the
Straits of Ormuz and the gateway for the Persian Gulf, he would have admired the
rocky outlines, like ruined fortifications, of the high cliffs that fall sheer into the
shallow sea. There is little shelter on this wild coast and the region was infested with
pirates, making navigation especially perilous. But the British had been keeping a
watch over this corridor to Bombay since the nineteenth century, while they consoli-
dated their empire in India. British frigates policed the coast and dealt with piracy.
British residents were installed in the Persian ports, and ties of friendship with the
sultan of Muscat had been renewed. Soon Bahrain and Kuwait were under British
occupation. When the British gained control over Basra in 1914, the Persian Gulf
effectively became a British lake. Getting to Naiband was therefore not very difficult,
even if the coast was still more or less swarming with pirates, and the desert with
hostile tribes. Perched on the top of a cliff, Naiband was home to a settled farming
community living off the proceeds of its date-palm trees and flocks. Naiband camp,
where Teague-Jones disembarked in 1917, was a vital source of water-supplies in the
area and therefore a place where people gathered.

In June 1917, when Teague-Jones received General Kirkpatrick's order from Simla
to stop Wassmuss at any price, General Sykes for his part was rather relieved to
receive trained reinforcements for the South Persia Rifles. To reinforce the SPR, the
16th Rajput regiment had been despatched from India, along with three cavalry
squadrons from Burma mounted on ponies. These were welcome reinforcements, for
in the spring of 1917 things were not looking bright for the British. At the end of
1916 General Sykes's attempt to open the Gulf road had ended in failure, and in the
south, in March 1917, his plans had to be put on hold because of the news of the
Russian Revolution. This was the context in which Wassmuss made his last moves,
and it was in order to foil them that Teague-Jones set off in pursuit. At the end of
1916 Wassmuss had left the hinterland of Bushire for Kazerun. He had lost weight,
and his hair had turned prematurely white; he had come to look so like a Persian that

the prospect of accidentally meeting an Englishman during his travels was of little concern to him. He persisted with his efforts in Tangistan, refusing to give up, still hoping that Sowlat al-Dawla or even the loyal Qawam al Molk would rise up against the interfering British. To reach Tangistan on the track of Wassmuss, Teague-Jones was obliged to take the western route across the Tang-e Zagh. The British were planning to make this route accessible to motor traffic, yet, as he chased Wassmuss through the narrow defiles of Tangistan, Teague-Jones was on horseback. The scene of his headlong hunt for Wassmuss was the spectacular coastline of southern Iran.

Tangistan, the theatre for Wassmuss's epic performance in southern Persia, deserves a detailed description. The mountain chains are made up of parallel lines of ridges and valleys, sealed off from each other except where a torrent has broken through a ridge to create a spectacular but impassable *tang* or gorge. To travel from one valley to the next one has therefore to climb over fearsome rocky cols, or *kotals*. The Kotal road from Bushire to Shiraz, which ran through the lowlands of Deshistan, the defiles and gorges of Tangistan, and from there to the enclosed high-altitude depressions of Serhad, was one of the principal routes along which Wassmuss travelled. The geographer Raoul Blanchard has left a description of this notorious route, which passed:

over terrifying paths which climb the mountain-sides: some like the bed of an Alpine torrent, others continually crumbling underfoot as one crosses a gypsum layer, and finally the 'Col Maudit', the accursed col, reached via a maze of narrow paths in the labyrinth of stratified marl and sandstone: it's like climbing an enormous staircase step by step.[20]

The British replaced this dreadful route in 1918–19 with a better track connecting Bushire with Shiraz, driveable by car, a road which Teague-Jones was to use ten years later during his circuit in Persia by car. A harsh country, naked and arid—where erosion has made fantastic shapes in the layers of gypsum and green or red sandstone—Tangistan stimulated Wassmuss's romantic imagination and Teague-Jones's hunting instincts.

Teague-Jones's mission was far from being the first in the hunt for Wassmuss. A Captain Noel, who also had experience of Persia and the North West Frontier Province, had preceded him, and it may be the case that he had also been accompanied by someone else. For his part Wassmuss, who had not had any contact with his compatriots since 1915, was joined in 1917 by three Germans who had come from Turkestan. One was to die at Ahram, but the second of the three was the famous Bruggmann, whom Teague-Jones caught and sent to India, where he was interned until the end of the war. Teague-Jones made a brief mention of this episode in his account of a Transcaucasian mission[21] which took him to Georgia in February 1921, on the eve of its Sovietisation. During a banquet attended by Noé Jordania, the representative from the French Mission, M. Chevalier, and the Germans von Rauscher, von Druffel, Anders and Commissioner Scheinmann, Teague-Jones recalls having exchanged a few words about Wassmuss and his companion with his neighbour at table:

THE PERSIAN GULF AND THE HUNT FOR 'MR WASSMUSS'

Von Druffel on my left was pretending politely to take an interest in our conversation but was looking ill at ease. He admitted to knowing no other language than his own, but he thawed somewhat when he found I spoke German, and warmed up considerably when he began to compare notes on our respective wartime activities in Persian, when I was trying to track down the elusive Herr Wassmuss:

— 'But you never caught him' he smiled rather maliciously.

— 'No but I caught his associate Bruggmann.'

— 'You did?' his smile vanished. 'I always wondered what happened to him.'

— 'He was shipped down to India' I said.

— 'Ach so' his smile returned. 'Gott sei dank. I thought he was dead.'

Wassmuss's other companion, Spiller, remained with Wassmuss until the end of his adventures. Wassmuss had redoubled his efforts at the end of 1917 and at the beginning of 1918, impelled by a major development: the signing of the Treaty of Brest-Litovsk, a separate peace which in Persia and elsewhere seemed to foretell German victory, and provided for the evacuation of Russian troops from Persia. Teague-Jones followed the faint track of Wassmuss's great cavalcades across Tangistan and the country of Kazerun, a Wassmuss who was still in high spirits and counting on the loyalty of the local tribes. But Wassmuss had not only lost his atlas, now fallen into Teague-Jones's hands, but had also lost sight of the general purpose of his mission. For although the signature of a separate peace with the Russians briefly revived German plans in Persia, the grand design dreamt of by William II of pan-German domination 'from Hamburg to the Persian Gulf', in which Wassmuss saw himself as an indispensable link in the chain, had had its day. Did Teague-Jones see the pointlessness of this mad chase across Tangistan? Or perhaps, like most of the British, he simply thought of Wassmuss as:

a murderer, and a low, skulking treacher. His pose of friendship for the Persians was a disgusting piece of hypocrisy. That was all there was to it. The more tolerant opinion was that he was a crazy fool, a romantic who had laid it on too thick, a fraud antique, as it were, that the Germans found they could palm off on the Persians.[22]

But although in 1918 Teague-Jones was to abandon the pursuit of the unimportant fugitive that Wassmuss had become, the latter's operational techniques were to serve as an inspiration to him on his new mission in the north of Persia, which began in the same year.

Persia and the Russian Revolution

The disintegration of the Persian state accelerated during the final year of the war, giving free rein to the hostile forces released not only by the Russian Revolution, with all its repercussions in the Caucasus, but also by increasing British interference, since Britain was in charge of the Caucasus from December 1917 onwards. When Teague-

Jones went to Meshed in northern Persia in May 1918, it was with a new mission in a new theatre of operations. The British were now less worried about the final German attempts to influence events in the Gulf than by the Bolshevik Revolution, which was not only leading to the disintegration of the Russian Empire, but was threatening to upset all the pieces on the Euro-Asiatic chessboard in the process. In signing the peace treaty of Brest-Litovsk (3 March 1918) the Bolshevik government agreed to the evacuation of the Russian army from Persian soil, and similarly yielded the districts of Kars and Ardahan to the Turks. But this renunciation of tsarist expansionary policy was a double-edged sword: in the eyes of the oriental specialists in the new regime, Persia could be one of the lands, perhaps the very first, where the dream of spreading the revolution could be realised. In the new version of the Great Game, therefore, Persia was an even more crucial piece, and it was from here that the British would seek to deploy their forces in the course of 1918 so as to intervene in Transcaucasia and Transcaspia. Teague-Jones's trajectory from his mission in the Persian Gulf to northern Persia is to be understood in this context, one in which the services of an agent who was a perfect Russian-speaker would be particularly useful. It is likely that he went back to Simla at the beginning of 1918 to be briefed on his new mission, returning to Persia via Baluchistan on the railway from Lahore or Quetta to Nushki and then Mashki Shah on the Persian frontier.

On the road to Meshed

The final year of the war was without doubt the hardest for Persia, a country which though neutral had not managed to stay out of the conflict. It was a paradoxical situation. Although Russian troops had officially withdrawn from Persian territory, the occupying Ottoman troops were still present in the north in Iranian Azerbaijan as far along as Zenjan, locally reinforced by Kurds, up to the Hamadan–Qazvin line which was held by the British. The Russian troop withdrawal confirmed British dominance in the country, but in reality the British only controlled part of the territory: Tehran, the eastern front held by the East Persia Cordon and the south which was held and pacified by the South Persia Rifles. The rest of the country, in particular the central provinces, was in the hands of local chiefs and bands of looters. The situation in Persia in 1918, with its damaged roads, broken bridges, a population suffering from severe famine and epidemics of influenza and typhoid, combined with an incompetent or absent state and financial debt and dependence, had all the necessary ingredients for a coup d'état or a revolution. Agitation in the northern provinces, in particular in Iranian Azerbaijan near the revolutionary centre of Baku, raised the spectre of Communist expansion, a fear made worse by a resurgence of the Jangali rebellion under Kuchak Khan in the Caspian region of Gilan.

In British eyes, therefore, Persia still had an essential role to play, but the zone of geostrategic interest to them was henceforth principally in the north of the country. Within this zone there was a considerable improvement in relations between the British and the Cossack brigade under Colonel Staroselsky,[23] who had remained loyal to the tsarist regime but was deeply anti-British by conviction. The Cossack brigade in Persia had received financial support from the British since October 1917; all its hopes were with the Whites and for the restoration of the imperial regime. Its mission was therefore to sabotage relations between Iran and the new Soviet regime, and to try to put down the Jangali rebellion. In March 1919 Norperforce (the name of the British military force deployed in northern Persia) under General Champain joined forces with Staroselsky's Cossack brigade with a view to launching a coordinated attack on the rebels. Additionally, to try to save the Caucasus, particularly Baku, from the twin threat of the Turks and the Bolsheviks, the British sent an expeditionary force—Dunsterforce—under General Dunsterville, which crossed Persia on the way to Baku without even notifying the Persian government. Finally, General Malleson's mission, Malmiss, was given orders to contain a possible Turco-German advance beyond the Caspian: from its position in northern Persia it was instructed to establish contacts with Transcaspia in order to stop the Turks reaching the port of Krasnovodsk and the Transcaspian Railway beyond it. Persia, which was itself on the brink of a revolutionary explosion, had thus become the rear base in the Allied powers' new fight against the Bolshevik regime. Teague-Jones's solo mission in the spring of 1918 was part of this picture.

Yet while this was a solo mission, HQ in Simla had in fact despatched several missions to northern Persia, some for operational intelligence, others intended to strengthen military capacity. When on 28 April 1918 Teague-Jones took the train from Nushki to the Mashki Shah terminus in the desert just the other side of the Indo-Persian frontier, he learned at Dalbandin that a certain Major Bingham was ahead of him with a caravan of no fewer than twelve camels carrying his personal baggage. Determined to ensure his creature comforts wherever he went, Bingham was quite clearly uninterested in keeping his mission discreet, and Teague-Jones drew some amusement from the fact. 'One of the original "Conspirators" from Delhi, Bingham was now also bound for Meshed, his duty consisting not so much in active intelligence work, as in laying the foundation for a possible military mission.'[24] Major Bingham was particularly prone to spreading pessimism among the British who had been posted to the region: according to him the Turks had crossed the Caucasus, were preparing to invade Central Asia and could appear at any moment in Sistan in fulfilment of Enver's pan-Turkic plan. According to Bingham 'there was absolutely nothing to stop them. Afghanistan would rise at a signal from the Turk and Baluchistan would follow suit. None of us poor devils on the East Persia Cordon stood the ghostliest chance of ever coming back alive.'[25] Teague-Jones left the train at the Mashki Shah terminus—the Quetta–Nushki line had been extended in 1916 in response to Russian construction of a line linking Merv to the North West Frontier of Afghanistan—where a driver at the wheel of a Ford was waiting for him, and then entered Persian territory. It was the beginning of an adventurous trip directly north across Persian Baluchistan and Sistan, in desert country where roads were few and far between:

I soon discovered that my Indian driver was a very raw hand at the game. His knowledge of motoring was even more elementary than mine. What was much more serious, he did not appear to have the vaguest knowledge of the road. As a matter of fact there *was* no road, nor was there even a track, save for the numerous goat tracks which criss-crossed the entire country and which were of course no use to anyone. I had a large-scale degree sheet and a compass with me, but this map was nearly responsible for leading me astray. Running across the map a dotted line represented the Indo-European Telegraph Line. This was shown running from the S.E. to N.W. I therefore decided to make straight north until we came across this telegraph line.[26]

This meant a further loss of time, as the map proved to be wrong yet again. But eventually Teague-Jones and his driver reached Saindak, where they decided to press without delay on kilometres of dreary road along the Afghan frontier to Robat, where General Dale, commanding the forces of the East Persia Cordon, was expected: 'This was the nearest I had ever been to Afghan territory and I made a point of crossing the line just to say I had actually been in Afghanistan.'[27]

It was a desolate country, forgotten by Allah, hostile to animals and plant life, where drought accompanied seasonal epidemics of a disease particularly deadly to camels, the indispensable means of transport. It was for this reason that the tribes removed their flocks during the summer months to regions which were held to be safer:

But war takes little account of such factors. Indian units of the East Persian had to be supplied and this was done by a system of regular camel convoys involving very large numbers of baggage animals. The tribesmen were reluctant to bring their beasts into the heat-stricken area and demanded exorbitant payment. This had to be met, but the casualty rate in every convoy was exceedingly high, and the terrible wastage of animal life was only too evident in the thousands of bleaching skeletons which marked this southerly section of the long caravan trail to Meshed.[28]

On arriving in Robat on 2 May 1918, almost at the same time as General Dale, Teague-Jones also met a certain Lieutenant Ward, a young subaltern whom he had first encountered at HQ in Delhi. Discreet, and ostensibly deep in study of maps of the terrain:

all anyone knew about him was that he had arrived with some instructions from the War Office. Ward himself did not vouchsafe any information about himself and the next day he had gone, as I understood to Peshawar on some business. I now discovered that he was bound in the same direction as myself. I was very pleased to find that I should have a companion, but very disturbed to hear from Ward that there was no means of transport ahead and that we should have to wait from ten to fourteen days at Robat before we could move up with the next convoy. Then we should only be able to advance in slow stages with the transport camels.[29]

Teague-Jones, who had no time to lose, immediately stressed the urgency of his mission, and asked General Dale for a car. The request was met with a categorical refusal from the general, who took no account of the urgency of the mission, nor of the fact that Teague-Jones was not a junior officer, but 'an independent Political Officer directly under the orders of Simla'.[30] Teague-Jones sent his superiors a long report on the route he had taken as far as Robat, as well as a letter describing

General Dale's uncooperative attitude. And while waiting for the camels needed for the next stage in the adventure, he had to possess himself of all the requisite courage and phlegm:

Robat is a pestilential godforsaken spot, the dust-impregnated atmosphere of which is rendered still more depressing by the myriad of flies. Never have I seen so many. I used to think they were bad enough on the N.W.Frontier, where the horses and water donkeys standing just outside one's door attracted them from far and near, but Robat in this respect stood quite alone. If in Frontier posts one slew one's flies in thousands, in Robat one slew them in tens of thousands. It was practically impossible to drink tea. One threw out the dregs of the first cup, and as one poured out the tea from the pot, the flies went in with it. They covered one's arms and one's neck, blackened the paper one was writing on and literally drove on to desperation. We were nearly all wearing nets over our faces, and when sitting about put them over our hands as well.[31]

At the end of a demanding camel journey, Teague-Jones and his companion finally reached Nasratabad, on the shores of Lake Hamun (see Map 1-B), the capital of Sistan, on 17 May 1918, where they were greeted by the British consul, Colonel Prideaux, whose immaculate white uniform contrasted with the filthy garb of the two travellers. Lake Hamun is currently suffering from an ecological catastrophe comparable with that of the Aral Sea, and has shrunk to four separate basins, but at the time it was estimated to have a surface area of 150,000 square miles, even though its dimensions were impossible to evaluate precisely because of the great variations resulting from weather conditions, the seasons or the year. Lake Hamun lies in a sensitive geostrategic zone where the frontiers of three countries meet—India (now Pakistan), Afghanistan and Persia. Two seasonal rivers run into it, the Halil and the Bampur, but the lake, which is essential for irrigation and for life in Sistan, has only one permanent tributary: the Hilmend, 'father of Sistan', is longer than the Loire, running from its source in the high mountains of Afghanistan as far as the enormous delta it has formed in the Hamun basin. The Persian–Afghan frontier runs across the lake, which is a vital water resource. In 1872 the British fixed the frontier line along the main arm of the Hilmend running into the delta. As a result two-thirds of the waters of the Hilmend delta in 1905 lay within Afghanistan, as against only a third for the most densely populated and cultivated region of Persian Sistan, thereby creating the geopolitical conditions for a 'water war' between the two countries. A sweetwater lake, Lake Hamun is like a gigantic pond which fills up in high-water season, precisely at the time that Teague-Jones passed by. In the absence of a ferry, the lake was crossed by means of *tutins*, rafts built from lengths of dry reeds tied together, and poled across the water. It took at least four hours to make the crossing, which would have been a good opportunity for the two men to observe the civilisation of the Sistan delta, were it not for the swarms of mosquitoes. The boatmen were Sayads, a fishing community living off the varied resources of the lake, who were the only men capable of guiding them through the channels that wound through the enormous reed-beds, several kilometres wide, known as *naizars*. Without pausing, the two men immediately set off for Neh, and reached Birjand on 20 May 1918. At Birjand they had a renewed encounter and a few skirmishes with the irascible General Gale, who had little interest in Teague-Jones's need to get to Meshed as soon as possible. The pair finally left again on horseback, and reached Kain (Qaen), and then Turbat-i-Heideri, where Russian influence was already visible in the dress—high boots and caftans—the goods on sale in the bazaar, and the shop signs, some of which were in Cyrillic script. Here Teague-Jones met the Russian consul, a certain Maximov, who had replaced the former tsarist consul, whose wife he also met; she had stayed behind because she had a house and orchard there, 'which was better than living under the Bolsheviks'. On 29 May 1918 Ward and Teague-Jones entered the holy city of Meshed, and went immediately to the consulate-general of Great Britain.

Meshed: Teague-Jones at the Turkestan frontier

In the spring of 1918 Meshed, the commercial capital of eastern Khorasan and the holy city of Persian Shiism, was home to a relatively large British colony, but it lacked a military mission. When Teague-Jones and Ward, his chance companion, arrived at Meshed, they had already been entrusted with solo missions beyond the frontier in Russian Turkestan. They had arrived ahead of Malmiss, the military mission under General Malleson, which left Quetta in June 1918 in the direction of Khorasan, taking the same route as Teague-Jones, whose reports had provided a detailed description of it. Malleson's military mission[32] arrived in mid-July 1918. Its objectives were to watch the development of events in Transcaspia—doubly threatened, by the Turks and the Bolsheviks—to take all necessary measures against possible penetration by enemy agents in western Afghanistan or Baluchistan, to keep an eye on Herat and, lastly, to use all means to prevent the Turks using the Transcaspian Railway, should Baku fall into the hands of Nuri Pasha's Green Army. Malleson, who was more a desk general than a field officer, had spent the major part of his career in the Indian Army intelligence services and on Lord Kitchener's staff from 1904 to 1914. As the author of a detailed study of communication routes in Central Asia, Malleson was highly knowledgeable with regard to Persia and Afghanistan:

his choice as a commander of the Mission to Meshed was evidently due to his exceptional knowledge and ability as an Intelligence officer, rather than his experience as a commander of troops in the field, a role that was clearly not foreseen in Simla when the project for sending a mission to north-east Persia was being considered.[33]

From July 1918 onwards, during the latter part of Teague-Jones's mission, General Malleson was to be an unavoidable intermediary. Teague-Jones, as we shall see, did not have much respect for him.

Meshed, the 'place of martyrdom' and also the tomb of Imam Reza (Ali ibn Musa al-Rida), a Shiite pilgrimage destination, was the religious and political nerve centre of Persia. The Russians had discovered this when they bombed Imam Reza's shrine in 1912, arousing lasting Shiite resentment. Meshed is the gateway to North East Persia, many times destroyed by invasions and by the terrible earthquakes which wreak havoc in the nearby mountains, and many times rebuilt. It is not far from Kuchan (Quchan), from which ran a post-road that crossed a high col in the Kopet Dagh, allowing access to Ashkhabad in Russian Turkestan, a road upgraded by the Russians in 1885. Its geographical location made Meshed the ideal rear base for all British missions of subversion in Russian Turkestan. A focal point for meetings, the British consulate-general was an enchanting paradise: a colonial house with white pillars leading to a patio, smothered in the exuberant vegetation of an English garden; magnificent roses, a vegetable garden, a cow, tennis and badminton courts—the attractions of the place were considerable after the hardship of the road that led to them. Teague-Jones was met at the door of the consulate by the military attaché, Colonel Redl—a very irritable character—with whom he immediately had a tête-a-tête conversation in which the purpose of Ward's mysterious mission was revealed. A would-be adventurer who had obtained a commission in the Rifle Brigade, Ward had made contact during a stay in London with the War Office, through the intermediary of an officer working in the Russian section of intelligence. On his own initiative Ward had succeeded in persuading the responsible authorities in the War Office to agree to his plan, which was that he should penetrate Transcaspian territory, blow up a major bridge between Ashkhabad and Krasnovodsk, and thus render the Transcaspian Railway useless in the event of a Turkish advance into the region:

As regards the technical question of actually destroying the bridge, Ward claimed to have had experience in dealing with explosives. Where he obtained this experience no one appears to have asked, but his word was taken for it and there it was. Ward was accordingly despatched with War Office blessing right round the world via Canada and Japan so that no one should suspect that his ultimate destination was Turkistan.[34]

He therefore arrived in Delhi, where Teague-Jones made his acquaintance, and as mentioned above:

he disappeared to Peshawar for a very hasty course of instruction in explosives, incidentally hurriedly brushing up his Pushto. It appeared that he had a case of explosives coming along somewhere behind him and at his urgent request Redl sent a wire down to the railhead to hurry it up. Ward's awful secret having been let out, there was no further question of secrecy between him and me. While admiring him for the way he had kept his affairs to himself, I could not help feeling that he had no possible chance of carrying out even a small portion of what he had gaily undertaken to do. In the first place he had no knowledge of any language save a very elementary knowledge of Pushto and some extremely risqué French songs. Secondly, while being quite practical in many ways, he lacked experience and seemed quite incapable of fending for himself out in the wilds. I am convinced that had I not taken him in tow at Robat, he would never have found his own way up to Meshed.[35]

The man in charge at Meshed was Colonel Grey, a typical modern consul according to Teague-Jones, who combined an aristocratic manner with good knowledge of the country. Grey had spent some time in the Persian Gulf and was a fluent speaker of French, Persian and Arabic. A nervy personality, he apparently found it very hard to bear the company of Colonel Redl, who instead of living in his own nearby house, just across the marvellous garden, had chosen to live in the consulate, where Mrs Redl was in charge of the smooth running of the household. Among the other British at Meshed in the spring of 1918 was Captain Sydney Jarvis, who with A. Gordon as companion had made an adventurous journey through revolutionary Russia. The two men, who had left Petrograd in March 1918, were among the soldiers who had been part of the British mission attached to Russian Army Headquarters, and were interpreters, Jarvis having been an engineer working for a British firm in Russia before the war. After the mission was dismantled in February 1918, Jarvis and Gordon appeared in Tiflis on 11 March 1918, where they made contact with the British military mission under Colonel Pike, and then in Baku on 5 April just as the last Europeans were preparing to flee. There, Jarvis and Gordon embarked on the steamer *Kokot*, disembarking at Krasnovodsk. On 21 April 1918 they were at Meshed, whence Jarvis then left for Tehran. According to Teague-Jones:

Redl had been impressed with Jarvis' experience of Russia which he himself lacked, and particularly with the fact that Jarvis had had recent experience of the post-revolutionary elements in Russia and had even had to talk to Bolsheviks. Redl had urged that Jarvis be kept in Meshed and it was understood that he would return shortly from Tehran.[36]

Before the arrival of Malmiss, a small Indian Army detachment, very badly equipped owing to General Gale's negligence, provided a reduced and singularly un-operational military presence, even though the British were faced with a number of complex challenges:

The question occupying the minds of both the Turks and ourselves at the beginning of June 1918 was firstly whether the Bolshevik authorities in Transcaspia would attempt to oppose a Turkish advance eastwards of the Caspian, and secondly, if the Bolsheviks did not attempt to oppose such advance, whether the British would be able to interpose any obstacle independently of the Bolsheviks. The Bolsheviks did not know themselves what attitude to adopt. At one moment they were all for fighting the Turk. The next moment, the peace treaty, prompted of course by Turkish and German money, would refuse to countenance any further fighting. Information also reached us that there was a number of German, Austrian and Turkish agents in Ashkhabad, who appeared to be in good terms with the Bolshevik commissars, but what their actual game was we were not in a position to know. Our intelligence from the other side of the frontier was disgracefully scanty and did not speak at all well for Redl's organisation. It was in fact a puzzle to me what Redl had been doing all this time, sitting in an important centre like Meshed, yet in total ignorance of what was really going on just over the frontier. Colonel Grey was well informed on the internal situation in Meshed and Khorassan in general, but I was surprised to find that he knew practically nothing about current events in Transcaspia. Indeed, he admitted frankly that he devoted his entire attention and interest to conditions and happenings in his own bailiwick and regarded developments in Russian territory as none of his business.[37]

In fact, although Teague-Jones's mission was to enter the territory of Russian Turkestan, he was also impelled to analyse local politics in the Meshed region, and to set up local networks which might be of use in the future. At Grey's request, he took a look at the activities of Tsentrosoyuz, a Russian commercial cooperative based in Moscow; at the beginning of June 1918 it had despatched a delegation of eight Russian Jews from Ashkhabad who, after a few days spent in Meshed, spread out into the neighbouring towns of Nishapur, Kuchan and Sabzawar. Their official mission was to buy a shipment of grain, grapes and cotton. At Kuchan, Khabat and Vaksin members of the delegation bought a *sarai*, a commercial warehouse, which Teague-Jones suspected of being used for other purposes. Having made an ally of the British commercial agent at Kuchan, an Armenian by the name of Hovsepiants, Teague-Jones busied himself by, on the one hand, buying a consignment of bread with which to feed the hungry in the town, and on the other by breaking into the *sarai* bought by the Soviet delegation in order to explore its secrets:

The *sarai* was an unusually large one and struck one at once with the advantages of its struc-ture from the point of view of turning it into a fort. It had the usual high walls round it, and what would in an ordinary *sarai* have been housing for mules and horses and store rooms for grain were large rooms with stone floors and wooden window frames. These improvements had only just been put in … One corner of the *sarai* had been built up and looked for all the world as though the owner intended posting a machine-gun there. Outside, the *sarai* looked like a typical frontier outpost, save that there were as yet no loopholes. The situation, too, was admirable for the purpose, as the *sarai* was in an isolated position on the very outskirts of the town facing along the main road.[38]

In other words, the commercial mission was acting for the secret services of Soviet Russia. This hypothesis was consistent with the activity of Bolshevik agents in Persia, on both sides of the porous frontier.[39] The place and time was also consistent with the strategy of using minorities in northern Persia which both the Russians and the British were attempting to pursue.

Teague-Jones also had to help a Ward 'full of his bridge, the destruction of which was, of course, the sole raison d'être of his tremendous journey halfway round the world', a mission whose urgency was felt all the more strongly in Simla as the Turks were now advancing in Transcaucasia. How could he reach Turkestan with the neces-sary supply of explosives without friends or accomplices? In the month of June 1918, Teague-Jones put considerable energy into finding or setting up networks of collabo-rators. The Armenians, whose commercial networks extended as far as Ashkhabad, and who could possibly constitute an urban militia of 700 men, were one option, but on reflection Teague-Jones discarded it. According to his own account, he evolved an even bolder plan, which involved buying the services of Kurdish brigands who could accompany him across the mountains on smugglers' paths as far as a predetermined point. All Ward would then have to do would be to blow up the track. In an effort to find 'the right kind of Kurdish brigand' he interviewed several individuals, among whom the most remarkable was the chieftain Khuda Verdi, known to his friends and enemies as 'Khuddu', an authentic cut-throat and highway robber, who was the boss of the smuggling trade between Persia and Transcaspia. With a cruel wolfish face under his enormous *papakh*, clothed in a long caftan from which two Circassian daggers protruded, Khuddu inspired Teague-Jones with reluctant respect and admiration. The Kurd immediately asked for help in eliminating one or two people, one of whom was the governor of Kuchan, whom he deemed impossible to assassinate himself because of his official position. While Teague-Jones assured him of his sincere sympathy, without giving any encouragement to his request, it quickly appeared that the Kurdish option had to be abandoned too:

From talking with Khuddu, however, I came to the conclusion that venturing into the hills with a party of cut-throats and a few mules laden with explosives was risky, but might be feasible as far as the frontier. On the other side however, the Kurds would be out of their own territory. They would be treated as raiders and the most I could expect them to do would be to dash to the railway, leave me and the stuff there and rush back over the frontier as quickly as they could. What would my position then be—stranded on the railwayline in the desert in hostile territory with a heavy load of explosives which I could do nothing with? I should be picked up by the first party of wandering Turkmans and either killed outright or taken into Ashkhabad and exhibited as a curio, or as a spy who had been fool enough to get himself caught. All this, mind you, provided I were not murdered in the Persian hills by the Kurds themselves.[40]

On his return to Meshed on 24 June 1918, Teague-Jones therefore resolved to put his latest conclusion to Redl: he proposed that he himself should go to Ashkhabad to assess the situation. With Simla's agreement, it was decided that Jarvis, the only one to have been in Russian territory recently, would go on ahead. On 3 July 1918 Teague-Jones, dressed as an Armenian merchant from Persia, and accompanied by his factotum Gulab Hussain, set off on the mountain road from the north-west of Meshed to Ashkhabad.

4

ASHKHABAD AND THE TRANSCASPIAN EPISODE

On 3 July 1918 Teague-Jones, Gulab Hussein and a servant, Din Mohammed, left
Meshed in the direction of Turkmenistan, riding on mules. In order to ensure their
safety, the two men had bought garments in the Meshed bazaar as disguises that
would be able to withstand local scrutiny. While Gulab Hussein could easily pass for
a Persian—born in India, he was a Shiite and spoke fluent Persian—Teague-Jones
had chosen the garb of an Armenian merchant. The costume he had devised consisted of a long coat with a heavy belt, sometimes worn under a capacious cloak. A
scarf and either a fur hat or a turban completed this Armenian costume, which had
been used as an informal passport in the Muslim East by European missionaries,
merchants and travellers since the sixteenth century.[1] By travelling in Armenian
dress, Teague-Jones, the field-agent, was harking back to an old tradition which
required this dress of Christians, whether they were ambassadors or monks, merchants or ordinary travellers. The three men and four mules loaded with essential
camping equipment set off across the hills in this prelude to their Transcaspian
adventures. The trek required them to travel lightly, but Teague-Jones had nevertheless brought a camp-bed so as to avoid the thin straw mattresses in the caravanserais,
a stove for Din Mohammed to use in preparing meals, and three *chagals*—goatskins—which had been brought from Delhi in case there was a shortage of water,
though water was plentiful in the area. Last of all Teague-Jones had been issued with
a considerable quantity of 'nikolaievskis', tsarist roubles, which were still legal tender
in some regions of revolutionary Russia in 1918. 'The lining of my coat was stiff
with notes, but the bulk of the money was in the third *chagal*. To anyone looking at
it, it appeared exactly the same as the other two, save that if you tilted it up no water
came out.'[2]

Beyond the hills lay the high mountains which separate the Persian region of
Khorasan from Transcaspia (see Map 1). Until Khakistar, a customs post on this caravan route, the walk was trouble-free, which allowed Teague-Jones leisure for observa-

tion and for scouting out flat terrain which might serve as a landing strip for planes. In Khakistar, at the quarantine control-post for travellers coming from Russia, where there was an outbreak of cholera, Teague-Jones happened to meet a certain 'Madame Popova', 'sister-in-law of a very charming woman whose acquaintance I had made in Meshed', who passed on some rather alarming news about Ashkhabad, which was still held by the Bolsheviks at the beginning of July 1918. What this lady said was partly confirmed by Jarvis on return from his mission in Ashkhabad. Jarvis, who was on his way back to Meshed, was able to give Teague-Jones a detailed report on the situation at Ashkhabad. The town, which was full of German and Turkish agents, was in Bolshevik hands. Jarvis managed to make friendly contact with them, without disabusing them of their unfounded belief in the presence of a British army corps at Meshed, poised to invade Transcaspia. He questioned them directly on the local Soviet's expectations of a Turkish invasion of Transcaspia, and the form such an invasion might take. In conclusion Jarvis had the impression that the Bolsheviks 'were hand-in-glove with the Germans and Turks who were undoubtedly very busy in Transcaspia'.[3]

The interview at Khakistar both focused and modified Teague-Jones's plans. He was well aware of the military value of cotton, which was extensively cultivated in Central Asia and used during the First World War in the manufacture of a powerful explosive, gun-cotton, a mixture of cotton and gunpowder. Rather than go straight to Ashkhabad, where Jarvis had just carried out a preliminary reconnaissance, he decided to go directly to Krasnovodsk, a port on the Caspian; it was also the railhead for the Transcaspian Railway, and its strategic position was vital for the realisation of a plan he had in mind—the organisation of a 'cotton conspiracy' against the Germans:

From now onwards I began to dream of cotton. I saw myself arriving at Krasnovodsk to find trainloads of cotton lying down by the docks and saw myself with Gulab Hussein pouring oil on it and setting fire to it by night. I developed this idea until I saw myself destroying the entire port of Krasnovodsk by fire and decided that if necessary I would do this and thus render the destruction of the bridge and all the trouble with the explosives unnecessary.[4]

To reach the first station on the Transcaspian line—Kaakhka, through which the train was scheduled to pass at 15.30—and then to press on to Krasnovodsk, were Teague-Jones's objectives on 6 July 1918. Thus began one of the most complicated chapters in his life as a field-agent, since the 'Transcaspian episode', as his friend C.H. Ellis called it, involved two interactive theatres of operations in the turbulent summer of 1918, Baku on the one hand and Transcaspia (see Map 1) on the other. The complexity of these events means that it is necessary to deal with events at Baku, where Teague-Jones went on many occasions in the summer of 1918, in the next chapter.

A secret mission at the gates of Central Asia in 1918

In the immediate aftermath of the revolution, Russian Turkestan, the future Soviet Turkmenistan, had none of the futurist décor that has been on show since the collapse of the Soviet Union. With none of the buildings in 'Persico-Palladian' style that were later to be built with gas and petroleum money by Bouygues Turkmen to the glory of the chief of the Turkmen nation, Saparmurat Niazov (1940–2006), Ashkhabad in 1918 was a dusty and backward little town in the heart of colonial Turkmenistan, entirely given up under Russian direction to the monoculture of cotton, the 'white gold' of Central Asia. The famous Transcaspian Railway was the means of introducing Teague-Jones to this harsh and largely desert country in the summer of 1918.

First impressions of Transcaspia

After an early morning arrival at Kaakhka station (see Map 1-A) on 7 July 1918, and determined to miss neither the train, nor the opening of the station buffet—the only place in the whole town where one could get a meal—Teague-Jones sat on a trunk waiting for the plume of steam from the Transcaspian train to appear in the eastern distance. On the horizon, the sun was rising over the Kopet Dagh mountains, along which the Transcaspian runs on this part of the frontier with Persia. In this encounter between modernity and primitive nature, the dazzling steel rails seemed incongruous in the surrounding desolation. They had nothing in common with Teague-Jones's childhood notions, built on stories of travel and adventure, on pictures and little leaflets inside chocolate bar-wrappers, about the epics of the Trans-Siberian and Transcaspian Railways. As a child in St Petersburg he had been present at parades where the tsar, surrounded by grand-dukes, took the salute from dashing Cossack and Turkmen cavalrymen. The impression they made was strong enough to stir a passion for the East. But the reality was disappointing, and the ordinary-looking railway was a long way from his childhood idea of it. 'Youthful impressions are strong and lasting, and to travel to Central Asia had thereafter remained one of my greatest ambitions. And now I was there and that was it!'[5]

The construction of the Transcaspian Railway line was carried out under the supervision of General M.N. Annenkov from 1880 onwards. The line was of strategic importance, enabling the political control and economic development of Turkestan, while providing the key to Central Asia in the Great Game between Russia and Great Britain. An instrument for opening up Russian Central Asia—it was intended to link up with existing railway lines in Siberia—the Transcaspian changed the way that space was organised, and helped to create new towns or develop existing ones along the line of its route. As the Caspian port of Uzun-Ada was not deep enough for large vessels, the port of Krasnovodsk in the north was chosen as the railhead. This entailed development work, the construction of a deep-water port and a railway station in an eclectic style which, for arriving travellers, conjured up the East they were about to encounter. The Transcaspian line runs from Krasnovodsk in a south-easterly direction across the Karakum Desert towards the Kopet Dagh mountains, passing through Kizil-Arvat, Ashkhabad and Kaakhka, very close to the Persian border. The line then bifurcates towards the north-east in the direction of Tashkent. It connected with Merv in 1885 and with Charjui in 1886, the gateway to the emirate of Bokhara, whose emir refused to allow admittance to the railway. Tashkent, the capital of the governorate, was reached in 1899. The route of the Transcaspian follows the mythical caravan route to Samarkand, and it stimulated a burst of growth in several towns—Ashkhabad, which was a town of 2,500 inhabitants in 1881, saw its population rise to nearly 20,000 in 1897—while marking the slow decline of caravan transport. For Teague-Jones, the important news was that there were large railway depots at Kizil-Arvat, repair workshops and an imported community of Russian railway employees.

Notwithstanding his disappointment, Teague-Jones was presented with the characteristic sight of Central Asia as soon as the train from Tashkent arrived at the station and a crowd got off to lay siege to the buffet:

Never have I seen such a sight. It might well have been a scene from one of the London musical comedies. There were Russian peasants in red shirts, Armenians and Persians, Cossacks and Red Soldiers, Sart traders and Bokhariots, Turkmans in their gigantic *papakhas*, while among the crowd were a number of pretty young girls and women in the latest Paris summer fashions. All this medley came crushing into the buffet and clamoured for glasses of tea, hunks of black bread and platters of soup. Somehow or other they all seemed to get served and Asiatic and European, Mongol and Muscovite sat down literally cheek by jowl, and satisfied their hunger.[6]

Once he had boarded the train, sitting in a window seat so as to try to spot strategic points along the line such as bridges and underground irrigation-conduits, Teague-Jones embarked on the first of a long series of voyages on board the Transcaspian. Throughout the summer of 1918 he travelled continually between Kaakhka, Ashkhabad, Krasnovodsk and, on the other side of the Caspian, Baku.[7] At Ashkhabad station, where there was a general stir, the train made a lengthy stop. Red Army soldiers boarded the train—high anxiety. Luckily for Teague-Jones the Reds were thoroughly drunk and contented themselves with pestering the travellers. Teague-Jones would return to Ashkhabad, 'a place of one's dreams', in fact an oasis which had been transformed by the Russian conquest into a colonial town, with rectilinear paved streets lined with acacias and divided into regular blocks, a municipal library and a technical training school for the railway. The town, a third of the population of which was Persian, among whom were many members of the Babi sect, also housed some embryonic industry, with cotton-cleaning workshops, tanneries, brickworks and a mineral water plant. As it happened, the only item that the famished Teague-Jones was able to buy there was a bottle of mineral water. After a long stop at the station, the train set off again. With a feeling of relief, Teague-Jones was able to resume his discreet observation of the rail-track, 'but beyond a few small culverts saw nothing of any interest and certainly nothing worth blowing up'.[8] Ward's famous bridge had to be located somewhere on the Krasnovodsk side. After nightfall, observation became impossible, and the train arrived at Krasnovodsk station after midnight. The Transcaspian railhead of Krasnovodsk numbered fewer than 10,000 inhabitants in 1918; set at the foot of bare hills hollowed out in places by gypsum mining, it was a place of burning heat on the shores of the Gulf, lapped by waters which are still clear. Although an obligatory trans-shipment destination for passengers and goods travelling between Transcaspia and the Caucasus, it could not be described as a hospitable town; drinking water came from distilled seawater, the place swarmed with scorpions and what fixed population there was, was tied to activity in and around the docks. The population was not local in origin, but was mostly comprised of Persians who had come looking for work as porters (*ambaly*). Teague-Jones did not stay for long before embarking for Baku. The events which drew him to the other side of the Caspian must however be seen in the context of the political situation of Transcaspia proper, to which he returned two days later, on 12 July 1918.

Once back at Krasnovodsk, Teague-Jones did not blow up the bridge, but set immediately to work on one of the objectives of his field-mission in Central Asia: obstructing the activity of German agents in the region by attacking the 'cotton question':

On my journey through from Kaakhka to Krasnovodsk, I had seen bales of cotton piled up on every wayside station. At Krasnovodsk the railway sidings were filled with truckloads of it, while in addition there were several huge dumps of neatly piled bales, both in the railway sidings and down by the quays. In Baku I had learned of the presence in Astrakhan of a German mission, whose problem it was to secure as much of the Turkistan cotton crop as they could get hold of. They had completely won over the Soviet authorities and the Baku Soviet were co-operating with them to the extent of sending over available shipping to Krasnovodsk for the transport of the cotton across the Caspian.[9]

With the help of a few contacts at Krasnovodsk, a certain Dr Arkannikov and in particular Nikolai Nikolaievich Semov, Teague-Jones managed in a single day to mount a 'cotton conspiracy' which would have even more useful consequences than blowing up a bridge. Due to its use in the manufacture of nitrocellulose and 'B Powder' (or 'poudre blanche' or Vieille Powder after its inventor, the French chemist Paul Vieille), which was used as an explosive and in ammunition for firearms such as the 1886 Lebel rifle (which was widely used during the First World War), cotton was a strategic material in great demand—hence the plot devised by Teague-Jones for diverting the shipment of cotton which the Germans at Krasnovodsk had just acquired and were loading on to ships leaving for Astrakhan. Thanks to the collaboration of a friend of Semov's who had access to the Krasnovodsk telegraph office, where break-downs were common, a plan was rapidly drawn up:

The scheme, therefore, was for the Krasnovodsk radio station to receive wirelessed instructions from Astrakhan, cancelling the loading of the ships, and for the station then to go out of action. D. could easily put it out of action and with the help of a little *bakshish* he did not anticipate much difficulty in getting the necessary message received and delivered to the local authorities in the proper manner.[10]

The message in question, correctly framed thanks to D's knowledge of the subject, ordered the Executive Committee of Krasnovodsk to put an immediate halt to the loading of cotton and to hold all available shipping for the transport of petrol and diesel-oil to Astrakhan. The plan was promptly put into action, with excellent results: in accordance with the false instructions from Astrakhan, loading was halted, the ships which had already been loaded were unloaded, and bales of cotton piled up on the quayside. The follow-up to this story would disclose another use for cotton several months later:

when military operations resolved themselves into a 'railway war' large numbers of bales came in useful as protection for trucks. There was a shortage of steel sheeting and the only sheet metal the railway workshops could produce was soft iron, which, of course, was not bullet resisting. One day a Russian railway engineer came to me with a scheme for using cotton as a protective lining for closed-in trucks and rendering them bullet proof and suitable for armoured trains. The idea seemed feasible enough and the finished specimen truck looked very imposing with its outer covering of sheet-iron, sinister looking loop-holes, and double walls, with a thick layer of cotton in between. I was invited to inspect this latest product of the Kizil Arvat railway workshops and a practical demonstration was arranged. It was suggested that the engineer and myself should shut ourselves inside the truck, whereupon fire would be opened on us from two machine guns. The engineer seemed quite willing to undergo the ordeal, but I suggested that the machine-guns should first fire at the truck while it was empty. They did so. We then went up and inspected and found that every bullet had gone clean through the truck. The cotton lining had only been pressed by hand [rather than hydraulically]![11]

Once back at Ashkhabad on 14 July 1918, still without having seen any evidence of a bridge, Teague-Jones learned that the Bolshevik authorities had been overthrown by a coalition of local railway workers. The coup d'état which had taken place on the evening of 12 July considerably modified the situation in this part of Central Asia. For Teague-Jones it was now a question of returning to Meshed as fast as possible so as to report on these developments, which might have favoured possible British action in the future. The return journey was an epic one, beset with as many extraordinary obstacles as the journey out: finding mounts and a muleteer at Kaakhka, crossing the frontier and getting through the quarantine formalities. Teague-Jones, convinced of the urgency of the situation, decided on a punishing night journey in company with a mount that was soon exhausted, and needed pulling, pushing and finally, at the end of the journey, practically carrying. At close to midnight, collapsing half-dead outside the gate of the consulate at Meshed, he found Redl, Jarvis and Bingham still up and ready to listen to his story. Teague-Jones inquired whether a report should be sent to India without delay:

'No, that's all right' said Redl. 'I forgot to mention, we have a General here now, just out from India. General Malleson has taken over the Mission. He's already gone to bed and I don't think he'd like to be disturbed. But he'll certainly want to see you in the morning!' A General! Gone to bed! Not to be disturbed![12]

Teague-Jones discovered at his own expense that the urgency of the situation in Transcaspia was not appreciated by everyone.

Transcaspia after the Russian Revolution: from the Red offensive to the emergence of a Turkmen power

What was new about this situation, and did it offer the British an opportunity to take action? The change of power at Ashkhabad followed the many disturbances experienced in Central Asia after the February 1917 Revolution. In Tashkent, after the fall of the tsar, the provisional government had deposed the governor-general of Turkestan, General Kuropatkin, and had replaced him with a commissar, a friend of Kerensky's. He kept this position until the Bolsheviks appeared in the region in November 1917, when he was replaced by 'Commissar' Kolesov.[13] It was a similar story at Ashkhabad, where a Soviet controlled by the Bolsheviks was set up and then dissolved. However, at Ashkhabad a new Soviet under more effective Bolshevik control—despite the support of a large section of the local Russian population for the Mensheviks—managed to hold on until July 1918. But in February of the same year the existence of forces hostile to Bolshevism was evidenced by the formation of a Turkestan anti-Red union, made up of Turkmen Jadids (Muslim modernist reformers), conservative Muslims and Russian Menshevik social-democrats under Oraz Serdar, one of the Turkmen chieftains who had resisted the Russian conquest at the Battle of Gök-Tepe (1881). After 17 June 1918 anti-Bolshevik movements appeared, originally at Kizil-Arvat, where Commissar Fralov was killed and his Red guards annihilated. There was another revolt at Ashkhabad, where the ruling Bolsheviks were arrested and killed on 12 July 1918. The movement spread like a trail of gunpowder all along the Transcaspian Railway, and within the space of a few days the whole region between Krasnovodsk and Charjui was freed from Bolshevik control.

This defeat left power in the hands of a new 'party', which although 'Menshevik' in name had no precise political line, and at Ashkhabad there was a Provisional Executive Committee of thirty members, most of whom were railway workers. The Bolsheviks, who had retreated to Tashkent, were rallying their forces so as to launch new offensives at Kaakhka, the nerve centre of the railway line, where the most violent conflicts were to take place. The agreement signed at Meshed on 19 August 1918 between the British military mission now directed by General Malleson and the Ashkhabad Executive Committee provided for British military assistance by means of troop reinforcements from India. Teague-Jones played no small part in the reaching of this agreement which, thanks to the rapid arrival of the Indian troops, managed to safeguard the position at Kaakhka. The Bolsheviks nonetheless advanced from Tashkent as far as Charjui, from which they launched a series of repeated attacks on Kaakhka in 1918. Dislodged from Merv, and soon progressively from Charjui, the Bolsheviks no longer seemed so threatening. In this relatively calm context, the Ashkhabad Committee formed the provisional government of Transcaspia on 5 November 1918. This government would be obliged to take account of the development of Muslim political elites, some of whom had rallied to the Jadist movement.

Two political currents had emerged within the Muslim population in Central Asia in the period since the revolution: a generally liberal 'progressive' tendency which had to some extent joined the constitutional-democratic (KD) mainstream, and a political/religious movement set up by the *shura*. The *shura* was composed of the leaders of ulemas and influential mullahs who were aiming not only at the propagation of Islam but also at giving it a political dimension, and sought to bring about the union of Muslim peoples, their liberation from the yoke of the infidel and the identification in the Koran of principles governing not only morality, but also public life. The 42nd sura of the Koran exhorts believers to conduct their affairs according to the principle of 'mutual consultation', the *shura*, which during the history of Muslim states had been interpreted by greatly differing institutions: Council of State, counsellors to the sovereign, parliament, Court of Justice and even, in Central Asia, the Soviet. Teague-Jones noted that the leaders of the *shura* appeared to favour the Germans politically, which brought them temporarily close to the Bolsheviks. But having gained power at the same time as the Bolsheviks, the influential ulemas in the *shura* soon displayed their fundamental disagreements. These had less to do with the anti-religious side of Bolshevism than with politics:

> The ulemas declared themselves to be the Mahomedan Government, and on the grounds that they were the elected representatives of the great majority of the population of Turkestan demanded that supreme control of the state be handed over to them. The Bolsheviks refused to recognise the Ulema, and appealed to the Mussulman working classes. The latter however remained loyal to their religious leaders, and supported the demand for power, proclaiming at the same time the autonomy of Turkestan. Thus nothing remained to the Bolsheviks but overthrow the Ulema. This they did.[14]

At the same time, different Muslim committees sprang up in Ashkhabad, then under Bolshevik control. Far from reproducing the lines of political fracture that had emerged during the October Revolution, the tendencies in nascent Turkmen nationalism derived from the colonialist situation in Central Asia. The two Ashkhabad committees, the Provincial Muslim Committee on the one hand, and the Municipal Executive Committee on the other, shared the objective of taking power in Transcaspia. But they differed with regard to the attitude that should be taken towards Russian protection. Some—like Mahtum Kuli Khan—a rich and influential chieftain—did not wish to intervene in Russia's internal affairs. Others, who were more nationalistic, wanted to take advantage of the weakening of Russian colonial power by establishing a Turkmen nation at the heart of an independent Republic of Turkestan. That was the option represented by Oraz Serdar, president of the Provincial Muslim Committee, backed by Ovazbaiev. 'Both were active propagators of the progressive movement. Both had strong pro-Turkish sympathies, and had as their party cry "Transcaspia for the Turkman".'[15] As for the Municipal Muslim Committee, it was presided over by two Caucasian Turks, Khanlar Beg Agaiev and Salman Askerov. The two committees were unable to survive the struggle with the local Bolsheviks in which they were soon engaged: the dissolution of the Shura-ul-Islam at Tashkent was soon followed by the dissolution of the two Ashkhabad committees, whose leaders were forced to flee. Khanlar Beg Agaiev and Salman Askerov escaped to the Caucasus, while Oraz Serdar and Ovazbaiev sought refuge in their villages. They would re-emerge to take an active part in the overthrow of Bolshevik power in July 1918, returning to Ashkhabad and a warm reception from the local Mensheviks. But the situation in Turkestan remained confused, the theatre for a civil war which not only pitted the Bolsheviks against their local adversaries, but also the Turkmen against the Russian colonialists, and the country against the town. The experience of the short-lived autonomous government of Khokand in December 1917, crushed by the Bolsheviks two months later, led Teague-Jones to comment that after:

the conflict with the Mussulmans at Tashkent and Khokand, the Bolsheviks entered on a general massacre of the native population. These excesses savoured more of pure hooliganism than of political movements. Mussulmans as a whole were branded as counter-revolutionaries. Well to do natives were robbed and killed. As a tribe the Sarts were the most wealthy, consequently the campaign was chiefly directed against them. The attack on Samarkand was organised by Fralov, who later came to a violent end at Kizil Arvat. A large number of Sarts were massacred and the town looted in the most barbaric manner. Similar treatment was meted out to Charjui, where the notorious Allah Yar fell on the town with his Turkmen robbers.[16]

Ashkhabad, which had been liberated from the Bolsheviks on 12 July 1918, barely five days after Teague-Jones had left it, now became the theatre for a political and military drama from which the British were able to benefit. Early in September 1918 there was a meeting of a new Turkmen assembly at Bezmein, a village near Ashkhabad. Soon named as the Central Turkmen Executive Committee, the assembly was directed by Ovazbaiev. Oraz Serdar for his part led the Turkmen valiantly in military operations against the Bolsheviks but, lacking artillery, the combined Turkmen and Menshevik forces were driven out of Bairam Ali, near Merv, a junction on the Transcaspian Railway line. Now under threat, Ashkhabad would have fallen again to the Bolsheviks without the intervention of the British troops based at Meshed. Under the terms of the agreement of 19 August 1918, a detachment of Indian troops advanced into Transcaspia and succeeded in stopping the Bolshevik advance before pushing them back into the region of Charjui. Both Teague-Jones and Ward took part in the Battle of Kaakha,[17] the outcome of which was decisive. Ward did not come out alive, while Teague-Jones, who received a serious thigh-wound, was left with a depressing impression of Menshevik incompetence and even of Turkmen treachery, since some of the shooting directed at him came from the rear. Indeed:

the arrival of British troops was looked on with very mixed feelings by the Turkoman, who were already beginning to consider themselves the principal power in Transcaspia, and who though themselves glad of the material assistance afforded by the British troops, could not but look on their presence in the country with a certain amount of suspicion. While the one desire of the great bulk of Turkoman was to have a restoration of peace and order in the country, the Progressive party were strongly pro-Turk in sympathy. The Turks were advancing victoriously in the Caucasus, the fall of Baku was imminent, and little doubt was entertained but that in a few weeks Turkish forces would appear in Transcaspia. Ideas of an autonomous Turkman khanate in the near future were strengthened. Enmity towards the British troops

81

however weakened as the Turkoman saw their fighting qualities, and realised that the position had been saved by them. There still remained the fear however that the British would occupy Transcaspia and thus rob the Turkman of what he was beginning to consider his lawful heritage.[18]

The climate of distrust of the British also dominated relations in this disparate coalition with the Russians, towards whom the Turkmen displayed their independence of spirit, particularly in the Turkmen Committee of Bezmein, on a daily basis. The common fear of a return of Bolshevism was thus the only cement capable of binding politically the representatives of these social groups and their divergent views. And it was to a Transcaspian government formed on this sort of basis that Teague-Jones became, on 30 August 1918, the political representative of Great Britain.

The brief history of a transient government: the Transcaspian government

The prehistory of the Transcaspian government follows the fall of the Bolsheviks on 12 July 1918, and is characterised by the 'railway legitimacy' which was the principal authority in a region with a highly confused political situation. Thus a rapidly formed committee of railway workers and employees soon found itself in charge of affairs without having any definite policies. 'No one knew what he was or what he stood for.'[19] The committee, which was baptised as an Executive Committee at the beginning of August, took on the functions of government; it was made up of representatives of different professional associations in Ashkhabad and other towns, and of other individuals chosen for their specific competences. Some of them were elected to membership of a praesidium with the right to initiate laws, whose members were 'commissars', following Bolshevik terminology. However, by the beginning of November what was henceforth known as the Provisional Transcaspian Government had taken firmer shape. It was made up of two entities, the Executive Committee and the Council of Directors. The Executive Committee had full executive powers, decided on general government policy, entered into relations with foreign powers and controlled the Council of Directors. The latter was purely an executive body made up of heads of department. It was responsible as a body to the Executive Committee and each head of department was responsible for all the activities of his department. Teague-Jones sketched some rather humorous portraits of the leaders of this Transcaspian government, with which he was now liaison officer:

The President of the Committee—somehow we could never bring ourselves to call him Prime Minister—was Comrade Funtikov. Before the coup d'état in July suddenly called him to play the role of village Hampden, Funtikov had never risen to anything higher than engine driver of the Central Asian Railway. In his proper sphere of life he had no doubt been a very worthy fellow and when sober probably a very good engine driver, but was no earthly use as a Prime Minister. He was very crude in his manners, extremely illiterate, but like so many of his kidney, painfully verbose and pretended to a certain skill in cheap rhetoric, so dear to all revolutionaries, particularly in Russia. His greatest weakness was drink, and although vodka and other strong beverages were supposed to be taboo, nevertheless, Funtikov—F-F-Funtikov as we generally called him, and he not infrequently called himself—was very rarely properly sober. I fancy he used to reason that drink helped his rhetoric. In point of fact, he rarely opened his mouth without making an ass of himself.[20]

As political representative in charge of all direct relations with and negotiations between the Transcaspian government and the Malleson mission—a position with which he was officially invested on 30 August 1918—Teague-Jones did not often have business with Funtikov. The interlocutor appointed by the Transcaspian government as 'foreign minister' was Lev Alexandrovich Zimin, a former primary school-teacher from Merv and an orientalist who was very knowledgeable about questions concerning the East and Islam. A Chekhovian personality, but rather irritable and narrow-minded, this right-wing member of the SR party was considered by Teague-Jones to be honest but without much talent for politics. In rare moments of discouragement, Teague-Jones would admit to having a fit of 'Ziminitis'. Another major figure, Kurilev, vice-president of the Executive Committee and a Russian by birth, was Funtikov's right-hand man and a gifted orator with considerable influence over the chairman and his administration:

Another railway employee, a fairly bright lad, much less ponderous than F-Funtikov and with a well-developed sense of humour. Kurilev revelled in the importance of his position. It gave him considerable prominence in the eyes of the population at large and of his railway comrades in particular. Furthermore it gave him the right to carry about with him a gigantic revolver, which he held cocked on his knee when sitting on a chair, or when driving about in his carriage. In addition to the revolver he carried about a large leather *porte-feuille* filled with numerous 'resolutions', 'proposals', 'schemes', 'estimates', and other documents. When in conversation he wished to refer to one or other of them he would turn out on the table all the contents of the portfolio, but somehow never succeed in finding what he was looking for. Kurilev liked to play the role of a strong silent man, but unfortunately he was neither strong nor silent and—I must add—was by no means brave. Though always employing such terms as 'stern action', 'repressive measures', and 'drastic punishment', I am positive he would not hurt a fly if he could help it and would certainly prefer to run away rather than face any personal danger.[21]

The other members of the government included Count Alexei I. Dorrer, the younger brother of a leading figure in the SR party, one of the earliest victims of the Bolshevik repression at Tashkent, whose title of 'Graf' brought a note of refinement to the scene. Teague-Jones thought that he was charming but weak; he seems to have been grateful for the care and hospitality offered by his wife, Countess Victoria Vladimirovna, when he was wounded. Another colourful member of the Transcaspian government, Dokhov—a typical SR according to Teague-Jones, all theory and no common-sense—was an inveterate bigamist and womaniser. His intrigues with women had brought him so much trouble in Ashkhabad that his nomination to Meshed as the permanent representative of the Transcaspian government was fortunately timed. The disparate alliance lacked an intelligence agent. Simion Lvovich Drujkin, a Jewish lawyer affiliated to the SR party, arrived in Krasnovodsk from

Astrakhan in mysterious and somewhat suspect circumstances on 10 September 1918 and made his way directly to Ashkhabad, where he made contact with Count Dorrer. After having cleaned out everyone suspected of being a Bolshevik agent at Ashkhabad, Simion Drujkin was appointed head of counter-espionage, and rapidly came to be considered one of the important figures in the Transcaspian government.

The Transcaspian government could not have functioned without military and financial assistance. In November 1918 an official agreement associated the Transcaspian government to a Caucasus/Caspian Union under the direction of General Bisherakov, who for the purposes of the agreement was appointed commander in chief of the united forces of the Caspian and the Caucasus. But this union of forces hostile to Bolshevism never existed on anything other than paper, and the hoped-for troop reinforcements never reached Ashkhabad. The government's finances, meanwhile, were in such a catastrophic state that at the end of December 1918 the government was forced to admit that it was unable to govern Transcaspia. Bolshevik propaganda was then deployed on a grand scale, while discontent spread, especially among the employees of the Transcaspian Railway who had not received their wages for months. The railway workers and staff were the first to be won over by this Red wave. On 1 January 1919 a meeting organised in Ashkhabad revealed not only the rising power of Bolshevism, but also the strength of anti-British feeling. In consequence the British authorities declared a state of emergency, and by agreement with the Transcaspian government formed a five-member Committee of Public Safety, whose priority was to repulse the Bolshevik advance. At the beginning of 1919 what was left of the Transcaspian government was hoping for help from Denikin's army in the Caucasus. Ashkhabad's position was becoming more and more difficult; in order to avoid depending on a hypothetical loan from abroad and, above all, in order to pay the railway employees, it became necessary to create a currency and print banknotes. As we shall see, Teague-Jones was both an observer and a participant in this tragic-comic 'Transcaspian episode'. After the British left in the spring of 1919, the Bolsheviks would have few problems in overcoming the White armies. Ashkhabad fell under their control in July 1919, Krasnovodsk in February 1920.

Reginald Teague-Jones: 'Political Representative in Transcaspia'

Though short—only a matter of a few months between the summer of 1918 and the spring of 1919—the Transcaspian episode had a central place in Teague-Jones's long life. The young field-agent formed discreet and lasting bonds of friendship with Jarvis and, especially, Ellis, both of whom were also active in British intelligence. There was no resemblance between these men and their contemporary, Lawrence of Arabia: no heroism or vainglory, still less any wise philosophising inspired by the tribes and the desert. Yet in a Turkmen East which positively discouraged any kind of romanticism, Teague-Jones still managed to find love. At least that is what is suggested by his marriage to the young and pretty Valya Alexeieva, whom he met between Krasnovodsk and Baku, and employed as his secretary at Ashkhabad before taking her off to

London. Teague-Jones married her after receiving permission from the military authorities. It was a military marriage, with a cavalry escort and festivities in the Russian style, washed down with plenty of vodka. Even though the marriage ended in divorce at the beginning of the 1920s, it is she whom Teague-Jones would seek out to share the end of his days in Plymouth sixty years later. The eloquence of this gesture says more than his enduring silence about this chapter in his private life. But at the end of 1918, Teague-Jones's main feeling was one of discouragement, the very opposite of the ecstasies of love, in the grip of the 'Transcaspian Blues', a time when his mission, looked at with a dispassionate eye, appeared to be completely absurd. At this point Teague-Jones was installed in his Ashkhabad HQ, where he had taken lodgings in a house rented by the Transcaspian government from a rich Persian merchant. On the first floor there was a large bedroom with a balcony, and on the ground floor, a reception room full of paintings of naked Circassian dancers, for which the proprietor of the place had a particular inclination:

This artist belonged to the starkly realistic school and his ladies were certainly very lovely and seductive and, during the heat of a Central Asian summer, no doubt calculatedly disturbing. But now we were in the depths of an abnormally rigorous winter and my household was still without fuel or firewood. I wore a wool-lined trench coat all day inside the house and spread it over my bed at night. Even indoors one's breath became visibly vaporised on the frosty air that pervaded the whole building.[22]

What sort of war was it at Ashkhabad in the winter of 1918, where Teague-Jones was both actor and spectator?

'This is a railway war'

As Teague-Jones repeats in his correspondence and reports, the Transcaspian war was a railway war. For the belligerents, Transcaspian on one side, Bolsheviks on the other, control of territory and military strategy depended on positions gained along the line. 'This is a railway war. Both forces live in trains and advance and retire only along the railway line. The first time we suggested leaving the line and marching over the flat, the Russians did not like the idea at all.'[23] In fact, controlling the steppe, the Turkmen domain, presented other kinds of problem, both strategic and political in nature. With its daily duel and repetitive formula, the railway war dominated the rest of the terrain in a desert zone where there were no roads and few water-points. This Transcaspian war, which Teague-Jones found amusing in a number of ways, was a mixture of the archaic and the modern. It was fought by British or Turkmen cavalry, though not to the exclusion of aerial reconnaissance, even if the Transcaspian forces only had a single aeroplane to fulfil all their needs. There were specific things about it which distinguish it from other railway theatres of operations such as South Africa during the Boer War, or the Western Front during the First World War.

On the Transcaspian side, armoured train no. 1 was a model of its kind. A metal fortress on wheels, armoured with metal and compressed cotton, it was composed of two flat-bed trucks in front heavily loaded with equipment and rails, followed by another flat-bed carrying the howitzer. Since there were no tunnels on the Transcaspian line, there were no height restrictions on the equipment. On the passenger carriage there were two machine-guns on the roof, and from this post the commander could both fire and send signals. Then came the powerful petrol-fired armoured locomotive, immediately followed by a fully armoured passenger carriage with weapon-slits, which served as offices and kitchen; behind these were two pilot trucks and a final flat-bed with a howitzer. This was the make-up of armoured train no. 1, on board which Teague-Jones frequently went up and down the stretch of the Transcaspian between Ashkhabad and Merv. In the opposing camp there were similar war-horses at the disposal of the Bolsheviks. The railway war consisted of daily manoeuvres in the neighbourhood of bends on the railway—in general on this section of the Transcaspian the length of a bend is between 300 and 500 *sagenes* (i.e. between roughly 600 and 1,000 metres). Teague-Jones's description of the daily ritual is full of humour:

War is beastly, but it also has its funny side, and quite the funniest side of this railway war was the daily duel of armoured trains … The Transcaspians possessed at this time three armoured trains, one of which mounted a howitzer taken from the fortress at Kushk and also a field gun and machine-guns. This was the principal 'battle train', the other two being kept in reserve. The Bolsheviks had similar armoured trains, but were believed to have heavier guns. In any case their shooting was execrable, so it made little difference. The daily operations were very simple. Between our position and the enemy's, the line made a bend and ran through a small cutting, which afforded a certain amount of cover. Armoured trains always liked bends and cuttings, for it enabled them to creep up out of sight of the enemy. Possibly like the ostrich with his head in the sand, they felt more secure. The Transcaspian train would advance bravely forth and puff and snort its way down the line to the 'home' end of the cutting. There it would stop just long enough to let off one round and would then promptly go into reverse and make straight for home. Local etiquette and the rules of the game then required the enemy to wait a little while, and after a reasonable pause their train would perform a similar evolution and fire its daily round at the Transcaspians. After watching this operation for a few days one understood perfectly the origin of that old phrase 'the daily round, the common task'. I must add that the shooting was wild and it was very unusual that any damage was done. The great advantage was that both sides had their bit of fun, there was no discomfort and honour was satisfied.[24]

This was not the case at Dushak station, a strategic position where the Transcaspian line made a dog-leg north-east towards Merv, Charjui and Samarkand. A Bolshevik train arrived there at the end of October 1918. The Transcaspians opened a barrage of shells in response and one of them hit their munitions wagon, causing terrible damage not only to the rolling stock but also to the station itself. At the end of the battle, the Bolsheviks had to withdraw as far as Karabata, the first station to the west of Merv, while the British were able to advance as far as Tejen, where Teague-Jones was able to assess the ravages caused by the Bolsheviks. As he wrote to his friend Ronald MacDonnell, who was based at Enzeli:

ASHKHABAD AND THE TRANSCASPIAN EPISODE

You cannot imagine the systematic way in which they looted Tejen. They even went to the trouble of cutting the locks and hinges out of doors. The place was practically burnt out. The Turkoman got in after the Bols had left and after murdering a number of the male population, carried off the women into the steppe. The same wholesale looting and pillaging has been carried on at Merv, until the place is literally denuded of everything of value. The Bolsheviks had every conceivable kind of loot stored in their trains even to the extent of grand pianos. Similarly their wives and families lived with them. It is a funny war.[25]

Lieutenant-Colonel Knollys,[26] who was in command of the 19th Punjabi Regiment, was based at Kaakha and was in constant correspondence with Teague-Jones. He also described the long train processions along the Transcaspian, preceded or followed as the case might be by the notorious armoured trains. Water was transported in enormous casks, the canteens were in open wagons, while the train carried men, horses, forage and food, weapons, printing-press for banknotes and, in the case of the Bolsheviks, the booty from their pillaging and a large number of women. In terms simply of the sexual attractions on offer, the Bolsheviks had an unarguably powerful advantage over the British, whose hospital trains with their teams of nurses and even a church-carriage presented a much more austere image. Teague-Jones allowed himself some ironic comments on the fact that the Bolsheviks transported their women with them:

I say their women but I must correct this, for as a matter of fact, most of the women were not theirs at all, at any rate not legitimately. Some of them, it is true, were voluntarily there. Some of them actually took part in the fighting and were occasionally found among the casualties. But many of the others, poor things, were there by force, conscripted wives and daughters of the Intelligentsia of Tashkent and elsewhere.[27]

This war of skirmishing soon gave rise to a tactical routine. Sheltered by a bend, the engine would groan and belch large clouds of steam at short intervals, providing a screen behind which the convoy could advance or retreat, forcing the enemy to shoot blind. Sabotage of the track by blowing up rails and ditches was also common practice, but the presence of experienced railway workers made rapid repairs possible. A craftier and more destructive tactic, apparently used by both camps, was to increase the gap between the rails so that the locomotive eventually crashed down between them. The most important distinction between the warring trains lay in the fuel they used. While the Transcaspians could in principle draw on the remaining petroleum stocks at Krasnovodsk, the Bolsheviks had to resort to a great variety of expedients to fire their engines. In the absence of diesel, they used the sparse brushwood growing in the Turkmen desert—*saksaul*—and further north, on the Aktyubinsk front, they adapted the engines for an improvised fuel in a way that prefigured future Soviet ecological problems: fish from the Aral Sea. At the end of 1918 the Transcaspians and Bolsheviks each controlled a section of the railway. The British had the strategic part of the Transcaspian from the Caspian to Dushak, running along the north-east escarpment of the Iranian plateau, a through route which if extended would finish up in India. The Bolsheviks for their part controlled, depending on their advances or retreats, the other section to the north of Dushak, Merv and Charjui. Of more commercial and administrative than strategic value, this part of the Transcaspian was to be linked later to the Transsiberian line, via the Aral Railway. It dominated the interior of Eurasia and access to Russia. The strategic town of Charjui controlled the Transcaspian Bridge over the Amu Darya River. But the straight track leading to it, which crossed the Karakum dunes, was the most difficult to capture, because the permanent threat from drifting sand had made it necessary as early as 1889 to raise the track by means of an embankment. This section of the Transcaspian, which needed more frequent clearing by bulldozer and where trains had to run fully exposed, was more problematic terrain for train warfare.

A railway government

As the British representative at Ashkhabad from 30 August 1918 onwards, Teague-Jones was the head at the local level of a railway government. In practice, the job of political officer was to conciliate the employees of the Transcaspian Railway, whose political role was just as critical as their practical contribution to train warfare. The workers and staff of the railway and of the railway workshops, assembled in the Soviets of Tashkent or Ashkhabad, had installed, and in some cases un-installed, the Bolsheviks in power. As the sole representatives of the Turkmen proletariat their political support and professional skills were indispensable for the maintenance of the British presence and for the prosecution of the railway war. They drove the trains and maintained them on a daily basis, repairing and inspecting each section of track and clearing away the sand which constantly drifted over it. It is not surprising, therefore, that the president of the Transcaspian government, Funtikov, was a train driver and that the same government's representative at Krasnovodsk, Vassili Kuhn, was a railway engineer. As political officer, Teague-Jones's job was to secure collaboration, in the face of a constant threat of strikes, from men whose wages and salaries had not been paid for months. On top of that he had to organise the provision of material necessities for the British and Indian troops arriving at Ashkhabad. These few months of incessant activity are very well documented, since, contrary to his normal practice, Teague-Jones kept his original correspondence. From his post at Ashkhabad he organised the British intervention in Transcaspia, maintaining permanent contact with Lieutenant-Colonel Fleming at Krasnovodsk, Lieutenant-Colonel Knollys at Kaakhka, and Redl at Meshed, the rear base for the Malleson mission.

The conditions meeting British and Indian forces upon arriving at Ashkhabad were poor: the Russian railway hospital was dirty and badly equipped, and the Russian staff, who had no experience of Hindus and their customs, were completely unable to cope in the absence of interpreters. They would be replaced to good effect by the staff of the Baku hospital, recently evacuated to Ashkhabad, some of whom were much more experienced Armenians. Food, rations, housing for officers and men were all matters in which Teague-Jones was absorbed in dealing with during October 1918. To Redl he confessed that 'the money in my charge for Secret Service purposes for objects which could in no ways be entitled Secret Service'.[28] A great part of the supplies came by rail from Krasnovodsk, where Fleming had daily arguments with Kuhn, the local representative of the Transcaspian government. In these times of war and revolution there was a general lack of money in Krasnovodsk as well as in Ashkhabad. The British authorities were therefore constantly receiving requests: would they make a loan to Enzeli so that the government could import a shipment of wood and rice from Persia? The weakness of the rouble against the Persian kran had to be considered, and then the reception of the shipment had to be organised, and some of it sent on to Ashkhabad where winter was approaching and there was a shortage of firewood. Charjui, on the banks of the Amu Darya, was the only wood-producing region and was in the hands of the Bolsheviks, and the prospect of winter was bleak because petrol and feed for beef-cattle and sheep were short. To Fleming, Teague-Jones wrote that:

the most vital question as far as we are concerned is the supply of benzine. There is as you know none in Transcaspia. The Committee lost their opportunity of purchasing it before the fall of Baku and now they are helpless. At present I am worrying them to send up a ship to Guriev (Atyrau),[29] where we know there is a considerable supply. The port will be frozen in a short time now, and we know that the Bolsheviks are also trying to get there, so we must make haste.[30]

The vital problem of supplies was further aggravated by the flood of refugees from Petrovsk, a port on the western shores of the Caspian (now known as Makhachkala), where General Bisherakov had assumed the command of the counter-revolutionary forces. Teague-Jones wrote about the problem to Fleming:

I confess I was getting rather anxious lest there should be a shortage, a fact which would do more to damage our prestige and make us unpopular than almost anything else. I do not know how far Kuhn has been successful in persuading Bisherakov to assist in the supply of grain from Petrovsk. Hitherto he has sent us several consignments, but with them he has sent equal consignments of refugees who more or less neutralize the advantages otherwise obtained.[31]

A few days later, Teague-Jones learned that Bisherakov now held only the immediate sector around Petrovsk, with 7,000 undisciplined and drunken men. At the end of October thirty steamers were waiting in the port of Petrovsk, ready for an immediate evacuation, an event which seemed likely in the light of Mme Bisherakov's recent arrival at Krasnovodsk. At Krasnovodsk, from 1 November onwards, the British authorities checked all vessels arriving from Petrovsk, only admitting those which really were bringing supplies, and summarily sending back all those carrying troops or refugees. This was another cause of tension between Teague-Jones and the members of the Ashkhabad Committee, which although prepared to allow the British exclusive control of Krasnovodsk, disputed their right to refuse entry to the port to Allied forces. An identical embargo was applied to vessels coming from Baku, which were suspected of carrying undesirable Bolsheviks in their cargoes. At Krasnovodsk as at Ashkhabad there had been a vigorous renewal of Bolshevik agitation in railway worker circles since the autumn of 1918.

Faced with increasing resistance from the railway workers and staff, weeks behind with their wages, Teague-Jones had to try to keep the Transcaspian government at arm's length in circumstances which were more and more hostile to the 'capitalist exploiters of the working masses'. Treated as an 'accursed representative of decadent imperialism', he had to find some way of managing, and to 'govern', a Transcaspia which had fallen into political chaos. Bolshevik propaganda put about by agents who had infiltrated under various guises—for example, primary schoolteachers at Kizil-Arvat—had to be countered by concrete arguments, such as support for the finances of the Transcaspian government, and above all by paying the wages of the railway employees. At the end of November 1918, at the instigation of the government of India, and with the approval of intelligence headquarters in Whitehall, it was decided to try money as an antidote to ideological subversion. The British mission on the ground did not have any:

but as there was no money available, [it was decided that] we should create some. In other words, it was decided that we should print our own currency in the form of promissory notes. We should issue notes of the face value of 500 roubles, and we were empowered to make a preliminary issue totalling, 5,000,000 roubles. This meant that we had to produce and issue exactly 10 000 notes. It was left to myself to put the scheme into practice.[32]

The first step was to print the notes, for which a satisfactory type of paper was needed. In Ashkhabad it was difficult in November 1918 to find the kind of water-marked paper which would discourage counterfeiting, and they consequently had to make do with very poor quality paper. Teague-Jones, who was very good at drawing, provided the simple design, using the elementary technical facilities of the local printers at Ashkhabad. The proliferation of new currencies in Central Asia during the civil war had encouraged new designs, particularly on the Bolshevik side. The British were keen to do the same, and with the means to hand succeeded in making up and then printing, in English, Russian and Turkmen, the famous Transcaspian roubles. Teague-Jones showed that he was up to the job. He supervised the trial efforts, watched over the printing, took steps to prevent fraud and kept the master documents under lock and key. He then had to sign by hand, in the presence of another officer, each of the 10,000 notes—though they were easy to forge and forged they soon were. Many sleepless nights were spent signing these derisory bits of paper, which were eagerly awaited by the local population, and without which the Transcaspian Railway would have quickly ceased to function. This palliative measure succeeded in saving the situation for a little while, to the point where even the dreary Zimin began to sound a bit more optimistic. Not so in Teague-Jones's case; he confided to Fleming in mid-December 1918:

We continue to carry on here. It is a hand to mouth sort of existence. The government is trying hard to gather a little power. Thanks to the presence here of our troops they are able to enforce a little more authority. I can however, already see a distinct increase in the feeling that 'better the Bolsheviks than the British', and we have a number of Bolshevik proclamations posted up in the town … I try not to be pessimistic, but the country cannot live without money. No government can stand that cannot feed and keep its subjects, and this government certainly cannot. Nous verrons is about all we can say at present.[33]

The role of the British representative in Transcaspia was difficult to maintain when there were delays in realising the financial aid which had been provided for under the terms of the August 1918 agreement. In the absence of any real British strategy in Transcaspia, or any clear objective which would require a stronger commitment on the part of the Malleson mission, particularly on the financial level, Teague-Jones was reduced to propping up a puppet government at the behest of a British military mission which increasingly seemed to be a big joke. His sense of absurdity but also of loneliness was reinforced by a short visit from Malleson and his team in mid-December, before they left again to spend Christmas at Meshed:

I regretted the departure of the Staff, in particular Ellis and Jarvis, for they were cheery and capable fellows and their presence acted on me like a tonic. Before their arrival I had become very stale and I was suffering from 'Blues Transcaspiana', otherwise a surfeit of 'Ziminitis'. I found myself taking life too seriously and I badly wanted a change, but with the arrival on the scene of these cheery lads my blues disappeared and I began to see the funny side of things again. Frankly, however, at this particular period, the funny side was becoming increasingly difficult to find.[34]

Building an intelligence network in Transcaspia

In addition to the business of government and administration, Teague-Jones was also expected to build a coherent system of intelligence in Transcaspia. Malmiss had no military function other than intelligence. Teague-Jones's solitary mission constituted one of its outposts, as did Percy Etherton's contemporaneous consulate at Kashgar,[35] which was watching political developments in Russian Central Asia from Xinjiang. As a British intelligence officer, Teague-Jones found himself at the centre of several networks of information. First there was the Committee of Ashkhabad, which was supposed to have a counter-espionage bureau, which Teague-Jones judged to be worthless and useless. A second network—with the mysterious designation of the 'TU Office'—covered the vast territory of Turkestan. Teague-Jones provides no organisational chart of the merchants, tribes, Europeans, White Russians and others that constituted it, but he considered it more effective. Its information reveals that Ashkhabad was teeming with Turkish agents, and constantly under threat from Bolshevik plots: in September 1918 there were at least 800 active Bolsheviks. The need to put in place a coherent system of counter-espionage required the amalgamation of the TU Office with the local Ashkhabad office, though the question of the British financial contribution was not clarified in the process. 'The argument put forward was that, with the present dangerous political situation, it was vital that all possible measures should be taken to cope with the ever increasing activities in our midst of enemy agents. This was only possible with money', as Teague-Jones wrote to Colonel Redl.[36] A third and separate organisation run by him personally was supposed to operate in the Caspian sector including Baku, to which he went on numerous occasions during this period. For Teague-Jones, the challenge was to unify the intelligence structure at Ashkhabad, and to obtain from Malleson and his superiors the necessary funding and a degree of freedom of action:

A scheme of counter-espionage, or to put it plainer, of Intelligence is indispensable. We must have it. So far the only work of any value has been carried on by our friends, who to give them their due have worked and [are] now working very hard, and not without good results, as the arrest of numerous individuals goes to show.[37]

The network of 'friends' was built on a handful of Britons—Ellis, Jarvis, and no doubt in addition Bailey, Gordon and Etherton—who had recruited their agents all over Central Asia as far as the limits of Xinjiang from among merchants, community elders (*aqsaqals*), White Russians and tribal chiefs.

From his privileged position at Ashkhabad, Teague-Jones was able to keep a watch on the Caspian to the west, and, to the east, the strategic frontier of Afghanistan, a neutral country in the First World War, but courted by a number of representatives of the belligerent powers. At the end of September 1918, he was briefed on the situation in Afghanistan by Colonel Zikov, the officer commanding a detachment at Kushk, a military post on the frontier between Russian Turkestan and Afghanistan, and the terminus for a strategic branch-line of the Transcaspian running due south from Merv, which had just fallen into the hands of the Bolsheviks. Most of his officers were savagely massacred, but Zikov had survived and managed to reach Merv thanks to the help of some Turkmen friends. Teague-Jones passed on his account to Meshed:

The Bolsheviks have taken large quantities of weapons and ammunitions from Kushk, including two 6 inch guns which they are now using on the Kaakhka front. Trains are running from Kushk to Merv. Zikov made his way through the latter place where he stayed ten days in hiding. According to him, words cannot describe the chaotic state of affairs there. The Bolsheviks have behaved with utmost savagery. The excesses of the Boxer rising pale into insignificance beside the awful cruelty practised by the Bolsheviks in Merv. They have apparently slaughtered without regard either to age or sex and have plundered in a wholesale manner that would do justice to the Huns. They have levied a 'contribution' of 250 thousand puds of corn on the wretched town and are busy removing to Tashkent everything of value. We hear of large numbers of trains standing at Dushak, but from the report of an individual who has just passed through there a large number of the wagons are filled with loot even to the extent of pianos.[38]

Teague-Jones also sent Zikov's personal analysis of the situation in Afghanistan to Colonel Redl:

Zikov, who has an intimate knowledge of the Afghan frontier gives as his opinion that there is no likelihood of Afghanistan coming into the war. He admits that German, Austrian and

Turkish agents are very active there but says that unless of course the Turks actually appeared in Transcaspia the Afghans are not in favour of interfering. Zikov reports the existence in the neighbourhood of Kushk (Afghanistan) of a mixed mounted detachment consisting of Afghans, Turkish and Austrian prisoners. This may of course simply mean that the prisoners have drifted there from Siberia and taken on in the ranks as the simplest way of earning a livelihood. The attitude of Afghan frontier officials is friendly to the Russians with the exception of the Bolsheviks, whom they look upon as brigands of the worst type.[39]

The forward military post at Kushk, only 66 miles from Herat, was strategically important. In order to keep a watch on political developments in Afghanistan, Teague-Jones set up a system of agents covering Ashkhabad and Herat, as well as Meymena, which is further to the north but still very close to the Russian frontier. From this system, set up in September 1918 to operate in difficult country, he could not expect any reports inside of a month; thereafter he would receive weekly reports, but in December he no longer had any agents left in Afghanistan. In the west Teague-Jones was promisingly placed at Ashkhabad for infiltrating a difficult sector of the frontier between Russian Turkestan and Persia, the Yomut country in the lower valley of the Atrek, where he also tried to set up an 'agency'. He set up the British intelligence system on the coast of the Caspian between September and December 1918: it depended on a network of agents both along the coast and in the district of Asterabad. Teague-Jones's mission as intelligence officer was not therefore solely confined to Turkestan. His field of investigations also included the frontier hinterlands of northern Persia and Afghanistan in the Russian zone of influence into which the British had never had the opportunity to venture.

Once a paid network of reliable informants had been recruited, who reported to him in writing or orally in Russian or Persian, Teague-Jones transferred the raw information to his working journal. There are very few of the original documents in his personal archives, since the basic rules of intelligence required them to be destroyed once they had come in. The communications system—telegraph, telephone and the Transcaspian Railway—allowed for the direct transmission of information between Teague-Jones at Ashkhabad, Lieutenant-Colonel Fleming at Krasnovodsk, Colonel Redl at the Meshed consulate and Lieutenant-Colonel Knollys further up the line at Kaakha. Besides cipher—indispensable, but time-consuming and unreliable owing to unpredictable breakdowns on the telegraph line between Krasnovodsk, Ashkhabad and Meshed—other modes of communication were employed depending on the level of confidentiality with which the information needed to be treated. Teague-Jones suggested pragmatically to Fleming that he send non-confidential messages in Russian or in English written in Russian script. 'No-one on the line knows English and there is little danger of such messages going wrong.'[40] These messages travelled daily by train between Krasnovodsk and Ashkhabad, carried by one or two men who had been given the shuttle job and a small sum of money to pay for their food on the journey. To the east of Ashkhabad this postal system functioned much less efficiently if Colonel Knollys' repeated complaints at Kaakha are to be believed, even though further up the Transcaspian line, near the front, rapid transmission of information was still possible. The British military mission in Transcaspia had a need on the ground for interpreters translating from Russian to English, a rare ability in Russia and rarer still in Transcaspia. Lieutenant-Colonel Knollys pressed Teague-Jones to find him interpreters, explaining that he could if necessary make do with a Russian–French interpreter. Their role in intelligence was crucial and they were very often Armenians whom Knollys dismissed as 'useless as they run when most wanted'.[41] Teague-Jones's reply is instructive:

The interpreters I have sent you are the only people I could find. A number have applied but they were absolutely useless. I have wired Enzeli asking them to help us. Krasnovodsk is also asking for interpreters. All the Russian speaking officers [who] were there with Colonel Battine have returned to Kazvin, and only one interpreter remains. I have found you two men here. One speaks French but I send him with much hesitation as he is now said to be a little insane. He does not look much of a specimen and I certainly would not pick him out of a crowd, but he is the best I can do. The other is a most promising man and when you have done with him I want him back please. He speaks English quite well also French and Turkish … Karibian came from Baku.[42]

Valya Alexeieva, who had also managed to escape from the disaster at Baku, arrived in Ashkhabad at the end of October. After disembarking at Enzeli from one of the last ships from Baku, she was easily able to resume contact with Teague-Jones through the intermediary of the British military mission, now commanded by General Thompson. In all probability she had already been engaged in every sense of the word by Teague-Jones since their meeting in the summer of 1918. It was therefore only natural that she should become the secretary to the British military mission at Ashkhabad, and she was probably able to carry out tasks other than those of a simple Russian shorthand-typist. Her arrival and that of Captain Haines, a British officer who had a working knowledge of Russian and who was put to work on logistics and organisational matters, were a considerable relief to Teague-Jones, who was labouring under the weight of so many duties that one wonders how he could find the time to write his reports, his daily correspondence and his working journal. At least now he could concentrate on 'matters of State'.

From improvisation to retreat: the Transcaspian episode

In the autumn of 1918, plunged into the chaos of a Turkmenistan racked by the strains of the revolution and the civil war, themselves a consequence of the great revolt of 1916, Teague-Jones found himself in an outpost which allowed him to observe not only military developments, but also and especially the political problems of Transcaspia. From 1918 onwards the central problem facing the authorities was that of the legitimate aspirations of the natives. The essential political issue was that of the Turkmen, whose emergent national identity had been channelled into different political streams and fractured by tribal struggles. Having been unavoidably confronted by the Turkmen question as soon as the Turkmen became involved in the

anti-Bolshevik struggle in Turkestan, Teague-Jones observed and listened to his informants and produced an expert report. Against the backdrop of the complex question
of Turkmen nationalism, a simple strategy for making use of this movement emerged.
From the British perspective it was essential to gain the collaboration and assistance
of the Turkmen during the crucial developments of the summer of 1918. This period
saw the revolt of the Basmachis (brigands) in the southern regions of Central Asia,
and the collapse for the time being of Turkish ambitions following the Ottoman
capitulation after the armistice signed at Mudros on 30 October 1918.

The Turkmen question: an instrumental strategy?

In the autumn of 1918, soon after his first few weeks as the political representative
of Great Britain in Transcaspia, Teague-Jones learned of the difficulties that the
Transcaspian authorities were experiencing with the Turkmen. Asked by Zimin for a
written opinion on the question, Teague-Jones was at pains to avoid giving advice to
the Transcaspian government, arguing his ignorance of the indigenous population,
with whose customs and language he admitted himself unfamiliar. Such modesty was
appropriately diplomatic when dealing with the Transcaspian government. However,
the long and documented notes on the Turkmen question that he sent to Lieutenant-
Colonel Knollys at Kaakhka—where the behaviour of the Turkmen during the battle
against the Bolsheviks had aroused justifiable suspicions of treachery—and to
Colonel Fleming at Krasnovodsk, prove that any gaps in his knowledge were quickly
filled. The British military authorities could not remain indifferent to the Turkmen
question. They had agreed a close military alliance on the front line with Colonel
Oraz Serdar, whose Turkmen regiments, even if they fought badly, were no worse
than the great majority of Russian conscripts. The Turkmen chieftains' desire for the
independence of a Transcaspia in which the majority of the population was Turkmen,
and the fact that Transcaspia was in the grip of increasing anarchy, could not leave
Teague-Jones indifferent. His sensitive understanding of tribal politics in a colonial
setting, which came from his experience in other territories, found a new field of
application in Transcaspia. The complex tribal chessboard was divided by a number
of fault-lines: anti-Bolsheviks against Jadids who had joined the Bolshevik cause;
anti-Russian sentiment against loyalty to the old regime; and tribal nationalism
against pro-Turkish sympathies. Teague-Jones for his part distinguished two tendencies among the Turkmen, which pit the 'party of the old regime' against the 'new
progressive party' whose most active and most Turcophile representative was
Ovazbaiev. The latter, a 'Young Turkmen' who had served in the ranks of the Turkmen
Regiment of the tsar's army, became the secretary of a Transcaspian Muslim
Committee after demobilisation. Although he had succeeded in recruiting a body of
armed men, Ovazbaiev did not wield much influence within the tribe.

The Khansha tribe, spread around Merv, was the oldest and most influential of the
Turkmen tribes, claiming authority over almost two-thirds of all Turkmen. The
female leader of the tribe had been killed by the Bolsheviks at Merv, and her son,

Yusuf Khan, who replaced her, was quickly eliminated shortly thereafter. This left the leadership of the tribe to Mahtum Quli Khan:

an old Turkman of the old school. He was a staunch supporter of the old regime and was convinced that the Russians would once more make their power felt throughout Turkistan. When the Turkman Committee was first formed, he was offered the post of President. He refused to accept it on the plea that he did not want to act against the Russians. He had lost influence since Ovazbaiev came to the fore, but still commanded a greater following than either Ovazbaiev or Haji Murat. His followers were, however, without arms and he was therefore more or less at the mercy of the most progressive party.[43]

The majority of Turkmen had rallied to the Khansha tribe and its conservative views, but Ovazbaiev's party, which Colonel Oraz Serdar joined, was distinctly Turcophile; Serdar enjoyed considerable prestige as the son of Tikma Sardar, the hero of the Turkmen resistance to the Russians at the Battle of Gök-Tepe in 1881. According to Teague-Jones, there was no doubt that Ovazbaiev was in communication with Turkish agents, and that he had succeeded in securing influence over Oraz Serdar, who was weak and easily influenced:

Ovazbaiev has really no established influence in the tribe but owing to a foolish mistake of the Committee in giving him a round sum of two millions not very long ago, he was enabled to collect around him a band of followers who will fight or not fight at his bidding. The view taken by the Committee is that Ovazbaiev will fight for them just so long as it pleases him and would turn on the Russians any moment he thought would pay him.[44]

Finally, another Turkmen chieftain, Haji Murat, a former lieutenant-colonel in the Turkmen Infantry Regiment in the Russian army, had served as commissar in the Bolshevik Soviet before its expulsion from Ashkhabad, and then became Oraz Serdar's chief assistant. A founder of the Turkmen Central Executive Committee in the village of Bezmein, a few miles from Ashkhabad, and later appointed a member of the Provisional Transcaspian Government, Haji Murat held very strong pro-Turkish views, at least until the Ottoman capitulation.

The rise of Turkish nationalism, mixed in nature though it was, combined with the growing desire for independence on the part of the Turkmen chieftains, presented a difficult problem for the political representative of Great Britain at Ashkhabad. At the front the British collaborated closely with Oraz Serdar, but some of the Turkmen under the leadership of Haji Murat were already parting company with the Transcaspian government. At the same time, the collapse of the Russian authorities was allowing free rein to the Turkmen tribes' instinct for pillage, and their activities were causing difficulties for the Transcaspian government: trains taken by storm by armed Turkmen, passengers robbed, armed attacks at the Ashkhabad bazaar, a raid at Tejen where the Russian population was massacred—all of these events were in the authentic tradition of Basmachi brigandry. Incapable of asserting its authority over the Turkmen chieftains, the Transcaspian government turned to Teague-Jones for advice and support:

Up to the present I had successfully avoided interfering in any question affecting the internal administration and I was particularly anxious not to get entangled in any such questions. I was impressed, however, with the potential dangers of this crisis between the Russians and the Turkmans and accordingly on October 28th I paid a hasty visit to the Front, then at Tejen, to discuss the whole matter with the military authorities.[45]

The visit consisted, on the one hand, in explaining the political picture among the Turkmen tribes to Colonel Knollys—who could not hold the front line without their cooperation—and on the other, calming down the anxieties of the same Turkmen who were convinced that the authorities at Ashkhabad in whose name they were expected to fight were in the process of snatching power from them. When Teague-Jones returned to Ashkhabad, he was informed of an incipient plot by Haji Murat and his Turkmen Committee against the Transcaspian authorities. It was a serious situation which called for all his diplomatic talents; he was obliged to go on horseback to Haji Murat's house, accompanied by two *sowars*, deal soothingly with his recriminations against the Transcaspian government and persuade him to accept a compromise. Although he was initially taken aback by this surprise visit, Haji Murat eventually allowed himself to be persuaded. For his part, Zimin, persuaded by Teague-Jones that the alliance with the Turkmen should be maintained at any price, had succeeded in persuading the other members of the Transcaspian government to adopt a more conciliatory attitude towards them. For the time being the 'Turkmen crisis' had been surmounted.

In January 1919 Teague-Jones carried out a further diplomatic mission to the Turkmen tribes in order to settle the rivalries between their chieftains at a time when the Transcaspian government had decided to allocate two seats to representatives of the Turkmen. Arriving by train from the more distant regions or on horseback from their respective *auls*, the delegations of Turkmen chieftains descended on Teague-Jones, in his salon decorated with naked dancers, who looked more incongruous than ever in the circumstances:

I had them all shown into the big room and as they came crowding in, many of them with daggers protruding from their waistbands, I could not help thinking of Ali Baba and the forty thieves. When they were all assembled, I joined them and mingled with the crowd. I recognised several tribal leaders. Haji Murat and Ovazbaiev were both there and introduced a number of other chieftains, presumably from among their own supporters. None of these spoke Russian but we managed to exchange salutations and compliments in Persian bolstered by my limited scraps of Turki. It was noticeable that the crowd had roughly divided itself into two sections, the one comprising the followers of Haji Murat and Ovazbaiev and the remainder centred upon Mahtum Quli Khan, with whom were a group of *aksakal* or tribal greybeards. Some of these were very fine looking men with pronounced Mongolian, though in many cases highly intelligent, features. It seemed clear that the older and better type of Tekke supported Mahtum Quli Khan and frankly I was very glad to see this, for it bore out what I had been repeatedly told, namely that, although he was less vocal and educated than Haji Murat, Mahtum Quli Khan still wielded much greater influence within the tribe.[46]

The objective of this double delegation of Turkmen was to get British support, for which each of them was contending against the other.

Against all expectations, Haji Murat and Ovazbaiev were elected at this critical moment in the life of the Transcaspian government, which had by now been reconstituted as the Committee of Public Safety. The political meaning of these nominations did not escape Teague-Jones, who would have preferred to see Ovazbaiev take a position of military leader at the front. And indeed, in January 1919 Ovazbaiev submitted a plan to Teague-Jones for the creation of an independent Turkmenistan, made up of a series of neighbouring principalities, or khanates, corresponding to areas of tribal influence in Transcaspia and in Turkestan as a whole. Starting from the principle that Great Britain had recognised de facto the independence of Azerbaijan, proclaimed on 27 May 1918, Ovazbaiev believed that Great Britain should similarly recognise the independence of Turkmenistan. An incredulous Teague-Jones examined the plan, which defined the zones of influence of the principal tribal chieftains:

Ovazbaiev would have his sphere of influence, Haji Murat would have his and there would be plenty of territory left for Aziz Khan of Tejen, for Allahyar the freebooter (who was supposed to have been hanged, but who was still very much alive) and Junaid Khan the ravager of Khiva. Even the Emir of Bokhara was included in the scheme, doubtless to give it tone.[47]

Teague-Jones could only temporise, laugh and offer cigarettes. As he lacked the boldness of a Lawrence of Arabia, he could not personally endorse this plan for an independent Turkmenistan, nor above all convince the British authorities to do so. But the two men nevertheless formed a genuine friendship. The exotic look of the Indian Army soldiers astonished the Turkmen, as did the 'almost brotherly' relationship between the British officers and the Indian *sepoys*:

I told him stories about India and about the North-West Frontier. He laughed when I told him we occasionally had trouble with our own tribes-people. 'There's going to be a good deal of that in this country before we've finished' he said. 'Do not forget that today every Turkman is armed. With the whole of the country in our hands …'

— 'Except the railway', I ventured.

— 'Well, except the railway; but what is the railway, after all? Our ancestors lived without it and in any case we have the whole of the steppe to move about in.'[48]

An intelligence service in Yomut country

Although Teague-Jones had managed to restore a degree of equilibrium in Ashkhabad, the reports which were reaching him from Krasnovodsk revealed the actual precariousness of the situation. At Krasnovodsk, where Bolshevik propaganda was gaining ground via the railway workshops, a coup d'état on 30 November 1918 nearly swept away Kuhn, the local representative of the Transcaspian government. As railhead for the Transcaspian line and strategic port on the Caspian, Krasnovodsk and the south-eastern shore of the Caspian beyond called for special vigilance. This was the territory of the Yomuts, the second most numerous Turkmen tribe after the Teke. In the eighteenth century the tribe had been based around the Khiva khanate, but in the nineteenth century it had settled lands further to the west as far as the Mangishlak Peninsula and the Persian shores of the Caspian. The Yomuts consequently held a strategic position along the frontier which ran along the Atrek, but also in the Gulf of Krasnovodsk where passage was obstructed by a great number of islands, among which the most important were the Yomut strongholds of Chekelen and Ogurchinski. Chekelen was the island domain of Yomutski Khan and had been turned into a proper weapon store: the Bolshevik agitators from Krasnovodsk were therefore seeking an alliance with him. The neighbouring island of Ogurchinski, on the other hand, served as a training camp for young Yomut recruits, who had originally been brought to white heat by the prospect of a Turkish invasion, and subsequently, after the Ottomans had capitulated, by the example of an independent Azerbaijan.

Teague-Jones and Fleming were concerned about the activities of these heavily armed Yomuts, who were capable of rising in the Asterabad region of northern Iran and setting the Turkmen steppe on fire at any moment. There was therefore a need for an intelligence service especially concerned with this sector of the Caspian. Teague-Jones had applied himself to this task from the middle of September onwards, recruiting a very valuable, and very expensive, agent known as 'Desiatnik', alias Chaika, whose pay he had to justify to Colonel Redl:

I also want to ask you about Intelligence in the Astarabad area, and on the Caspian littoral to the south of Krasnovodsk. When I received instructions in the middle of September to take up Caspian Sea intelligence, I took steps to get into touch with various people I knew in Baku, and who were at that time in Petrovsk. As however I was unable to go personally to Krasnovodsk I never actually got into touch with them, and, with the change in the political situation, I dropped work in that direction. The South Caspian littoral however demanded, and in my opinion still demands attention. I organized a scheme of intelligence agents at a number of places both on the coast and in the Astarabad district. I calculated that this scheme would cost me about 7.000 Roubles a month actual pay of agents plus about half that sum incidental expenses. The head agent is a man whom I call Desyatnik. He is well known in those parts, and I know him very fairly well myself. He has sent in a number of quite useful reports … Desyatnik points out that owing to the fall in the value of the Rouble he has been obliged to pay his agents considerably more than the sums he told me he thought would suffice … Do we still attach importance to intelligence from those parts, or rather, sufficient importance to justify the expenditure of this sum?[49]

After the defeat of the Ottomans, the Turks no longer presented a threat and a general Yomut uprising seemed less likely. This raised the question as to whether he should he keep the agent 'Desyatnik', alias Chaika, and with him the network of five intelligence agents between Asterabad, Bandar-e Gaz in Persia and Hassan Quli on the other side of the frontier in Turkmen country. At first unsure, Teague-Jones expressed his convictions on the subject to Fleming:

I certainly think that as long as we have any troops here, we should watch the Yomut steppe very carefully. I agree with you that there is trouble brewing in that quarter. I thought for a time that with the downfall of Turkey the local Mussulman would realise that the game was lost, and give up their dream of pan-Islamic rule. Far from it. Each day further convinces them of the hopeless weakness of the Russians and the feeling in favour of self-rule is becoming continually stronger. The only thing that can keep things in order in Transcaspia is a strong hand, and that is at present lacking.[50]

Agent Chaika, a Russian colonist involved in trade in Bandar-e Gaz, could still be useful, even if it was no longer a question of watching the activities of Turkish agents but rather of keeping track of the level of support among the Yomuts for Turkmen independence. The system set up by Teague-Jones worked brilliantly. Chaika's reports—which his commissioning officer deemed to be of very high quality—arrived with regularity. Chaika entrusted them to the captains of boats plying the route between Hassan Kuli and Krasnovodsk, who passed them on by hand to N.N. Semov, the trusted British contact in Krasnovodsk.

In light of the passing of the Turkish threat, but with the continued presence of the Bolshevik danger, the British were now confronted with political choices given that their presence was no longer justified by the First World War but was now a case of 'foreign intervention' against the Reds. From this point onwards the expression of Turkmen nationalism had instrumental value, even if both Fleming and Teague-Jones were deeply distrustful of the Turkmen tribes, not to say contemptuous. In practice the priority was to disarm the Yomuts as far as possible. On 16 December 1918 Fleming was authorised by Norperforce to disarm the islanders of Chekelen and Ogurchinski and proposed to organise 'a raid and clear up things there. The possibility of so many arms so near Krasnovodsk makes things uncomfortable.'[51] But at the end of December the clean-up operation, which had been continually deferred, had still not taken place due to a lack of a suitable steamer. 'Had I a boat like the Perlaga I could disarm them and this would clear the air here,'[52] he wrote to Teague-Jones. In the meantime the disturbances continued at Chekelen, where Turkmen from three local villages had burned all the telegraph posts and all the wooden structures on the oilfields, seriously endangering work there. The British tried to contain the disturbances and carried out arrests in Yomut country in the neighbourhood of the port of Hassan Quli and of the Persian frontier. It was left to Teague-Jones, who had no illusions about the professions of friendship made by the Turkmen chieftains after the Ottoman surrender, to provide a political analysis of the situation:

Previously preserving a 'standoffish' attitude, they now showed a keen desire of making our acquaintance, and incidentally of course probing our policy. They came to the conclusion that we were at any rate much more tolerant than the Russians, and the fact that we have more or less recognised the Azerbaijan Government in Baku served as a ground for believing that the British would support the Turkman in Transcaspia even against the Russians if necessary. Ovazbaiev, who is a hot headed individual and represents no section of the Turkman community save his own Turkman detachment, became so positive of our support that he gave open utterance to what he considered to be Turkman aims, but which are in reality nothing more than the personal ambitions of Ovazbaiev. Thus the formation of a government here the great majority of which would be Turkman or Caucasian Turks, and the immediate despatch of a representative to the European peace conference seemed quite possible with British assistance. As a private individual the vapourings of Ovazbaiev are harmless, but when he suddenly got himself nominated by the Turkman as a member of the Committee of Public Safety it seemed high time to check him. He was therefore told definitely that under no circumstances would we allow him to enter the committee if our relations with the latter were to continue, after receiving some fatherly advice to the effect that he would do better to return to the front and refrain from dabbling in politics, Ovazbaiev departed. The feeling now on the part of the Turkman 'intelligentsia' as represented by H. Murat, Ovazbaiev & Cº is one of disappointment and disillusionment. They realise that our interpretation of the theory of the self determination of peoples does not include the raising of a savage tribe to the status of a civilised nation, and they are again thrown on their own resources.[53]

Malmiss: game over

The Transcaspian episode, an improvised military campaign during the last year of the First World War, 'without clearly defined plan or policy',[54] and with few human or financial resources, has left no trails of glory in the annals of British military history. It may nonetheless be seen as emblematic of a certain *modus operandi*: British power in this period was not deployed on a massive scale, but made use of a few individuals on the ground who were trusted in their capacity to improvise more or less freely. This was certainly the case for Teague-Jones, who was left to operate alone as political agent in Ashkhabad, facing difficulties with his own hierarchy. It was not that Teague-Jones was disrespectful, but while he appreciated General Dunsterville's humour and phlegm, he allowed himself to paint a less than flattering, not to say frankly critical, portrait of General Malleson, his military and intelligence superior. Malleson, whose career between 1904 and 1914 had been in intelligence at Indian Army HQ and in Lord Kitchener's team, was familiar with Persian and Afghan affairs.[55] He had notably visited Kabul with Sir Louis Dane's mission in 1904 and carried out a complete study of the communications system in Central Asia. Apart from serving a short period in East Africa in 1915–16 against the Germans, the main part of his military career had been spent as a desk general. According to the careful formulation of Charles H. Ellis, Teague-Jones's friend and colleague, he had a reputation for being obstinate, unsociable, wrapped up in his work and meticulous in the extreme. Ellis adds that the very appointment of Malleson revealed the nature of Malmiss as an intelligence mission rather than a military combat mission. Teague-Jones notes critically that his 'main quality lay in his cleverness in picking other people's brains and turning to his own advantage the work of others. This had been his reputation before and it was certainly substantiated during his command in Meshed and Transcaspia.'[56] He also mentions that the cipher service detested Malleson's interminable telegrams for despatch to India, which kept it in action night and day. 'It became notorious that any statement by any casual agent or camel driver in the bazaar would be made the subject of a long foolscap wire',[57] Teague-Jones continues. And indeed one of the things of which Malleson was proud was that he had put in place an exceptionally effective intelligence network. He claimed to have placed men wherever he judged them necessary, on every train and in every station along the Transcaspian line. Yet he seemed to prefer staying in the comfortable surroundings of Meshed to the field, where he was only to appear for the first time on 24 November 1918 before disappearing again; he did not visit his troops again for another three months. Given these circumstances it is not hard to understand why Teague-Jones's hyperactivity and enterprising spirit were severely tested by his sense of a vacuum at the heart of Malmiss, a feeling which was generally shared:

To anyone with a sense of humour, the Mission itself was one big joke. I do not think the General himself had much sense of humour. I upset him badly one day at breakfast by remarking that I thought the tea was too weak. It transpired that the teapot I had picked up contained his own special brew of some super blend of pure Darjeeling which he kept exclusively to himself. The General growled and made some caustic remark about the inability of some people to discern a really good tea when they came across one.[58]

Nor did General Malleson's very limited sense of humour incline him to take any pleasure in meeting the various shades of revolutionary within the Transcaspian government, demagogues whom he looked on—whether Bolsheviks, Mensheviks or SR—with equal mistrust. At the end of December 1918 he received an entreaty from Zimin for the resources to enable an advance by British and Transcaspian troops from Merv to Charjui.[59] The position on the Amu Darya was held at the time by the Bolsheviks. At Charjui the Transcaspian Railway crosses the Amu Darya by a bridge, the first part of which was built of wood. The river is the biggest and fastest-flowing in Central Asia, its waters swollen by its many tributaries arising in the snows of the Pamir and on the western slopes of the Hindu Kush. With no other possible crossing within 200 versts, Charjui was an obvious strategic position, which had the additional merit of allowing direct communication with Bokhara, where a population exhausted by the Bolshevik occupation was likely to welcome the British with open arms. According to Zimin, 'General Malleson, during his visit to the front was assured of this personally by Oraz Serdar the Commander in Chief, as personal friend of the Emir of Bokhara.'[60] The Transcaspian government's minister for foreign affairs added that such a troop movement on the part of the British would not engender feelings of hostility in Afghanistan, as the British seemed to fear:

The Transcaspian Government is in constant touch with Herat, and the latest reports received from there show everything to be perfectly quiet, with the prestige of the British to be higher than ever before. If the Afghans remained loyal in spite of German agents during the time when Great Britain was at war, there can be no possible grounds for fearing complications with them now when England appears as the most powerful nation in the world.[61]

This, with the errors of judgement it contained—a third Anglo-Afghan war broke out in May 1919 despite these optimistic predictions—and its geopolitical reasoning, was the grandiose plan which Zimin the orientalist—an anti-imperialist and anti-British revolutionary at heart—submitted to Malleson on 22 December 1918, just before the Transcaspian government was confronted with a final internal crisis. In January 1919, at their lowest ebb, the Transcaspian forces seemed to have lost all hope of an Allied intervention. Why did the Allies who were occupying the Caucasus and Baku assert that they were unable to send just one aeroplane and two heavy guns to the Transcaspian front when, on the other side of the front line, the Bolshevik troops seemed about to abandon their positions?

At the end of January 1919, Teague-Jones's intelligence harvest[62] revealed that the Bolsheviks were not in a good position. According to one of his agents who reported an account from a deserter, the Bolshevik forces, which were divided into four mounted detachments, and equipped with machine-guns (some of which were unusable), did not amount to more than 7,000 men. The majority were Magyars and Kirgiz, but there were also Russians, Armenians, Persians and a small number of Turkmen, and many demoralised Muslims who were ready to give themselves up at the slightest hint of failure. The Bolshevik army on the ground lacked a unified command. Each detachment decided independently whether or not to go on the attack, but they all practised a unanimous policy of pillage and seizure of livestock in the villages, while in the towns of Samarkand and Tashkent the shortages of petroleum, wood and vital foodstuffs had made rationing necessary. 'Numbers of people are dying from hunger and cold in Tashkent. The inhabitants as a whole are praying for the early arrival of the British', Teague-Jones's agent reported:

The Reds have practically no reserves in the rear, and practically all their troops are on the sector of the line between Uch-Adji and Charjui. The opinion of the Bolsheviks themselves is that if a circumventing movement were carried out against them, they would be forced to retreat, and if they did so it would be the end of them as a force.

If this information was reliable—which seems likely since Teague-Jones kept this document in his personal files—then it is impossible to avoid the conclusion that the British decision to withdraw, taken on the advice of General Milne, who replaced Malleson in February 1919, did not stem from an unfavourable balance of forces on the ground but from a political decision to limit the British zone of responsibility to Transcaucasia. In any event, the three independent republics of Georgia, Armenia and Azerbaijan were made subject to the authority of General Thomson, who was in charge of Azerbaijan and of Dagestan, and also of General Forestier-Walker who was based at Batumi and responsible for maintaining order in Armenia and Georgia. It is therefore not surprising to find Teague-Jones in Transcaucasia from 1919 to 1921.

For the time being, the Transcaspian episode was over. It was an inglorious episode, as Teague-Jones was well aware; he clearly informed General Milne of the fate which would befall Transcaspia when the British troops began their retreat:

General Milne's final question was what would happen if we withdrew our troops? My reply was that without a doubt the Transcaspian resistance would immediately crumble and the Bolsheviks would reoccupy the whole of the country. I then mentioned the petition to the British Government for the continued cooperation of our troops and the appeal of the Transcaspians on humanitarian grounds and made out as strong a case as I could in favour of our standing by them a little longer.[63]

But Teague-Jones was only a modest political agent and not a decision-maker. It was with feelings of sadness mixed with bitterness that he had to leave Transcaspia, with the last marks of distinction with which the Transcaspian government was able to honour him: a special train and a delegation of railway workers and civilians expressing their profound recognition of everything that had been done, or rather attempted. Teague-Jones also received a farewell gift from the hands of Haji Murat to express the gratitude and respect of the Turkmen tribes: a whip which had belonged personally to his father, a Teke chieftain who had wielded it at the Battle of Gök-Tepe. Teague-Jones kept this gift until it was stolen sixty years later during his final voyage from Marbella to Plymouth. This, then, was how the British abandoned a theatre of activities now seen as marginal. They left this part of Central Asia to its fate and to its inevitable Sovietisation, even though the geostrategic importance of this area between Russian, China, India and Iran has consistently manifested itself, right up into the twenty-first century:

I watched the flat, desolate landscape glide past me with mixed feelings of relief and sadness. For years, since early boyhood, it had been in my dream to get to Central Asia. True, I had seen only a small part of it, and that in anything but favourable circumstances, but I still felt the spell of its ancient charm. Perhaps one day I might revisit it under happier conditions, but for the present I had seen enough. The Transcaspian dream had begun in tragedy and was ending in tragedy. Ring down the Curtain![64]

5

THE LEGEND OF THE TWENTY-SIX COMMISSARS

TEAGUE-JONES, HERO OR VILLAIN?

*'It was on such a night
In such a mist,
That we were gunned down
By a squad of Englishmen.'*[1]

'The train arrived at Kizil-Arvat—two hundred and eighty-two versts away from the Caspian, at thirteen minutes past seven in the evening, instead of at seven. This slight delay provoked thirteen expostulations from the Baron, one a minute.'[2]

Baku, January 1990. Amid the disturbances accompanying the gradual collapse of the Soviet Empire and the Armenia/Azeri clash, exacerbated by the question of Nagorno-Karabakh, a group of excited demonstrators wreck a Soviet monument. In the group of statues sculpted out of red granite, one figure stands out clearly, that of Stepan Shahumian, one of the first Bolsheviks, a companion of Lenin. The heroic and sacrificial pose was the sculptor Merkurov's attempt at evoking, following the best principles of socialist realism, the execution of twenty-six commissars in the desert of Karakum on 20 September 1918. The monument symbolised the duration of the Soviet regime—commissioned in November 1923, it was erected in February 1958 in the Square of the 26 Commissars at Baku. Its destruction erased an important chapter in the history of the revolution in Transcaucasia, at any rate the one in the revolutionary catechism which was supposed to illustrate both the dawn of the revolutionary era and the solidarity of all Caucasian peoples. With the end of the Soviet regime in 1990–1 the Baku demonstrators, heated to fever-pitch by the conflict in Nagorno-Karabakh, were attacking not only a symbol of Soviet power but also their Armenian neighbour, for seven of the 'twenty-six commissars'—an expres-

105

sion which one has to use for the sake of convenience, even if this group of fugitives escaping from the Commune of Baku was made up neither solely of commissars nor even of Bolsheviks—celebrated by the monument were in fact Armenians. The dismantling of the legend of the twenty-six commissars is connected to one of the most striking periods in the life of Reginald Teague-Jones. Cast as the central figure in the enquiry mounted by the Soviet authorities, and as the principal culprit, Teague-Jones was to incarnate all the misdeeds of British imperialism. The affair of the execution of the twenty-six commissars, an episode from the earliest revolutionary days in Transcaucasia and Central Asia, raised to epic rank by a voluminous and unanimous Soviet historiography, lies within the triple context of the end of the First World War, foreign intervention in the last sector of the Eastern front in Transcaucasia and the Great Game in Central Asia. The personal involvement of Teague-Jones, demonised by Soviet propaganda and haunted all his life by the gloomy spectre of the twenty-six commissars, elicited an attempt to revise the historical account from Brian Pearce, who from the 1980s onwards set about writing a meticulous and systematic counter-investigation. More recently, the exhumation at Baku of the remains of the twenty-six commissars in 2009 has given rise in Azerbaijan, in Armenia and in Russia to commentaries which throw doubt on the traditional thesis of British culpability. It remains to set the stage, that of a war in a remote theatre of operations where the railway was the essential military and political key. So what happened at the 207th verst of the Transcaspian line to Ashkhabad, between the stations at Pereval and Akhsha-Kuyma, on 20 September 1918? To understand, it is necessary to go back in time and space, for the story begins in Baku at the end of the First World War.

Baku: 1918

The country before the battle

At the turn of the century the frontier town of Baku, situated on the borders of the Russian and Ottoman empires and of Persia, served as the principal port of Transcaucasia and was the petroleum capital of the world, a place of critical geostrategic importance (see Map 4). Due to the geographical protection afforded by the Absheron Peninsula, which projects like a spear-head into the Caspian, at the bottom of a bay sheltered by a chain of islands, Baku was the widely seen as the best harbour in the Caspian. When seen from a distance on the approach from Krasnovodsk, the gateway to Central Asia and head of the Transcaspian Railway line, Baku looks like a kind of oriental Riviera, one which Reginald Teague-Jones frequently photographed during his Transcaspian journeys. But the illusion was only short-lived, for since the nineteenth century the town had been the site of widespread petroleum exploration and exploitation. The phenomena of 'eternal fire' and oil-gushers on the Absheron Peninsula arose from the geomorphologic features of the landscape—the oil-bearing rock (*petrolea*), layered in bands within folds of sand and porous sandstone, would build up under the pressure of gases which accumulated at the top of convex deposits, and these gases would escape when erosion or drilling brought them into contact with the exterior. All along the top of these cavernous spaces the gas or crude oil which had escaped gave rise to the 'eternal fire'. Since the end of the nineteenth century prospecting and exploitation in Baku had focused on two convex deposits, at Balaxany to the north of the town, and at Bibi-Eybat to the south. Following the introduction of drilling in Baku in 1872 a forest of derricks had sprouted in the area of these two deposits, the ground around which was sometimes burst open by gushers of crude mixed with stones and sand jetting up to 100 metres high, flooding the surrounding area and sometimes setting off large-scale and formidable conflagrations. The growth of Baku's petroleum industry was due to the by-products yielded from distillation. Because of its composition it yielded abundant quantities of *mazout*—a Russian term for the product which in the form of *mazout* or fuel oil henceforth provided competition for coal—and oils for lubrication, a naturally occurring characteristic which distinguishes Baku petroleum from American petroleum. Petroleum from Baku, transported to Astrakhan and thence by ship on the Volga and its tributaries, destined for Russia and the export trade, supplied the pre-war Russian Empire with lighting fuel, petroleum and lubricants, and especially fuel for industry, steamships and a good half of all the empire's railways.

Baku was formally annexed to the Russian Empire in 1813. The city was subsequently awarded the status of administrative capital by the Russians, which accounts for the first phase of growth, the population of the town rising from 8,000 inhabitants in 1850 to 14,500 in 1870. But it was thanks to the petroleum boom at the end of the nineteenth century that the town of Baku really mushroomed, its population increasing from 111,094 in 1897 to 260,000 in 1917. This demographic growth and the accompanying expansion of petroleum development—with a production of 11 million tons Baku became the world's leading producer of petroleum in 1901—contributed to the extension of the urban area, which now incorporated the surrounding Tatar villages, for the majority of the population governed by Baku is Muslim. On the other hand, the urban population was becoming more and more cosmopolitan as the petroleum industry had attracted workers and peasants from Russia, Ukraine and Armenia, and had also stimulated a massive influx of 'Persians' who lived and worked in wretched conditions. Some of the figures in the petroleum boom, audacious entrepreneurs, real capitalist pioneers, had built fabulous fortunes in Baku, whether they were Armenian like Der Gukasov (founder of the Caspian Company), Mantashev, Khatisov, Lianosov or Avetisov, Jewish like Solomon, or Azeri like Nagiev, Tagiev and Asadulaev. These operators from Transcaucasia nevertheless faced formidable competitors from abroad. The Paris Rothschilds, the founders of the 'Société industrielle et commerciale de la Caspienne et de la mer Noire', had invested enormous sums of capital in Baku and by 1889 they controlled half of all its exports. Similarly, in 1879 the three Nobel brothers (Alfred, Emil, Ludwig), the sons of an inventor living in Russia, had set up the '*Société anonyme d'exploitation du napthe Nobel Frères*' (Nobel Brothers' Oil Production Association), a company with Russian status whose emblem was the Temple of the Fire-Worshippers at Suraxany.

Baku is a city of two parts, one of which fits within the other 'like the kernel in a fruit' in the words of Kurban Said,[3] whose well-known love-story *Ali and Nino* takes place almost entirely in Baku during the First World War. The inner city, an old Islamic town surrounded by ramparts, was a huddle of low houses and a labyrinth of alleys climbing up to the citadel and the palace of the Sirvan-Shahs. The outer town, which was born in the boom, is clearly distinct from the old, with its straight streets, buildings with facades of dressed stone, pavements, boutiques and trams. Street signs testify to a zoning of communities, distinguishing the Muslim quarter to the east of the old town from the Armenian quarter (*Armenikend*) to the north-east. In the European town the administrative quarter was separate from the business quarter, the centre where the real economic decisions were made; located in the latter were the banks and the headquarters of industrial companies, trading houses, churches, printing presses, as well as palatial mansions built by petroleum magnates, who were fervently eclectic in their tastes. Thus the Ismaïla mansion built for Nagiev is a reproduction of the layout of the Palazzo Contarini in Venice, while Tagiev's residence draws on the style of the Italian Renaissance. The source of their underlying fortunes was only a few versts from the centre amid the forest of derricks of Bibi-Eybat, Balakhani, Sabunchi, Ramani, and in the refineries of the Black Town (*tcherny gorod*), the smoke-blackened streets of which sweated soot and the stench of petroleum. The majority of the petroleum workforce lived where they worked—in makeshift shelters, in nooks and crannies, in repulsive underground dens, in communal barracks—offering the miserable spectacle of a true lumpenproletariat. Not far from there, between the White Town and the Black Town, stands the famous Villa Petrolea which belonged to the Nobel brothers, a compound of modern buildings where the Nobels sometimes stayed, which included residential buildings, a theatre and a clubhouse for administrative staff, all set in a vast park surrounded by a tall perimeter wall, an oasis preserved and irrigated at great cost by desalinated seawater.

Baku: the geostrategic prize

Teague-Jones's mission, aimed in part at establishing contact with the anti-Bolshevik forces in the Transcaspian region, reflected the changing shape of the British intervention. The British expeditions—Dunsterforce and Malmiss—had initially been launched in order to block a possible German–Turkish thrust across the Caucasus towards India and Afghanistan. But they now became the first steps in the foreign intervention against the Bolshevik regime. In 1963, probably in an attempt at reassurance, Ellis wrote that neither of these missions had been planned as an anti-Bolshevik manoeuvre, any more than they were a consequence of the opposing interests of Great Britain and Russia in the Great Game: 'As military operations, they were tactical moves, undertaken with the minimum of troops to cope with an emergency brought about by the Russian collapse and an enemy advance eastwards in which involvement with the revolutionary and counter-revolutionary forces in Russian territory could hardly be avoided.'[4]

THE LEGEND OF THE TWENTY-SIX COMMISSARS

The conquest of Baku had been among the symbolic war aims of the supporters of Pan-Turkism and of some of the Young Turks since November 1914, but the town had only really become a strategic objective in October 1917, with the collapse of the Caucasian front and its subsequent abandonment by Russian forces (see Map 3). The minister of war, Enver Pasha, despatched the Ottoman Army in February 1918 with the objectives of liberating the irredentist territories (Kars, Ardahan and Batumi), stimulating a Muslim uprising and marching on Baku and Central Asia. In the confusion reigning in Transcaucasia in 1918, drifting between civil war, foreign intervention and temporary success for the nationalist movements, Baku had become a strategic prize. In order to contain the Turkish advance, the British attempted an operation from the other direction, Persia, under the command of General Dunsterville, whose expeditionary corps briefly entered the town in August 1918 after an epic crossing of the Caspian. 'A British General on the Caspian, the only sea unploughed before by the British keels, on board a ship named after a South-African president and whilom enemy, sailing from a Persian port, under the Serbian flag, to relieve from the Turks a body of Armenians in a revolutionary Russian town', as Teague-Jones reported Dunsterville's humorous words.[5]

As a signatory to the Treaty of Brest-Litovsk Germany had in the meantime agreed with the Bolshevik government to take control of Baku and the oilfields before the Turks could take the town,[6] which explains why the British were considering the destruction of the petroleum plants[7] by aerial bombardment at the beginning of August 1918. Teague-Jones recalls the strange combination of circumstances which led to the presence of the Germans in Baku in August 1918:

The Government of Germany had concluded an agreement with Moscow over the control of Baku and the oilfields there. Consequently a German military mission was sent via Astrakhan to Baku. It seemed needless to foresee any complications either for Moscow or for Berlin, since both the towns of Astrakhan and Baku were controlled by the Communists in June 1918. Thus the German plan was to take control of Baku before their Turkish allies could conquer the town. The mission embarked by boat at Astrakhan towards the end of July. Neither the Germans nor the Bolshevik Committee of Astrakhan were yet aware that the SR dictators had put an end to the Bolshevik regime in Baku. On August 4th the German mission arrived at Baku and secretly disembarked at the quay, and to their great surprise its members were rapidly arrested and put under lock and key.[8]

The British plans for a bombardment were abandoned on the eve of Dunsterville's entry into Baku: such a measure would have estranged the Tatar workers, already reputed to be pro-Turk, from the British authorities. Above all, the agreement concluded at Meshed between the English and a short-lived 'Transcaspian Government' with the aim of warding off 'the danger of the Bolsheviks and the Turco-Germans' is yet more evidence of the importance given to the defence of Baku, 'the gateway to Russian Central Asia on which depends a large part of the economic life and military power of Russian Turkestan and Transcaspia'. In exchange for strategic facilities in the Caspian area—control of the port of Krasnovodsk and of the Transcaspian Railway—

the British undertook to supply military help to the Transcaspian government, to defend Baku to the end, and to evacuate so far as possible all stocks of fuel oil and naphtha to the further shore of the Caspian at Krasnovodsk.[9]

Accordingly, on 2 August 1918 Teague-Jones explored the bay of Ufra, only a few kilometres from Krasnovodsk, where the storage facilities of the main petrol companies were housed, so as to evaluate the level of stocks and the means of procuring fuel in the event of Baku becoming occupied by the enemy. He would have prepared a circumstantial report on the question, supported by photographs, on the basis of information supplied by Vladimir N. Alexeiev, father of the young Valya whom he had recently met.[10] For during the summer of 1918 Teague-Jones, on solitary mission in Central Asia, travelled by train at least six times between Ashkhabad and Krasnovodsk. And on three occasions in extravagantly improbable circumstances he took the *parokhod* (steamship) linking Krasnovodsk and Baku. Arriving at the end of a testing storm on the Caspian, a famished Teague-Jones disembarked at Baku on 10 July 1918 in a city under siege and in need of everything. In the Hotel Europe the Armenian waiters asked him anxiously 'when the British were coming to save them' and Teague-Jones, after his meeting with the British consul, MacDonnell, soon summed up the situation as 'a pretty kettle of fish'.[11] At the political level the situation was inextricably difficult, since in July 1918 five different 'governments'— Bolsheviks, the Centro-Caspian Dictatorship, the Armenians, the Caspian Fleet and the anti-Bolsheviks—were confronting each other in a city which was in the grip of exceptional pressures. In fact, urban society in Baku had never really been peaceful since the 1905 Revolution—inter-ethnic tension had culminated in the violent conflict of the Armenian/Tatar wars, and strike action had also been incessant in the period between 1905 and the outbreak of the First World War. From the onset of the war, as prisoners and refugees streamed towards Baku, the Caucasian front thus became a test of the loyalty of the Azeri population in the Russian Empire. The first flows of population were determined by the victorious advance of the Russian army in Eastern Anatolia. Confined to barracks built on the arid island of Nargin, which lies across the bay of Baku, the Ottoman prisoners of war were isolated from the urban population of Baku where the majority of the Tatar population might well have felt a spirit of solidarity with them. Few of them managed to survive the typhoid epidemics which were sweeping Russia at the time. Some of the Armenian refugees, for their part, who had escaped the genocide of 1915 and had then dispersed throughout Transcaucasia, finished up in Baku. Products of the initial victories of the Russian armies, these first population streams were bound to heighten urban tensions. Finally, Baku witnessed the arrival of soldiers who had been demobilised from the Russian army, who could not return home because the lines of communication had been cut.[12]

The siege of Baku

Under siege from outside by the Army of Islam, the city was also under internal siege from a large part of the Tatar population, whose loyalties were with the 'enemy' at the gates. A Tatar army corps of 8,000 men formed at the beginning of 1918 would join forces with the Army of Islam during the victorious advance of the Turkish troops on Baku. All the cab-drivers in the besieged town disappeared at the same time, returning to the neighbouring Tatar villages to await the arrival of the Turks. On Teague-Jones's first visit to Baku on 10 July 1918 the Turks were no more than 40 miles away, and the forces which were supposed to oppose them were showing all the signs of disintegration. In Baku the besieged population was suffering from a lack of food and water, since the Turks, who understood the basic principles of siege strategy, had cut the supply pipe from Sholar, necessitating the re-commissioning of the old seawater desalination boilers.[13] It was in Baku, a colonial city at the southern limits of the Russian Empire, where an emergent Azeri nationalism—distinct from pan-Islamism and pan-Turkism[14]—confronted the nationalism of Armenia, whose population in 1917 in Baku numbered 67,000. The third largest 'Armenian city' after Constantinople and Tiflis, the cohesion of its Armenian community vis-à-vis the Azeris was enhanced by the fortunes of some of the petroleum kings. These magnates employed thousands of immigrant Armenian staff in their firms, thereby contributing to the reinforcement of the 'ethnicity' of the petroleum companies, and consequently sharpening social competition between the communities. The anti-Armenian pogroms and fire of August 1905, during the appalling Armeno-Tatar war of 1905–6, had ended with the destruction of almost all the oil-wells belonging to Armenian companies, putting their Armenian workmen out of work and obliging them to return to their villages. In 1918 these memories were even more vivid because feelings of fear and hatred of the Turk had been exacerbated by the deportation and extermination of the Armenians of Eastern Anatolia in 1915, and by the advance of the Army of Islam during the spring and summer of 1918 (see Map 3). Since the end of 1917 all population groups in Baku—Russians, Muslims, Georgians and Armenians— had provided themselves with national councils. The National Armenian Council of Baku, which was presided over by a Dashnak, Abraham Gulghandanian, had set up a political and military structure with a militia formed of trained recruits. This contingent of 4,000 men, composed of Armenian soldiers demobilised from the Austro-German front, had the task of ensuring the self-defence of the Armenian population in the event of a Tatar attack. Thus during the famous 'March Days' of 1918 the rebellion of the Muslims and the Musavat party against the Baku Soviet was put down by the Bolsheviks only with the help of this militia, mainly made up of Dashnaks, entailing 3,000 deaths—mostly Muslim—and the pillage of those Muslim quarters of the town into which the Armenian militia had penetrated. The massacres committed during the 'March Days' called for reprisals and heralded a new flaring up of urban warfare with the onset of the Baku siege.

It was at the end of July 1918 that Teague-Jones made his reappearance in Baku: his duty was to report on the situation, although the city was cut off from the rest of the Caucasus and no longer had telegraphic communication with Enzeli in Persia. On board the steamer *Arkanghelsk* on 30 July, Teague-Jones had occasion to meet Valya Alexeieva, a young Russian from Krasnovodsk—her family lived at Ufra where her father Vladimir Nikolaievich seems to have had some responsibility for managing petroleum stocks—who was going to join her uncle, an employee of the Nobel business in Baku. After accompanying Valya to her uncle's house in the Black Town, Teague-Jones found that the town was in a state of panic. The rumour of an imminent entry into the town by the Turks, who were already massed at the gates, drove thousands of Armenians to the port, seeking any possible means of escape and a passage by steamer. Teague-Jones for his part went in search of a map of Baku's harbour defences. His plan, to which Malleson had given his approval at Meshed, was to leave the attackers a harbour which had been mined and rendered useless. With a few regrets for Valya Alexeieva, living within the confines of the Black Town where it would now be difficult to go looking for her, he mingled, disguised as a merchant, with the crowd of refugees, who were principally Armenians hoping to escape by ship. 'I knew that everyone leaving the port was subjected to a strict search and I knew quite well that a suspicious individual like myself, for I was still in a nondescript trader's dress, found with an important military map in his possession would be shot immediately.'[15] And things in fact nearly went wrong when he found himself confronted by a Red who was prepared to intercept any young and qualified man capable of being sent to the front for the defence of Baku. On 1 August 1918 Teague-Jones was nonetheless back in Krasnovodsk, and on 3 August once again in Ashkhabad.

During the whole of August and until the first weeks of September 1918 there was violent fighting in the west of the town, in the neighbourhood of the Tatar quarters of Chemberikend and the Wolf Gate, between the Turks and the defenders of Baku who had been joined, since the beginning of August, by the expeditionary force commanded by Dunsterville. Equally fearful of intervention by the Tatar inhabitants of the Baku suburbs and of the entry of the Turkish soldiers, the Armenian population of Baku knew in advance the fate which would await it if the town should fall. Upon learning that the first detachments of Dunsterforce had entered Baku, Teague-Jones landed again at the quay on 7 August 1918. In the Hotel Europe he immediately met Colonels Stokes and Keyworth, who were in charge of the Dunsterforce advance party. During this first encounter at the top of the hotel's main staircase, Teague-Jones learned of the tragic-comic events on 1 August which had saved Baku from the Turks at the eleventh hour. The Turks, confident of victory, marched in a slow and leisurely fashion down the neighbouring hills instead of advancing rapidly. The extraordinary military commissar for the Baku region, Grigori K. Petrov, was busy collecting arms and ammunition with a view to evacuation. 'Petrov was known to be a moody individual, with the temperament of a prima donna, and totally unpredictable in behaviour. Instead of embarking the guns he now trained them on the Turks and opened fire. The enemy were entirely taken by surprise and beat a hurried retreat.' Adding to the general confusion, a steamer which had arrived from Astrakhan with a good number of German officers on board demanding to be shown the way to Turkish Army Headquarters was met with a cold reception. Teague-Jones eventually learned from Valya Alexeieva that the Tatars had almost succeeded in occupying the Black Town, where she was staying with her uncle. 'I do not think any of them had felt very happy about it, as the part they lived in was one of the Armenian centres, and the Tatars could not always be relied upon to discriminate whom they were massacring',[16] Teague-Jones noted with his usual phlegm.

While evolving military operations had almost miraculously enabled a temporary postponement of the inevitable outcome, the political situation in Baku, although still very complex, had itself evolved considerably in Teague-Jones's absence. On 26 July 1918 a coup d'état had put an end to the Bolshevik government—the famous 'Baku Commune'—and put in its place a 'Centro-Caspian Dictatorship'. It is necessary to look backwards briefly here in order to understand the context of an event which was to prove of crucial importance in Teague-Jones's life. As was also the case in Petrograd, the February 1917 Revolution had created a system of dual power in Baku: on the one hand a municipal Duma dominated by the liberals, and on the other hand a moderate worker Soviet in which all socialist tendencies were represented. However, the real power was in the streets, where workers and soldiers were becoming radicalised under the influence of the Soviet orators. The latter were in a minority and feebly represented in the Baku Soviet, which was dominated by the SR, the Mensheviks and the Armenian Dashnaks. During the spring and the summer of 1918, Bolshevik influence began to spread. Led by Stepan Shahumian, a counter-theorist of national autonomy, and a Georgian Bolshevik, Prokofij Djaparidze, director of the local RSDWP (Russian Social Democratic Worker's Party) organisation during the 1905 Revolution and secretary of the Union of Petroleum Workers from 1906 to 1909, the Bolsheviks profited from discontent among the workers. Having gained a certain degree of prestige after the success of the general strike on 27 September 1917, the Bolsheviks, under the leadership of Shahumian (who was now named the commissar for Caucasian affairs by Lenin), did not press for armed insurrection after October 1917 as at Petrograd. In favour of maintaining the coalition of left-wing parties at Baku, Shahumian denounced the 'defensive war', while the Muslims and the Musavat awaited the arrival of the Turks in order to rid themselves of the Bolsheviks (whose representatives were drawn from other ethnic groups) and their tactical allies at Baku, the Armenian Dashnaks. This opportunistic alliance succeeded in overcoming the resistance of the Baku Muslims in March 1918, with the 'March Days' terminating in the temporary victory of the Bolsheviks and the Dashnaks in a town which had been partially deserted by the Muslim population.

These are the events which opened the way to a brief episode, glorified by Soviet historians as the 'Baku Commune' by analogy with the Paris Commune, during which, from April to July 1918, the Bolsheviks and the left SR took control of the Baku Soviet, and undertook a short experiment in municipal government. Formed on 25 April 1918, the Council of People's Commissars, all of them Bolsheviks or left SR, and presided over by Shahumian, had as its proclaimed objective the installation of Soviet power in Transcaucasia. It proceeded to nationalise the fisheries and the Caspian fleet, as well as the petroleum industry and privately owned land, hastily applied measures which further disrupted production and supplies and displeased the liberal bourgeoisie and socialist moderates. In May 1918 the Baku Commune denounced the 'act of treason' towards Soviet Russia represented by the Federal Transcaucasian Republic's declaration of independence, and refused to recognise the independence of Georgia, Armenia and Azerbaijan. When, during the summer of 1918, Baku was the last remaining city resisting the Ottoman forces, a sort of municipal army constituted by authority of the Commune, whose members had mostly come from the Armenian militia—10,000 to 12,000 men wrested from the authority of the Armenian National Council—took the name of the Red Army. Armenians made up 70 per cent of the members of this Red Army which appeared determined to defend Baku, although this did not prevent a defeat at the hands of regular Ottoman troops near the river Kura (27–30 June 1918). In July, when Turkish troops were at the gates of Baku, there was a debate in the Soviet on the question of British intervention, which Shahumian was forced to accept[17] on a majority of twenty-three votes in favour. At the invitation of a 'Centro-Caspian Dictatorship', established on 26 July 1918 and set up by the right-wing SR, supported by the Dashnaks and the Mensheviks, Dunsterforce entered the town with the mission of taking control of the Caspian Fleet, ensuring the defence of Baku and control over Krasnovodsk. Thus ended the short life of the Baku Commune on 26 July 1918, subsequently glorified by Soviet historians as the forerunner of Bolshevik power in the Caucasus two years later. Of the fatal destiny of the twenty-six commissars there will be much to say later in these pages.

From this point on, Teague-Jones, who was still in the shabby disguise of a street-merchant, had to assume duties of a more official nature in his relations with Dunsterforce. As one of the rare Russophone English officers capable of ensuring accuracy in conversational interchanges with the Russian or Armenian officers, and due to his knowledge of this particularly complex terrain, Teague-Jones would remain close to Dunsterville throughout almost all of the British occupation of Baku, for he did not simply act as translator or diplomat at local level. From the time of Dunsterville's arrival at Enzeli on board the *Kruger* on 17 August 1918, Teague-Jones says that he added to his usual duties those of an intelligence officer:

In this capacity I was personally responsible for obtaining all intelligence and for this purpose enrolled a number of agents. I had been working at intelligence for about ten days when Colonel Stokes told me that Malleson had been 'raising Cain' about my not having returned to Transcaspia. He had received several wires from Meshed demanding my immediate return, but had replied regretting his inability to allow me to go. Malleson thereupon wired to Simla, who in turn wired to Dunsterville. The latter replied protesting, but Malleson retorted quoting the very serious situation in Transcaspia and insisted that my presence was most urgently required in Ashkhabad.[18]

Teague-Jones, who did not disguise his lack of enthusiasm for Malleson and his obvious sympathy for Dunsterville, was obliged to leave Baku at the most critical moment. Adding to this bitter disappointment, which is expressed in his journal, was probably the silent one of being separated from Valya. Teague-Jones says no more about this relationship, but one can sense that the special light in which the tragic-comic events of Baku appeared could only be produced by a combination of the Russian sense of the absurd and the English sense of humour. Teague-Jones therefore left Baku on 24 August 1918:

While it had frequently assumed the appearance of a comedy, the drama of Baku had never for a moment been free from the atmosphere of a tragedy. The more casual among us playing actual roles in the drama were at times inclined to laugh at some of its grotesque and fantastic phases, yet we were nevertheless constantly weighed down with the presentiment of impending disaster.[19]

Indeed, two days after his departure, on 26 August 1918, the Army of Islam launched a decisive assault on the most weakly defended sector in Baku.[20]

After abandoning their HQ in the Hotel Europe, which was regularly on the receiving end of the Turkish batteries, the British evacuated Baku by sea on 13 September. The Armenians tried to escape at the same time on the few boats still moored at the quays of Black Town. Baku fell into the hands of the Army of Islam on 15 September. The Turkish high command gave free rein to some of its troops and to the Tatar population which was hungry for vengeance. For three days and three nights they spread throughout the town, massacring the population of Armenikend, raping women, abducting young girls and pillaging. The 'September massacres' ultimately resulted in around 15,000 deaths. In an effort to escape the massacre some Armenians sought refuge in the grounds of the Villa Petrolea (see Map 4) two or three versts away from the town. The *usadba* (domain) of the Nobel brothers in its immense park surrounded by a high stone wall seemed a safe refuge, particularly since the members of the firm's administration who lived there with their families were for the most part foreigners.[21] At the end of the three days, an order was given to stop the slaughter. The Turkish command erected scaffolds in different quarters of the town and threatened hanging for those caught in any further killings. Thus:

it was only on the morning of the 17th that the Turkish command sent in its police and vigorously repressed the disorder. Some Turkish soldiers—about twenty of them—and some Tatars were hanged or shot and their bodies exposed in public places. It would have been simpler and more humane to send the military police in before the troops, but the Turks wanted to make this goodwill gesture to their Tatar auxiliaries, by allowing them to murder and pillage for two days.[22]

In Baku, where the deserted streets and ruined houses offered the spectacle of a ghost town, the Turkish command made its quarters[23] in October 1918 in houses belonging to rich Armenians who had been spared the destruction. So 'in the general disintegration of political and social order in 1918 ethnic loyalties re-emerged in Baku with a new force'.[24] The capture of Baku by the Army of Islam set off an Armenian exodus escaping to Persia in fear of further massacres. According to the French vice-consul at Resht, there were 8,000 Armenian refugees from Baku in Enzeli at the beginning of October 1918.[25]

The drama of the twenty-six commissars: the anatomy of an execution

On the edge of the Karakum desert, on the Transcaspian railroad about half-way between Krasnovodsk and Kizil-Arvat, stands a mournful funeral stone which, during the Soviet era, every train passing along this line was in the habit of saluting with blasts on the whistle. Despite the complete desolation of the scene, lost in the vast dry emptiness of the *barkhans*, those sandy dunes of the Karakum blown here by the great winds of the north, where the only plants are struggling thorn-bushes and the famous *saksaul* whose deep and vigorous roots have the virtue, much sought after in the vicinity of the railroad, of anchoring the shifting ground, the spot is one of the sacred places of Soviet civilisation. The monument, which is located on the very place where the twenty-six commissars of Baku were executed, lists the names of the martyred commissars and denounces the guilt of the British imperialists, as well as that of the SR and the Mensheviks. The monument erected in November 1932, unmoved by the furnace heat of summer or the great winds that blow, makes tangible one of the fundamental events in the story of the revolution. At Krasnovodsk, the departure point for the Transcaspian line and for this tragedy, a museum of the twenty-six commissars in Lenin Square in this Caspian port completes the educational apparatus intended for the edification of the Turkmen masses. The event that took place here on 20 September 1918 is of striking importance, and its consequences would weigh heavily on the life of Reginald Teague-Jones, who was directly charged with the crime by the Soviet authorities. His change of name in May 1922—when he became Ronald Sinclair—and the fear which it appears he felt until the end of his life that the Bolsheviks would come to settle accounts with him, testify to the gravity of the charge even though at the time he does not seem to have attached particular significance to this event, which was one among many he experienced.

A political drama with a railway ending

I was the driver of the train on board which the Commissars of Baku, under arrest, had left Krasnovodsk in the direction of Poltoratsk. The prisoners were in the postal wagon, while in the other wagon, a second class one, were the members of the strike committee of Krasnovodsk and the Turkmen command. The train was composed of two wagons in total. At Pereval station, Germash and a guard came and sat next to me. On the stretch between Pereval and Akcha-Kuym, on Germash's orders I stopped the train. Among the members of the committee present were Germash, Sedykh, Piotrovich (Ashkhabad) and others whose names I don't know. The persons under arrest were taken out of the wagon at this spot, and led behind the hill. I was not present at the execution. The bodies were buried on the spot. The train was stationary for 45 to 50 minutes. We then went on to Poltoratsk. We were arrested at about 12 at Kyzil-Arvat. The arrest was in the morning. With me in the locomotive was my assistant Kurachev Alexander. The train I drove from Poltorask to Krasnovodsk was composed of the same two wagons.[26]

Shchegoliutin's statement, which is one of the rare pieces of first-hand evidence regarding the execution of the twenty-six commissars of Baku, adds resonance to the

116

evidence of Alexei Dirdikin, a railway worker on the Transcaspian line, whose presence at the dawn of this day of 20 September 1918 allows us to picture the scene.[27] Shortly before dawn, Dirdikin had been walking along the Transcaspian line when he was surprised by the sound of a train coming from Krasnovodsk. Travelling with no headlights, the unexpected train at such an early hour of the morning frightened the man, who hid behind a bush. Rather than travelling onwards, the train came to a silent halt in the dim light. The door of one of the wagons immediately opened. Guards and then a group of prisoners with their hands tied behind their backs—the twenty-six commissars—went down on to the track. An order was barked out and the prisoners were led towards the dunes in the desert close by. They were lined up at the top of the crest, some blindfolded, others not. Some of them protested, but the order to fire had already been given. Those who survived were pitilessly finished off. The bodies were dragged to the bottom of the dune, a few spadefuls of sand were thrown over them, and the guards who were about to re-join the train threw a last look around when they spotted the railway worker still in hiding. Embarrassed, he looked questioningly at them, but was immediately warned to stay silent. Despite their menacing attitude, the guards nonetheless resumed their places on board the train, which made off in a hurry for Ashkhabad, leaving the terrified railway worker behind. Hastily returning home, he fell in with a group of railway employees whom he knew well. He related the story to them and returned with them to the place of execution. Horrified by what they discovered, the men quickly dug some graves, muttered a few prayers, and rapidly left the spot, firmly deciding to speak to no one about their macabre discovery. On the following day, the lifeless body of Alexei Dirdikin was discovered nearby.

The scene painted by this evidence, which is uncorroborated, has an almost cinematic quality—its sense of tragedy recalls the scene in Nikolai Shengalaia's film *The 26 Commissars* (1932). The execution of the twenty-six commissars was a key chapter in the revolutionary epic; it features hero-martyrs in real life second-order figures among the Transcaucasian Bolsheviks (seven Armenians, nine Russians, two Georgians, four Jews, a Latvian, a Greek and two Azeris), with the exception of Stepan Shahumian, who had been close to Lenin and had attracted attention before the war for his radical positions on the national question, and their executioners who remain unidentified to this day. How was the myth of the twenty-six commissars created? How did Reginald Teague-Jones come to figure as the main actor in the scenario mounted by the Soviet authorities during the 1920s? Why, finally, did the thesis of British guilt ultimately supplant every other hypothesis so far as the Soviet authorities were concerned, even the rather more likely one of SR and Menshevik responsibility?[28]

The affair of the twenty-six commissars, the subject of a prolific Soviet historiography denouncing British imperialism and its incarnation in the person of Teague-Jones, was the subject of a systematic counter-enquiry carried out in the 1980s by Brian Pearce. According to Pearce:

although the record of what actually happened is not as complete or as clear as could be wished, there is no room for doubt that the Soviet story is false. Nobody, one might suppose, who had read the various (and varying) Soviet accounts of the fate of the 26 commissars can have failed to notice the contradictions and impossibilities in them.[29]

Brian Pearce's conviction, that of a scholar of the revolutionary period of Russian history, and a former communist, was forged at the end of a minute investigation based on systematic research into the Soviet archives. However, to understand the affair of the twenty-six commissars in which Teague-Jones found himself involved, it is necessary to return to the extremely complicated situation which reigned in Baku from the middle of July 1918 onwards.

In mid-July the Turkish troops were at the gates of Baku and were besieging the town. Since 25 April, the Baku Commune, that is to say the Council of Commissars of the People of Baku, had been carrying out an experiment in municipal administration in a situation of particular confusion. To exorcise defeatism, Stepan Shahumian had subordinated all organs of the Baku Soviet to the Cheka, but he was unable to prevent the SR and the Dashnaks, who were obsessed with the imminence of a new Armenian tragedy, from demanding an appeal to the British. Dunsterville, at the head of a column of 1,500 men, had arrived at Enzeli, a Persian port on the Caspian.[30] His mission was to hinder German and Turkish penetration in the Caucasus, to protect Baku and to forestall any attempt to cross the Caspian.

On 25 July there was a critical debate in the Baku Soviet. For Stepan Shahumian, who had received a clear warning from Stalin about 'Franco-British imperialism', an appeal to the British would mean cutting ties with Soviet Russia[31] and submitting to British tutelage. On the other hand, according to the Dashnaks and the supporters of British intervention who did not necessarily wish to break with Soviet central power, if Baku fell into the hands of the Turks, the city would be lost to Russia in any event. When the historic vote of 25 July 1918 took place the Baku Soviet voted by a small majority in favour of British intervention, contrary to the views of Stepan Shahumian, the SR and Dashnaks of the left. The Turkish attack began on 30 July. On the following day the twenty-six commissars of Baku were obliged to cede power to a right-wing SR 'Centro-Caspian Dictatorship', which was supported by the Dashnaks and the Mensheviks. There was a renewal of resistance in the circumstances described above until the arrival of Dunsterforce on 17 August 1918. What became of the twenty-six commissars during this period? With or without the consent of the Centro-Caspian Dictatorship, the Bolsheviks were intending to evacuate troops and arms to Astrakhan so as to put them at the disposal of Soviet Russia. In Anastas Mikoyan's words:

In the afternoon of August 14th, 17 boats carrying our troops and armaments left the port of Baku one after another. The *Kolesnikov* led the way. It was carrying on board the people's Commissars and a number of other officials. At the quayside we said our farewells, thinking that they would have a good voyage. We left before the departure of the last boats. At any moment one of the 'Dictatorship's' squads could have burst onto the scene and arrested us ...

THE LEGEND OF THE TWENTY-SIX COMMISSARS

On August 14th vessels under the command of the 'Dictatorship' began the pursuit of the Soviet boats. They succeeded in intercepting first four and then all the remainder near the island of Zhiloi, and brought them forcibly back to the military harbour. The troops were disarmed, and sent on to Astrakhan on the same boats. The Baku commissars and other leading figures, 35 people in all, were arrested and imprisoned.[32]

Imprisoned from 14 August onwards, they could only listen to the hammering of the approaching Turkish batteries as the final battle for Baku began at the beginning of September.

In his memoirs, Mikoyan recounts in detail the approaches he made to the members of the Centro-Caspian Dictatorship with the aim of procuring the release of the commissars, whose fate had to be decided before the arrival of the Turks. Although a decision had been made several days earlier to refer them to a court martial, with the impending arrival of the Turks A. Velunts sent an order to Lev Dalin, assistant to the head of Counter-Espionage, to evacuate the 'Baku Commissars'. In reality this group comprised fifteen 'commissars', not all of whom were Bolsheviks, and some junior officials of the Baku Commune, including some who were just drivers. Finally, at the last moment Mikoyan managed to have the prisoners released and ensured their safety for the time being by embarking them on the *Turkmen*, a ship commanded by a Dashnak captain, Tatevos Amirian (Amirov), brother of Arsen Amirian, one of the twenty-six commissars. In his memoirs Mikoyan goes on to say: 'We made our way to the quay to find the boat in question. On Amirov's orders, the upper deck and the officer's cabin had been reserved for the Commissars and their companions. Amirov installed himself in the same quarters. The boat was ready to leave at any moment'[33] for an uncertain but fatal destination. This was the beginning of a journey, or rather a wandering trek, across the Caspian. With its boatload of refugees, sailors and Bolsheviks, the steamer *Turkmen* encapsulated, in its cargo of political and social tensions, the drama of the Russian Revolution, the civil war and foreign intervention. A ship which had gone astray, just like Transcaucasia and Transcaspia, fragments of which had been detached from imperial Russia by the October Revolution in 1917, the *Turkmen* was a floating theatre of this age of war and revolution, carrying into Caspian waters the complexity of the political game in the Caucasus. In a context where anarchy and improvisation were the deciding factors in practically every decision, pinning down the diffused responsibilities of the actors in the drama of the twenty-six commissars is a nigh on impossible task. Nonetheless, official Soviet accounts have always put the accent on British responsibility and on that of Teague-Jones in particular. This is an incitement to scrutinise the chain of events more closely.

Passengers for Krasnovodsk

The voyage of the twenty-six commissars in company with other individuals favourable to the Bolshevik regime on board the *Turkmen* from Baku to Krasnovodsk, the Turkmen port on the eastern bank of the Caspian, before the drama of their execution deep in desert country, is an established fact. The story of the circumstances under which the commissars embarked, summarily dealt with in the first Soviet accounts as an operation carried out under the control of the British forces directed by Dunsterville, has since been considerably modified.[34] However, the Soviet version of the facts remains that the steamer which was destined for Astrakhan, where the Bolsheviks would have found a safe refuge, was diverted towards Krasnovodsk, a port controlled by forces hostile to the Soviet regime, on the orders of two English officers who were also on board. This diversion to Krasnovodsk, a fatal preliminary to the drama of the twenty-six commissars, is a historical episode on which Brian Pearce sought to cast light by uncovering the traces of these two officers, whose presence is mentioned in Dunsterville's memoirs, *The Adventures of Dunsterforce* (1920). They were Major H.B. Suttor and Sergeant A.L. Bullen, both members of the Australian contingent, who had remained behind at Baku after the evacuation of Dunsterforce and had embarked with the flood of refugees seeking safety at Krasnovodsk. The presence of these two officers on board the ship allowed Soviet historians to provide a plausible explanation for a diversion towards a destination where, on all the evidence, the twenty-six commissars and their comrades would not be welcome, since Krasnovodsk was controlled at the time by anti-Soviet forces. It is thanks to Brian Pearce that Major Suttor's report,[35] the only direct testimony from a passenger on board the *Turkmen*, was rediscovered and published.

Suttor, who with Bullen had witnessed the fall of Baku and the first massacres of Armenians, was horrified to discover at Sabunchi station, on the morning of 15 September, the corpses of 200 to 300 Armenians, men, women and children who had been massacred by the Tatars. Suttor and his companion, caught in the general shambles while heavy fighting continued in the area of the Black Town, arrived on 15 September at the centre of Baku, where chaos reigned. Petroleum fires were burning, shells were falling on all sides, the crowd, panicked by the bullets which were whistling from every side, was running in all directions and attempting to climb on board the last two departing steamers, which were already low in the water with the mass of escapers. Neither officer had a chance of getting on board, but a new round of shelling from the Turks created the expected diversion: they managed to climb on to a ship which had already weighed anchor but which was still held at the quay by two mooring ropes. The crew of the *Turkmen* repeated the manoeuvre four times in succession, raising the anchor and then lowering it again, in an attempt to return to the quay. It later appeared that the ship which the Bolsheviks had boarded was waiting for seven more of their companions who had stayed behind in the hell of Baku. While this was going on, the two English officers whose identity had now been discovered were on the receiving end of their shipmates' hostility. They were told to leave the ship—but how?—and finally Suttor decided to speak to the captain:

The bridge was crowded with Bolsheviks who didn't look pleased at my appearance, later I discovered Sharmeon (Shahumian), Petrov and Arganski (Djaparidze) were amongst the crowd. The Captain (Tatevos Amirian?), who spoke English fairly well, told me he had to go where these people directed, he didn't seem to like his position and warned me to be careful.

I told him I had ordered my men (?) to shoot the first man on the bridge who interfered with me, and asked him to interpret to the others. He said the Bolsheviks had two machine guns aboard and as far as he was concerned he was powerless. He further informed me that the Bolsheviks were endeavouring to make arrangements with the Turks to be allowed to return to Baku with a guarantee that they would not be interfered with.

And indeed, again according to Suttor's evidence, the *Turkmen*'s erratic path across the Caspian suggests that negotiations were taking place: after heading north at full steam for four hours, the *Turkmen* dropped anchor near a lighthouse, and then set off again due south. Suttor and his companion concluded that the Bolsheviks had reached an agreement with Baku, which was now in Turkish hands. Apparently resigned to their fate, Suttor and his companion decided that with this prospect in view a bit of rest and sleep were required. When woken abruptly by a Bolshevik two hours later, Suttor immediately realised from the position of the stars that the *Turkmen* was now running due north:

The Bolshevik who wakened me questioned me as to where I wanted to go, his English was not so good but I understood a certain amount of Russian. He talked a lot about water but as I couldn't gather his meaning we went along to the Captain and I discovered they were short of water and that the Bolsheviks wanted to go to Astrakhan, but the Captain could not manage it on account of the water shortage.[36]

The circumstances described here by Suttor differ significantly from those put forward by Mikoyan, who maintains that in these revolutionary times power was in the hands of the Soviet. Now, the sailors' Soviet on the *Turkmen*, mostly consisting of SR, had apparently decided to set sail for Krasnovodsk because there was no shortage of food there as there was at Astrakhan. Despite Shahumian's efforts:

the sailors were obstinately determined, and did not wish to submit to anyone else's advice. The ship's engineer, a dyed-in-the-wool counter-revolutionary, laid down the law on his terms. Moreover the refugees on board and many of the soldiers supported the attitude taken by the ship's committee. They were all against us: the crew, the armed soldiers and the refugees who filled the whole ship (except the upper deck). We only learned later what a feverish campaign had been mounted among the soldiers and refugees by the Dashnak commanders, who were in cahoots with two English officers from General Dunsterville's detachment who were on board.[37]

In Suttor's considerably different version, he does indeed report a conversation with a Bolshevik, and admits, with a mixture of pride and naivety, to a crafty manoeuvre. Questioned about the number of British troops stationed at Krasnovodsk, knowing that the port of Petrovsk (Makhachkala, nowadays the capital of Dagestan) was held by General Bisherakov, an opponent of the Bolsheviks, and having in any case no wish to go to Astrakhan, Suttor replied that the British had evacuated Krasnovodsk at the same time as Baku. He stuck to this assertion throughout the interrogation despite knowing that it was completely false. He states that the Bolsheviks did not look as if they believed him, but his conscience was untroubled nonetheless; exhausted, he went off again to get some sleep. When he awoke on the morning of 16 September, the sun was rising directly in front of the ship, so the *Turkmen* was therefore sailing due east towards Krasnovodsk. On arrival at their destination on the evening of the same day:

a searchlight was flashed on us as we entered a tug came within hailing distance and ordered the anchor to be dropped immediately and that no one was to leave the ship. As the tug came along-side I called out that I was a British Officer and I dropped aboard. We were at once taken to a cabin below, where I found Col. Battine and even to him I had some difficulty in proving my identity.[38]

The two English officers were finally disembarked while the *Turkmen* was directed to the little port of Ufra not far from Krasnovodsk.

In the extraordinarily clear waters off the coast of the Krasnovodsk Peninsula, where lines of dry hills divide up the land, Teague-Jones had enjoyed a delightful swim a few weeks earlier, and had subsequently gathered some useful information about Ufra's petroleum stocks from Vladimir Nikolaievich Alexeiev, Valya's father. Far from the colourful crowd on the quays of Krasnovodsk which Teague-Jones had photographed earlier in 1918, where tall Turkmen hats mingled with Russian caps and a few British military caps, the *Turkmen* arrived at its final destination at Ufra two and a half miles further on. Mikoyan recalls the surprising scene on arrival:

On both sides of the quay files of soldiers in Turkmen headgear were drawn up, with mounted bayonets, and standing in front two or three officers, a militia detachment, and shock troops of the local SR. A little behind stood an English gun battery and several English officers were walking up and down the quayside, among them the two officers who had now left the ship; however they did not involve themselves openly in anything going on. … We went back to the officers' cabin. Shahumian declared that, in the circumstances, the best thing would be to go down and mingle with the refugees, to try to get past the check-points, to get to the town and to hide there with a view to making for Astrakhan or Tashkent.[39]

Did the commissars really hope to get by? It was unlikely, and the reception committee organised by Kuhn at Ufra rapidly proceeded to arrest them. The news was immediately sent to Ashkhabad where Teague-Jones was present at the time, and caused a tremendous stir at Krasnovodsk. Kuhn, who was the local anti-Bolshevik representative, and the Krasnovodsk committee faced a problem: the local prison was already full, and the prospect of holding prisoners who included high-ranking Bolsheviks such as Shahumian presented a risk of political destabilisation. The decision was therefore one for higher authorities, that is to say the Transcaspian government based at Ashkhabad and their British ally. It is at this precise point in the affair of the twenty-six commissars that Teague-Jones, who was in contact with the Turkmen political world, made his entry on stage.

Diminished responsibilities

As a liaison and information officer on the staff of General Malleson's mission, which was based at Meshed in northern Iran, Teague Jones had been sent on a solo mission

122

to Turkmenistan and Baku during the summer of 1918 to establish relations with and conduct negotiations between the Ashkhabad Committee—the executive committee of the Transcaspian government—and Malleson's mission—Malmiss—at Meshed. It was a difficult task in view of the nature of his interlocutors, starting with Funtikov, president of the executive committee of the Centro-Caspian Dictatorship, a train-driver on the Transcaspian Railway, who had been propelled into the position of 'prime minister', and his deputy Kurilev, who was also a railway employee. Teague-Jones's mission in Turkmenistan was to construct an intelligence system worthy of the name, so as to stymie the dual threat from the Turks and the Bolsheviks. There was also the question of keeping an eye on the activities of the Transcaspian government, which was in a state of permanent crisis on the military, political and economic fronts. 'Needless to say, if I never obtained any rest, I cannot complain that there was any monotony',[40] he recalls in his journals. At the time when the twenty-six commissars disembarked at Krasnovodsk, Teague-Jones was in Ashkhabad, having taken part in violent fighting against the Reds at Kaakha, further east on the Transcaspian line. He was limping on crutches after being wounded in the leg on 29 August 1918, a fact which at the very least invalidates the film version of events in Nikolai Shengalaia's *The 26 Commissars*, where Teague-Jones is shown helping to carry out the order of execution in the dunes of the Karakum Desert and where, armed with a revolver, he pursued the last surviving commissar, leaving deep traces in the sand.

So far as it is possible to judge from the collection of telegrams held in the archives of the Imperial War Museum in London, the problem of the twenty-six commissars was far from being Teague-Jones's main preoccupation at the end of September 1918. That was no doubt his principal mistake, for it was after he had made an early exit from one of the meetings of the Ashkhabad Committee that, in his absence, the fate of the twenty-six commissars had been decided. The Transcaspian authorities at Ashkhabad were no keener than Kuhn at Krasnovodsk to take charge of these prisoners. Was not the prison at Ashkhabad, like the one at Krasnovodsk, full to bursting? They nonetheless took the step of sending a telegram to the representative of the Transcaspian government at Meshed asking him to request instructions from General Malleson on the fate of the twenty-six commissars who were under arrest. Teague-Jones himself had only learned of the arrest of the commissars on 18 September, and had also sent the information to General Malleson. According to the latter, the commissars were to be handed over to the British authorities and eventually evacuated to India. Dokhov undertook to transmit this wish to the Ashkhabad government, though he expressed a few doubts since, according to him, it was more than likely that the prisoners had already been shot. For his part, General Malleson sent Teague-Jones a telegram on 18 September confirming that he had given his instructions to the Transcaspian government delegate at Meshed, and asking in return that he should telegraph the intentions of the Transcaspian government in this matter. He telegraphed the following information to the commander in chief of the General Staff at Simla on the same day: 'Ashkhabad government is being asked to hand over the above mentioned leaders to me for despatch to India as their presence in

Transcaspia is most dangerous at present time when probably fully half Russians are preparing to turn their coats once more at the slightest sign of enemy success.'[41] Malleson had probably been informed of the extremely volatile state of local politics by Teague-Jones, his one and only intelligence agent. At Ashkhabad Teague-Jones had been summoned by Funtikov to a meeting on the evening of 18 September, at which the fate of the commissars, still unresolved, was to be decided. Teague-Jones describes this decisive yet absurd event in the letter of justification[42] which he wrote in 1922:

I attended the meeting. There were present the President, Funtikov, the Deputy President, Kurilev, the Foreign Minister Zimin and one or two others whom I cannot remember. The committee having assembled, the President (who was in a semi-intoxicated condition) made a statement to the effect that they had been informed from Meshed that General Malleson had declined to take over the prisoners, or, at any rate, had expressed his disinclination to do so, and had told the Ashkhabad representative that their Government must make its own arrangements. It was then argued that the local prison was full, that Krasnovodsk had refused to keep the prisoners for the same reason, and that therefore there was no alternative but to shoot them. This suggestion was opposed by Zimin, but was supported by Funtikov and Kurilev. The arguments continued endlessly and finally I left the meeting before anything had really been definitely decided.

It was only the following evening after some hard questioning that Funtikov informed Teague-Jones that it had been decided to shoot them and that Kurilev had been sent to Krasnovodsk the night before to make the necessary arrangements. Funtikov, in one of his rare sober moments, and without resorting to any of his tire-some rhetorical catch-phrases, told Teague-Jones three days later that 'the majority of the prisoners had been quietly shot', a formula which Teague-Jones repeated to General Malleson on 23 September. He in turn telegraphed India with the informa-tion that the '26 Bolshevik leaders'—a misnomer—had been shot, and only a few less important Bolsheviks spared.

According to Brian Pearce, the list of the twenty-six prisoners selected for execu-tion was in a document drawn up by the Krasnovodsk authorities at the time of their arrest. This document from the Baku prison contained the names of the prisoners to whom food parcels were to be supplied. Its nature explains why, fortuitously, some lesser political personalities figured among the twenty-six to be executed, while oth-ers, above all the young Anastas Mikoyan, escaped death. Anyway, in General Malleson's view, possibly repeating Teague-Jones's analysis, the execution was 'politi-cally advantageous as it means Ashkhabad Government have burnt their boats as regards Bolsheviks'[43] and that no volte-face was now open to them. The story is only comprehensible if one bears in mind the degree of the violence deployed by the Reds during their advance in this precise period from Tashkent towards the Turkmen steppe and the Afghan frontier. That was the main concern. Indeed, it was about this that Teague-Jones wrote to Colonel Redl at Meshed on 24 September. By this time the affair of the twenty-six commissars seems to have already been forgotten. Reporting the general tenor of a conversation with Zikov at Kushk on the Afghan frontier, Teague-Jones mentions atrocities committed by the Reds: 'The latter place was taken by the Bolsheviks and most of his officers were murdered. He himself only escaped through the assistance of friendly Turkomans.'[44]

This and other news show that September 1918 was a turning point. The British presence, initially motivated by the continuing war with the Ottoman Empire and Germany, made it possible to fight another war, a war of foreign intervention against Bolshevik Russia, 'Churchill's Crusade', in the words of the English historian Clifford Kinvig.[45] The execution of the twenty-six commissars, which according to Teague Jones cannot in any way be attributed to the British authorities, but rather to the SR members of the Centro-Caspian Dictatorship, belongs in this context. The Soviet authorities' accusation that Great Britain in general and Teague-Jones in particular were the responsible parties in the affair of the twenty-six commissars is also only comprehensible in this context. Why did the Soviet authorities disregard the obvious responsibility of the SR members, namely Funtikov, Kurilov, Zimin, Dokhov and Kuhn, who were nonetheless charged and executed later, in order to focus on the British? There is one obvious reason: to characterise the execution of the twenty-six commissars as the inaugural act in the British intervention against the Soviet regime. Out of a fortuitous crime, born of a string of unforeseeable events and improvised decisions made between two shots of vodka, the execution of the twenty-six commissars became an exemplary political crime, illustrating British imperial high-handedness. The accusation subsequently centred on Teague-Jones as a result of Funtikov's evidence, in prison in the spring of 1919, to the ex-SR Vadim Chaikin. Funtikov was trying to save his skin, while the Soviet authorities, who were probably aware of Teague-Jones's activities, took the opportunity to finger an English agent who had shown exceptional ability on Russian soil. Teague-Jones almost certainly had no responsibility for the execution of the twenty-six commissars other than the fact that he had left a meeting that was dragging on before it had come to an end. The guilty figure with the blood of the twenty-six commissars on his hands, a story built up over the years by Soviet authorities, served the double function of propaganda and neutralisation. By examining the stages in the construction of the Soviet case file, it is possible to evaluate the real effect of the affair of the twenty-six commissars on Teague-Jones's life and subsequent career. But first it is necessary to examine the lengthy prosecution dossier.

'A malicious propaganda legend' (Teague-Jones, November 1979)

In an interview, Ann Randall, the nurse who cared for Ronald Sinclair at the end of his life at Charlton House, gave the following recollection: 'The day when the back-yard door was broken, he exclaimed: oh! the Bolsheviks will come and get me ... He was really frightened and that was the first time I heard about the Bolsheviks.'[46] Were these words merely the ramblings of an old man? Or did they express a genuine fear? Was Ronald Sinclair the perpetually uneasy, watchful, innocent hero, or rather anti-hero, of a spy novel, pursued by the emissaries of Stalin? It is not a picture which quite fits the freedom of movement of our protagonist, who throughout his life ranged all over the world, and indeed often came close to the Soviet border areas. His only precaution was to make a simple change of name in May 1922 when Vadim Chaikin's accusatory book was published. But during his lifetime Reginald Teague-Jones, now Ronald Sinclair, never sought to add to what he had said when he asked for official Foreign Office protection in 1922. At the time he asked for an official denial from the Soviet authorities, together with the destruction of Chaikin's book *History of the Revolution*, the first volume of which was devoted entirely to the execution of the twenty-six commissars;[47] and he even considered a claim for libel 'at such time as there shall be a civilized and responsible government in Russia'.

Ronald Sinclair, who was present during the twilight years of the Soviet empire and who disappeared at practically the same time as the USSR, never had the opportunity to make a demand for moral reparation. Fifty years after the affair he discreetly discouraged—without however denying his identity—the historian Brian Pearce from attempting to clarify and refute the Soviet version of events. Pearce, who, following in C.H. Ellis's traces, was undertaking a revision of Soviet history and putting the 'Transcaspian episode' in proper context, managed to trace Teague-Jones, now Ronald Sinclair, in 1979. He sent him a detailed letter, asking for precise information not only on the affair of the twenty-six commissars, but also on his subsequent career. For, as he said in his letter, if one were to dismantle the Soviet version of the affair, one must be assumed to have an idea of the kind of man 'whom the Soviets have made the central figure in their sensational crime-story'.[48] Although the enquiry was framed in precise and well-polished terms, the reply was polite and totally discouraging. Teague-Jones refused to supply any more details regarding the course of events in the tragedy of the twenty-six commissars—Pearce had invited him to give his reasons for his early departure from the fatal meeting of the Ashkhabad Committee—and merely repeated what he had clearly stated in 1922. No British authority of the period, nor a fortiori himself, had been involved in the tragedy of the twenty-six commissars, an affair which had been exclusively Russian from the outset. 'Moreover, there can be no doubt in your own mind that those responsible for concocting and putting out mendacious accusations and building them up into a malicious propaganda legend, have done so while fully aware how completely devoid of truth and substance they were',[49] he wrote in 1979. He then talked of the unsuitability of returning to the affair, and of prudence:

By resuscitating this matter, as you say you propose to do, by publishing articles, or even a book, (a book! When the British authorities' attitude to this situation can be fully recorded in three short paragraphs!) you must yourself be well aware that such publication, while serving no useful purpose to anybody, would have the inevitable effect of inflaming passions and of provoking yet another outburst of hostile accusations, and this at a time when the British Government is striving to preserve peaceful and, if possible, amicable relations with the Kremlin.[50]

Whether springing from reasons of diplomacy or official secrecy, his refusal to speak more openly about the history of the twenty-six commissars was also linked to personal considerations about which we know little. David Footman, a former agent for the SIS to whom Brian Pearce sent Sinclair's letter, commented briefly 'The old boy still seems full of spirit.' But even if untrue, the tale of the twenty-six commissars turned Teague-Jones's existence upside down. Its near-cinematic construction is worth a closer look since, even if founded on a fiction, it succeeded in neutralising an intelligence agent on the territory in which he excelled from 1921 to 1922 onwards. The foreign intervention was coming to an end, and so far as we know Teague-Jones never returned to Russia.

The origins of the Soviet case: Vadim Chaikin's inquiry

The legend of Teague-Jones's guilt originally rested on Chaikin's book, which was published in 1922. It is a lengthy work that is difficult to navigate, stuffed with annexes, eye-witness accounts, records of interviews, telegrams and archive documents; but a guiding thread nonetheless runs through it.[51] Although the title promises a history of the Russian Revolution, the subject matter of the volume in question is in fact the execution of the twenty-six commissars of Baku. The book is the result of a local inquiry carried out in Transcaspia in 1919 by Vadim Chaikin, member of the Central Committee of the Socialist Revolutionary party (SR party) and deputy of the Constituent Assembly of Fergana, in a particular context: after the tragic death of the twenty-six commissars in September 1918, the situation in Transcaspia had changed yet again. Although the greater part of Turkestan and Tashkent were now under Red control, the British had resumed control over Baku while, on the other side of the Caspian, Malleson's mission, formerly based in Meshed in Iran, had advanced as far as Ashkhabad. In January 1919 conflicts between Russian and Turkmen elements within the Centro-Caspian Dictatorship had led the British to support a coup, which brought about the fall of Funtikov and of some of his companions, and their imprisonment at Ashkhabad. After they had been driven out of Central Asia by the Bolshevik advance, Chaikin arrived in Baku at the beginning of 1919 in the company of Mustapha Chokaiev, a Muslim dignitary who had led the autonomous government in Kokand, which had recently been abolished by the Reds. The two set up a 'Committee for the Convocation of a Constituent Assembly for Turkestan' and requested aid from the Allied powers.

With this as their declared object, they crossed the Caspian in order to meet General Malleson at Ashkhabad and request his support. But, as Chaikin himself admitted, the mission had been ordered by the Mensheviks and the Baku SR with the aim of elucidating the circumstances behind the murder of the twenty-six commissars. It appears that rumours were circulating in Baku that the act had been one of political vengeance by one or other of the parties. On arrival in Ashkhabad, the two men divided their efforts. While Chokaiev went off to meet General Malleson, Chaikin went to visit Zimin from the SR, one of the sole survivors of the previous government—who, it will be recalled, Teague-Jones had mentioned as the only member of the Ashkhabad Committee who had opposed the execution of the twenty-six commissars—and who had been kept on as minister for foreign affairs. On the latter's recommendation, Chaikin was authorised to go to the prison at Ashkhabad and meet Funtikov, without the British authorities making the slightest objection. The transcript of this conversation in the Ashkhabad jail, under the eyes of Indian soldiers, is the starting point for the accusation against Teague-Jones. Although initially very suspicious, the prisoner of Ashkhabad and his companion in misfortune, Sedykh, were more forthcoming to Chaikin when the latter shared his reservations about the new government and in particular told them of the real reasons for his visit. After giving them a day for reflection, Chaikin returned to the prison on 2 March 1919, when he was able to take delivery of a deposition written by Funtikov and counter-signed by Sedykh.[52]

Funtikov's muddled deposition, running to five paragraphs in three pages, exculpates him of any responsibility for the execution of the twenty-six commissars. Who then was responsible for the fatal decision? According to him, the chief information officer for the Transcaspian government, a certain Drujkin, had joined forces with Teague-Jones in the execution of the commissars. They were intending to camouflage their crime by pretending that the twenty-six commissars had been evacuated to India via Meshed, and Funtikov insists that he felt powerless to prevent the execution which took place on the Transcaspian railroad 207 versts from Krasnovodsk. In the absence of their consent he declared that he was unable to name the people who had taken the train that day—essentially Russians and Turkmens who belonged to no particular party—in order to carry out the dreadful task. Finally, after the execution, and on their return to Ashkhabad, Drujkin and Teague-Jones allegedly expressed their open satisfaction to Funtikov. Brian Pearce, who has commented in extensive detail on Chaikin's text, rightly notes that in this first version of events, which was aimed at removing the suspicions which then surrounded the SR, Drujkin shares the role of principal offender with Teague-Jones. As it happens, this same Drujkin had been one of the architects of the coup which had ended with Funtikov's imprisonment, thereby making him an ideal scapegoat for the SR. Zimin's even vaguer deposition, also taken on 2 March 1919, adds to the confusion. Zimin declares that he had never been made aware of the execution and that he did not know who had ordered the murder, but that Teague-Jones appeared to have been informed of the execution and that it seemed to have the approval of the British mission. Armed with these statements, which were procured without any interference from the British authorities, Chaikin returned to Baku in March 1919. There he met Anastas Mikoyan, who had miraculously been saved from the Krasnovodsk adventure—had he not, unlike the twenty-six commissars, escaped the death train?—and who was extraordinarily interested by this member of the SR whom he did not much respect but whose inquiry offered some interesting nuisance value. Mikoyan's account is as follows:

In March 1919, Vadim Chaikin arrived at Baku just after we had been released from prison. He was an experienced lawyer, a member of the Central Committee of the SR party, and on their list of elected members in the Constituent Assembly for Turkestan. He succeeded in organising a meeting with me, which took place in a clandestine apartment. Chaikin told me that he had spent more than a month in the Transcaspian zone and had tried to untangle the real circumstances surrounding the execution of the Baku commissars. He had done so both as a jurist and as a member of his party, so as to satisfy himself personally that no member of his party in government had a hand in this crime. He wished to be the first to unmask the guilty if such there were, and in doing so wash away the disgrace which had covered the whole SR party in which he had faith even if he did not approve of all its actions. Chaikin was convinced that if the English command had not been behind the SR members of the Transcaspian government, the latter would never have dared to go as far as they had. In conclusion, Chaikin declared to me that he saw it as a moral duty to organise an international campaign to unmask those responsible and bring them to justice, whether they were Russian or English citizens. These were not just empty words, Chaikin immediately took effective steps in this direction both at Baku and at Tiflis, and we supported him to the best of our ability.[53]

The purport of Mikoyan's evidence is clear; he was too intelligent a politician not to be sceptical about the possibility of identifying those who were truly responsible for the affair, but he also judged that Chaikin's inquiry had come at a good time for the agitprop campaign against British imperialism which the Bolsheviks were carrying out in Transcaucasia. In the three independent republics of Azerbaijan, Armenia and Georgia there were parties in power—Musavatists, Dashnaks and Mensheviks—who were hostile to them and who were supported in varying degrees by France and Great Britain.

Chaikin was summoned to Tiflis to appear before General Thomson and justify his allegations. Unimpressed, Thomson brought the interview to an end with a surprise confrontation between Drujkin and Chaikin. Dead to any sense of shame, Chaikin left the room to his adversary's protests that he had been slandered. However, the British authorities took no further action against Chaikin: apparently no one wanted to pay any more attention to a man in quest of publicity and with such low credibility. That was a mistake, since Chaikin's tale had made its way—possibly thanks to Mikoyan—from the semi-clandestine Bolsheviks of Baku all the way to the high-ranking Bolsheviks of Soviet Russia. The broadcast on 21 April by Chicherin, the commissar for foreign affairs, marked a new turn in the propaganda campaign which the Bolsheviks were planning. Chicherin picked up Chaikin's story, and accused the British government, with Teague-Jones at the forefront of the accusation. The following are extracts from Chicherin's broadcast:

It has been conclusively established that … the British officer Reginald Teague-Jones, together with some Russian Transcaspian counter-revolutionaries, fulfilling the desire of the British military mission, decided secretly to murder the commissars, who had been brought from Baku. An official communiqué issued at the time stated that the commissars had been taken to India, but, in fact, the train carrying them had been stopped at a lonely place in the desert, where the escort provided by the British military authorities and the Russian counter-revolutionaries carried out the order which had been given them to shoot the prisoners and bury them in the sand.[54]

Chicherin's broadcast was published two days later in *Izvestia*. It appeared on the same day as an article by Stalin, then commissar for the nationalities, drawing on a

Baku newspaper's account of Chaikin's story. Whether deliberately or otherwise, Stalin added some striking details and made some striking omissions. Reginald Teague-Jones, the man who had coldly ordered the execution, now became the actual murderer of the twenty-six commissars. Stalin had no hesitation in writing that the commissars had been shot 'by the British Captain Teague-Jones on the night of 20th September 1918 on the road from Krasnovodsk to Ashkhabad to which he was convoying them as war prisoners'.[55] Chaikin's inquiry continued to lead a life of its own until the publication of the book in Moscow in 1922. It is worth noting that the SR trial began at the same time, one of the first great show trials of the Lenin era, yet the affair of the twenty-six commissars played no part whatsoever in the case for the prosecution. However, none of the SR members who was involved, whether closely or distantly, in the affair of the twenty-six commissars, including Chaikin himself (who was deported and probably executed in 1941), was to survive the ensuing round of executions. Finally, on 4 May 1922, Reginald Teague-Jones became Ronald Sinclair by deed poll.

Shot or decapitated?

After the Sovietisation of Transcaucasia, and particularly of Azerbaijan (27–8 April 1920), the affair of the twenty-six commissars became a real affair of state, the memories and martyrs of which were established and then sustained in the popular imagination by the new Bolshevik authorities. In September 1920 the Congress of the Peoples of the East (1–8 September 1920) took place in Baku, attended by delegates from thirty-eight different countries, among them the American journalist John Reed and Enver Pasha, who was to head the Basmachi insurrection against the Soviets in Bokhara in 1921. On the same occasion the remains of the twenty-six commissars were repatriated with great ceremony. After a procession which began in Ashkhabad station in funerary wagons adorned with revolutionary slogans, the remains of the commissars took the return route on the Transcaspian Railway, and thence by boat from Krasnovodsk to Baku, where they were greeted by a large crowd. In Liberty Square the decorations for the Congress of the Peoples of the East had been replaced by dark shades of mourning drapery. The arriving coffins, accompanied first by a disorderly crowd and then moving at the orderly pace of officialdom, heralded the birth of a new political mythology and the legitimation of the new Soviet power in Transcaucasia. The speaker was Nariman Narimanov:

Today we bring back to the land of Soviet Azerbaijan the best among us, our dear comrades who remained faithful to their revolutionary mission to the very end. These inflexible and honest heroes were destroyed at the hands of England, the England which is always talking of its humanity. Here is the result of that humanity: 26 graves. Here the East can see clearly what that humanity is made of. May the East learn the lesson. But the hour of punishment has come. Yesterday the East, united in congress, swore to join forces to overcome these global conspirators, and soon the plundered East will awake and throw off the yoke from its shoulders. Sleep well dear comrades, the idea for which you fought will bring light to the whole world.[56]

THE LEGEND OF THE TWENTY-SIX COMMISSARS

Great preparations were made in setting the urban scene at Baku for the Congress of the Peoples of the East and for the funerals which contributed a moment of solemnity to this event. The newly paved town of 1920 had effaced the memory of the town which had crumbled in 1918. There were posters and satirical images put up by the Kaurosta,[57] electrical illuminations and triumphal arches swathed in metres of material taken from the Tagiev factory, while the hall of the Mailov theatre, the Baku opera house which had been founded by the rich Armenian Mailian family and chosen as the site of the Congress, had been converted to suggest the entry to a mosque with minaret and dome.[58] In these surroundings where requisitioned oriental carpets—every family in the town had been obliged to contribute a minimum of three carpets—were the background for lithographs of Bolshevik heroes and images of the twenty-six martyred commissars, in a hall stuffed with people to the point of suffocation, Zinoviev's speech against capitalism and imperialism rang out like a call to holy war:

It is time to declare a holy war against the English and French capitalists. Comrades, remember what these brigands are doing in the world. … Comrades, the question of holy war has been much at issue in recent times. The capitalists tried to represent their war as sacred and made the people believe it. When they spoke in 1914–1916 of a holy war, it was only a bluff. But now comrades you must proclaim here a real holy war against the French and English brigands, against capitalism … Comrades, brothers, the time has come for you to proclaim with a loud voice holy war against all the brigands and oppressors. International communism demands it of you today and says to you: Brothers, we call on you to declare holy war first of all against the English (prolonged applause).[59]

Another event reported with satisfaction by the *Kommunist* newspaper, the ceremonial burning of effigies representing European and American imperialism, took place in one of Baku's principal public spaces:

In the middle of the square were dummies representing Lloyd George, Millerand, Wilson, they were very good imitations with black suits, decorations, ribbons, an inquisitive wind fluttered their clothes. The executioner sat down next to them, with a bottle of petrol in his hands. When he had been given the tribunal's order to begin, he made the three dummies sniff the oil which they had so much enjoyed getting from Baku. He then threw the petrol in their faces and they began to burn. Lloyd George's briefcase, which was full of inflammable material, fell to the ground among the cheering crowd. The first to be consumed by the fire was Millerand, who sat there like a decapitated Louis XVI, because the dummy's head fell off and rolled off the scaffold. Then it was Lloyd George's turn. He fell off his chair like a man whose heart had broken. But Wilson lasted longer, which shows that America is not as close to revolution as England and France. After the fire had been extinguished, the soldiers withdrew. Everything that happened in this ceremony was an identical image of the French Revolution, only there was no *Caramaniola* (guillotine).

In these times of holy war, how could the affair of the twenty-six commissars not have been raised at the Congress of the Peoples of the East? In his speech, Narimanov did not fail to allude to it and to British guilt, in the process adding several 'improve-

ments' to Chaikin's version. At this point Soviet historiography abandoned all historical probability:

Until September 14th our dear comrades proudly, bravely and honourably remained at their
posts down to the last moment and then, when the Turks drew near, the Menshevik and
Dashnak traitors allowed them to leave for Astrakhan. While they were on their way, these
same traitors arrested them and changed their ship's course to Krasnovodsk. Our comrades
fell into the hands of the British scoundrels and were shot by them over there, between
Ashkhabad and Kizyl-Arvat.[60]

As Brian Pearce notes, every single element in this declaration is false, up to and
including the place of execution.

While Great Britain, and in particular Reginald Teague-Jones, were the subjects of
condemnation by international communism and the revolutionary East, the affair of
the twenty-six commissars was also exploited by the Commissariat for Foreign Affairs
as a way of turning down certain British requests. The demand for an inquiry into
the C.F. Davison affair, that of an English businessman executed by the Cheka at
Petrograd in 1920, was refused on the grounds that such a demand would naturally
call forth a similar demarche on the part of the Soviet government 'to examine the
evidence against innumerable Russian citizens executed by the British authorities
prior to the signing of the Anglo-Russian Trade Agreement'.[61] In May 1923 the
'Curzon ultimatum' again called the Soviet authorities' attention to the Davison case
and to that of Mrs Stan Harding, an English lady who had been unjustly imprisoned.
The request provoked some furious speeches, notably one from Trotsky to the
Congress of Metalworkers which denounced Teague-Jones as the man responsible for
ordering the murder, but which mixed up General Thomson with General Malleson.
Meanwhile, the judicial process which was to lead to the elimination of all the local
protagonists in the affair of the twenty-six commissars was still contributing to the
publicity surrounding the charge against Teague-Jones. This judicial process, itself
bathed in publicity and published in the form of selected extracts by the Communist
Party of Azerbaijan in 1928,[62] was a three-stage affair. In the first phase, during a
session of the revolutionary military court of the Turkestan Front, presided over by a
certain comrade Fonshtein and held from 19 to 26 April 1921, forty-one witnesses
were heard. Then came the Funtikov trial. Fate had caught up with Funtikov, who
had been freed at the last minute in 1919 from Ashkhabad prison when the anti-
Bolsheviks had evacuated the town, and had succeeded in surviving incognito in
European Russia until his arrest by the GPU at the beginning of 1925. This explains
why his trial in Baku, the second in the affair of the twenty-six commissars, was not
held until 11–27 April 1926. For eleven days this session of the Supreme Court of
the USSR, which was to result in Funtikov's execution, examined not only the circumstances of the death of the twenty-six commissars, but also the wider story of
British intervention in Transcaucasia and Transcaspia. Funtikov retracted his statement in front of Judge Cameron, and although Chaikin's written testimony was part
of the evidence in the case, he declared that he had never been aware of the execution

plan. Was this a prefiguration of the Stalinist trials? The accused tried to justify himself, protested his innocence and attempted to hold fast to his reconstruction of an evidential chain which led inevitably to Teague-Jones's guilt.

The Funtikov trial was not the last: there was a third trial at Baku from 1 to 6 March 1927. This time the Supreme Court of the Soviet Republic of Azerbaijan was trying one of Funtikov's henchmen, the train-driver Shchhegoliutin, whose testimony was mentioned above. The driver, who appeared to be innocent and had probably been subjected to fewer pressures, made no mention of the presence on the 'death train' of either an English officer or of Funtikov, although he knew the latter by sight. Without going into the details of the case files, which were to lead to the straightforward elimination of all the protagonists in the case of the twenty-six commissars, however closely or loosely connected, it is not hard to guess at the pressures exerted on the witnesses. The figure of Teague-Jones as torturer and oppressor, demonised as intended, emerges from even the least important witness statements. For example, I.K. Khrabov, an assistant machinist on the Transcaspian Railway,[63] declared that he knew the name of Teague-Jones, whom he had seen before the murder of the twenty-six commissars. At some point before the execution he claimed to have witnessed a scene in which Teague-Jones was dragging a sepoy by the hair— although it is difficult to recognise him from this kind of caricature, in these accounts Teague-Jones was a brutal and unscrupulous officer, an agent of colonial oppression: the devilish symbol of British imperialism.

New developments have further lifted the veil on the 'mystery of the twenty-six commissars' in the period since the collapse of the Soviet Union. Brian Pearce, an assiduous reader of the Soviet press, mentions the evidence of a certain Suren Gazarian, who was imprisoned at Orel in 1940–1 and one of whose cell companions was none other than Vadim A. Chaikin, fifty-five years old at the time and a former member of the central committee of the SR party. Chaikin is said to have talked of his political past, and to have confided to Gazarian, who had been arrested during the 1937 purges, that Brodsky's painting gave a false impression of the execution of the twenty-six commissars: they were not shot, but decapitated by a single executioner, a Turkmen.[64] This version of events, which if corroborated would conclusively clear Teague-Jones, agrees with the information which Baku recently supplied to the National Archive of Armenia. The Baku authorities, probably with the aim of drawing a line under a 'foreign' affair in which the main actor, Stepan Shahumian, was an Armenian, apparently decided to take a decisive step. A radio broadcast from Yerevan devoted to Stepan Shahumian[65] revealed that:

in reality there was never any kind of fusillade. That had simply been an invention. The 26 commissars were not shot, they were decapitated like common bandits. And their death was at the hands of a single executioner, a Turkmen of great height and prodigious strength. It was this Turkmen who decapitated them all with his sabre. The trench where the bodies and severed heads of the 26 commissars were buried was opened in the presence of a delegation representing the Central Executive Committee of the Russian Federation, along with a special commission. It was decided to conceal the truth from the people, because there was nothing heroic about it. And the scene of the shooting was invented: the commissars striking a heroic attitude, as though there were a witness present to hear their last cries. The Central Committee commissioned the painter Brodsky to paint this picture.

The painter's canvas had to be an edifying one, since the Turkmen sabre had fallen at a very inconvenient moment, just when Baku was making resonant speeches of solidarity directed at the revolutionary East. How could it be possible to establish the posthumous fame of the twenty-six commissars, the main instrument for legitimising Soviet power in Transcaucasia in 1920, if in reality the responsibility for this horrific execution lay with a Turkmen? The atrocity reported here by two different sources seems to leave no room whatsoever for British involvement. Were the unfortunate prisoners buried up to their necks in the sand, apparently a widespread practice in Central Asia, before their heads were calmly cut off? Only the report of the special committee which organised the transfer of the remains in September 1920 can furnish precise answers to this question, together with the conclusive proof of Teague-Jones's innocence. The decision taken at Baku in January 2009 to dismantle the funerary monument for the twenty-six commissars and to transfer their remains to the Kovtsan cemetery,[66] well outside the town centre, led to another revelation because the remains of only twenty-three bodies could be found. The evidence that Stepan Shahumian's remains were not present immediately revived another story: that the English had not shot all the commissars, and that Shahumian had been deported to India, a suggestion which was firmly rejected by his granddaughter Tatiana Shahumian, director of the Institute for Oriental Studies at the Moscow Academy of Sciences. According to her, her grandfather's absence could be attributed to a profanation of the grave at the end of 1980s during the worst moments of the Armeno-Azeri clashes.[67]

The culprit on stage: Teague-Jones in Soviet iconography

The twenty-six commissars have a prominent place in Soviet martyrology. Interestingly, the monument to the twenty-six commissars constitutes a kind of inauguration of the reign of statues[68]—representing officially famous figures, alive or dead—which was to characterise Soviet civilisation. When in July 1923 the Foreign Office was informed by Moscow that a monument to the twenty-six commissars was to be put up in Baku, and when the monument was actually unveiled on the sixth anniversary of the 'Tragedy of Ashka-Kuim' on 24 September 1924, the twenty-six commissars were beginning their career as models for sculptures and monuments named after them throughout the Soviet lands. We do not know the earliest form of the monument, since work on erecting the 'definitive' version of the group of statues sculpted by Merkurov on the Square of the 26 Commissars at Baku only really began in February 1958. The commemorative pillar at the scene of the crime in Turkmenistan was put up in 1932, but the Baku monument apparently suffered some delay; Merkurov's work, which began in 1924, was only completed in 1946. Sergei D. Merkurov, an official artist who was famous throughout the USSR for his statues of Lenin and Stalin in granite, marble and bronze, had been entrusted with the project—never actually realised—for a colossal statue of Lenin, 100 metres high, which was to tower over the Palace of the Soviets. Born into a family of Greek merchants at Andropolis, Merkurov enjoyed the prestige of having trained in Europe, indeed in Paris, since he was said to have spent time before the war in Rodin's studio. It is not possible to form a visual judgement today of the monument which Merkurov sculpted in honour of the twenty-six commissars because the granite relief was destroyed in the circumstances described at the beginning of this chapter. Merkurov's monument must be disentangled from the complex memorial to the twenty-six commissars which was unveiled at Baku in September 1968, on the fiftieth anniversary of the event. To try to form an exact idea of the way it was placed, one has to turn to some of the few photographs of the Baku monument: it is not easy to work out how the group of statues fitted into the 1958 monument, or whether it made a distinct ensemble. It is possible, however, to examine Merkurov's relief carving: the sculptor's classical training is visible both in the forms and in the diagonally ascending composition of this dramatic and theatrical work, where a clearly recognisable Stepan Shahumian stands out. Although the relief features the twenty-six commissars—if indeed there are exactly twenty-six on the monument, which is hard to tell—realistically enough, particularly in the case of some of the faces which have been taken from photographs, no place has been given to an executioner or to an English officer. The naked bodies in Merkurov's relief, which are carefully posed, may have some of the rhetoric of socialist realism, but it is essentially a symbolic monument from which the figure of Teague-Jones is absent.

However, Teague-Jones, along with other English officers, does seem to have been depicted in the large (285cm x 176.5cm) painting by Isaac C. Brodsky (1884–1939) entitled *The Execution of the 26 Commissars* (1925) held by the Museum of Fine Arts at Volgograd. Brodsky had been a pupil of the great Russian painter Ilya Repin, the head of the 'Wanderers' school, under whom he completed his years of apprenticeship from 1902 to 1907. At the beginning of the 1920s he embarked on a cycle of large historical works entitled *The Revolution in Russia*, of which the painting of the execution of the twenty-six commissars forms part. He had previously painted *The Opening of the Second Congress of the Comintern* (1920–4) and the monumental canvas of the twenty-six commissars was soon to be followed by *Lenin's Speech to the Workers of the Putilov Factories* (1926). In this cycle of official paintings, the picture showing the execution of the twenty-six commissars is interesting both from an iconographic and a historical point of view. Brodsky is understood to have taken the initiative in choosing the subject of this great pseudo-historical painting and proposing it to Kirov, then secretary of the Communist Party of Azerbaijan. Kirov warmly encouraged the project and put the necessary documents and materials at the artist's disposal, thus orchestrating the political message, while for its part the praesidium of the Baku Soviet assumed oversight of the work. In his initial description of the project,[69] Brodsky had declared his intention of depicting Kuhn, Kurilev and other actors in the drama, without any mention of a British participant. But when he sent a preparatory sketch of the painting to the Baku Soviet, the authorities told him that 'it did not sufficiently show the participation of the English in the execution'. The three English officers eventually shown in profile in the painting, depicted as cynical and arrogant observers, represent the wish of the artist or his clients to personify British imperialism. One of them is clearly intended to represent Teague-Jones imperturbably watching the fusillade taking place.

This type of historical painting in the Soviet era drew its realistic qualities from the fact that the artist had worked like a real journalist, basing himself on precise documentation. Just like Repin, his teacher, Brodsky knew how to paint scenes containing large numbers of people, even crowds, while distinguishing individual personalities—among the forty characters in the picture one can easily recognise Shahumian, Zevin, Aziz-Bekov, Fioletov, Korganov—by means of portraits based on photographs. It is known that the artist did not have a comparable image to draw on in painting Teague-Jones, but in spite of the imaginary character of the scene, the physical type of the English officers shown is not too far from reality. To set the heroic scene, Brodsky, who had visited the site of the executions, painted a dramatic countryside. The bare desert under a pre-dawn sky with a faint hint of sunrise is a fitting setting for the event, which is depicted in a palette of pale and misty blues and pinks. In this setting, which perhaps also symbolises the dawn of the new era, the silhouettes of the commissars who are still on their feet stand out sharply. In the official myth, they are supposed to have died shouting 'Long live Communism' and indeed the artist has shown them in a theatrical pose of defiance and protest. Brodsky's painting, which won the approval of Voroshilov and was presented at the celebration of the 200th anniversary of the Academy of Sciences in 1925, was exhibited in a number of Soviet cities. In Georgia there was a request for a copy—Brodsky took the opportunity of making some minor changes to the left-hand side of the painting so as to make the image of the English officers more distinct—which could be put on permanent exhibition. Could it have been this picture, a realist picture of a fantasy scene, a picture with near-cinematic qualities, that Nikolai Shengalaia once saw at the Tiflis museum?

Nikolai Shengalaia's 1932 film *The 26 Commissars*, which was 'dedicated to the heroic proletariat of Baku', is a kind of culmination of propaganda imagery relating to the affair of the twenty-six commissars. Although the film, which was clearly influenced by Eisenstein and by Dziga Vertov's production techniques,[70] has some aesthetic merits, it is riddled with historical errors. This propaganda film distorts the complex chain of events with a series of improbabilities; it is actually more a fresco of the revolutionary struggles at Baku than the story of the twenty-six commissars as suggested by the title. As a historical fiction whose central theme is the denunciation of British imperialism it is nonetheless a fascinating document in the history of Soviet cinematic propaganda. Shengalaia inevitably felt compelled to incarnate the British in immediately identifiable and stereotypical characters. Teague-Jones thus appears in the cast list as 'Captain Johnson', played by Kh. Ts. Veranikov. Alongside him 'General Denvil' stands for General Dunsterville, and is played by the actor

THE LEGEND OF THE TWENTY-SIX COMMISSARS

R.I. Riazanov, a giant of a man with Slavic features. As this is a silent film with minimal subtitled dialogue, the screenplay gives the character of Teague-Jones (alias Johnson) the role of henchman and cold-blooded executant of Dunsterville's wishes. It is the latter who gives 'Johnson' the order, heavy with unspoken meaning, 'to help with the evacuation of the prisoners to India'. Easily recognisable, he is present at the execution of the twenty-six commissars—there is even a marker by the track to indicate the now legendary 207th verst of the Transcaspian line—without however being shown as one of the executioners. By using a montage of shots which alternate images of the chase in the dunes—a man with a pistol in his hand finishes off one of the commissars—with marks in the sand, close-ups of 'Johnson's' face and shots of petroleum spouting at Baku, the film points to the identity of the only culprit, who is 'Johnson'. His role as a cold, cynical and cruel Englishman leaves no room for doubt in the eyes of the spectator, who has been enjoined to see in this execution, 'in the heart of Asia in the sands of Turkmenistan', a wider conflict underlying it, one which is recalled on the final screen: 'Remember Stepan's (Shahumian's) declaration to the Soviet: with the arrival of the English the imperialists' fight for petroleum has begun.' The arrival of three armoured trains—named Azizbekov, Shahumian and Djaparidze—at Baku station, bombarding the steamer carrying away the retreating British, brings the film to its conclusion: 'Long live Soviet Azerbaijan!'

It is unlikely that Teague-Jones ever saw Shengalaia's film. He would no doubt have been greatly interested to see himself portrayed as a big-bellied, cruel Englishman, far different from the man he really was. Shengalaia's film, which limits the responsibility for the execution to Teague-Jones while leaving his character singularly silent and inactive, is largely representative of the generality of Soviet arguments in the case of the twenty-six commissars, which was above all a propaganda case; the crude way in which it was projected had a durable effect on Soviet–British relations and did undeniable damage to the man who was its principal target. With much patience and determination, Brian Pearce has demonstrated the extreme unlikelihood of Teague-Jones's personal responsibility for the execution of the twenty-six commissars, and the inconsistencies in the charges levelled against him. One question remains, however: to what extent was the identity of Teague-Jones, who was described as 'a very important agent' in Central Asia, known to the Soviet authorities? The answer will only ever be found in the Russian archives. On the British side, the Foreign Office has consistently stuck to the same position, including in 1930–1[71] when the USSR announced its intention to raise the question of British responsibility in the tragedy of the twenty-six commissars once again. The British position was set out at the time as follows:

It appears that not only was there no responsibility attaching to the British authorities in this matter, but that, on the contrary, so far as we are concerned in the affair at all, we wished to have the men surrendered to us—presumably with a view to interning them in India, as was done with other Soviet officials at that time.

Let us leave the last word with Ellis, a friend of Teague-Jones, a fragment of whose autobiography appears in the file for Major T.S.W. Jarvis held at the British Library:

In 1962 (?) I was an interpreter to a British firm exhibiting at a Trades Fair in Sokolniki (Moscow). One day a group of VIPs (from the Kremlin) visited the stands and just before they left our stand Mikoyan complimented me on my Russian, we exchanged a few words and as a parting shot I said to him: 'Yes, Excellency, many things have happened since events in Baku'. He looked startled but retained his composure and just smiled when I bowed to him on his departure.[72]

The same Mikoyan, who managed to survive all the vicissitudes of Soviet history to de-Stalinisation, was to mention C.H. Ellis's work, *The Transcaspian Episode*, in his memoirs, concluding: 'There is no subterfuge by means of which the English imperialists can escape. They will never be able to wash away the shame of the tragic end of the 26 commissars.'[73] So what could that smile have meant?

6

THE RETREAT OF THE WHITE ARMIES

FROM CONSTANTINOPLE TO THE CAUCASUS (1919–21)

'One's head is like a soupkettle simmering on the back of a stove. Thoughts move slowly about in a thick gravy of stupor. A second's glimpse of a war-map with little flags. Russian, Turkish, British. What a fine game it is. The little flags move back and forth. Livelier than chess. Then the secret intelligence map. Such extraordinary cleverness. We'll exploit the religion of A to make him fight B, we'll buy up the big men of D so that they'll attack A in the rear, then when everybody's down we'll neatly carve up the map.'

John dos Passos, *Orient Express*, New York: Harper & Brothers, 1927, p. 62

In February 1919 Reginald Teague-Jones left Ashkhabad a disappointed and disillusioned man. So much completely wasted energy, with so little material support, had preceded the British decision to withdraw, a decision which was shortly followed by the predicted Sovietisation of Turkmenistan. With the end of the First World War, and with no new assignment as yet, Teague-Jones returned to London with Valya to a temporary home at 80 Philbeach Gardens near Earls Court in South West London. He was in a state of uncertainty. In his pocket was a letter of recommendation from his friend and colleague at Meshed and Ashkhabad, T.S.W. Jarvis. It commended Teague-Jones—he was using the pseudonym Ronald Sinclair by this point—to Jarvis's brother, C.S. Jarvis, who held an important post at the War Office after having served during the First World War in France, Egypt and Palestine. He was later to become governor of Sinai—an administrative entity which formed part of the British Mandate in Palestine—and seemed likely to be able to steer Teague-Jones towards a new job which could make full use of his abilities. T.S.W. Jarvis summed up Teague-Jones's qualities for his brother as follows:

The bearer of this letter is Captain Ronald Sinclair, now on sick leave in England. I would just like you to put the following facts to the right quarter, as he is too modest to tell you himself. I have served with Ronald Sinclair on this Mission for seven months. You may know something of the difficulties we have been up against, perhaps, if I call to mind that we were here before all those highly organised and fitted out military expeditions to Archangelsk and Siberia were thought of. With no credit, a handful of troops and only the Indian Government to which one could appeal, you can take my word for it that many a time we were absolutely dejected and in despair. You will remember that our Western boundary was Krasnovodsk, and as you know, the Turkish troops and German staff were in Baku and had vessels on the Caspian. Our eastern boundary was the Front against the Turkistan Bolsheviks. Our lines of communication were 1400 miles of desert to India. Well, anyhow, all is OK now, and no one has done more to bring it about than Ronald Sinclair. Speaking Russian perfectly, he was brought up in Petrograd, and knowing the Indian troops and Indian Administration absolutely, you can form an idea of the value his services were. For seven months he has been the symbol of British prestige and authority in Transcaspia. As you know, the G.O.C. mission and his staff, including your brother, had our HQ in Meshed, Persia, and so every order and every line of Intelligence came through Ronald Sinclair. He has made and unmade governments and workmen committees and is esteemed by all classes of the population. If you know of any job in connection with Russia, the Caucasus, of Asia Minor, whatever the work is, and one man can do it, that man is Ronald Sinclair. As you know, I consider I know something about Russians of the new school, after my experiences of 1917 and 1918, but I honestly say there are many jobs I would not attempt to tackle, but would recommend Ronald Sinclair for every time. Please bring these facts to any quarter you think would be advantageous to Ronald Sinclair. Also introduce him to Alec Layard and Colonel Byrns.[1]

Of the affair of the twenty-six commissars, and the circumstances which had led Teague-Jones to operate under another name from 1919 onwards, T.S.W. Jarvis breathes not a word.

A nest of spies in Constantinople

In February 1919, after leaving Ashkhabad, Teague-Jones took a train on the now familiar Transcaspian line to Krasnovodsk. Time was short, since London had demanded his early return to arrange the details of a new assignment. To take a steamer and cross the Caspian and then disembark at a Baku ravaged by the passage of the Turks had now become a routine trip, which did not appear to occasion even slight feelings of regret on Teague-Jones's part. At the Hotel Europe, where he met McDonnell, he spent an uncomfortable night in an establishment which had been ruined by the war. It hardly mattered, as he had little time to linger in the city, which had become the capital of independent Azerbaijan. He immediately took a train on the line between Baku and Batumi on the Black Sea. It was a slow journey, with numerous stops as the train crossed Azerbaijan and Georgia, allowing Teague-Jones to see how the countryside of Transcaucasia looked under a covering of winter snow. The line ran across the Kura plain along the foothills of the Caucasus Mountains, then climbed boldly into the mountains at Kanja before crossing into Georgia. Further stops were Tbilisi, Gori, Kutaisi, Samtredia and then finally Batumi. At Batumi Teague-Jones embarked on a stinking old boat which had been used to transport cattle from South America. The journey across the Black Sea and into the Bosphorus was therefore far from a pleasure cruise. After a short stop at Constantinople, the ship sailed down the Dardanelles and on to Salonika. There Teague-Jones embarked on the *Glengorn Castle*, a hospital ship which took him to Tilbury at the mouth of the Thames Estuary, within easy reach of Central London, where the management of His Majesty's Intelligence Service were expecting him.

In the ruins of the Ottoman Empire: Constantinople in 1919

Thanks to a short holiday in London, whether in the form of sick-leave, a honey-moon with Valya or a set of business meetings in Whitehall and the Mall, Teague-Jones was able to introduce himself and probably find a home for Valya in one of the intelligence services where Russian-speakers were particularly sought-after. At the War Office he met C.S. Jarvis and some of the top brass from the Foreign Office and the India Office, which were still on a war footing. Although the First World War was indeed over, a Russia deep in civil war was still a subject of major preoccupation, while in the Near and Middle East, notably in Palestine, the British were facing new disturbances. Among the different territories where British power was engaged, Teague-Jones could be of particular use on the southern borders of Russia. In July 1919 the White armies under General Denikin had advanced across the northern Caucasus and were massing their forces for a march on Moscow. The situation seemed to be turning in favour of the Whites to the point where experts in London and Paris were forecasting the victory of the anti-Bolshevik forces and the imminence of the Soviet downfall:

Since Denikin was headed for Moscow, it was decided that I should go along as political observer and since he appeared to be advancing rapidly, I must lose not a moment to catch up with him. Arrangements were quickly made, but just as two years previously it had been easy for the Brass Hats at Headquarters to urge haste, it was impossible to travel quickly with the disorganised state of transport in war-torn Europe. It took me sixteen days to reach Constantinople, only to learn that in the meantime the tide of the Russian Civil War was turned and, instead of Denikin advancing on Moscow, he and his White Army were in retreat heading for the Crimea and the Black Sea.

Teague-Jones's job was to be both political observer and liaison office between the high commissioner—a British ambassador was to be nominated a little later—and British naval and military forces in the Black Sea area: 'My duties also entailed liaison with General Denikin and his successor, General Wrangel, and I likewise maintained relations with the British occupation authorities in Batum and Tiflis.'[2] In October 1919 the southwards retreat of Denikin and the Whites towards the Black Sea clearly worried the British authorities based in Transcaucasia; the military reverse aroused fears of a rapid advance by the Reds in Transcaucasia. Teague-Jones recalls that:

the experts found it necessary to revise their earlier forecasts of an impending Soviet collapse. Instead, they now foresaw the probability of a determined red Army drive to overrun the three break-away states of Azerbaijan, Armenia and Georgia, and bring them back into the Soviet fold. Circumstances pointed to Azerbaijan as being the most vulnerable to attack …[3]

Although Nuri Pasha's Army of Islam had continued on its drive towards the east for a while, the Mudros Armistice (30 October 1918) which marked the defeat of the Ottoman Empire had given the British presence a solid foothold in practically all regions of the Ottoman Empire as well as in Transcaucasia. The Armistice conditions which Britain had imposed on both its enemies and its allies prefigured the extremely tough conditions of the Treaty of Sèvres, against which Mustafa Kemal was to raise the banner of his 'War of Independence'. On top of the immediate demobilisation of the Ottoman Army, the confiscation of its fleet and the surrender of those of its forces which were still active in Arab territory, the Armistice imposed the opening of the Dardanelles and the Bosphorus and their occupation by the Allies, along with free access to the Black Sea. The Mudros Armistice thus made the Allies masters of Turkey with the exception of north-east Anatolia, where they had decided not to send troops because of the difficulties in communication. Under Article 15 of the Armistice Allied officers were to take charge of all the railways, including those sections of the Transcaucasian line currently under Turkish control, which were to be put entirely at the free disposal of the Allied authorities, taking into account the needs of the population. It followed from this clause that the Allies had the right to occupy Batumi, and that Turkey would make no objection to the Allied occupation of Baku.[4] British troops controlled Constantinople and the straits, and occupied the principal Black Sea ports including Batumi, where a division was fighting the Reds.

At the end of the summer of 1919, when Teague-Jones disembarked for the second time at Constantinople, the capital of the Ottoman Empire had been under an occupation regime orchestrated by the Allied high commissioners, Admiral Arthur G. Calthorpe and Louis Franchet d'Espèrey. However, it was with Calthorpe's replacement as high commissioner, John de Robeck, that Teague-Jones was to serve as liaison officer from August 1919 onwards. From then on his activities centred round the British embassy in Constantinople to which Sir Horace Rumbold was appointed in 1920. The latter was the interlocutor with the government of Sultan Mehmet VI, led by Ferid Pasha, a strong supporter of the British, but lacking in any real political abilities. Caught between the Allied plan to transform Turkey into a rump state with only a 'blind' coastline on the Black Sea, and Mustafa Kemal's nationalist programme which was soon to deprive him of all legitimacy, the sultan, while lacking political power, still enjoyed the religious prestige belonging to the caliph. Teague-Jones's main business was not with him, even though he visited the Seraglio several times during his stay in Constantinople. His visits moved him principally to commentaries on its architecture:[5]

It is not perhaps, quite accurate to suggest that the Seraglio is nothing but a confused medley of inconsequent and disconnected kiosks. A considerable part consists of courts and quadrangles as regular as those of an Oxford college, it is only as one approaches the arcana of the Palace that symmetry begins to make way for a more picturesque variety.[6]

142

General Wrangel, photographed by Reginald Teague-Jones off Crimea, 17 October 1920: 'A magnificent soldier sets off', p. 149 (© Imperial War Museum).

A young Reginald Teague-Jones in St Petersburg around the time of the 1905 Revolution (Private collection).

Valia Alexeieva, first wife of Reginald Teague-Jones, towards 1918 (Private collection).

A Turkmen wearing a papakh. Photographed by Reginald Teague-Jones in Achkhabad in 1919 (©
Imperial War Museum).

North West Frontier, Shirani Country in 1915. Photographed by Reginald Teague-Jones (© Imperial War Museum).

Transcaspia, Reginald Teague-Jones inspects a badly damaged Bolshevik train in 1918 (© Imperial War Museum).

Transcaspia, the railway station at Kaakhka in 1918. In the centre, Reginald Teague-Jones injured after the battle of Kaakhka (© Imperial War Museum).

Shirani Country, a patrol by the Frontier Constabulary in 1914-1915 (© Imperial War Museum).

An Imperial Airways flight between London and Karachi, 1929 (© Imperial War Museum).

Baluchi chiefs photographed by Reginald Teague-Jones in 1915 (© Imperial War Museum).

The Frontier Constabulary on patrol in Shirani Country, North West Frontier, 1916 (© Imperial War Museum).

In a *nullah*, Waziristan, 1915. Photographed by Reginald Teague-Jones (© Imperial War Museum).

11th May, 1950

My dear 4-Star General:

Look who is looking in our mirror!

A distinguished looking gentlemen, I MUST say!

Very kind regards,

Yours,

Constance Calenberg

CC/hs

Ronald Sinclair, Esq.,
British Consulate
350 Fifth Avenue
New York, n.Y.

A letter from an admirer to a "distinguished" gentleman (Private collection).

Reginald Teague-Jones's reflection is captured in a mirror, New York, 1950 (Private collection).

Reginald Teague-Jones at the end of the 1940s (Private collection).

Evidence of the innocuous diplomatic relationship between the representative of British power and the caliph, a 'metrical version of Sir Horace Rumbold's despatch to Lord Curzon, describing his first interview with the Caliph on February 27, 1923', is among Teague-Jones's papers.[7] It summons up with determined humour the vacuity of the Seraglio and of the exchanges with the last titular holder of the spiritual power of Islam.[8]

'Beefsteaks à la Hoover-Nansen'

In 1919 Constantinople was not yet the megalopolis which Istanbul has become in the twenty-first century. With a million inhabitants, only half of whom were Muslims, the city still had a number of minority populations, principally Greeks, Armenians and Jews. The occupation, which began with the entry of the French on 12 November 1918 and the British the following day, allowed the victors in the First World War to establish themselves in every sector of the city between Europe and Asia. The resulting tensions were irreconcilable since, while the minorities were delighted, the Turkish population felt humiliated. The fall of Constantinople and the entry of General Franchet d'Espèrey on a white horse on 8 February 1919 seemed to echo the entry of Mehmet the Conqueror in 1453, five centuries earlier. In 1919 the fall of Byzantium and of Constantinople, the city which Dostoyevsky said 'should be ours', was no longer food for the imperialist fantasies of the Russian heirs of the Slav dream. Russians fleeing Bolshevik Russia, whether as ordinary refugees or aristocrats, soldiers or diplomats, nonetheless thronged there in large numbers. Once they had arrived in Constantinople, there was no work for these cohorts of refugees, men and women alike, in a city where there was not even enough to go round for its ordinary citizens. The penniless refugees would soon be taken under the wing of charities and international organisations. The streets of Constantinople were swarming with escaped Russian soldiers who were looking to survive through small-scale street trading: cigarettes, newspapers, postcards and old books were their meagre wares. Among the amateurs and professionals selling their paintings of nudes or sunsets on the Grande Rue at Pera where Teague-Jones was living, it was not unusual to see a refugee who had managed to get all or part of his library out via the Crimea trying to sell his books, one at a time, for a few piastres to American or English passers-by.

Every category of expatriate Russian seemed to have ended up in the streets of Pera—for the most part poor and destitute, a few managed to open cafés and bars. For years the Russians contributed a vivid nightlife to Constantinople. From the sleaziest sailors' café on the quays, on the edges of the red-light district, to the smartest café such as Le Moscovite—the most popular address in Pera—the Russian establishments brought a liveliness, an atmosphere, indeed a whole economy of excess which had hitherto been lacking in Constantinople. Elmer Davis, a reporter for *The New York Times*, drew an evocative picture:

The best café in Constantinople is the Moscovite. It is owned and operated by a few Russians who had little money, and furnishes a living for a good many Russians who have none. Not such a brilliant living at that. The prices are rather less than would have been charged by a New York restaurant of the same class before prohibition: still, it is enough to enable the staff to keep going. There is an elaborate cabaret fairly good, though obviously most of it amateur, singers trained for the drawing room, dancing girls who studied the ballet as practice in eurhythmics. The waitresses are girls—young women rather—Russian aristocrats; a General's daughter, the wife of a Colonel of the Guards, a lady who before the war owned the only Rolls-Royce in Russia, and so on, at least if the casual visitor may believe what the residents tell him. And, if the residents may be believed, these girls are virtuous. Most of them are supporting husbands, fathers or children out of their earnings as waitresses.[9]

A judgement which the journalist rapidly qualifies, mentioning less smart cafés where the girls depended for their livelihood on a less virtuous kind of trade; the Russian blondes swept all before them. Whether it was the deposed aristocrats now taking orders in the bars, the artists who had gone astray or the ordinary prostitutes, no one described Russian society in Constantinople in these years better than Georges Simenon, who had a talent for rendering the murky atmosphere of the brothel, the intrigues of the spies, the unsavoury settling of scores and the assassinations.

Teague-Jones lived alongside this society, and even if he hardly had the time or the taste for a life of debauchery, he still enjoyed the pleasures which Constantinople had to offer, including the leisure to frequent, at the proper distance for an experienced agent, a colourful interloper society made up of vivid déclassé personalities. Among the papers which he kept from this period are a few menus skilfully sketched on paper napkins which caricature, in a distinctly anti-Semitic way, receptions at the Russian embassy in Constantinople. One guesses at a cheerful band of Englishmen sitting round a table of stuffed mussels or grilled fish, a rice pudding or an oriental pastry, laughing like schoolboys over Russian intrigues. The menus always begin with traditional *zakuskis* washed down with vodka, followed by fish soup or 'œufs à la provençale à la Gagarin', pan-fried steak, lamb cutlets with all the trimmings or 'beefsteaks à la Hoover-Nansen' before finishing with 'gâteaux à la mode du général Wrangel'. On one of them there is a drawing of a man in three-piece suit with a Semitic profile, the very picture of a Bolshevik agent, who visits the Russian embassy and issues the following warning: 'Major? Look here, I do dislike this company of scoundrels in the Embassy. They are "no good", "Tchernosotteniki"!'[10] The Russian embassy did indeed bring all of émigré Russia together. The ambassador's sumptuous residence, witness to an era when Russia coveted Constantinople and the straits, had no financial sources of support and was full from the basement to the attics of Russian officers and homeless refugees. According to Elmer Davis:

it is, in effect, a home for the unemployed. The Wrangels live in a corner of the building and stow away as many of the army as they can. In that fact is perhaps some suggestion of the reason why soldiers and civilians, officers and privates, men and women, of the lost tribes driven into exile from Crimea look up to General Wrangel as more than a commander, almost as a father. He is a good shepherd for a flock of sorely troubled sheep. And it is no doubt due in some degree to his example that the Russian exiles have hung together so well.[11]

THE RETREAT OF THE WHITE ARMIES

There were certainly loyal supporters, but also webs of intrigue around the White generals and Prince Gagarin, who lived under the shadow of plots and infiltration by Bolshevik agents. People had been shaken by the assassination of General Romanovski, the commander of Denikin's army, in the embassy's billiard-room in April 1920, shortly after the defeat of the Whites in the Crimea. If a general could be assassinated with shots from a revolver in a room next to the one in which the ambassador, General Denikin and some other friends were doing some quiet planning, it meant that the Russian embassy was not a safe place. General Denikin and his wife were therefore transferred on to a British ship under British protection. At the beginning of his stay in Constantinople, General Wrangel lived on his yacht until it was accidentally sunk in suspicious circumstances by an Italian steamer coming from the Black Sea. It was not that this kind of accident was uncommon in the Bosphorus, but there had never been one in the zone reserved for the Russian ships. The episode was all the more unusual in that a Russian was at the helm of the Italian steamer. In any event, at the end of 1921, after the accident, in which there were no victims other than the yacht which sank to the bottom of the sea, General Wrangel and his wife, Baroness Wrangel, decided to live inside the Russian embassy in Constantinople. There was a short-lived rumour that Baroness Wrangel had lost her priceless jewels in the wreck, but the rumour soon died, since the Baroness had in fact disposed of her jewellery a long time previously.

Although his humanitarian work also served as cover, Teague-Jones was actively involved in providing help for refugees and was in constant touch with Baroness Wrangel.[12] Absorbed in her philanthropic work on behalf of the Russian refugees at Constantinople, she was devoting all her energies to the British Refugee Relief Committee of Constantinople, and occasionally visiting her husband, who in the spring of 1920 had launched a final offensive against the Reds in the Crimea. Teague-Jones was close to her 'particularly in those early days of the evacuation tragedy, when her energy, devotion and loyalty to her country, her husband and her fellow refugees won the admiration and affection of all who knew her'.[13] Teague-Jones worked for the British Refugee Relief Committee throughout his stay in Constantinople, and especially from November 1920 onwards. This involved constant collaboration with the French, because the British were only responsible for food and supplies, while housing was exclusively a French responsibility. In his notebooks Teague-Jones recalls that:

as I was the only member of our Relief Committee speaking both fluent French and Russian, I could not very well refuse to act as liaison between the Committee and the French authorities on all matters affecting the refugees. This brought me into constant and close relations with the French medical, transportation and other services. Our relations were consistently friendly and cooperative. However, with the passing of the weeks I noticed a marked falling off in the French enthusiasm for their work with the Russians. They had been unfortunate in the class of military refugees they had placed in the Tuzla camp. They were a rough and ill-disciplined crowd and after some initial troubles the French had been glad to borrow the services of an experienced British commandant in the person of Colonel Walshe ... I could feel that my French friends were rapidly becoming disillusioned with this whole Russian refugees business. The French government had no doubt thought, like many others, that they were backing a winner when they decided literally overnight to grant de facto recognition to the Wrangel administration. They doubtless considered it a smart move to anticipate the Anglo-Saxons and thereby secure a favourable position with, as they thought, the future rulers of Russia. Now they were beginning to realise that not only had they backed the wrong horse, but they had got themselves involved in responsibilities far too heavy for them to carry. Their dream had turned into a nightmare, and they now seek ways of cutting down these responsibilities and, who knows, eventually perhaps, renounce them altogether.[14]

The French had for example set up schools for thousands of exiled children as well as for illiterate adults. While the achievement was evidence of French know-how, the main concern of the Russian refugees was the lack of food. Furs and diamonds had gone a long while ago. If there was still a silver dish or cigarette case to sell, or a faded ball gown or some other object testifying to the splendours of the past, it was quickly put on show and sold in the Russian bazaar in Constantinople.

A meeting with General Wrangel

Teague-Jones's mission at Constantinople was not confined to helping refugees and collaborating with Baroness Wrangel's good works. One of the political elements of his mission was to ensure liaison with General Denikin, and later with General Wrangel, two White generals, soldiers rather than politicians, whom their close advisers recognised as being cast in completely different moulds. At the end of 1921 there were many who believed that the Whites would have been able to march on Moscow if General Wrangel had been in command in the Crimea from the beginning of the offensive rather than General Denikin. Struve, the foreign minister in the Wrangel government since Denikin's abdication at the end of March 1920, was also of this opinion. Struve had been a supporter of General Wrangel from the outset, and saw in him the only person capable of restoring order to the anti-Bolshevik movement and making a success of the counter-offensive against the Reds. The Wrangel government's diplomatic relationships were therefore extremely complex. The weakness of the Whites made pragmatism obligatory. This was not lacking in Struve's plan, his objective being to realise a 'Two-Russia' policy which would have allowed Wrangel to take part in the negotiations with Soviet Russia.[15] It was also necessary to win the diplomatic and economic support of the Allies. As we have seen, Teague-Jones had a rather sceptical view of the speed with which the French had recognised the Wrangel government, a haste which was not a true reflection of the hesitations of the French government, whose:

different polices were determined by a number of contradictory considerations, of which the most important was perhaps the difficulty of knowing who would be most capable of ensuring compensation for the French assets seized in Russia in 1917–1918: the Soviet Government or the Whites? Whichever was the case, neither England nor France believed that Bolshevism could be an international problem, which is why neither was willing to give the kind of support to the anti-Bolshevik leadership which was essential for Struve's strategy.[16]

THE RETREAT OF THE WHITE ARMIES

In fact, French military support was based on proposed engagements of an extremely onerous kind which the Wrangel government would never have been able to honour. Furthermore, on 2 April 1920 Great Britain had announced that it would no longer support the anti-Bolshevik armed forces and that it was asking for an immediate truce with Soviet Russia.

According to Struve:

the brusque reversal of English policy in favour of an agreement with the Bolsheviks can be explained by events in Persia and the arrival of Krasin. The new policy, which has been criticised even in England, may change; however, so far as stimulating a European movement as envisaged in telegram 515 is concerned, one must not rely on it. Maklakov and I had an interview today with Millerand. He declares categorically that at present the policy of France remains unchanged. Nevertheless he must be given help to support us. As for the British requests, it is better to respond to them without irritation as friendly advice with which it is impossible for us to conform. We must without fail make the English understand the absolute impossibility for us of entering into direct talks with the Bolsheviks. Mediation based on a capitulation or even on an amnesty is equally impossible. On the other hand, it is necessary to envisage the possibility of talks at a later date based on recognition of the inviolability of our territory and Cossack territory, and on the liquidation of political groupings in the Caucasus, which is a matter of interest to the English themselves. At that point we could counter English proposals for a capitulation with conditions which would be acceptable to us and capable of satisfying the army. This point of view is one with which the French have no quarrel. What matters for us is the clarity and firmness of our internal policy, as described in my telegram to you, and a sincere willingness to act in concert with the Poles.[17]

This, then, was the context of Teague-Jones's mission at a point when Great Britain, out of pragmatic considerations, was preparing once more to embrace a prudent policy of non-commitment. It was an informal mission, on the margins of official diplomacy, for although Teague-Jones looked rather sceptically on the question of recognising the Wrangel government, he was sympathetic to the general as a person and to the historic drama that was playing out in the Crimea.

Teague-Jones actually met Wrangel on board a British ship off the Crimea on 17 October 1920. Impressed by the grandeur and tragedy of General Wrangel's personality, as he disclosed the circumstances of the forthcoming White defeat, Teague-Jones would preserve the memory of this meeting. General Wrangel was easily recognisable with his long, lean figure, aristocratic features and distinguished profile, and was the complete physical opposite of the members of the Soviet government whose caricatures appeared frequently in Teague-Jones's personal papers. Struck with the general's good looks, Teague-Jones took his photograph at the end of the meeting described below. Wrangel, who had no illusions about the outcome of the conflict with the Reds, had by mid-October 1920 already drawn the inevitable conclusion: the Whites would lose because the Reds were in the process of considerably strengthening their forces. He confided to Teague-Jones that:

it is true that their casualties are considerably greater than our own, but they are able to draw on fresh reserves which we cannot and they are in a position to keep up a tremendous pressure on our defences. Up till a few days ago I continued to be optimistic, and was even confident that I could continue to hold Perekop which, as you know, is a narrow neck which 10 000 determined men ought to be able to hold against several times that number. But just lately, we have been having abnormally cold weather for so early in the winter. A few days ago the ice was already forming on the winding channels which flank the actual Perekop. Then it became clear to me that within a couple of weeks at the most, the enemy would be able to cross the ice and bring up their artillery and transport, and launch attacks at any of the scores of different points. With their overwhelming superiority in numbers, we could not possibly hope to hold them. These are cold, bitter cold facts. Curiously, not many people seem to have thought of the ice problem, yet, but they soon will. Therefore I have to prepare for the worst. If the Perekop goes, then in a matter of days the whole of the Crimea will be overrun. We shall fight rearguard actions all the way to Sevastopol but there we will be literally pushed into the sea.

To this rather pessimistic conclusion the general then added:

I want you to please explain the situation clearly to General Harrington and warn him that while I cannot even guess how many, or indeed how few, of our wounded we may be able to evacuate by sea, I have hesitated to begin requisitioning shipping for fear of starting a general panic but the probability is that many thousands of sick and wounded military, not to mention civilian refugees, will flood to Constantinople during the next few weeks. We will certainly fight to the very last, but that, briefly, is the warning I want you to convey to your people in Constantinople. And now I must hurry back to the front.[18]

These poignant words underline the strategic importance of Perekop, a village on the isthmus that links the Crimea with the rest of Ukraine. A fortified place, Perekop occupied a commanding position over the Crimean Khanate. In 1736, during one of the Russo-Turkish wars, the Russians had taken the fortifications of Perekop by assault, leaving the Tatar fortress in ruins, and dealing a severe blow to the independence of the Crimean Khanate. Perekop, in line with General Wrangel's pessimistic predictions, did indeed prove to be the key event in the civil war, at the end of which the Reds succeeded in pushing the White Army out of the Crimea. The village, which was the southernmost on the isthmus which separates the Gulfs of Karkinitsk and Sivash, was practically wiped off the map after it had been razed to the ground by the Red Army. In 1932 the Soviet authorities were to build a new Perekop, Krasnoperekopsk ('Perekop the Red'), positioned this time some 30 kilometres further south at the southern end of the isthmus.

Upon resuming his account of this historic interview, Teague-Jones depicts the urgent atmosphere. All this, he recalls:

had been said very quickly, and I gave my word to carry out the General's wishes. We went out on deck and were joined by the Captain. He assured us there was no hurry, for he had kept the sailing time open. 'Would His Excellency do him and his ship the honour of a parting drink'? But the General declined with thanks and begged to defer the pleasure for a future occasion. Meanwhile the sun was nearing the horizon, but the deck was still bathed in sunlight. I had my camera in my brief case and I felt a sudden impulse. 'Will you please do me a favour and allow me to take a quick photograph? I am sure the Baroness would like to have

148

one.' The General smiled. 'Very well, then, but please make it a quick one'. So I snapped him as he stood on the deck. Minutes later he shook hands with the Commander and myself and he was formally 'Piped away' into his waiting launch.

The Skipper and I watched the tall slim figure descending with steady step and head erect until with a parting salute he boarded the naval pinnace which promptly cast off and headed at full speed for the shore.

'There goes a magnificent soldier' I said. 'Yes' the Commander agreed, 'and a very brave man. And now let's go and drink to his health and wish him all the luck that he's going to need so badly'.[19]

Such is the story of Teague-Jones's photograph of Wrangel, taken at dusk on 17 October 1920.

General Wrangel's prophecy of events in the Crimea was borne out in the weeks that followed his brief meeting with Teague-Jones. Perekop, which Wrangel had hoped would hold out for a considerable time because of its fortifications, was almost completely destroyed by continuous Red attacks. Worse than the Reds was the cold, which had reached record levels (up to–16C): due to their inadequate clothing, the Whites died of cold when they did not die fighting. At the end of November Wrangel confessed to having lost, in two weeks, around 25,000 men killed, wounded or sick out of the 50,000 available to him on this front. But he could draw some pleasure from his success in evacuating his men by sea: 130,000 of them were to arrive at Tsargrad—his name for Constantinople—in November 1920. Wrangel told Struve[20] that, despite the retreat, he felt a moral satisfaction such as he had never felt after his most brilliant victories, since all the essentials had been saved during the evacuation, and above all the morale of the troops had been preserved intact:

My briefest appearance, even in the harbour here, is greeted by hurrahs from all the ships whose like I never heard either at Velikoknajeska or at Tsaritsyn. If this time Europe does not remain blind, and if, having finally understood the threat to the world which Bolshevism represents, it allows us to keep the Army, our retreat can be transformed into victory.[21]

Tragically, events in Transcaucasia, which Teague-Jones was to witness in 1920–1, were to prove the contrary.

The Caucasian imbroglio

How had the situation evolved in this region, one judged by Teague-Jones to be of vital importance? Following their logic of restoring the empire, the Whites were planning to reconquer the Russian Empire via the Crimea and the Caucasus, where three independent republics had been established in the period since 1918. In fact, in the wake of the October 1917 Revolution and the desertion of Russian soldiers, the Caucasus front had collapsed, opening a breach into which the Ottoman Army had plunged.[22] The Ottoman offensive launched by Enver Pasha, the minister for war, had as its objective the liberation of the irredentist Turkish lands (Kars, Ardahan,

Batumi) which had been seized by Russia, raising the Muslim populations, reaching Baku and, from there, conquering Central Asia. Under a Convention for Allied Activity in Russia, signed on 23 December 1917, France and Britain agreed on the allocation of two zones of influence. While the Crimea was to be for the French, the Caucasus and Transcaucasia went to Great Britain, whose task was to organise and sustain resistance to the Turks and the Bolsheviks in a zone between the Black and the Caspian Seas. The organisation of nationalist forces in Transcaucasia—Georgian, Armenian and Azeri military units—had not only failed to stop the Turkish offensive, but had revealed the profound divergences separating the three nationalities in Transcaucasia. In the spring of 1918 only the Armenians had shown themselves determined to fight against the Turkish threat, waging a real 'Armeno-Turkish war', while at Baku the Azeris were on the contrary getting ready to welcome them with open arms. The Treaty of Brest-Litovsk, of 3 March 1918, signed by Russia and the Central Powers, stipulated the return to the Ottoman Empire of Kars, Ardahan and Batumi, taking no account of the wishes of the peoples of Transcaucasia who were now driven to secession. At first this took the form of a short-lived Transcaucasian Federation, whose independence was demanded by the Turks on 9 April 1918; the collapse which swiftly followed gave birth to three independent republics. Georgia, which had obtained German protection against the Turks, proclaimed its independence on 26 May 1918, followed by Azerbaijan on 27 May 1918. The National Armenian Council was almost forcibly constrained to proclaim the independence of Armenia on 28 May 1918, the very day that at Sardarabad, on the plain of Ararat, the Armenians managed to halt the Turks at the gates of Yerevan. It was a holding battle, not a victory. In reality it was the Turks, masters of the field, who dictated the terms of the Treaty of Batumi, signed on 4 June 1918. They were draconian so far as Armenia was concerned, reducing its territory to a miniscule area of 10,000 square kilometres. Although Georgia came off slightly better, Turkish favours naturally went to Azerbaijan, which was gratified with a treaty of friendship. During the summer of 1918, while Teague-Jones was shuttling non-stop between Krasnovodsk and Baku, the Turkish objective was to take Baku with the help of the Azeris. In the manuscript history of his mission in the Caucasus, Teague-Jones recalls that the sole sources of information for the British were the reports emanating from the British mission in Tiflis commanded by Colonel Pike. The mission's existence was brutally cut short by the arrival of the Germans in Tiflis, and it was obliged to fall back on Vladikavkaz in the North Caucasus, where Pike perished at the hands of the Bolsheviks.

Back to Baku

The end of the First World War put a stop to the German and Turkish race to Baku. The three Transcaucasian republics could now consolidate their positions. The defeat of the Ottomans allowed the British to reoccupy Azerbaijan, where a national Azeri identity was beginning to emerge. For its part, Armenia succeeded in enlarging its territory by annexing the provinces of Kars and Ardahan. In Georgia the Menshevik party, which had gained widespread popular support, devoted itself to building the Georgian state. The three republics were pluralist parliamentary democracies inspired by the Western model, and governed by socialist and/or nationalist parties hostile to Bolshevism: the Mensheviks in Georgia, the Dashnaks (the Revolutionary Armenian Federation) in Armenia and the Musavat in Azerbaijan. All three faced considerable internal difficulties, but in Armenia, totally enclosed geographically and cut off from the world, submerged by refugees and orphans from the genocide in 1915, the economic and social situation was particularly severe during the winter of 1918–19, when famine and epidemics began to spread. Soon caught in a vice between the Soviet threat and the Turkish war of independence led by Mustafa Kemal, the three republics were also confronted with the question of their borders. As in the Balkans, it was difficult to reconcile the conflicting territorial aspirations of each of the Transcaucasian nations. The issue resulted in a short war between Armenia and Georgia in 1918, and a permanent state of conflict between Armenia and Azerbaijan. From 1918 to 1921 there was violent fighting between Armenians and Azeris for possession of the three adjoining provinces of Nakhichevan, Zangezur and Nagorno-Karabakh. For both Armenians and Azeris what was at stake was the construction of a true national territory.

In 1919, at the time of the Paris Peace Conference, the three Transcaucasian republics waited for Allied recognition of their independence. But for a variety of reasons this was slow in coming. The British and French were in no hurry to recognise the independence of the Transcaucasian republics so long as there was hope of a victory for Denikin. On 16 June 1919 Georgia and Azerbaijan signed a mutual defence pact against a return of White Russian imperialism, which Armenia refused to join. It was only when the defeat of the Whites was beyond doubt that the Allied Supreme Council recognised Georgia and Azerbaijan de facto, followed by Armenia a week later. But in a parallel move, the Allies decided not to send any troops to Transcaucasia to forestall the very real threat of a Bolshevik invasion, but instead only to help with arms and supplies. In accordance with the new direction of British policy—Lloyd George was of the belief that the whole of the Caucasus should belong to the Soviet sphere of influence—the last British troops evacuated Batumi on 9 July 1920, leaving the Transcaucasian nations to their pre-ordained fate. But the absence of military support did not signify a lack of political interest. How otherwise can one explain Teague-Jones's presence in the Caucasus at a time when the territory had once again been abandoned by Great Britain? In truth, despite the withdrawal of British troops, the British presence had not altogether vanished. A political mission under Sir Oliver Wardrop had been installed at Tiflis, and it was under its auspices that Teague-Jones carried out missions in Transcaucasia which are recorded in 100 unpublished pages in his personal records. His was an intelligence rather than an operational mission, unlike some of his time as a political agent in Transcaspia, as Transcaucasia had largely been left to its own devices since the beginning of 1920.

In Teague-Jones's archives in the British Library there is a brown box file holding pages of carbon copies. It is labelled 'Secret' and contains several dozen pages in

Teague-Jones's handwriting about the situation in the Caucasus and Central Asia between 1918 and 1922. It is a logbook, the only one he is known to have preserved. It is of inestimable value even though it is a collection of fragments and brief notes, as he is putting down his analyses in the heat of the moment, with no self-censorship and none of his customary professional revisions. The file also reflects, in its disorder, the chaotic sequence of military events and the methods of the intelligence agent, revealing Teague-Jones's personal views, which are pragmatic and are often discreetly or indeed openly in disagreement with decisions taken by the politicians in London. For since the retreat from Transcaspia—and even more since the retreat from Transcaucasia—the Reds had been advancing. In February 1920 Krasnovodsk fell into their hands: this predictable event marked the Sovietisation of Transcaspia, but it also had the potential to affect Transcaucasia, on the eastern side of the Caspian. In the months preceding the evacuation of the Caucasus by the British, Teague-Jones offers the following prediction:

Much depends on the immediate attitude of the government of Azerbaïjan. In some time past the Transcaspian Bolsheviks have been at pains to impress upon the Azerbaijanis that their aims in regard to pan-Islamism are common and that a linking up of the two governments on the Caspian will be the first important step towards the achievement of these aims. It appears possible therefore that the Baku Government may at once come to terms with the Reds in Krasnovodsk. On the other hand should they not wish to do this—the Bolshevik party in Baku is so strong that the Azerbaijanis may find their hands forced. The main factor is the attitude of the shipping—if intercourse by ship with Krasnovodsk is allowed then Bolshevism in Baku may be considered inevitable. The opinion of a number of people is that in the event of an outbreak of Bolshevism in Baku—or in the case of the Turkistan Bolsheviks obtaining a footing there the German influence behind the Reds will insist on the latter coming to terms with the Azerbaijanis—and leaving them who are Turks and the allies of Germany to run their own country, the Bolsheviks meanwhile contenting themselves in the linking up with Georgia. The latter country is admittedly ripe for a spontaneous outbreak of Bolshevism at the present moment, even without awaiting the actual linking up with the Turkistan Bolsheviks and should such outbreak take place then a simultaneous movement might be expected in Batum, where for many reasons the soil is more fertile for Bolshevism than it was some twelve months ago. The opinion has been expressed by many people that the only hope of saving the Caucasus is for the British to move forward troops into Baku and hold the Caspian. It is thought that with the British in the Caspian there would be no fighting and the Red advance in a westerly direction at all events stopped. If we do not hold Baku and with it incidentally the entire Caucasus, then there is little point in our endeavouring to hold Batum alone.[23]

Teague-Jones's sketch of the political forces within Transcaucasia shows the variety of possible options in the event of a future British presence in the Caucasian and Transcaucasian regions. In Azerbaijan, the Musavat, whose main leader was Rasul Zade, represented the nationalist movement, which was in favour of the independence of Azerbaijan, but also of concluding a treaty with Turkey. This party, whose existence went back to the notorious Armeno-Tatar wars of 1905, and was born to a large extent out of a reaction to Armenian nationalism as represented by the Dashnak party, was intransigently pro-Turk. Moreover, after the collapse of the Russian front in the Caucasus in 1917, the Musavatists had succeeded in opening an invasion route for the Ottoman Army, allowing Nuri Pasha to establish his headquarters at Elizabetpol. Although the Musavat was the dominant party in the government of independent Azerbaijan, they nonetheless had to reckon with the Ittihad, a pro-Turk party whose intrigues at a time when a Soviet–Kemalist alliance was secretly beginning to take shape were interesting in the highest degree to Teague-Jones. In his notebook he writes that:

the political aims of Itihad are directed towards the founding of a pan-islamic empire with its centre in Asia Minor. The party includes among its adherents in Baku a number of Young Turks. Nuri pasha himself has of late definitely thrown in his lot with this party and is striving to oust from power the Mussavat in order to render supreme the pan-Islamic Ittihad. The latter's plan of campaign is to cooperate closely with Mustafa Kemal in creating a state of anarchy throughout Turkey in Asia and the Caucasus and thus thwart the Allied powers in their efforts to enforce the execution of the peace terms with Turkey. At the present moment they consider it to their interest to cooperate with the growing threat of Bolshevism and German intrigue with a view to rendering insecure the rear of the Volunteer Army. Hence the active measures now being taken by the Mussavat to cause anti-Russian risings in Daghestan, and to foster in every possible way bitter anti-Russian feeling among the population of Azerbaijan. All this of course with the deliberate intention of causing an outburst of Moslem feeling which should result in the expulsion of all foreigners, Russians included, from the Caucasus. In accordance with these plans we have thus seen how when certain bolsheviks had been arrested by the Azerbaijan Government their release was persistently demanded and ultimately obtained by the Ittihadists. Nuri Pasha and Karabekoff have been actively agitating against the Government in the districts, their agitation taking the form of emphasising the corrupters and bad administration of the Mussavatists and asserting that there could never be peace or welfare without the outside assistance of the Turks.[24]

In opposition to these two parties the Hummet, principally composed of SR and SD, did not play a major role in Azerbaijani politics, although it showed a clear leaning towards Bolshevism and represented the extreme left among Muslim revolutionaries. But it did not exist as a regional party anywhere in Transcaucasia, unlike the Mensheviks in Georgia. The Transcaucasian Bolsheviks were affiliated without exception to the pan-Russian Bolshevik party, but they were also able to draw on local agitators and propaganda resources. For Teague-Jones, it was the social conditions in the Caucasus that explained the Bolshevik's popularity; the Bolsheviks enjoyed strong support among the proletariat of Baku, while in the provinces the Tatar population was manifesting discontent with the local authorities, which had been dominated by the Beks since the tsarist era. Their feudal and corrupt form of government had remained unchanged, as had their privileges, which they continued to exercise within their domains. Thus in independent Musavatist Azerbaijan the climate of social discontent present throughout the towns and countryside favoured the rise in pro-Bolshevik sentiment. Elsewhere in Transcaucasia, and particularly in Georgia, a poor country depending on external aid, without any industry or agriculture worthy of the name:

the vast majority of the population are ready to welcome the Bolsheviks as their preservers. Georgia is in ignorance of the real nature of Soviet control and believes readily the glowing promises of free bread, housing and clothing, held out to her by the Bolshevik agents. With the arrival of Soviet troops the poorer classes which include practically the entire population look forward with eagerness to taking the power into their own hands and putting an end to their present miserable state of existence.[25]

Teague-Jones also analysed the case of Dagestan, where there were extreme social tensions: landless peasants on the plains, Muslim brotherhoods in the mountains which had often been infiltrated by Bolshevik agitators, pro-Turk sentiment; altogether the region, like Azerbaijan, seemed to be hesitating between two allegiances, the Soviet and the Turkish.

How could the British, in the face of such detailed but discouraging reports, deal with the situation?

From all the evidence to hand it must be accepted that the Bolsheviks intend overrunning Transcaucasia. Whether this will materially affect the Pan Islamic situation or not, the result will be a blow to Allied prestige which will be nothing short of disastrous. The Allies and primarily the British will lose their access to a considerable area of country, which they might if they wished definitely control. To save the situation immediate action is called for. Bolshevism threatens the very existence of the independent Caucasian states and the danger can only be met by an immediate coalition of Azerbaijan, Georgia and Armenia, strongly supported by the Allies. The latter must play a strong hand—not for the mere philanthropic defence of smaller nations, but because their own interests and the existence at least of the British Empire demand it. The issues appear quite clear—a general flare up and anarchy throughout the Caucasus or prompt and effective intervention by the Allies.[26]

However, the withdrawal of British troops from Batumi in the summer of 1920 coincided with a new phase in British politics instigated by Lloyd George, who was in favour of resuming trade with Soviet Russia[27] (his speech in the House of Commons on 7 June 1920 provoked a hearty round of laughter when he remarked: 'this country has opened up most of the cannibal trade in the world'). Although Moscow recognised Georgia on 7 May 1920 and Armenia on 28 October 1920, while in November 1920 the League of Nations refused to admit them as members, these were essentially matters of tactics. The republics of Transcaucasia, squeezed in a vice between the Red Army and Mustafa Kemal's army, had only a few months of independence left to live. Teague-Jones was present for the end-game in Transcaucasia.

Georgia on the eve of the Red invasion

In January 1921 Teague-Jones, in company with Captain Rienold, left Constantinople on a mission to Georgia. At Batumi, where he took the train to Tbilisi (Tiflis), he was immediately made aware of the return to the region of the Bolsheviks, who had been driven out in 1918:

We found to our amusement that the other coupé separated from us by a partition door, was occupied by the Bolshevik mission from Batum, consisting of two evil faced Jews and an equally unpleasant Jewess. We dozed comfortably for the night, and awoke [at] daybreak to a strange silence. The windows were covered with ice, and it was with difficulty that we could make out a blurred landscape deeply buried in snow which was still falling steadily.[28]

In Tbilisi Teague-Jones was met by the British representative, Colonel Stokes, who was in charge of the British military mission in Transcaucasia. The mission was housed in a mansion belonging to a rich Georgian, Arkady Khostaria, who had obtained a petroleum concession in the north of Persia from the tsar in 1916. Khostaria, a wealthy eccentric, had ordered a leopard's head and an elephant's head from Rowland Ward, the London taxidermists, as decorations for his house. Teague-Jones seems to have enjoyed the pleasures of the cosmopolitan city of Tbilisi, the capital of independent Georgia, and the political and cultural capital of the Caucasus, which was about to fall into Bolshevik hands. The prime minister of the independent Republic of Armenia, Alexander Khatisian, had been mayor of Tbilisi before the war, recalling an era when the Armenians were almost a majority in the city. Teague-Jones found time to explore the city built on the encircling slopes of the Kura Valley, crossing from Sololaki to Avlabari on the other side of the river, where there was an Armenian church and theatre, and passing through the picturesque quarter of Abanotubani, with its baths. Stokes took Teague-Jones for a lunch, during which they flirted assiduously with the Postovskaya sisters. Teague-Jones suggested that Stokes would eventually marry one of them, but he does not say how much he was smitten by the charms of the other sister. The city seemed hospitable, the women prepossessing and far from shy. There was a dinner with the Melikovs, one of the old families descended from a princely Tbilisi dynasty, and then an evening at the opera. And it was not the quality of the performance of Don Giovanni which held Teague-Jones's attention that evening, for the audience was the real show:

The opera house was a surprisingly fine building and would have done justice to many a larger European city, but the most striking thing about it was the audience. The house was filled to capacity, and never have I seen before or since so many beautiful women and such a brightly coloured assembly of people in any one building. Even in my early days in St Petersburg when I had been taken to an Imperial ball, I had never seen anything quite so striking. There had been, perhaps more glitter and magnificence, but here in this Tiflis opera house I swear there was more real beauty per square foot of floor space then in the Imperial capital.[29]

The stay at Tbilisi continued on this festive note. On the evening of 1 February 1921, Stokes gave a dinner for some officers at which Teague-Jones met the elderly General Georgy Orbeliani. There was a banquet on the occasion of the de jure recognition of Georgia's independence: the dinner, which was presided over by Noé Jordania, the president of the Council of Ministers, provided an opportunity for Teague-Jones to do the rounds of the foreign diplomatic representatives in Georgia. Apart from the British, and Commissar Scheinmann, representing the RSFSR (the Russian Federative Soviet Republic), he also met M. Chevalier from the French mission. The presence of a large number of Germans, among them von Rauscher, von Druffel and Anders, was a reminder of the protectorate over independent Georgia which Germany had formerly exercised. Von Druffel had been in Persia during the war, which gave Teague-Jones another chance to talk about Wassmuss and the fate of his right-hand man Bruggmann, who had been sent off to India after Teague-Jones's success in arresting him. It was not an abstemious occasion, one toast following another, and Teague-Jones could hear Alshibai, the former Georgian representative in Azerbaijan who was sitting on the other side of the table, assuring his next door neighbour von Rauscher that in the very near future the Tatar population would revolt and massacre the Russians. The day after this banquet there was a reception for the Georgians at the British mission. Teague-Jones's own mission was over. He had to return to Batumi where Captain Seymour was expecting him. They dined together and he passed over his news. Then he embarked on the destroyer *HMS Trinidad* which took him back, via Trebizond, to Constantinople on 17 February 1921. Almost as soon as he arrived, he learned of the sudden deterioration of the situation in the Caucasus, the arrival of the Bolsheviks in Georgia (11–12 February 1921) and the anti-Soviet insurrection in Armenia (18 February 1921). There was nothing for it but to retrace his steps: Teague-Jones was back in Batumi in the early hours of the morning of 27 February 1921. It was icy cold, the sun was shining on the snow, and in the distance the mountains of Ajaria, the outlying spurs of the Lesser Caucasus, were sparkling, reminding Teague-Jones of hunting expeditions in the high mountains of Kashmir. At Batumi, Captain Seymour of the *Calypso* was amused to see him back so soon, and told him at once that the French on the *Waldeck-Rousseau* had bombarded houses all along the coast. As for Colonel Stokes, who had been evacuated to Batumi at the same time as British subjects, refugees and persons under British protection, he exclaimed: 'What! Back already? You seem determined to run into trouble!'[30]

Stokes told Teague-Jones that before leaving Tiflis he had an interview with Kiazim Bey—General Karabekir—representing the Kemalists. During the conversation the latter disclosed that he was open to a compromise with the Georgians over the territorial status of Batumi.[31] The British mission, which had now fallen back on Batumi, had been housed in a residence formerly occupied by the Soviet consulate. The building was in a deplorable state and the abandoned files were of no interest, but Teague-Jones noticed the presence of some items of archaeological interest, a portrait of Nicholas II and a seal belonging to the Imperial Counter-Espionage Department. At Batumi, he lunched with Stokes, whose morale was at rock-bottom. The British commissar for Transcaucasia had always been an ardent defender of the cause of the independent republics. He had argued to the British authorities that Georgia and Armenia were prepared to fight against the Bolsheviks in defence of their independence, and that they therefore deserved British support. The fall of the Mensheviks in Georgia and of the Dashnaks in Armenia left the men in the field with little hope for the future and the impression that London had abandoned them mid-mission:

Stokes and I lunched in La France restaurant. We discussed the latest situation and could not see a single bright spot in it. Stokes, usually so cheerful, was very gloomy. He could not help likening the situation to Baku. There was no Armenian population to be massacred, but the Bolsheviks, though they might spare the Georgians, would deal ruthlessly with any of the Russian intelligentsia and their families who could not get away, and the Red troops would loot the town. Some very ugly stories of Red excesses in Tiflis were already coming through, but the air was full of rumours, and it was very difficult to know what was really happening.[32]

In the absence of reliable sources, their best informant was to be a Russian journalist, met through a London editor friend, who had already supplied a number of reliable reports containing first-hand news while Teague-Jones was in Constantinople. As he expected, his agent was able to give him a mass of detail that was impossible to obtain from official communiqués; he made a number of brief notes with the intention of writing them up on board ship while they were still fresh in his memory, and it may be this information that Teague-Jones confided to his brown notebook. In the meantime he had to ensure the safety of his journalist, who let it be known that this was probably his last journey to the Caucasus. The British mission ensured his protection by doing what was necessary to allow him to get out of Batumi.

Once Teague-Jones had a clearer view of the situation and of the imminent disaster, he went into town to do some shopping. He could not leave Batumi without a few bottles of his favourite Georgian wine from the vineyards of Kakhetia. His supplier in Batumi was a Greek merchant, but Teague-Jones arrived at his shop just as the Greek was about to take flight to the harbour; he explained that he had already sent off his wife and children and that he now had to flee himself. His main worry was that the Italian ship's captain would demand an exorbitant price for his passage. 'I regret you are going,' Teague-Jones said calmly,

'because I wanted some Kakhetian wine.' 'How much money have you got?' he rapped out. I told him I had exactly one English five-pound note. 'Give it to me', he said almost breathlessly. 'It will save my life, for with it I will have enough to get my passage'. 'Yes, but what about my wine?' 'Wine?' he gave a wild, almost hysterical, laugh. 'Wine? Look my friend. You give that five pounds and the whole store is yours. Tomorrow the Reds will be in, and they'll loot it anyway'. He glanced at his watch. 'There's just time. I'll come back to the shop with you, but come quickly. I dare not lose that ship; she sails in a couple of hours time'. He led the way breathlessly and I followed, not quite sure whether I was dreaming or that the man was mad. We reached the store, a vast cellar of a place, several steps down below street level. A couple of Adjar muslim assistants had been left in charge. Wine stores invariably employed Muslims because they could be trusted not to touch or pilfer alcohol.[33]

The Greek merchant was not lying; Teague-Jones was free to have all his stock. He advised him to forget about the Kakhetia wine in favour of more valuable liqueurs. He had some Shustov Imperial, reputed to be the best cognac in the world. Not to mention cases of Scotch whisky, which would require the help of the shop-assistant to transport. 'And now, says the Greek, please give me that five pounds. You don't know what it means to me and I can't feel secure until I have it right here inside this pocket.' Teague-Jones gave it to him, marvelling at his luck, and then immediately felt remorse: had he not behaved like a vulgar war-profiteer? But the Greek merchant absolved him of any scruples, since the goods were lost in any case, and the shop would be pillaged by the Red Army or destroyed by the Turks. He still had to track down some boats to carry the cases to the ship, where cargo of this kind was not authorised, and find ways of persuading the captain of the *Calypso* to take the cases on board along with the refugees. Once back in Constantinople, Teague-Jones was able to entertain his guests lavishly, but the tragic-comedy of the retreat from Batumi did not obscure the essence of the matter, the Red Army's advance into Georgia.

After boarding the *Calypso* in Batumi harbour, where the departure siren was already sounding on the morning of 28 February 1921, Teague-Jones shut himself up somewhere quiet and began to draft an accurate account[34] of the Red advance into Georgia:

The first phase of the Georgian tragedy concluded with the capture of Tiflis by the Bolsheviks and we are now witnessing what appears to be the culminating phase. In my last letter written a few days ago I gave you a sketch of the circumstances attending the commencement of hostilities and the assumed reasons of such hostilities. There is little to add: the Bolsheviks hold Tiflis and are making an effort to advance down the Black Sea coastal area to Batum. Up to yesterday the Red troops were still being held up at a place called Novi Athon (Athou) some ten miles northwards along the coast from Sukhumi. The Georgians had drafted reinforcements to that front, but I do not think they have any real hope of holding the enemy long. Some Bolshevik prisoners taken in that area presented a miserable spectacle. They were almost all boys aged 16–18 years, literally starving and ill clad—their clothing being all in tatters. They had long since lost all morale if they had ever had any and they told a piteous story which one cannot help believing of how they had been forcibly mobilised in their villages in the North of Russia and drafted down to the Caucasus to fight. They were treated as slaves and definitely told that they could choose between the Georgian bayonets or their own machine guns. The Red troops on the Black Sea front are now being reinforced from the Terek but the new material is said to be no better in quality and if the Georgian troops would only put their backs into it they would beat the Reds. The latter are adopting their usual tactics of outflanking their opponents and coming down in their near. It was in this manner, I understand that Gagri was occupied.

There was a marked paucity of detailed news from the Tiflis front. The Georgians were holding a line at Mtskhet, 20 miles west of the capital, where the Vladikavkaz road comes down from the north. There are excellent defensible positions there if the Georgians have the time and the skill to organise them. Latest reports stated that the Georgian staff intended withdrawing still further to Gori which is a very considerable distance further west along the railway line. The Georgian government have withdrawn to Kutais but I do not think they feel very safe there and if the Reds reach Poti there will be nothing to prevent them advancing up the railway line to Kutais. The general opinion is that Georgia is doomed and during the last two days there has been a marked deterioration in the morale of the Georgian troops, resulting in an increase of desertion. The success of the Bolsheviks is generally attributed to two main factors, a preponderance of artillery and cavalry. In both these arms the Georgians are very weak and are very limited in ammunition. It is now quite clear what the immediate plans of the Bolsheviks will be having captured Tiflis it is most probable that they will detach as many troops as they can spare and draft them to the Turkish front to liquidate the trouble in Armenia and also it is said push the Turks back to the frontiers of 1914. An intercepted order from Moscow to Scheinmann, the late Bolshevik representative in Tiflis supports this view. Apparently Baku had concluded that Tiflis had been already captured by the Reds on the 20th February and definite instructions were therefore sent to Scheinmann to fortify Tiflis and [to] draft troops to the Armenian front. This order may possibly account for the fact that the Bolsheviks have so far shown no inclination to advance westwards from Tiflis, though this [is] also explicable by the fact that the Red troops are doubtless busily engaged in looting Tiflis. At the same time my own personal impression is that with the capture of Tiflis, the Reds have carried out their major project of obtaining possession of the Armenian railway and of the Georgian capital and will not press further westwards. They may consider that the further conquest of the country can be more easily attained by an advance along the coast on to Batum. I think there can be no shadow of doubt as to the Red's intentions to occupy Batum. If only to prevent the Turks getting in before them. At the moment of writing (I am in Batum at present) Batum is anybody's town. The elements in the question are (1) the Georgian garrison which is by no means a strong one (2) the local Bolsheviks who have always been a well organised and numerous body but whose organisations have been badly weakened by the strong measures recently taken against them by the Georgians (3) the local Moslems whose aim is to establish their own autonomy who in their time have been bitterly anti-Georgian but who seem to consider at present that Georgian administration is with all its faults infinitely preferable to either the Bolsheviks or the Turks. Finally we have the Turks themselves. The latter are extremely problematical, and at the present moment it is absolutely impossible to foretell what exactly will happen. The general wish of the better classes of the population, Georgian Russian and Moslem alike, is that the Turks will step in and save the town and themselves from the scourge of Bolshevism. The population is praying for the Turk to come in. But will he? Yesterday a new arrival appeared in the person of a Kemalist delegate from Trebizond who informed the Georgian governor that he had been specially sent by the Nationalists to assure the Georgians that the Turks entertained no hostile intentions as regards Batum. He denied the rumours current for some time past that the Turks are concentrating troops in the coast.

Yet these Turkish assurances did not totally convince the population. In fact the Turks, taking advantage of Georgian difficulties and in order to attain additional ammunition in any bargaining with the Bolsheviks, had presented the Georgian government with an ultimatum demanding the occupation of the districts of Ardahan and Artvin as well as of the region of Batumi on 23 February.[35] This was how things stood when Teague-Jones left Georgia.

As he was back in Constantinople on 2 March 1921, Teague-Jones was not present during the invasion of Georgia that took place over the following three weeks. The Georgian government was hemmed in by the 80,000-strong Red Army advancing from the north and along the Black Sea Coast, and in the absence of any effective help from the Allies it had no option but to enter into truce negotiations which were concluded on 18 March in the presence of the representatives of the RSFSR, Enukidze and Svanidze. Two days previously, the Georgian Parliament, which had withdrawn to Batumi, had voted to move the government of independent Georgia abroad. Like the Greek merchant who had earlier dispensed a bounty of wines and spirits to Teague-Jones, Noé Jordania and the other Menshevik leaders embarked on an Italian ship at Batumi. The latter city, where the defence was directed by the military governor, Zakharia Aslanovich Mdivani, had surrendered to the Turks on 11 March, but Mdivani had evacuated it under pressure from the Revkom[36] in the city, which was evidence of a degree of Soviet–Turkish understanding. It was the end of the game for the British—Colonel Stokes arrived in his turn at Constantinople on 23 March—but not for the German mission which, Teague-Jones recalls, had always maintained friendly relations with the Bolsheviks; and indeed they were soon back in the Georgian capital, now in Soviet hands. With the re-conquest of Transcaucasia by Soviet Russia in mind, he notes: 'plus ça change, plus c'est la même chose'.

The view from Mount Ararat (February 1921)

There are numerous notes in Teague-Jones's journal on the general situation in Transcaucasia and the North Caucasus at the start of 1921, including detailed information on troop movements and on the number, equipment and position of the Red and Kemalist divisions respectively. Armenia, caught between the Kemalist hammer and the Soviet anvil and threatened with obliteration, had been Sovietised on 29 November 1920, bringing the experience of the Dashnak government to an end. The wholly unresisted invasion of Armenia by the XIth Red Army has been presented in Soviet historiography as an 'anti-Turkish offensive' and not as the pure and simple act of annexation it was. However, in February 1921 the Red Army, busy with the Sovietisation of Georgia, had disappeared from Armenia, leaving only a small number of troops on the territory as a covering force. Elsewhere, in the North Caucasus behind the Red Army, in Dagestan, Russia, Ukraine and Turkestan, disturbances and anti-Soviet insurrections multiplied. Red Army units posted at Ekaterinodar, Armavir, Stavropol and Vladikavkaz were suddenly recalled to the heart of Russian territory, to Ukraine and to the frontiers of Poland. Teague-Jones notes that:

this sudden change of plan coinciding with rumours of risings in Russia acted as an impulse to insurgent bands in the North Caucasus who have apparently sprung into activity throughout the North Caucasus from the Black Sea Coast to the Caspian. The coast road from Novorossisk to Tuapse is said to have been occupied by insurgents and fighting is reported between Reds and partisans in many of the villages. The garrison at Novorossisk has been greatly reduced and consists of remains of the Xth Army which has been partly merged into the Terek shock units and is partly distributed over the towns of the North Caucasus[37] [such as Anapa, Ekaterinodar, Maykop, Kavkazskaya and Stavropol].

With rumours of revolts in the North Caucasus, and peasant insurrections in the provinces of Saratov, Samara, Tambov and Orlov, Soviet power appeared not to have put down firm roots anywhere. The Armenian uprising of 18 February 1921, at which Teague-Jones was not present, but which he described from his Georgian vantage-point, was part of this general context and of the Soviet power vacuum during the short period while the XIth Red Army was intervening militarily in Georgia. Under the presidency of Simon Vratsian a revolutionary government, which was essentially made up of Dashnaks, took the name of 'Committee of Public Safety' while in the south-west, in the Zanzegur Mountains, a 'Mountain Republic of Armenia', a Dashnak place of refuge, embodied the resistance to Sovietisation. Teague-Jones bears witness to this development in his journal, noting that Zanzegur 'is now free of Bolshevik troops and has assumed a quasi-independent attitude under the control of Ter Minassian late minister of war in Armenia who is said to be form-ing some sort of a government'.[38] From what Khatissian said during his interview at Tiflis, Teague-Jones gathers that Ruben Ter Minassian[39] was ready to advance into Armenia and to march on Yerevan at the head of the Mountain Republic of Armenia:

He is at present deterred from starting an offensive by the fear that the Turk may make this an excuse for a further advance. The Dashnak Committee would like Britain to intervene and bring about a Turko-Armenian treaty, merely to guarantee the neutrality of the Turks in the event of Armenian bolshevik hostilities.[40]

The Sovietisation of Armenia, which was accomplished in two stages, in November 1920 and April 1921, was not an example of proletarian revolution. It took place in the pivotal year of 1921 which saw the birth of the Soviet–Turkish entente. It brought the territorial and strategic interests of Soviet Russia in the East into conflict with those of Kemalist Turkey: having already annexed the city and fortress of Kars, the Turks occupied Alexandropol in Armenia, and maintained detachments all along the railway line to Yerevan. In his journal, Teague-Jones notes the positions held by the Bolsheviks: they consisted simply of a battalion of troops based at Amamly and another battalion of 500 soldiers at Karakilis. A few, mainly cavalry units, were based in the areas of Voskresenka, Bakizend, Nikitna, Dilijan and, north of Lake Sevan (Lake Gochka), at Semenovka, Elenovka and Karakir. The Bolshevik presence was therefore not a massive one, and Teague-Jones notes that, in contrast, the bulk of the Armenian artillery was still available and that, in particular, the 1st Armenian infan-try regiment, which was still intact, had not been demobilised. In the confused situ-ation in the winter of 1921, Armenian territory had been split into different entities. In the north, small detachments of Georgian troops still present in the area were keeping the civil administration going, although the new Soviet Armenian authorities had ordered them to withdraw. South of Zangezur, at Meghri on the Iranian frontier, Ruben Ter Minassian had formed an independent government which had completely eluded Bolshevik control, while after a Dashnak congress at Tadev on 26 April 1921 a 'Mountain Republic of Armenia' was formed under the leadership of the militant Dashnak, Nejdeh. In Nakhichevan in the south-west the situation was complicated by clashes between Turkish and Bolshevik detachments.

In the winter of 1920 to 1921 Teague-Jones's analysis was as follows:

At the present moment all interest centres in the solution of the Armenian problem and everything will depend on the attitude to be adopted by Soviet Russia. That the Bolshevik leaders are both deeply concerned at the seriousness of the problem and are also of different opinions as to its solution is evident from telegraphic conversation which took place in December 26th between Mravian and Atabekoff, Armenian representatives who had arrived at Baku from Moscow and the Armenian Minister for Foreign Affairs in Erivan, Bekzadian.

161

The above representatives who had interviewed both Lenin and Trotsky in Moscow stated that the former had declared that Russia has no intention of allowing the Armenian question to become a casus belli with any power, particularly with the Turkish Nationalists. Russia did not want to fight at present and could not fight. All that she could do would be to help Armenia in supplies and money and concentrate sufficient Red troops in the country to exercise a moral influence over the Nationalists. ... Trotsky held the opposite view that the strategic importance of Armenia was far too great to be jeopardised. A Red Army must be raised and organised in Armenia which would enable that country to be used to advantage by Russia in any future operations in which she might be implicated in that part of the world. As a means of organising the Red Army, Trotsky proposed to russify Armenia by transferring to Russia all Armenian officers serving in Armenia and replace them by Russians. The situation in Armenia as described by Bekzadian is very bad. There was a shortage of bread and the country was in a chaotic state. Relations between the Bolsheviks and the Turks left much to be desired. The latter were interfering in the internal affairs, were violating frontiers and holding up grain trains. The presence of the Turks in Alexandropol was unbearable to the Armenian Soviet authorities who were most anxious for the Bolsheviks to expel them and occupy Alexandropol themselves, or at least establish a combined occupation of that town. The above statement by the Armenian Foreign Commissar is a startling admission of the anxiety of the Armenian Soviet authorities regarding the situation in that country. The entire question resolves itself into whether the Bolsheviks intend to hold Armenia with Red troops or not, or to be more explicit, whether they are able to occupy Armenia with Red Troops or not.[41]

To this question Teague-Jones responds with a negative, since in the precise context of early 1921, in the gap between the two Sovietisations of Armenia, everything still seemed possible. As Lenin had declared that Soviet Russia would not fight against Turkey for Armenia, the Bolsheviks, he notes:

would be unable to maintain themselves in Armenia at all and they would have to face the alternative of taking up a defensive line in the highlands of Eastern Armenia or of retreating right back to Baku. Of the two alternatives the latter is the more probable in that should the Bolsheviks actually be forced into hostilities against the Turks, the Moslem rising which is often predicted in Azerbaijan and Daghestan would most certainly take place and with communications threatened on every side the Bolsheviks would be unable to hold Azerbaijan and would be forced back to the Caspian.[42]

Was this a likely scenario? Or did it instead reflect wishful thinking on the part of Teague-Jones, who, as things currently stood, continued to envisage opportunities for an active British policy? In February 1921 the situation in Transcaucasia made such a first-hand assessment conceivable, even though it was to be shown as mistaken, since Armenia was to be thoroughly Sovietised for a second time in April 1921. The Soviet–Turkish entente, confirmed by the signature on 16 March 1921 of the Treaty of Moscow between Soviet Russia and Kemalist Turkey, explains the Sovietisation of Transcaucasia. Teague-Jones was well aware of the consequences, even if he privately regretted Great Britain's abandonment of the strategic and military system constructed in 1919 for the protection of India. He felt it all the more bitterly because he was one of the creators of this system in Transcaspia. But from now on, in London as at Simla, at Westminster as in Whitehall, those in charge of British politics rejected any idea of a 'forward policy'. It is in the context of dismantling the military empire that the British presence in Transcaucasia was brought to an end, in accordance with the change in diplomatic thinking and the acceptance of the Kemalist movement. Leafing through Teague-Jones's journal, one cannot help but be struck by the lucidity of his analysis of the Soviet–Turkish entente.

Teague-Jones and the Soviet–Turkish entente

The complex sequence of events which led to the delineation of the Soviet–Turkish frontier in 1921 is not solely of interest because of the accompanying sacrifice of the three Transcaucasian republics' independence. It constitutes one of the most important chapters in the history of international relations following the Great War, given the strategic importance of the region, which was destined to be one of the active fronts in the cold war throughout the twentieth century. The entente between the Bolsheviks and the Kemalists, the first signs of which Teague-Jones had spotted during his posting in Constantinople, is an essential part of events: it is known that London was given precise information on all the preliminary contacts in reports from the British High Commission based on evidence from its agents[43] in Constantinople. Teague-Jones's journal, which contains drafts of notes on this subject, is therefore an interesting source, particularly since London never disseminated this information, which presaged the early obsolescence of the Treaty of Sèvres (10 August 1920), which had been imposed on Turkey by the Allies. The annulment of the Treaty of Sèvres was in fact Mustafa Kemal's prime ambition. For him, the existence of an Armenian Republic constituted by the four vilayets of Van, Bitlis, Diarbekir and Erzerum was out of the question. Moreover, the Soviet–Turkish entente allowed the Kemalists to reclaim the former vilayets of Kars and Ardahan which the Russians had annexed in 1878, and additionally to annex the Mount Ararat region which since that date had stood as a symbol of the Armenian nation. The Soviet–Turkish entente also determined the ways in which the Sovietisation of Transcaucasia was accomplished internally: Armenia was transformed into a Soviet Republic with a miniscule land-area, sundered from the disputed regions of Nagorno-Karabakh and Nakhichevan, which were allocated to Azerbaijan at the request of Turkey. Finally, the rapprochement between Kemalists and Bolsheviks, dictated by pragmatism rather than ideology, allowed the Turkish nationalists to draw on Soviet financial and military assistance, a factor which was to prove conclusive in the last act of Mustafa Kemal's military victory, the decisive triumph over the Greeks in Asia Minor in 1922.

A confluence of interests

When he was posted to the British High Commission in Constantinople in 1919, Teague-Jones was one of the agents who knew the most about the developing situation in Turkey. At this point, he recalls:

the Kemalist revolt was beginning to gather strength in Anatolia, but its importance had been greatly underestimated by the Allies. Mr Lloyd George was much more impressed by the claims of M. Venizelos that his Greek troops could deal effectively with the clique of young rebel Turks headed by Mustafa Kemal. It was a fatal misjudgement. A second miscalculation by the Allies was the effect produced by the excessively severe terms of the Treaty of Sèvres, coupled with the fact that the Allies preferred to deal with the discredited old Ottoman regime rather than with the Turkish Nationalists. The Sultan was induced to sign the Treaty, but the immediate result was to create a surge of popular sympathy away from himself and his regime, of Mustafa Kemal and his nationalists. It was at this point that the Moscow leaders saw their great opportunity. They were convinced that Britain and her allies were backing the wrong horse, that the Ottoman regime was finished, and that the Kemalist Nationalists were the coming power. Moscow lost no time in recognising the nationalists as the new government of Turkey.[44]

Although written sometime after the event, these perceptive lines in Teague-Jones's autobiographical account of his missions in Transcaucasia reflect his view of the situation at the time. While he was operating between Constantinople and Batumi, and even during his stay in Tiflis, Teague-Jones was unable to reach Anatolia to make an evaluation of the political and military strength of the Kemalist movement. However, he kept himself fully informed through a network of agents and secret sources in Georgia. In his files there are carefully drawn maps with legends in Russian, annexed to intelligence reports which have been removed. The maps, which Teague-Jones could not bring himself to destroy, relate to a variety of subjects—one is a description of the Greek and Turkish positions in the battle of Afion-Karahisar, another a map of Ajaria. As for the reports assessing the Kemalist forces massed on the frontiers of Transcaucasia in 1920, these emanate from the Georgian intelligence services, and one may legitimately ask to what extent they may not themselves have been infiltrated by Bolshevik Russian or German agents.

In December 1920 a note about the Turkish forces concentrated on the Georgian and Armenian frontiers gives a very precise idea of the regiments at the disposal of Kiazim Karabekir, the commander of the Caucasus front who had made his headquarters at Kars. There were three infantry divisions commanded by Colonels Hamid Bey, Javid Bey and Osman Nuri Bey which, together with two battalions of Tatars from Azerbaijan, constituted an imposing force. Mass mobilisation of Kemal's army was still under way, for Teague-Jones notes in his journal that the 4th infantry division was in the process of formation and 'composed of Agbabi tatars who are considered good fighting material and mounted Kurd detachments under Teimur Aga, total 4000 men'.[45] In this inventory of military forces one can observe the 'multi-ethnic' character—or at any rate the variety of the 'Tatar' elements—of an army called on to serve the nationalist Turkish cause. The army was in the process of being built, notably at Erzinjan where a Vth Army Corps was being constituted in the region of Trebizond—on the shores of the Black Sea near the Georgian frontier—and where 43,000 new soldiers were being mobilised on a mainly voluntary basis, despite a considerable wave of desertions. Some 25,000 soldiers from all branches of the army together with some irregular troops had massed on the Georgian frontier in the Batumi district and were preparing for a march on Batumi. Apart from the detail of munitions and military equipment for each division, their strengths and weaknesses—including the lack of armoured cars except at Alexandropol and Igdir—Teague-Jones notes the presence of a certain number of German officers at Trebizond, where 'there is one Company of Sappers under the command of a German officer with two other German subordinate officers'.[46] According to the same Georgian source, there were also Germans at Kars, where it had been possible to identify five German officers, thirty instructors and a number of mechanics, the great majority German, all busy reorganising the Turkish heavy artillery.

Even more interesting for Teague-Jones than the position and number of Turkish divisions massed on the frontiers of Transcaucasia were the phases in the Soviet–Turkish rapprochement and Mustafa Kemal's 'multilateral' diplomacy. In the rough draft of a note probably written at the end of 1922, he recalls that:

in the beginning Mustafa Kemal adopted a policy of playing the East against the West, in other words the Bolsheviks against the Entente. During last summer he made a definite effort to win over the Entente. After the disavowal of Bekir Sami Bey, he decided to delay initial steps in the direction of France pending the results of Major Henry's visit to Angora. When he saw that this mission had no official recognition, he turned towards France and Franklin-Bouillon. He rapidly succeeded in winning over the latter, who were only too eager to meet the Nationalists owing to French commitments in Syria and Cilicia. At the same time, negotiations were commenced with M. Tuozzi the Italian representative. In this way Mustafa Kemal thought by winning over two of the Allies he might compel Britain to join him. In this Mustafa Kemal was soon disillusioned. Britain refused to follow France's lead and Italy withdrew her representative. Russia viewed the Franklin Bouillon Treaty as a breach of faith on the part of Turkey, whom she accused of going back on the Turco-Soviet treaty of March 1921. Mustafa Kemal however, had just completed his successful defence against the Greeks, and felt himself in a strong position. While still negotiating the final phases of the Franklin Bouillon Treaty he entered into simultaneous pourparlers with the Caucasian states. His intention was to conclude separate treaties with them, but in this he was strongly opposed by the Bolsheviks and the pourparlers materialised in the form of the Kars Agreement (October 13th 1921) [signed between Turkey and the three Soviet Transcaucasian republics, in the presence and with the agreement of the representative of Soviet Russia].

A little further on, Teague-Jones alludes to the role of Enver Pasha, an ardent pan-Turkist and rival of Mustafa Kemal, in exile since the end of the First World War, who had arranged with the Bolsheviks that they should supply munitions to the nationalists in Anatolia. Before being sent by Moscow on a mission to Turkestan in 1921 to bring the Basmachi revolt to an end—a cause which he was eventually to espouse before disappearing in July 1922—Enver stayed for a while near Batumi with the Ajars, whom he tried to unite to form an independent Muslim state. The Soviet attempt to replace Mustafa Kemal with Enver Pasha seems to have taken place in this period:

Disillusioned in Kemal, who if backed up by the Entente must naturally become a dangerous enemy of the Moscow Government, whose real policy, as the Turks are well aware, is to obtain control of the Straits, the Bolsheviks attempted an abortive coup both in Angora and Batum. The intended object of the coup was to oust Mustafa Kemal and replace him by Enver Pasha, so that the Soviet policy could be carried out by a Dictator who owed his position entirely to Soviet assistance. Though Mustafa Kemal weathered this storm, he was immediately subjected to a serious attack over the fundamental law of the constitution. The opportunity was seized to attack his position as Dictator on all sides. After a speech of extraordinary vigour he managed to retrieve the day, but his position had been shaken to its foundations. Mustafa Kemal then realised that he was in a very weak position. England was opposed to him, Italy was negatively neutral, and the Bouillon Agreement was not producing the anticipated advantages from France for which he had hoped. This combination of facts decided him to throw in his lot with the Soviet Government by the signature of the Turco-Ukrainian Agreement. The latter was in every way tantamount to a second treaty of friendship with Moscow as also a ratification of the Kars Agreement. Mustafa Kemal had now capitulated to Moscow, and the opposition to him in the Nationalist Assembly automatically disappeared. One of the first steps of the Bolsheviks has been to institute consulates in a number of centres in Anatolia including even such outlying places as Adana and Mersina. Mustafa Kemal had always been so thoroughly opposed to Communism in any form, that this permission for the establishment of the above consulates shows very clearly the change in his relations with the Soviet Government.[47]

Mustafa Kemal's multilateral diplomacy, playing on the Soviet alliance on one side, and on Franco-British rivalry in the Near East on the other, finally succeeded in its objective. After the French evacuation of Cilicia, under the Franklin-Bouillon Agreement of 20 October 1921, came the victory against the Greeks in Asia Minor at the Battle of Sakaria from 23 August to 13 September 1921, which set in motion the Greek Army's general retreat. The revision of the Treaty of Sèvres (which none of the parliaments of the signatory powers had ratified), the creation of a Turkish nation-state in Anatolia, the abolition of the Capitulations and the re-establishment of Turkish sovereignty over eastern Thrace and the Straits were to be the great victories at the Conference of Lausanne which opened in November 1922. These events had an effect on Teague-Jones's strategic thinking about the Muslim world and possible strategies for the British Empire. In particular, his observation of Soviet policy in Ajaria convinced him of the importance of the Muslim factor.

Ajaria: a strategic position on the Soviet–Turkish frontier

Teague-Jones's method of entering Transcaucasia had been through its two ports. In 1918 he was in Baku on the Caspian. In 1920 he was at Batumi, a port on the Black Sea, the export route for petroleum from Azerbaijan via pipeline or railway tanker-wagons. Batumi, a bone of contention between the Turks and the Soviets, occupied a strategic position. What happened at Batumi and in Ajaria after the British evacuation? What forms did the occupation of Batumi take, and how did they lead to the Sovietisation of Ajaria? Teague-Jones was interested in these questions, to which some manuscript notes in his journal are devoted. They describe an essential chapter in Soviet policy towards the nationalities. After Teague-Jones's departure at the end of

THE RETREAT OF THE WHITE ARMIES

February 1921—which brings to mind the desperate flight of the Greek merchant—Batumi was at first briefly occupied by the Turks, whose interest in the region can be explained by history and geography. Ajaria, a part of legendary Colchis where Jason was a visitor, and incorporated into the Georgian kingdom in the eleventh century, had been conquered by the Ottomans in 1614, a conquest which led to the conversion of the Ajars to Islam. In 1878, at the outcome of the Russo-Turkish War, Ajaria and the districts of Kars and Ardahan were lost by the Ottomans to the Russians. From this perspective, the Turks saw the occupation of Batumi as a re-conquest. The Turkish occupation was a brief one: it involved a few short skirmishes with Russian troops and preceded the Red Army's entry into Batumi by only a few days. Once the Turks had withdrawn to the other bank of the Chorokh, Batumi was left under the protection of Soviet Georgia. But the way in which Ajaria was Sovietised had to take account of the conditions imposed by the Turks in the Treaty of Kars, which specified that Ajaria would be incorporated into Soviet Georgia on condition that that the Muslims of Ajaria were given autonomous status. The Turkish demand superficially corresponded with Soviet policy for the nationalities, which divided nations and nationalities according to a strict administrative hierarchy. But with a nuance in this case, in that it was the religious factor, Islam, and not the ethno-linguistic factor, which distinguished the population of Ajaria from that of Georgia. Despite the militant atheism of the Bolshevik leadership, the latter relied on Muslim identity when creating the specific administrative entity of Ajaria:

As the Russians had given independence[48] to the small nations, the inhabitants of Batum demanded to be independent and thereupon elected their national Assembly. Their leaders were Husni Effendi, Osman Bey, Shakir Bey and other local dignitaries. These men were under the influence of Turkey. A committee was formed by Averpetadze the chief of police and Husni Aliev for the purpose of sending propagandists to the villages. So as to diminish the power and influence of the Assembly, the Tiflis government proposed to send three members to each Government Department with a view to common administration of Georgia and Ajaristan. The Assembly thinking it better accepted this proposal. But some time later they understood that they had made a mistake, because it decreased their power.[49]

In March 1922 Teague-Jones still had informers in the Georgian Menshevik intelligence services, who were able to intercept a report from the Revkom of Batumi to the Revkom of Tiflis on the means of reinforcing Soviet power in Ajaria. He quickly translated and made a note of the gist of the intercepted report:

According to accumulative evidence collected by the Batum Revkom, the Kemalists are endeavouring to increase their influence through Adjaria. There is ample and definite proof that numbers of Turkish soldiery who were driven out of Batum on the occupation of that town by the Red Army remained scattered among the villages of Ajaria and have been carrying on an active propaganda campaign in favour of Mustafa Kemal and the Nationalist government. The work of the Batum Revkom has been rendered very difficult by many causes. For a long time it enjoyed no popularity whatever in the rural districts … A close study of the question has convinced the Batum Revkom that the population of Ajaria is practically entirely in the hands of its Mullahs and other religious leaders and that therefore it is essential to get these latter into our hands. This can best be accomplished by sanctioning a sum of money to be placed at the disposal of the Batum Revkom with which to subsidise the Ajarian Mullahs. One of the most important steps is to effect the expulsions of the Beks from the country, and in this the Mullahs could give valuable assistance by using their influence in the different committees. Until this is done, and until we have the Mullah class on our side, Soviet Government will never obtain a firm footing in the land.[50]

In its reply to this request, the Tiflis Revkom agreed to allocate these sums in support of agitation among the mullahs of Ajaria, while the Bolsheviks orchestrated a vast campaign against the Beks. Many of the latter indeed left Ajaria, and their lands were immediately seized and redistributed. Teague-Jones was particularly struck by the Bolsheviks' pro-Muslim policy, which was being given one of its first trial runs in Ajaria and Central Asia. The Bolsheviks had plans for building mosques and Koranic schools and by these means were seeking to appear as the champions of Islam in the Caucasus. At the same time the Muslims of Ajaria were said, according to certain informants, to have appointed their own religious leader (Sheikh ul-Islam), arguing that they had lost all direct contact with the Caliphate (or what was left of it in 1922) now that they were cut off from Turkey. Finally, the position of the autonomous Republic of Ajaria—whether within the planned Caucasian Federation or within Soviet Georgia—was still undecided, given that:

the Russian Bolsheviks favour the first solution in that they wish to keep Batum and Ajaria out of the influence of Georgia. The population of Ajaria are inclined more towards Turkey than either towards Georgia or Russia and are anxious to have their own independent republic. Their autonomy is at present a mere face. They have their own Ajarian Revkom but this is nothing more than a powerless appendage of the Batum Revkom, which, latter really has all the power in his hands.[51]

These notes, made a few months before the establishment of the Soviet Socialist Republic of Ajaria, show the extent to which Teague-Jones was aware of the Muslim factor at a time when, on both the ideological front—the People's Congress of the People's of the East met at Baku from 1 to 8 September 1920—and on the political front, the Bolsheviks were being particularly accommodating to Muslims.

Plans for a Muslim policy: an Alliance counter-strategy against Russia

For Teague-Jones, Ajaria in 1921 rounded off a series of experiences of the Muslim world. From the North West Frontier to Baluchistan, from Turkmenistan to Ajaria, he had become convinced of the importance of the Muslim factor and of its potential for preserving a British sphere of influence in Central Asia. On his return to London during the summer of 1922, he met Sir Arthur Hirtzel, one of the most influential figures in the Foreign Office at the time. The two men discussed Soviet policy towards Central Asia and Islam. The note[52] written by Teague-Jones—henceforth Ronald Sinclair—for Sir Arthur Hirtzel, is a follow-up to this private conversation.

It expresses his personal views on the possibility of, indeed the need for, an Anglo-Muslim alliance against Russia. Although disclaiming any expert knowledge, the paper to some extent foreshadows the tactics tried in the 1980s by the United States, when the latter gave its support to the mujahedin during the Soviet occupation of Afghanistan. The Central Asia region—widely defined—was, and remains, a geostrategic pivot, around which it was possible to conceive of three different policies: an Anglo-Russian alliance which would be to the detriment of the independence of Muslim countries, a Russo-Muslim alliance against British power in the East, and lastly an Anglo-Islamic combination against Russian influence. In his note, Teague-Jones enlarges on all these possibilities.

The first, an Anglo-Russian alliance, seemed to him to depend entirely on 'the degree of good faith existing between ourselves and Russia', a possibility which he considers with no apparent emotion, despite the difficulties of his personal involvement in the affair of the twenty-six commissars. Such an arrangement would make it possible to return to the pre-1914 division of zones of influence:

The Persian question could be settled again to our mutual satisfaction just as well now it was in 1907. The Persians might not accept such a settlement quite so quietly now as they did then, but with the only two powers that matter, Russia and Britain in accord, their outcry would be in vain.

A return to the 1907 zones of influence, though ideal in principle, would be impracticable given the hostile Soviet policy towards Great Britain:

Never during the whole course of history perhaps, with the exception of such hostile feeling as is inevitably conjured up between belligerents in time of war, or between communities as a result of blood feuds or vendettas, has one nation so persistently and so systematically worked up a feeling on the part of his subjects of hatred towards another foreign nation, as has Soviet Russia towards Great-Britain. No amount of peaceful and patient negotiation, no Trade Agreements have in any way reduced that hostility, and one cannot but feel that whatever action we may take as a nation towards creating closer relations with Russia, such action will be repudiated and thwarted by the Russian Soviet Government. The latter are determined to regard Capitalist and Imperialist Britain as Russia's deadliest enemy … The Bolsheviks have failed to kindle the fire in India which they fondly supposed would burn us out of Asia, but they have successfully poisoned the minds of the whole Central Asia against us.

In 1922 there was nothing to indicate that the Soviet Union would survive, or, if it did, whether its stance towards Britain would change. Even so, Teague-Jones rejected the possibility of an alliance with the monarchist forces: how could the supporters of imperial restoration ally themselves with Great Britain, which had participated in dismantling the Russian Empire at the end of the First World War? In pursuing his analysis, Teague-Jones's tone is frankly critical when it comes to the incoherencies of British policy in relation to Central Asia and Transcaucasia:

We began by intervening and having done a great deal towards prolonging and embittering the struggle, we abandoned the cause we had originally supported, and immediately commenced to coquet with the other side. Our attitude, one cannot call it a policy, has been nothing but one long sequence of inconsistency. We fought the Bolsheviks but we were not at war with them. We deliberately obstructed them when we were at peace with them. We treated with them when they flagrantly deceived us. We profess to be friendly while they are openly and actively hostile. We have gained no prestige or friendship in the eyes of the Bolsheviks, and we have lost whatever prestige we had in the eyes of the remainder of the Russian people.

There is a degree of emotion in this strongly worded critique which contrasts with the more diplomatic language that was typically used in reports submitted to the Foreign Office. Teague-Jones was a territorial imperialist by conviction and professional experience: his earlier adventures in Transcaspia and Transcaucasia brought him up against the incoherence of British policy and reinforced his visceral anti-Bolshevism. A coherent policy towards the power and defence of the British Empire therefore ruled out an Anglo-Russian entente in Central Asia as inconceivable.

The second of the eventualities that Teague-Jones envisaged, a Russo-Muslim alliance, was not theoretical: it had in fact been actively realised since the Baku Congress by the Bolsheviks, who were hoping that the flame of revolution would burst forth in the Muslim East. But after arming the Central Asian hordes and supporting the revolt of the Muslim peoples, did the Bolsheviks, who were following a policy of revolutionary subversion on the approaches to British India, not risk seeing this revolt turn against themselves? The rising of the rebel Basmachis at Bukhara in 1921–2, and the check they gave to the forces of the Red Army, seemed to confirm this interpretation:

In any case, it would be extremely inconvenient for us to have a Central Asia which would continue as it is at present, a refuge for all the discontented elements of Asia. Surely it must be in our interests to have a friendly Central Asia, utilised neither as a field of agitation against us, nor as a refuge and training ground for our enemies and political outcasts.

It followed therefore that an Anglo-Muslim alliance was the only possible alternative counter to Bolshevik Russia: the British must win the support of the Muslim populations now, at this precise moment of the anti-Red revolt in Turkestan, and formulate a proper Muslim policy which took account of 'our own Muslims' in India and the adjoining countries. Teague-Jones suggests putting this policy into practice among the Muslims of India, Afghanistan, Turkestan (including Bokhara and Khiva), Persia and Turkey. His starting proposal was that those responsible in the Foreign Office should take a close interest in the revolt in Turkestan, and provide themselves with the means to carry out 'passive propaganda', not openly pro-British, but subtly anti-Russian. There should be a kind of competition with the Russians in Central Asia in terms of colonial policy. If the cotton monoculture and the railway in Turkestan are in Bolshevik hands and completely out of local control, the British must demonstrate the positive example—about which Teague-Jones has not the slightest of doubts—of colonial India:

If the Turkestani communists knew that in India, under the regime of the tyrannous British, there were railways working whose employees of all grades were Indians of the country, and that there were also cotton mills in India worked largely by Indians, and that India exported and sold her own complete manufactures, these facts alone (one could quote them in thousands) would go far to change the popular idea of British tyranny and at the same time increase the tension between Moscow and Turkestan.

By contesting the Russian and Bolshevik presence in Turkestan it would be possible to remove Afghanistan from Russian influence and move towards a regional restructuring on the basis of commercial relations. A treaty with Afghanistan would allow India to supply Turkestan with imports and to take carpets, sheepskins and dried fruit from Central Asia in return. Teague-Jones was certain that the development of trade along these lines would make Turkestan economically independent of Russia. Following this chain of reasoning, he instances, without developing it further, the case of Turkey: still bound to the Soviet regime in an unnatural relationship, its release should be easy to manage. For Teague-Jones, the British would have to beat the Bolsheviks in the field of Muslim policy if British influence in Central Asia was to be saved:

We must remember that the Bolshevik policy in the East is aggressive but it is bluff. The claim of the Soviets to be the champions of Islam, is, as we know, an empty bubble. Why not prick it, and demonstrate its emptiness to the millions of Moslems enslaved by the Russian Bolsheviks throughout the whilom Russian Empire. The Bolsheviks are cowards, and the whole of their policy is based on cowardice. They are afraid to death of the Moslems, therefore they distract their attention from themselves and divert their rage against the British ... The Soviet Government have profited at our expense by proclaiming themselves the champions of Islam, and ourselves the enslavers of it. Let us now challenge them for the championship, and turn the tables on them.

This hastily written note from an impenitent imperialist was to have no practical consequences. The different officials responsible in the Foreign Office and Whitehall through whose hands it passed all advised caution. To Teague-Jones's proposals for boldness, the no doubt justified response was that he overestimated the effects of propaganda, and that initiatives of this kind end by rebounding on their authors. The most that might be done would be to invite Turkestanis to India to demonstrate the benefits of the British administration. He was thought to have gone too far in considering Islam to be the pivotal factor in possible future policy. Even Sir Arthur Hirtzel, despite the fact that he passed the report on to the SIS, took the same line. 'Thus although the indeterminate situation in Central Asia involves a considerable element of danger, it would seem that the only practicable course is to do nothing.'[53] Another official went one further:

We cannot join the Bolsheviks in going for the Moslem, God forbid. We cannot violate the Trade Agreement ... Any recrudescence of imperialistic expansion by us in Central Asia would be unlucrative, would attract the hatred of the Moslems as well as the hatred and suspicion of the Russians (present and future regimes). It would be contrary to the whole tendency of the age.[54]

There could be no better demonstration of the gap between the relatively lowly field agent and the politician in this era of British imperial withdrawal. The Turkestan revolt suggested the potential utility of financing an intelligence network and gathering all information that might be useful. But as Sir Arthur Hirtzel wrote to the head of SIS, 'There does not therefore seem to be anything more for us to do.'[55] 'Do nothing.' The instruction, which has the ring of a doctrine, was a turning-point in Teague-Jones's career.

7

RONALD SINCLAIR, IMPERIAL TRAVELLER

'Finance! Things are coming back to finance now all the time. What finance is doing, where it's going, what it's supporting, how far hidden it is. There are people you know, people in the past who had power and brains and their power and brains bought the money and means, and some of their activities were secret, but we've got to find out about them. Find out who their secrets passed to, who they've been handed down to, who may be running things now.'

Agatha Christie, *Postern of Fate*, London: Collins, 2003, p. 159

In 1922 Ronald Sinclair's career took a decisive turn. This year, which saw the unleashing of Soviet propaganda against 'the assassin of the 26 Baku commissars', was also the year in which the British intelligence services made deep cuts for budgetary reasons in their permanent staff. Teague-Jones, who had been an intelligence officer in time of war—a role which continued in the Caucasus and Turkey until 1922— became an unofficial agent in the intra-war period, paid out of private intelligence service funds. The change did not imply any withdrawal of support on the part of the hierarchy, for whom he was a high-quality political agent and field operative, but was in line with the transformation of British intelligence which began in the second half of the nineteenth century. The British Empire was based on a convergence of interests between the worlds of politics and business. It gave birth to an alliance, as secret as it was effective, between big city bankers and financiers, ministers in different departments, representatives of industries of national importance and the various heads of intelligence. The historian William Engdahl underlines the particular nature of the British intelligence services, which he describes as functioning as 'a secret, Masonic-like network which wove together the immense powers of British banking, shipping, industry and government'.[1] This permeability between business, industry, politics and intelligence meant that it was logical to ask finance and industry to pay for intelligence missions with a commercial, political and strategic focus. Between the two wars, the intelligence services, which were subject to budgetary pressures from the early 1920s on, seem to have resorted to this solution on a considerable scale, thereby underlining the essentially mercantile and commercial character of British imperialism.

In 1922 Reginald Teague-Jones finally disappeared, becoming Ronald Sinclair. Simultaneously the intelligence services were notified to proceed to staff reductions 'from time to time, as soon in each case as possible'.[2] Services dependent on the India Office, which had been reduced to economising on postage stamps, were briefed on these drastic economy measures, 'arrangements which are considered to be sufficient if the activities of Indian revolutionaries and their associates in Europe do not become more pronounced than they are at present'.[3] The case of Teague-Jones, who had joined a service answerable to the government of India in 1910, was bound up with the complex relationship between the India Office in London and the government of India. In the IPI archives[4] there is a secret report which mentions the economy measures taken by the Indian secret services in 1921. They apparently culminated in the abolition of a system which had been carefully developed since 1911, and in the sudden dismissal of many agents who had given exceptional service during the war. Teague-Jones was part of the contingent of secret agents tossed overboard at the beginning of the 1920s, the view in London henceforth being that the intelligence system created in India is 'most valuable but not vital'. Although there may have been some within the secret services who were offended by the British government's lack of good faith towards their best agents, the sacrifice nonetheless took place in a specific context. In the years 1920–1, British India, which had supplied a million and a half men during the conflict, was going through a severe economic, monetary and budgetary crisis. This demanded, among other measures, an attempt to link the rupee to sterling and the implementation of a policy of budgetary austerity, which involved dismissing its intelligence agents with a mere nine weeks' notice. This was a major turning-point for Ronald Sinclair since, while he continued to provide intelligence, his missions were now at the behest of and financed by private entrepreneurs, including the 'Lancashire lobby'. The arrangement was probably a profitable one for him, judging by the comfortable fortune that he left at his death, an amount which he could not have saved simply from his official salary. Through it he gained freedom of movement, an apparent lack of financial worries, and above all a life rich in adventure and the unexpected.

'Zobeida and I': a Persian Odyssey

From 1922 to 1939 Ronald Teague-Jones, alias Ronald Sinclair, travelled around the British Empire and its 'informal' adjoining territories. From India to the Middle East, from East Africa to South East Asia, his journeys were for the purposes of pleasure, trade and intelligence. He was not enamoured of luxury; by temperament and training an English sportsman, he was used to putting up with all kinds of conditions. Moreover, he was exceptionally familiar with Persia, Baluchistan and

North East India, across which he drove alone from Beirut to Bombay at the wheel of an ordinary Model A Ford, which he christened 'Zobeida'. So in 1926 he embarked on a solitary trip—the complete antithesis to André Citroën's highly publicised 'Croisière Jaune'—financed, he says, by 'English manufacturers'. Two years later, Sinclair repeated the exploit by making the return journey from Bombay to London in a car supplied by William Morris. Following in the steps of Teague-Jones, Sinclair journeyed across the new country which became Iran in 1926. He describes the trip in a story published by the London publishers Gollancz as *Adventures in Persia* a few months before his death in 1988. His editor, David Burnett, who was fascinated by the author's personality and exuberant imagination, viewed the story as semi-fictional, obscuring the political aims of the journey. However, the vivid, spirited and humorous narrative, frustratingly discreet in places, offers easily decipherable clues to a piece of coded autobiography.

An opaque mission in Iran for a combination of partners

In the account of his adventures in Persia, Teague-Jones explains in a few lines the circumstances which led him to accept the mission. A certain 'Jim Bradley'—the name is obviously a fiction—at the Board of Trade had been contacted by an important group of representatives of British manufacturers, who were looking for a man who could study and report on current trading conditions in Iran. They had naturally turned to the Board of Trade:

Jim must have recommended me strongly for I was given a friendly reception at my meeting with the directors. They explained that they wanted a person with experience in Persia, someone who could speak the language, to go out and visit the principal towns and business centres and send home reports on market conditions and trade possibilities in general. I could decide what places to visit and how I travelled. For expenses I could draw on credits in the Imperial Bank of Persia, and the bank had been asked to instruct their local managers to accord me any assistance I needed. The terms offered were generous and altogether it was a most tempting assignment. I accepted without hesitation. It was agreed that I would have two weeks in which to make my preparations. My new colleagues stood me an excellent farewell luncheon, I shook hands, they wished me luck.[5]

Contrary to David Burnett's assumption, the role of this group of English manufacturers was not pure invention, even if it has proved impossible to find any trace of a mission to Persia in 1926 in the Board of Trade's archives. The Lancashire textile industry, traditionally exporters to India, had been exposed to higher and higher import tariffs since the beginning of the 1920s. Moreover, the sector was suffering from Japanese competition in India, and had been badly hit again in 1925 when the British authorities in India, yielding to pressure from Indian producers, abolished indirect taxes on Indian cotton products, thereby increasing their price attractions: the Manchester manufacturers could now only hope for some benefit from imperial preference, or else turn to other export markets. Hence Teague-Jones's mission to Persia on behalf of a London firm with the vague name of Eastern Exporters.

Technically this was not just cover, since he was in practice inquiring into trade in the bazaars and caravanserais. But Teague-Jones's expertise went beyond the needs of an enquiry of this kind. His journey took place at a key moment in Persia's political history, the accession of the Pahlavi dynasty. He was in Tehran on 25 April 1926, the day of Reza Khan's coronation ceremony and of the birth of Iran. The role of the bazaar in this country was of primary political importance during the constitutionalist revolution of 1905–8. Simultaneously investigating commercial possibilities and political developments was a simple matter of conversing with a few Armenian carpet merchants in the Tabriz bazaar—good sources of information when they were not being paid by the Soviets—over a glass of tea. The mission, as he himself said, suited him perfectly: it was a question of sending reports on commercial matters to the textile manufacturers and on political and strategic matters to the DIB (Delhi Intelligence Bureau) and the secret service authorities in London.

Industry, trade and information, three partners sharing closely combined interests, were also united by the immense power of British banking. The Imperial Bank of Persia (Bank-e shâhi) had been an active force in the building of the 'informal' British Empire. Its director, who had a dual responsibility for intelligence and finance, saw to the needs of Teague-Jones's mission by issuing instructions to the managers of local branches in the principal Persian towns. The bank had been the instrument of British imperialism in Persia ever since its founding in 1889 by the son of Baron Julius Reuter. In 1872 the latter had obtained a monopoly in Persia for railway and tram construction, coal and metal mining, dams, bridges, a national bank, the farming of customs duties, and several other sectors. The Imperial Bank of Persia had not carried out the railway plans—a field in which the Russians had successfully intervened in 1887—but enjoyed the immense privilege of a monopoly on the printing of paper money, while investing in a good number of other sectors. It responded to the shah's wish for a state bank, but it acted as much on behalf of the British shareholders as an agent for Foreign Office influence. The Imperial Bank of Persia's political leanings varied from time to time depending on the shareholders or the dominant groups within the bank—David Sassoon's Eastern Trading House, for example, owned 30 per cent of the shares and had a seat on the board. But it always acted in the British interest, and its directors were agents with influence even if they were not members of the intelligence services.

Before beginning his journey, Teague-Jones had a meeting with one of the executive officers—the board had its seat in London but the executive director of the bank was based in Tehran—a meeting which he relates as an anecdote, but which confirms the intrinsic bond between the bank and the world of intelligence:

Before leaving London I had lunched with a top executive of the Imperial Bank of Persia at his club. Afterwards we had sat over coffee near a large window overlooking Pall Mall and continued to discuss my forthcoming journey. I had asked for some final tips for the road. 'You know the language and you're no stranger to the East', the director said, 'but there's one piece of advice I can give you. Never, never sleep in an Iranian caravanserai or local inn. In a big town the bank manager or the consul will always be glad to put you up. We've written to all our branch managers, informing them of your journey. We have a branch in every sizeable town as you know, and you should make a point of calling on them at once, advising them in advance where possible—but never, never stay in a caravanserai. They're filthy and full of typhus germs. If you cannot reach a town with a bank manager, then sleep out in the open, no matter what the weather'. I did not tell him that I had slept in caravanserais in eastern Iran and had resolved never to do so again, but promised to take his advice, and I had written to the Kermanshah manager from Baghdad, informing him of my journey and expected date of arrival.[6]

This salutary advice from an Englishman of the sort who enjoyed outdoor life and camping—during his previous stays Teague-Jones had already tried staying in caravanserais—is also an indication of the close links between the branches of the Imperial Bank of Persia. In the south of the country, the Shiraz, Bushire and Isfahan branches were mainly interested in the development of trade between Iran, Britain and British India, and particularly in the export of Iranian opium to China and the British colony of Singapore. In the north, the Tabriz, Meshed and Resht branches financed Russo-Persian trade, particularly exports of rice and cotton to Russia. During the 1920s the Imperial Bank of Persia continued to support the development of Soviet–Iranian commercial relations: the Meshed branch took care of the export of cotton and wool to the Soviet Union, while the branch at Resht dealt with Soviet commercial organisations over the export of rice, cotton and dried fruit to the USSR.[7] In other words the British were able, by means of banking activity, to keep a watchful eye on the movements of Bolshevik agents who often infiltrated the north of Iran as commercial representatives. The interlocking of the management structures[8] in banking and trade with the intelligence domain seems to have been behind Teague-Jones's mission to Persia.

The mission had multiple objectives. It was certainly an investigation of market potential on behalf of British industrialists, but it also involved crossing Persian territory from west to east and from north to south in order to test whether cars could use the routes in remote areas like Baluchistan, a territory then on the frontier of the British Empire. Great Britain had been searching for a strategic route which would allow a rapid connection between India and its sphere of interest in the Middle East since the end of the First World War. It was a question of creating an artery which could be used both for trade and transport, and for the supplying of troops out of India. The continental route implied crossing Iran and securing its territory. It was to be backed up by an air link, provided by Imperial Airways; Teague-Jones was to be one of their first passengers. A simple reconnaissance mission then, for which Teague Jones, in the guise of Ronald Sinclair, had all the necessary abilities. He spoke fluent Persian, and knew the difficult areas between Baluchistan and Khorasan, which he had travelled through in 1918 by mule or camel, like the back of his hand. He was also sufficiently familiar with the methods used by Bolshevik agents to be able to form a precise impression of Soviet infiltration in Iran, the importance of which would be revealed at the beginning of the 1930s when the memoirs of the GPU defector G. Agabekov were published.[9]

Levantine encounters

It was mid-January 1926 when Teague-Jones, having reached Genoa from London, embarked on an Italian steamer. He was alone, since Valya seems to have already disappeared from his life some years previously. A few days later he was in Beirut, the departure point for a land cruise which was to follow the line of the great caravan routes across the Middle East. The account of his adventures in Persia opens on a picture postcard view. Beirut under the French Mandate, where the sight of the old town, which had yet to be demolished in order to make way for Ecochard's urban development, and of the surrounding hills covered in luxuriant orange and lemon trees, olives and larches, moved every traveller arriving by sea to exclaim with enthusiasm. Teague-Jones was no exception; the beauty of the countryside was breathtaking, and the town, which still bore the stamp of its Ottoman past, reminded him of Constantinople. At Beirut, Teague-Jones only had one friend, a certain 'Emil Mattar', who was there to welcome him warmly on his arrival. Trained to be discreet, and skilled in dropping hints, Teague-Jones does not give his contacts' real names, but it is nonetheless worth noting that among the many Emil Mattars still living in Beirut there was one who was Lebanon's first ambassador in New York.[10] But he was not the Emil Mattar mentioned in Teague-Jones's account; the choice of synonym instead signifies his friend's Greek extraction, a distinctive element in the Maronite elite under the French Mandate. Whether fictional or real, the Emil Mattar whom Teague-Jones says he last met three years previously—he was working as a barman in a South Kensington pub—is an attractive character, built like a film-star. Tall, with brown hair, broad shoulders and thick-arched eyebrows, one visualises him as having the appearance of Gregory Peck. Teague-Jones certainly thought that he must have caused many a feminine heart to flutter, and was inwardly astonished that this handsome businessman in his thirties was not yet married. He lays out for Emil, but not for the reader, the details of his mission. The report of the conversation is elliptical and only one remark: 'Generally speaking, would you say the French are popular?' stands out as suggesting that 'Emil' works for British intelligence. Teague-Jones asks him for an introduction to Norman Nairn, the great veteran of the desert road connecting Beirut to Baghdad by motorised convoy.

With his desert jacket and shorts, desert tan and bright blue eyes, Norman Nairn (1894–1968) also looked like a movie hero. A New Zealander who had served in the army under General Allenby during the war, Nairn had stayed in the Middle East after he was demobilised. Nairn was convinced that it was possible to cross the desert from Beirut to Baghdad by motorised transport, and enjoyed the support of Ibn Bassam, a rich Arab merchant who had amassed a considerable fortune in the transport of gold between Damascus and Baghdad, and who knew all the routes through the Syrian Desert. This was the era of the very first crossings of the desert by car. In December 1921 the American writer John Dos Passos had reached the Iraqi town of Ramadi, on the west bank of the Euphrates, in a Model T Ford. The following year saw a successful car journey from Damascus to Baghdad. In 1923, with the support of the British authorities in Mandate Iraq, Nairn won a contract for the postal service between Baghdad and Haifa. There the post was put on to a train to Port-Said, achieving the link between Iraq and Egypt in only sixty hours, at a time when the sea route took twenty-four days. Nairn had literally revolutionised the means of communication, and the French Mandate authorities quickly entrusted him with their own postal traffic between Damascus and Baghdad, until the day in 1925 when they encouraged the creation of a competitor for Nairn—only too obviously an agent under British influence—the Compagnie orientale des transports. The French organisation which used the route via Palmyra and Kubaisa was fairly efficient; it had the monopoly over the motor road the far side of Baghdad, and even provided a connection once a fortnight with Tehran. Against this background of a Franco-British struggle for control over the strategic routes in the Middle East, Nairn had not only managed to merge his own organisation with the Compagnie orientale des transports, but to control the majority of the shares, thus reducing the French government to the status of minority partner. Teague-Jones, who seems to have had a very full picture of Norman Nairn's activities and his strategic development plans, adds that 'the company's activities have now increased to a point where the British Government has acquired a substantial measure of indirect control through the holdings of various major banks'.[11]

The 'Nairn route', which in less than a decade had won a solid reputation for efficiency and safety—in 1924 he had transported the shah of Persia and his suite across the desert—had begun with a weekly crossing by two vehicles. From 1926 on he had a dozen vehicles available, which were American- rather than British-made for reasons of clearance and power. The drivers on the Nairn route[12] were real desert veterans, all former British soldiers, with a reputation for endurance and devotion that was unrivalled throughout the Middle East. They ensured the safety of their passengers on the old caravan routes, constantly threatened with attacks from the Bedouin tribes, which could easily spot the tyre-tracks on the desert sand. The fact that Nairn carried money and gold on behalf of various banks tended to arouse Bedouin greed—the drivers had consequently worked out a subsidy system, under which a third of the revenues from the postal service were paid to the Bedouin tribes by an influential Baghdad merchant.[13] The Nairn route thus provided an essential and secure strategic connection, until the time when a full reconnaissance of the Syrian Desert made it possible to open an air link between Cairo and Baghdad as had been agreed at the Cairo Conference in 1921. In 1929, Nairn's company proposed the opening of an air link between Damascus and Baghdad.[14] Later, in 1936, Nairn provided an auxiliary service to the IPC (Iraq Petroleum Company), transporting workmen and technicians to the production sites. All this suggests that Teague-Jones's mission in Persia, besides reconnoitring possible road links, may have had something to do with the establishment of the air connection between Karachi and Baghdad via Persian airspace. A few years later, Teague-Jones took film and photographs of the route on board the inaugural flight of Imperial Airways' *City of Tehran*.

For Teague-Jones a meeting with Nairn to ask for advice and help was indispensable. Nairn, who was fully informed about political affairs—the French authorities were currently engaged in dealing with a Druze revolt—and their practical implications—the need to take the northern route via Homs and Palmyra—gave Teague-Jones some further advice. If he was planning to attempt the crossing of Iran by car, he must get one in Beirut and not wait until he was in Baghdad. He was given the name of a reputable garage-owner to whom he described his plan:

'There', he pointed to a small shiny black car parked away in a corner. It was an A-model Ford, first cousin to the famous Model-T. I was intrigued by the name ZOBEIDA painted in neat white letters on one door. He explained that the car had belonged to a French officer who had been transferred. It had not run many kilometres and was almost new. The price was low, he said, because the Lebanese preferred big, powerful cars which could run up the mountain roads in top gear. He assured me that for Iran the small Ford was more suitable. He himself had been up there and knew that country. Except in the few large cities, there were no facilities for repairs or servicing, and the extra high clearance of this particular model and its light weight were big advantages in rough country.[15]

So Teague-Jones's first meeting with his plain little Zobeida, a light car, ideal for a country with no roads, was governed by purely practical considerations. As the kilometres went by the relationship was to turn sentimental—*Zobeida and I* was the original title of his adventures.[16]

Across the Syrian Desert

After a French police inspection, the Nairn convoy moved off from its departure point, the Beirut military depot, actually a former caravanserai, in a braying of horns and sirens. The Nairn coach and several satellite vehicles were in front. Behind, at the wheel of Zobeida, Teague-Jones 'realis[ed] with a sense of inferiority that Zobeida was the smallest, the lowest-powered and the lowest-priced vehicle in the whole caravan'.[17] Tripoli, Homs, Palmyra, a delightfully exotic journey in Syrian Mandate territory, dense with the archaeological history of thousands of years. At the wheel of Zobeida, whose water and oil levels he had to check constantly along with the tyre pressures, Teague-Jones proceeded at a slower pace than the forty other vehicles in the caravan. While driving in a kind of historical reverie along the sun-baked road, a series [of] images came to his mind: a Roman legionary exhausted by a forced march to Berytus, the caravanserais of the old Silk Road, now used as staging-posts by the motorised caravan. There was a feeling of a world coming to an end in the face of modern civilisation. Teague-Jones was particularly aware of this aspect as he photographed camels and donkeys, the traditional users of a route that was as old as humanity. And silk was a topical issue, for the camels were carrying loads of uprooted mulberry trees: silk production had been facing stiff competition since the early 1920s from artificial silk and silk imports from Japan. Homs, Emesa, Queen Zenobia, Palmyra, the chariots of Aurelian's army, Teague-Jones's reverie was brutally interrupted by a violent lurch, fortunately with no serious consequences.

RONALD SINCLAIR, IMPERIAL TRAVELLER

Nairn's caravan passed through the Valley of the Tombs before reaching Palmyra:

The track, which was the ancient caravan route, emerged from the Vale of the Tombs into the open plain. Immediately ahead, and spreading out over the desert, was Palmyra itself, a vision of tawny golden colonnades extending from one central massive pile of the great temple of Bel, the sun god. I had not thought to see anything so spectacular as the scene which now lay before me. I had expected a ruined city. Ancient cities, wherever they may be located, always seem to possess certain features in common. But Palmyra was different. Here, except round the base of the temple itself, there was no confusion of tumbled masonry, no disorderly collection of decapitated columns, none of the piles of rubble which mark the ravages of earthquake or invader. Here there were far-reaching colonnades of marble pillars and archways standing intact and erect in their original alignment. The first impression was of a well-planned city, which the builders, for some reason or other, had never completed. There was no suggestion of violence. Here the enemy had been gradual decay. As the population had decreased or moved away, the desert had stepped in and cleaned up. The result was a scene of graceful beauty rather than chaotic grandeur.[18]

Teague-Jones and Zobeida followed the desert track and finally succeeded in reaching the bank of the Euphrates at Hit. The convoy then turned south, along the Mesopotamian invasion and conquest route, passed through Ramadi, crossed the Euphrates at Fallujah, and arrived at Baghdad. Although he relates some amusing anecdotes about his stay in Baghdad, Teague-Jones spent little time visiting the Iraqi capital. There were few archaeological remains from the era of the Caliphate. There were, it is true, some picturesque sights, such as the Street of the Amarah Silverworkers in the bazaar, or the *gufas* on the Tigris—round coracle-type boats made of goat- or sheepskin, the origins of which lie in biblical times—but Teague-Jones was mainly concerned with the preparations for his journey. It is here that his odyssey really started, at the Hotel Maude in Baghdad, where Nairn's manager had reserved him a room. He had to find a servant, driver and mechanic, in other words a Persian-speaking factotum who could accompany him for the whole or at least part of his Persian tour. After several amusing and fruitless interviews, he ended up hiring Abdul Samad, a Persian from Isfahan, who had travelled to Baghdad to look for work:

He had tried different jobs and the last one had been with a garage. He produced a much thumbed piece of paper in support of this. I could barely decipher the name of the garage and accepted it for what it was worth. He said he knew the road as far as Isfahan quite well and was less well acquainted with the country as far as Shiraz. Beyond that he had never been and never wished to go. It was all *biaban*—a wild and desolate land. However, if Allah so willed, he would go with me to *akhir-i-dunya*, the end of the earth.[19]

So Abdul joined the crew of Zobeida as general handyman: he turned out to be a better cook than he was a driver or mechanic. Nonetheless, the real journey could now begin. The north-east road out of Baghdad led to Qasr-e Shirin on the Persian border. Teague-Jones once again took an old trade route which he found oddly free of traffic:

I had expected to meet a fair amount of motor traffic on the way, for the road we were following was the ancient trade route which had linked the Great Silk Road through Central Asia. But save for a few isolated trucks and cars within the outskirts of Baghdad, all we met were occasional strings of camels, packhorses and mules. I was surprised that for such a main highway there was no properly made road, only a dirt track tramped hard by generations of flat-footed camel and the foot of man. Though motor traffic had not been heavy, it had already carved out two deep lines of wheel tracks, formed mainly in wet weather when the surface was soft and yielding.[20]

Soon Zobeida and her crew of two began the climb up to the Iranian plateau, leaving the flat lands of Mesopotamia behind. They travelled without problems through the eastern fringes of Persia, which are part of Iranian Kurdistan and populated largely by Kurds. It is here that Teague-Jones's new adventures in Persia began.

Persian adventures: to India by the back door

To the plucky throbbing of Zobeida's engine, Teague-Jones advanced into a part of Persia's territory that he did not have a chance to explore during his previous missions in 1917–18. It was not exactly a voyage into uncharted territory, nor did it have the introspective and metaphysical quality of Nicolas Bouvier's extraordinary travel account *L'usage du monde*, published in English as *The Way of the World*, twenty-five years later. Unlike Nicolas Bouvier's journey, the programme for this trip did not include Afghanistan and the Khyber Pass, but finished in a crossing of the Baluchistan desert and a test of the feasibility of a land route to India by the backdoor. It is both an adventure story, for Teague-Jones had two or three brushes with emergency, and an autobiography in code, based on travel diaries which he kept for a while before destroying. Its originality lies with the personality of the author, for whom the country of Persia is familiar rather than exotic, and who observes men, animals and countryside with the sympathy, humour and perception peculiar to the eccentric English traveller.

Kurdistan to Iranian Azerbaijan: assessing Soviet influence

From the Iranian border to Kermanshah, Zobeida traversed the southern part of Iranian Kurdistan, a zone with such a dangerous reputation for travellers that the frontier authorities insisted that they carry an escort. In fact, during the time of Reza Shah the struggle against tribalism and nomadism had become a priority for the Iranian state, which was engaged in a policy of systematic repression. Already heavily laden despite having reduced travel and camping baggage—Teague-Jones had been obliged to take on plenteous reserves of petrol, oil and water against the long stages ahead—Zobeida struggled to make it to the top of her first real climb, the Patak Pass, the entrance to the Iranian plateau. The track used by muleteers and camel-drivers called for constant watchfulness on the part of the driver—Teague Jones discovered at this point that Abdul had never driven a car in his life—happily compensated by his companion's conversation. The austere and desolate Zagros mountain country reminded Teague-Jones of the rocky slopes of the North West Frontier, and while the track rose in endless bends, Abdul related his story.

He was a more unusual person than Teague-Jones had supposed. His father was a lettered man who had been secretary (*Mirza*) to the deputy governor of Shiraz. Intrigues had caused his father to be transferred to Isfahan, where the young Abdul had been educated and had learned to read and write. After his parents' death while he was still very young, Abdul had been spotted as he left a mosque by a respectable Saiyid wearing a green turban, called Meshedi Abbas, the guardian of a saint's tomb on the very road that the travellers were now taking. The tomb on this relatively busy road was a source of income for the old man, who wanted to employ Abdul to help him with the work: maintaining and embellishing the tomb, serving travellers with water and hubble-bubbles, harvesting the few coins they offered in return, such were Abdul's tasks in this holy and secluded place by the side of the road. But the solitude of the place weighed heavily on the young man, who decided one day to leave his master. The Saiyid, who was saddened by this decision, made him promise to stay until the end of the main pilgrimage season, after which Abdul set off on an old donkey in the direction of Hamadan. The donkey, which had been bought from some passing member of a caravan, was old and tired—so much so that the poor beast died on the road in the neighbourhood of Hamadan. Abdul, distraught, sat down on the edge of the road next to the corpse of his donkey. What was to be done? While the flies began to buzz around the poor donkey, he had an idea. He would bury the donkey and make a mausoleum of his tomb. From a small nearby spring he could provide water to travellers and pilgrims, and beneath a tree he could unfold his carpet and pray to Allah.

The stratagem was apparently sufficiently ingenious for Abdul to harvest enough coins, thrown to him by passing muleteers and camel-drivers. Even if none of them remembered the existence on this section of the road of the tomb of such a distinguished holy man—as his pilgrimage venture grew Abdul had enhanced and embellished his mausoleum—it had become customary to think of the tomb of Abdul's donkey as that of a particularly influential saint. One day, Abdul saw an old man coming down the road towards him whom he immediately recognised as his old master. The old man was up against it: after heavy mountain rains, the stream had burst its banks and swept away the tomb he had been guarding. Surprised to find Abdul in such a prosperous state next to another mausoleum of which he had no memory, the old man started asking questions. 'Tell me, my son, how did you manage to become warden of such an important shrine? I do not recall seeing this when last I came down this road many summers ago. Who is the saint who lies in this very fine tomb?'[21] Embarrassed, Abdul mumbled a reply, then admitted the subterfuge. He then realised that he had never asked the identity of the saint whose tomb his old master had looked after. Now that the waters had swept it away, the old man in his turn was free to admit the truth: he murmured in Abdul's ear that it belonged to his camel!

The road continued to climb as far as Hamadan. Ecbatana, the ancient capital of the Medes, conquered by Cyrus and then by Alexander the Great in 330, has a grey and monotonous look to the traveller. The Ecbatana tell has few grand ruins other than the gigantic statue of a lion, only disappointing remains of dry brick walls, a poor stimulus to the imagination. Welcomed by the manager of the local branch of the Imperial Bank of Persia, Teague-Jones was briefed by him on matters on which he does not enlarge. The whole of the following day was spent talking to city notables and the most prominent merchants:

I found them friendly, but parochial in their interests and generally ill-informed on anything beyond their own immediate boundaries. This was not surprising when one considered that even the smallest Iranian towns are to a great extent self-sufficient in their daily needs. Each bazaar is a small-scale replica of the larger markets. Each possesses its own source of local produce, its native crafts and industry, its metal-workers, tanners, shoemakers, dyers, spinners and weavers, millers, butchers, bakers and the rest of them. This limits their need for contact with the outside world, and, lacking such contact, they are thrown back upon their own society, and are slow to open up to a stranger, particularly to a *feringhi*.[22]

After Hamadan, the road ran towards Qazvin, then directly north towards Tabriz, the capital of Iranian Azerbaijan, very close to the Soviet frontier. It was a monotonous country, of villages and *chaikhanas* (tea-houses), where Russian influence was increasingly discernible: particularly so where the means of transport were concerned, since a good number of *fourgons*—a kind of wagon—were being driven in the opposite direction, vehicles of Russian origin drawn by four horses harnessed abreast. These *fourgons*, travelling in convoy, transported products imported from Russia: cotton goods, sugar, petrol or kerosene from Baku. 'Some of the southbound caravans we met were laden with Russian benzene or kerosene packed in big sheet-iron drums, each containing some forty pounds of weight of fuel. These had all been shipped from across the Caspian from the Baku refineries',[23] Teague-Jones notes in passing. The drivers of the convoys were invariably hostile and sinister-looking Tatars from Azerbaijan, very different in appearance from the much more friendly Persian drivers. Soon Zobeida's crew reached Qazvin: once more, the approaches to the town were disappointing and in no way reflected its strategic position on the crossroads of four main routes: Tehran and Khorasan, Resht and the Caspian, Tabriz and the Caucasus, Hamadan and Iraq. From Qazvin to Tabriz, the road ran north-west for nearly 400 kilometres. At first it passed through irrigated agricultural land, with flourishing orchards, and there was then a particularly difficult stretch between Zenjan and Meyaneh. Zobeida struggled to get up the long ascent of Kafkan Ruh leading to Tabriz. There, Teague-Jones was welcomed by the British consul, 'Charlie Stevens', who had been in post at Tabriz for many years, and had a legendary reputation for hospitality.

There is no trace of 'Charlie Stevens' at Tabriz in the British consular archives. The man in question is very probably Ernest Bristow, who had been the consul there for several years. In 1920 he had been present in Tabriz during the revolt led by

Mohammad Khiabani, who had taken control of the police and the city administration in the name of the 'democrats', and had reported on the intrigues of the German consul, Kurt Wüstrow, who was fiercely hostile to the British. He:

was not only a marvellous host, but also a veritable mine of information on a wide range of subjects. He enjoyed friendly relations with Iranian officialdom from the Governor downwards, and in addition had a host of Iranian friends in both business and social circles. I met a number of these and learned a great deal from them and from one prominent merchant in particular. He gave me valuable information regarding the import and export trade with the Caucasus and was well informed about conditions in Iran generally.[24]

Tabriz was the capital of Iranian Azerbaijan and the second city of Iran, close to the Soviet frontier and the Soviet Socialist Republic of Azerbaijan. Its history in Persia had been one of turbulence, indeed of separatist movements, as was to be the case again twenty years later at the end of the Second World War when it came under the protection of the occupying Red Army. But at the time of Teague-Jones's visit to Tabriz, Reza Shah's centralising policy, together with the normalisation of relations between Iran and the Soviet Union—a treaty of neutrality and guarantee was signed in October 1927—had put a limit to the danger of Soviet influence. This was now confined to the commercial arena and to the infiltration of Soviet agents among the minorities[25]—principally the Armenians and Azeris—who formed the nucleus of the Iranian Communist Party.

The Tabriz bazaar had played an important part in the constitutionalist revolution, which in December 1905 had obliged the shah to concede a constitution and the installation of a parliament, the Majlis. Teague-Jones was bound to have been aware of these facts when he went to visit the bazaar at Tabriz in order to find material for his report. Unfortunately he does not record the substance of his conversations with the merchants in the bazaar, contenting himself with a physical description:

The Tabriz bazaars are of the enclosed pattern, built on the same model as those of Tehran and Isfahan. Here are the mysterious labyrinths of long dark passages, dependent for illumination upon apertures in the lofty vaulted roof. Shafts of sunlight pierced the clouds of dust, stirred up and held in suspension by the constant movement of the milling throng, and appearing as golden columns in the semi-darkness. The main passages have numerous narrower ones branching off them, and all are lined on either side by a continuous row of shops and stalls. Most of these are little more than cubicles, about twenty feet square, but many of them have a second cubicle as store-room or office in the rear and in some cases these open onto a paved courtyard or even into a full-size caravanserai, where the merchandise is carried in and off-loaded from the caravan or pack animals, literally in the merchant's own backyard.[26]

After Iranian Azerbaijan, Teague-Jones's plan was to visit the Caspian coast, the Gilan region around Resht where the Jangali rebellion had broken out in 1915. The guerrilla movement and revolt, directed against both Russia and Britain, led by Mullah Mirza Kuchuk Khan (1878–1921), took its name from the subtropical rain-forest (*jangal* means jungle) which covers this part of the Caspian coast, close to the Caucasus, that hothouse for revolutionaries. Teague-Jones could not fail to be drawn to the Gilan. It was true that the Jangali revolt was no more than a memory—it had been forcefully repressed by Reza Khan, then minister of war, in the autumn of 1921—but it seemed to him that a visit to a region in the Caspian area that he had not seen in 1918/19 was essential for his grand tour of Iranian territory. He abandoned his original plan of visiting the surroundings of Lake Urmia and instead returned to Qazvin before striking due north towards Resht and Enzeli. To reach the plains of the Caspian coast, he had to cross the Elburz range of mountains via the Manjil Pass. Here there was a perilous moment thanks to a *fourgon* in an oncoming convoy. It was one of Teague-Jones's abiding memories:

The Manjil Pass? Gracious. Very narrow track, a lot of dust, radiator boiling, I heard a jingling of bells and round a bend came a native cart drawn by four horses. They took a dislike to my car, got very prancy, so I pulled over and deliberately ditched and found myself hanging half over a precipice. I was saved by the front axle and the gear box. If I had sneezed I'd have gone over.[27]

As it was pointless to hope for any help from the Tatar drivers, who went on their way regardless, Teague-Jones and Abdul managed to haul Zobeida up and set her back on the road with help from local villagers. Once in Resht, where he was welcomed by the British vice-consul, he assessed the Soviet presence in the region. Russian interest in the southern part of the Caspian was discernible through the presence of a commercial mission which had probably disembarked from one of the ancient Soviet vessels arriving at Enzeli, and in the existence of the caviar industry. In the tropical heat, against a background of rusting Soviet ships, Teague-Jones made a few notes, photographed a gunboat to the annoyance of the crew, then set off again on the road to Tehran.

Iran from north to south: Tehran to Bushire

In the period since the end of the First World War and Teague-Jones's last visit, the Persian capital had been the theatre of major political upheavals following a coup d'état by Reza Khan, a Persian soldier in command of the Cossack Brigade, who was said to have come to power thanks to secret support from the War Office.[28] On 21 February 1921 his men had seized Tehran. In April 1921, following a reshuffle of the shah's government, he had become commander in chief, and shortly afterwards minister of defence. His revolutionary plan was to reform Persia from top to bottom, to put an end to the current state of anarchy and to re-establish state control by restoring the authority of the state and asserting nationalist principles. Reza Khan had promised General Edmund Ironside—who was reputed to be the direct inspiration behind the Qazvin conspiracy—that he would not interfere with the Qajar succession, whose last and perpetually absent representative, Ahmad Shah, lived abroad in luxurious circumstances. However, in October 1925 the Majlis declared that the Qajars had ceased to exist, and shortly afterwards a specially elected constituent assembly entrusted the crown to Reza Khan and his descendants. A new dynasty, the Pahlavis, was born, and with it Iran, a nation whose name its new sovereign managed to impose on foreign chancelleries ten years later.

Teague-Jones arrived in Tehran on the eve of the coronation of Reza Shah on 25 April 1926. 'On my arrival in Tehran, there was much talk in official circles about the new Shah's impending coronation but few signs of excitement in the city itself. The common people seemed to be taking things very quietly and going about their business as usual.'[29] Teague-Jones had a number of connections in Tehran—whom he does not name—inside a British legation which was buzzing with preparations for the coronation. The ambassador, Sir Percy Loraine, was in London, but his wife Louise Loraine and Vita Sackville-West were heavily involved in the coronation ceremony. Since there was no real tradition of this kind of event in Iran, they were guided by descriptions of the symbols of royal power—thrones, daggers, crowns, sceptres and so on—deployed at the coronation of George V, and the two ladies even painted the coronation hall rose-pink. Teague-Jones says almost nothing about the louche, eccentric, aristocratic British diplomatic society in Tehran. He simply mentions a particular friendship with the 'Commercial Attaché' with whom he stayed in Tehran. This was no doubt the new chargé d'affaires and counsellor, Harold Nicolson, who had been posted the previous year to Tehran, arriving with his wife, the capricious poet and novelist Vita Sackville-West. Harold Nicolson had been born in Tehran, where his father had also been chargé d'affaires, and had embarked on a Foreign Office career while nursing literary and artistic ambitions.

Teague-Jones's stay with the unconventional couple would undoubtedly have offered some pleasant distractions, but he says nothing about it. His account chronicles neither worldly diplomatic society in Tehran, nor the escapades of a free-living couple who enjoyed a number of homosexual liaisons. Instead it provides a lively portrait of the merchants and dealers of Tehran:

I spent many hours daily, seated in their offices or squatting in their serais, discussing in leisurely tempo almost anything from the import of cotton goods and export of goatskins and dried apricots, to such diverse matters as whether motor transport will eventually supplant camel and mule, and the vexed question of chemical versus vegetable dyes in the carpet-weaving industry; all this, of course, while consuming innumerable glasses of hot sweet tea, to a background accompaniment of grumbling camels, cursing mule-drivers, and the soporific bubbling of water-pipes. Meanwhile I accumulated a mass of miscellaneous notes, which I later condensed into reports for my London friends.[30]

At the home of a Jewish dealer in Manchester cotton goods, Teague-Jones encountered modern Persian womanhood, neither a fiery *houri*, nor a veiled matron. She was:

a handsome, dark-eyed woman, many years younger than her husband. She had a graceful figure and a pleasant and vivacious manner. Her curly black hair was cut in a bob, which emphasised the fine curve of her neck and enhanced her youthful appearance. She wore an orange-coloured silk blouse of western design, open at the throat, and girdled at her waist with a narrow belt of gilded leather. The only oriental items of her dress were her baggy trousers of dark-blue silk. Her feet were clad in dainty golden leather sandals which looked as though they had come direct from Fifth Avenue or Rue de la Paix, and she had pink lacquered toenails. Her jewellery consisted of a pair of jade ear-rings with a necklace to match and a plain gold wedding ring.[31]

Elegant Western simplicity, a discreetly erotic unveiling of face and body—there is in this portrait of a modern Iranian Muslim woman of the 1920s something expressive of all the later paradoxes and changes in twentieth-century Iranian society. Teague-Jones was naturally very aware of her, not just because he was instantly captivated by her charm, but also because her story was emblematic. The Jewish merchant had made her his mistress after having saved her in desperate circumstances from stoning in a distant village, where her jealous husband had heard a rumour of adultery. Under her chador the woman had turned out to be beautiful, young and attractive. He had brought her back to Tehran and lived with her until rumours had spread in the neighbourhood and come to the ears of the religious authorities. Since marriage between a Jew and a Muslim was inconceivable, the merchant had reached a compromise with the mullah, who could not be bribed in view of the stage the affair had reached. According to this arrangement, the merchant would publicly renounce his faith, convert to Islam and marry his wife under Islamic law. Since then they had been living together in a state of perfect happiness. As for the woman, her social trajectory from village to capital city summed up the paradoxes of Iranian society, already modern within the home, patriarchal and traditional outside it, capable of finding, as in this case, a viable compromise within Islamic law.

But now Teague-Jones had come to the end of his stay. With Abdul still beside him, he set off again in Zobeida, heading for Qom and Isfahan. Through a dreary khaki-coloured landscape—the word *kaki* means of the earth, earthy in Persian—the road ran on southwards. This road, or what passed for one, was beset with every kind of obstacle for motorised vehicles, from the irrigation channels dug directly across it, creating dangerous ruts, to the tyre-puncturing donkey-shoes cast by donkeys and mules on the track. The state of the Persian roads was a matter of constant concern for the British intelligence services, particularly in the period since the end of the First World War. Information about them derived not only from 'secret' intelligence but also from real-life anecdotes. Like Teague-Jones, Vita Sackville-West talks about the difficulties of the travel routes in Persia and the presence on the 'roads' of the corpses of donkeys and camels. But whereas she was moved by sympathy for the animals, Teague-Jones was only concerned with the practical inconveniences they created for car drivers. Qom, the holy city and religious centre for Shiism, eventually appeared on the horizon, looking disappointingly drab:

Apart from the great mosque with the shrine, on which the city's fame is based, there is nothing to distinguish Qom from any other medium-sized township, unless it is the unusually large number of caravanserais for the convenience of pilgrims and for the bodies of their dead relatives brought to the holy city for interment.[32]

In 1923 the Iraqi ulemas—at the time, the Shiites were in revolt against the British Mandate in Iraq—had arrived at Qom, which had become an alternative centre of power near the Iranian capital. The religious authorities were afraid that Reza Shah might introduce a secular, anti-religious reform programme in Persia comparable to that brought about by Mustafa Kemal in Turkey:

Even today Qom still retains the reputation of being the centre of much religious bigotry, and it was Mohamed Ishaq in Tehran who told me that the new Shah, Reza Pahlavi, would have to be very careful in his avowed intention to introduce reforms along the lines of those formulated by Mustafa Kemal in Turkey, and most particularly in regard to that extremely delicate question, the emancipation of women. Otherwise he would inevitably incur the hostility of the fanatical elements in Qom, who were capable of creating very serious trouble throughout the country. In times of internal unrest, the holy city would almost certainly be a dangerous trouble spot.[33]

On his arrival in Isfahan, Teague-Jones could not find enough to say about the beauty of the monuments bequeathed by Shah Abbas I (1587–1629) to the town which he transformed into his imperial capital. Isfahan, which seemed a sleepy place, far from the modern world and the machine age, was a green city, lined with poplars and *chenars* (the oriental plane-tree which Teague-Jones considered the finest of trees), and also a blue city, the blue of the tiles and the window-frames, the incomparable azure of the sky. In Isfahan, Teague-Jones stayed with the manager of the local branch of the Imperial Bank of Persia. He wandered in the alleys, walked about the maidan and the bazaar, and took photographs and films of scenes of daily life, like an ethnographer. In the evening, as was his usual practice, he noted down his impressions in a diary. The character whom he chose to highlight from his encounters at Isfahan was an Armenian merchant, whom he calls 'Tutunjian', who lived at Nor Julfa ('New Julfa') in the neighbouring Isfahan suburb. In the town of Nor Julfa, founded by Shah Abbas, a remarkable community of Armenian merchants had developed. The inhabitants originally came from Julfa, a flourishing trading town on the left bank of the Araxes—nowadays lying within the autonomous Republic of Nakhichevan, part of Azerbaijan—but had been deported following Persian victories over the Ottomans. The forced deportation of the Armenians and their settlement at 'New Julfa' was part of a large-scale economic plan. By moving the international network of Armenian merchants to the capital, Isfahan, Persia would be able to profit from the kind of economic prosperity which Armenian know-how and the networks of Armenian merchants in the silk and silver trades could alone ensure. Tutunjian soberly related the facts to Teague-Jones, mentioning the compulsory nature of the huge deportation, whose numbers have not been accurately computed by historians.[34] But he also talked of the sequestered past of the Armenian merchants, since at Nor Julfa, a new town with a main avenue, parallel streets and quarters dominated by one merchant dynasty or another, they constituted a privileged class under the shah's personal protection, kept isolated from the Muslim population. Tutunjian explains to Teague-Jones that:

to avoid friction with the Moslem religious elements in Isfahan the Christian Armenians were compelled to live strictly within the limits of their new colony and were forbidden to do business in Isfahan. 'Is the ban still in force today?' I asked. 'It remained in force for three hundred years, but now under the present regime it has been relaxed, and our merchants and tradespeople are moving freely to the modern commercial quarter on the other side of the river.'[35]

In Persia there were close and long-standing connections between intelligence and trade networks. Teague-Jones only talks of the international reach of this merchant, whose business extends as far as Paris, London and New York; he does not disclose the precise tenor of the 'very useful' information that he provides over a cup of tea and a glass of locally made Armenian wine, a Christian minority privilege in a Muslim country.

The two men resumed their journey in Zobeida: the fantastic vision of Izad Khast, looking like a stone ship stranded in a dried canyon, Abadeh, Persepolis, and on down towards Shiraz, the capital of Fars. During his mission in the Persian Gulf in 1921, Teague-Jones had not had the opportunity to go to Shiraz, whose name is emblematic of all Persia. But the reality did not live up to expectations. While there, Teague-Jones enjoyed the hospitality of his old friend the British consul:

who had spent much of his service in Iran, and spoke the language with unusual fluency. He was one of those popular Englishmen—Sir Percy Sykes was another outstanding example— who had lost their hearts to the country and its people, and had earned the reputation of being 'more Persian than the Persians'.[36]

Although delighted by Shiraz and by the many possible archaeological excursions in the neighbourhood—Achmaenid ruins at Pasargadae, Naqshi-i-Rustom, Persepolis and Istakhr—Teague-Jones did not have much time for tourism. His objective was to push on southwards as far as the Persian Gulf and Bushire. His aim in returning to Bushire was to make a detailed report on the current state of the terrible Kotal route where, ten years previously—as Teague-Jones well remembered—Wassmuss had been on the road; and the latter had returned to Bushire in 1924. Did Teague-Jones intend to meet him? In any case, nothing could affect his determination to press on to Bushire, not even the heavy rains and landslips which had recently made the route even more difficult, and crossing the terrible passes even more perilous:

The road continued bad in many places. Zobeida boiled furiously as she struggled up the long gradients in bottom gear, and several times I thought I would never reach the top of the pass. But the view from the summit was worth the effort, and I was rewarded with a grand panorama of bare brown mountain ranges decreasing successively in height, until they dwindled to mere foothills and lost themselves in the coastal haze of the Persian Gulf.[37]

Teague-Jones's readers are not told any more about Bushire. Apart from Wassmuss, who was a shadow of his former self by now, the British were worrying about a possible resumption of German activity in the region. Germany had become so aggressive in the Iranian market that, the following year, the Junkers company opened the first air link between Enzeli, Tehran and Bushire. Teague-Jones had just managed the same journey by land, from the Caspian to the Persian Gulf. It was an axis of fundamental importance in a land still without proper roads, but where Reza Shah, for reasons of economic nationalism, was to start building a trans-Iranian railway in 1927: things were looking up for the north–south axis. The British for their part were attempting to establish the need for an east–west railway line, from Khanaqin on the Iraqi frontier as far as Tehran, via Hamadan.[38] Teague-Jones's tour thus fits into the geopolitical battle over the planning and construction of communication routes on Iranian territory.

Iran from west to east: return to Baluchistan

The consul at Shiraz and Teague-Jones disagreed about the route. The consul, who wanted to steer the traveller towards the safest route, favoured the road to the north which made a long detour via Yezd. Teague Jones on the other hand wanted to take the southern route from Shiraz to Kerman via Niriz, which was reputed to be the worst bandit lair in the region. The direct, and shortest, road had been partly repaired by the British during the First World War but had since fallen into disuse. No telegraph line, no militia posts, plenty of highway robbers, it was definitely an excellent introduction to the Iranian East, 'a land forgotten by Allah'. Despite his sincere attachment to Teague-Jones, Abdul refused to venture into it. It was therefore necessary to hire another servant, who would rapidly turn out to be a less amenable and dependable companion. There were more punctures from mule-shoes, a resort to mustard-oil to lubricate Zobeida's engine—since the new factotum had forgotten to load a precious oil-can—errors in finding the right direction, the departure of the unreliable servant and an inevitable attack from bandits, as well as many other exploits, which Zobeida and Teague-Jones, now on their own, performed together on their way to Kerman. The original plan for the journey was to go to Zahedan and then to make due north for Meshed in Khorasan—a road that Teague-Jones had already travelled on foot and by mule in 1918—before returning to Tehran. He was familiar with this difficult and boring route, which had been the prelude to his adventures in Russian Turkestan. It was a dreary prospect, happily transformed by a providential telegram:

It was from the board of directors. They thanked me for my last batch of reports and requested me to proceed as soon as convenient to India, to look into their existing organisation there, and in countries further east. I should advise them when I eventually reached Bombay. This sudden development was as welcome as it was unexpected, and had happened most opportunely, since it absolved me from the long and monotonous trek up to Meshed. Now the question presented itself, how should I 'proceed' to India? Normally this would mean returning to Tehran, then down the road through Kirmanshah to Baghdad, thence to Basra and by sea to Bombay. As I subsequently learned, this is what the directors in London assumed I would do. The thought occurred to me of going through Afghanistan. This had long been a dream of mine, but I discarded the idea at once as impracticable. Permits would be necessary, and to procure these would entail much delay. This would be entirely inconsistent with 'proceeding as soon as convenient' to Bombay. There was just one alternative. I could bypass Afghanistan and reach India 'by the back door' by continuing eastward from Kirman. This seemed to be the obvious solution, for to me it appeared ridiculous to go all the way back across the Iranian plateau, when the road ahead would be so very much shorter.[39]

The decision was an audacious one. It took Teague-Jones beyond the ruins of the fantastic fortress at Bam and across the Dasht-e Lut, literally the 'empty desert', a sterile terrain where the trail quickly petered out and then disappeared in the banks of sand, salt and rock. The desert, 480 kilometres long and 320 kilometres wide, puts huge obstacles in the traveller's way: the dry ground is shifting or ridged, the heat is overpowering, and in springtime, the exact time of Teague-Jones's journey, there are violent storms. At that time the Dasht-e Lut had not been fully explored, and the few explorers who had ventured into it had described the special features which made it unsuitable for car travel: a surface of gravel and clay layers, inset with ridges of salt. A fearful desert, but also a solid frontier between central Persia and Afghanistan, the Dasht-e Lut surpasses the Gobi and the Kizil-Kum, which according to Khanikov are fertile prairies in comparison. The desert in front of Zobeida was different from the Syrian Desert. For a car, it was a question of 'navigating' on an immense sheet of dry and salty mud: a *kevir* is in fact a lake where a solid sheet has replaced the previous liquid one. Teague-Jones describes the surface of the desert as being completely flat, covered in a fine layer of gravel. Underneath there was very fine and powdery sand into which one could easily sink, and in places the sands were really in motion. These factors in combination provided Zobeida with a very tough ordeal. Her radiator was practically incandescent and she stalled continually despite her driver's encouragements. What with storms, shifting sands, and frequently getting stuck, the situation in this territory forgotten by Allah often seemed hopeless ... until a providential puncture gave Teague-Jones the idea of deflating the tyres as far as he could, which ultimately made it possible for Zobeida to overcome the sands of the Lut.

Exhausted by the ordeals he had been through, Teague-Jones sees on the horizon, through the shimmering mirage, an indistinct shape:

Distances are deceptive in the desert, especially with the mirage playing tricks with one's eyesight. The object quickly became more distinct, though still ethereal and seemingly suspended in air. Minutes later it resolved itself into a solid body in the form of a circular lofty tower, rising some sixty or more feet from the surrounding desert, like a red-brick lighthouse in a mud-coloured ocean.[40]

The magnificent apparition was none other than the Mil-i-Nadiri, Nadir's tower, a watchtower and also a kind of fortified boundary-post, supposedly built at the time of Nadir Shah (1736–1747) on the caravan route across the Dasht-e Lut. The tower, which stands in the lonely desert at a place called Fahraj—nowadays a village—was a fascinating sight. Teague-Jones took a photograph of it, making sure that Zobeida was in the frame. The tower allowed him to get his bearings and to resume navigation in the direction of Zahedan. In Baluchistan he was forced to struggle with another violent storm. Further on, the track reappeared, but was blocked by landslips or boulders. Her driver literally had to build a road for Zobeida to run on. But little by little there was a change in the country; mountains appeared on the distant horizon, and for the first time since the tower of Nadir there were signs of human presence. Among the more ghastly of the traps lying in wait for poor Zobeida, all described with determined humour, was the putrid corpse of a camel, which provided a different experience of soft terrain.

However, the journey now took a turn for the better as the driver's morale had returned, and in the distance he could make out the recognisable shape of Kuh-Malik-Siah, a real boundary post raised above the desert flats, a landmark at a point where the frontiers of Persia, Afghanistan and India (now Pakistan) meet. The view from the mountain promised an early arrival at Zahedan, known at the time as Duzdab, 'Thieves' Water': still a tricky journey in a country which even today swarms with raiders, bandits and smugglers. The Baluchistan town was small and out of the way, an Iranian frontier-post and the railway terminus for the line to Quetta. Teague-Jones and Zobeida had triumphed! As he was already familiar with the Indian part of Baluchistan, Teague-Jones allowed himself to be persuaded by a railway official to load Zobeida on to a wagon and take the train leaving for Quetta. After all, he had accomplished a personal sporting coup as the first car-driver to make a solo crossing of the desert from Kerman. So Zobeida was hoisted aboard, but she and Teague-Jones made a triumphal entry into the Quetta cantonment on all her four wheels. Just as she did so, one of her tyres exploded, a noisy epilogue to her Persian adventures. Zobeida would not travel this road again, but Teague-Jones did, taking the road from Bombay to London in 1928 in a car which this time would be supplied by William Morris.

The colonial eye behind the camera

In his account of his Persian adventures, Teague-Jones mentions other missions on behalf of the 'British manufacturers', which led him to make later journeys 'in countries further east'. He seems to have continued to use India as a partial base at the end of the 1920s, but he pushed on further east, to Ceylon, Burma, Thailand and Singapore, the latter a British commercial stronghold and nerve centre of influence in Asia. It is not easy to disentangle the political from the touristic aims of these journeys. There are few or no written documents in the archives, but there are many photographs and films produced by Teague-Jones and held by the Imperial War Museum which bear witness to his travels. It was already clear that he had artistic gifts as an excellent draughtsman, amateur painter and good photographer. In the 1920s Teague-Jones added a cine-camera to his travelling equipment and his talents in this field are obvious. His considerable collection of photographs displays a taste for the 'ethnographic portrait'. His films are an animated extension of and complement to these scenes and landscapes, a sort of motion-picture sketchbook in which he experiments with the basics of cinematographic technique while casting his eye over the colonial Orient. Trained to have a photographic memory—the principal quality in a good spy, according to John Buchan—Teague-Jones explores the otherness of the world with close sympathy. The nineteen reels of amateur film bequeathed to the Imperial War Museum make it possible to attempt a reconstruction of the way he saw the world, which adds considerably to the biography of a professional observer. Teague-Jones's cine-camera is sensitive to gestures, such as those of the Indian 'gondoliers' on Lake Dal whose sculling entails a curious rotary movement of the leg holding the oar, women using their spinning-wheels, the fisherman casting his net, the Indian potter, barber, weaver or road-mender—one digs with his spade while his assistant uses a rope attached to the spade to help, the sublime and sometimes comical manual techniques that are intrinsic to craftsmanship and human intelligence.

Teague-Jones's camera-eye and his close-ups allow him to capture his tribal subjects in Kenya and Tanganyika; he catches the movements of the bodies, the dances and the rhythms. In the Middle East, in Egypt or in Palestine, where people have a certain reticence about being photographed, the cine-camera's presence is more discreet, hidden or peeping over a slope. It can then capture fascinating street scenes: the baker, the craftsman, the public scribe in the Arab quarter of the Old City of Jerusalem in the 1930s, the extraordinary social variety and contrasts of a Cairo street. In order to catch reality and to observe the passers-by, whether human or animal—in the East in the 1930s donkeys and camels were still the kings of the road—Teague-Jones sometimes likes to wait in ambush at the side of the road or at a town-gate, by a church-door or in the corner of a mosque. He works to a set plan, taking his shots to the rhythm of small events as they happen. The reels of film, bearing the patina of time, in black and white and occasionally in colour, disclose a particular way of seeing the colonial world, and illuminate the inner world of Teague-Jones himself. He is, no doubt, filming as an amateur and for his own pleasure, but his 'filmography' reminds one to some extent of the banker Albert Kahn's film *Archives of the Planet* and his aim of filming everything so as to compile an inventory of a world that was soon to disappear.

A Cairo idyll …

Teague-Jones's journeys from India across the British Empire proliferated after the 1920s. He only made occasional appearances in London to see his employers, whether in Whitehall or industry, and to deal with administrative and banking business for the mysterious 'Eastern Exporters' at Mitre Court, off Fleet Street, to which, for a time, he arranged for his post to be forwarded. He is likely to have taken advantage of his stays in London to go to some of the meetings of the Royal Geographical Society, of which he was a member, although he did not give a talk himself, even though his recent crossing of the Dasht-e Lut would have merited an account to the members of the prestigious Society. In July 1933, however, it was for personal reasons that he returned to London. It was to put an end, secretly, to his marriage with Valya Alexeieva, making official a separation which in practice had existed for several years. No more would be heard of this marriage until 1988, when

Teague-Jones revealed its existence to the manager of Charlton House. It was a marriage which belonged to his youth and his adventures in the intelligence world, intimately bound up with his identity as Reginald Teague-Jones, who had now 'disappeared', and whose existence must never be disclosed to anyone, not even to his new wife. It was in Cairo, in October 1933, that Teague-Jones (Ronald Sinclair) married Elsa (Taddie) Danecker, daughter of a German engineer, Hermann Ferdinand Danecker.[41]

Nothing is known of the circumstances in which Teague-Jones met this tall and attractive German lady from a good family. Had she left Germany after Hitler's accession to power? Had she been living in Egypt with her own family for some time previously? In any case the man who married Elsa Danecker was a mature 44-year-old, and she for that matter was no longer a girl. Even if Teague Jones may not have told her all his secrets, beginning with his true identity, they embarked together on a life apparently untrammelled by any material constraint. The couple were to have no children and were relatively well-off. Until the Second World War, which they were to spend in New York, Reginald Teague-Jones and Taddie, or rather 'Ron' and Taddie, spent most of their time travelling in Egypt, Palestine, Ceylon, India, Burma, Singapore and Thailand. From India they travelled by liner via Aden and Mombasa to go on safari in Kenya and Tanganyika. They made an attractive couple, with no geographical or family ties, who drew a constantly renewed flow of friends from every kind of background. They were a couple open to others, and put a high value on relationships, friendships and new encounters. As was normal in good society, Taddie kept a visitors' book throughout her life for her guests to sign and comment in. As for Teague-Jones, he had an address-book which was constantly updated, containing very detailed notes—a vice of his professional training—on the people whose names appeared in it. Such and such a woman met on a steamship journey, such and such a couple 'with a very charming wife' encountered at a dinner on a given date. The foundations of this second marriage were grounded in the pleasures of society life, in leisure activities and in travel. The question of what they lived on remains something of a mystery, however. Perhaps Taddie had some private family income, while Teague-Jones must have continued to carry out 'commercial missions' while doing a bit of journalism, evidenced by the occasional article in the *Illustrated Weekly of India* during the 1930s.

Of Teague-Jones's stay in Egypt we know neither its length nor, apart from the marriage performed at the British consulate, its purpose. It is possible that he had instructions from the Manchester manufacturers on business relating to cotton or to the textile industry, just as it is also possible that his presence in Cairo can be accounted for by a specific intelligence mission to do with German policy in the Middle East. Despite the declaration of Egyptian independence in 1922, Britain was continuing to exercise an informal protectorate in Egypt. To the disgust of the Wafd nationalists under Saad Zaghlul, the famous 'four reservations' ensured that the British continued to exercise power in order to safeguard communications in the British Empire, the defence of Egypt against direct or indirect foreign aggression, the

protection of foreign interests and the existence of the Anglo-Egyptian condomin-
ium in the Sudan. Thus despite independence and Saad Zaghlul's electoral success
in 1924 the British presence was still as solidly established as ever on the Suez Canal
and in Sudan, the country where the headwaters of the Nile lie. In the 1930s Britain
thus retained full freedom of action in Egypt. And Cairo, where the British had set
up an 'Arab Bureau' during the First World War, had become the headquarters for
the British presence throughout the Middle East. At the time of the Cairo
Conference in 1921, held under the auspices of Winston Churchill, then colonial
secretary, General Allenby, Colonel Lawrence, Gertrude Bell and Sir Percy Cox had,
amid the ruins of the Ottoman Empire, determined the shape of Britain's new possessions in the Middle East. Despite local resistance Britain had installed its own
clients in every country, giving the crown of Iraq to Prince Faisal, son of Sherif
Hussein of Mecca, and that of Trans-Jordan to Prince Abdullah. With Palestine now
under the British Mandate, Britain controlled a continuous territory from Jerusalem
to Baghdad, though not without betraying the Arab cause which Lawrence had
ardently supported during the war. Teague-Jones's view of Lawrence of Arabia is
interesting. His reported comments in a work by Harry B. Ellis suggest that Teague-
Jones endorsed the vitriolic portrait of the hero of Arab politics, to whom he was
opposed in every way:

As a member of the Arab Bureau Lawrence had been concerned, if only peripherally, with
the fostering of the revolt, and Storrs took him to the Hedjaz, partly for his engaging company, partly for his judgement. Lawrence was only an obscure and ill-groomed captain, but
he attended the Jeddah talks and so impressed the Arabs by his knowledge of Turkish disposi-
tions that Abdullah exclaimed to Storrs perhaps a little irritably: 'Is this man God, to know
everything?' The Prince and the captain were of similar age and equal force of character and
did not much like each other. Lawrence thought Abdullah 'too clever'. Abdullah wrote later
that he was suspicious of Lawrence's influence among the tribes but added that 'through the
money he spent and the words he talked he became the uncrowned king of the Arabs'. To
the Western mind of the 1920's 1930's, Lawrence was a symbol of Anglo-Arab romance; but
Hussein himself was never easy with Lawrence and Faysal apparently regarded him, at least
in retrospect, with more curiosity than hero-worship. He made his mark at the Jeddah discussions, nevertheless, and was consequently appointed liaison officer with Faisal's forces,
then encamped upon the coast. From the beginning of 1917 he was intimately associated
with all the fortunes of the revolt, inspiring its aura of high romance and panache, and proving himself the most brilliant of its guerrillas. He was a puzzle from the start and so he has
remained. It was a Bedouin who, in a moment of inspired lucidity, dubbed him 'the world's
imp'. Like the British, the Arabs never mastered his character, never quite knew whether he
was a charlatan or genius. The more astute of them must have realised soon enough that he
was a poseur, a man with a gift for blarney and self-advertisement; but like everyone else they
usually found themselves caught in the spell of his extraordinary personality. As Churchill
said of him 'he always reigned over those with whom he came into contact'; and indeed, it
must have been hard to resist the magic of Lawrence in the desert, with his long-drawn
melancholy face alert beneath its head-cloth, and his slim sinewy figure preposterously
caparisoned.[42]

RONALD SINCLAIR, IMPERIAL TRAVELLER

There are many reasons, other than his honeymoon or tourism, why Teague-Jones may have been drawn to Egypt and the sizeable British community in Cairo, a world of its own with an Anglo-Egyptian elite—such as Sir Thomas Russell Pasha, head of the Cairo police—that was actively involved in every sector of the Egyptian economy. The British in Cairo ran the Egyptian railways, were irrigation inspectors, teachers, merchants, doctors, bankers or businessmen. The couple may have passed their wedding-night at the famous Shepheard's Hotel or at Mena House near the Pyramids, and frequented the most select British places in Cairo: the embassy at Garden City, with its gardens stretching directly down to the Nile, and the Gezira Sporting Club at Zamalek. They explored the Delta and the Gizeh plateau together, and spent a lazy afternoon by the roadside in an oasis beside the Nile watching the peasants, donkeys and feluccas go by. Teague-Jones, perhaps with Taddie's help, wrote an article[43] about the archaeological tragedy of the day, that of the famous Temple of Philae at the entrance to the first cataract of the Nile. Building work on the first Aswan Dam, erected by the British in 1908, subsequently raised and reinforced twice, in 1912 and 1933, had caused the flooding of the Temple of Isis which Nectanibis had built. With the help of wonderful photographs taken by a professional German photographer, E.R. Bachmann, which show the flooded kiosk, entrance and pylons of the Temple of Isis, Teague-Jones's article is a plea for the rescue of Philae. The majestic pylons, the harmonious columns, the colours, sumptuous blues, greens and yellows which have survived the centuries, were all these to disappear forever beneath the waters? That is the substance of the argument, which compares E.R. Bachmann's photos with those of Lehnert and Landrock (whose photography shop had been a Cairo institution ever since the two German photographers had set up in 1924), which show the state of the Temple of Isis before the flooding.

At this time it was easy to travel from Egypt to Palestine and Jerusalem. It was the Palestine of the Mandate, where the British were struggling with the Arab revolt and the Zionist question: the incident at the Wailing Wall in 1929 had set off a decade of tensions and violent incidents which grew steadily worse as Jewish immigration increased. It was Jerusalem within its old walls that Teague-Jones filmed at the Lion Gate, which opens on the eastern side of the wall, facing the Mount of Olives. This was a provincial city where there was much coming and going on the Via Dolorosa of donkeys, children, venerable greybeards, Bedouin, dignitaries, women returning from the spring with large containers balanced on their heads. In the Muslim quarter of the Old City, Teague-Jones watched, unobserved, men smoking their *narguilehs* (hookah) in cafés, the everyday business of the little shops in the markets, silent conversations on doorsteps, venerable greybeards passing by. Oddly, he filmed nothing in the Jewish quarter, nothing in the Jewish colonies in the rest of Palestine, which he visited nonetheless, and not even the holy places, other than the Dome of the Rock, seen from the Mount of Olives. This fact is worth mentioning, since Teague-Jones may have been sent to Palestine on a specific mission. Germany's aggressive pro-Arab policy following Hitler's assumption of power and its open support for the mufti of Jerusalem, Haji Amin el-Husseini, were sources of British anxiety. Teague-

Jones, who had some experience of German agents, and moreover a German wife, may have been the right man for the situation. Although there is no archival source to support this hypothesis, the text of a talk he gave many years later makes it possible to discern how he perceived Arabism. In 1958 he gave an outline of the contemporary history of the Arabs, in the form of a schoolroom story, to the members of a New Jersey Rotary Club:

Once upon a time, many years ago, before World War One, while the Turks still ruled the whole of the Arabian Peninsula, including what is now called Israel and Syria, there was an old saying current among the Arabs that Turkish rule, which lasted nearly 400 years, would finally come to an end when 'a White Prophet would come from the West who would make the waters of the Nile flow to Jerusalem'. Well, that sounded a very remote sort of prophecy, but the strange thing is that it did come true in 1918. The British forces pushed up from the Nile delta, the Turks retreating before them, until Jerusalem was occupied. The British commander was General Allenby. The Arabs never could pronounce that name and always called him Al-Nabbi, which in Arabic means 'The Prophet'! And to keep his troops supplied with water as they advanced, the engineers laid a pipe-line and pumped fresh Nile water all the way up to Jerusalem. And so the prophecy was fulfilled. The Turks were finally defeated, Arabia was liberated, and the Arabs all said Wah! Wah! and praised Allah and the White Prophet. But after that, things did not work out quite so well. Instead of getting what they had hoped for and had been promised—one single united Arab state—they found Arab lands were all being cut into numerous separate states, and placed under different rulers, mostly under Western control. Then, one day, some years later, I was in Bagdad, and an influential Arab sheikh who had fought with Lawrence against the Turks complained bitterly to me about the ill-treatment of the Arabs. It had been a betrayal, he said, to divide up the Arabs. And then he added 'but since you Christians divided even the Almighty into three parts, small wonder that you've carved up us Arabs!' And then he added in a very serious tone: 'But mark my words: one day a leader will arise among us, and then we will drive you out, and at last we will have an empire of our own'. That was many years ago, and it seemed a very small incident at the time, but in the light of more recent happenings, it begins to look like another prophecy in process of being fulfilled.[44]

Teague-Jones refers here to Nasser and his attempt to assert himself from 1956 onwards as leader of the Arab world. The passage is also of interest because it confirms retrospectively the political nature of Teague-Jones's movements in the Middle East in the inter-war years.

A passenger of Imperial Airways

As he explored the roads and caravan routes from the Middle East to India, Teague-Jones, who was alert to the way in which the modern era was transforming life generally, had the feeling that he was travelling through a world in the process of vanishing. In the very near future motorised transport would compete with 1,000-year-old modes of transport, and the wide spread of technology heralded the end of the 'traditional' societies he knew from India to Persia, and from Iraq to Egypt. He was particularly aware of this situation because the purpose of his missions was probably to reconnoitre continental land routes—as he did in Persia—but also the air links which were to perfect communications acròss the British Empire. After the First World War, the British looked at various plans for direct links between the Mediterranean—thanks to the Mandate in Palestine, they now controlled the port of Haifa—and India. It was a question of a main strategic route which would consolidate British positions and make it feasible to safeguard the territorial continuity of British possessions from Palestine to India via Mandate Iraq and Persia. According to Morton B. Stratton:

a great strategic route was in the making that would consolidate the British position in the Middle-East, open a new artery for commerce and speed troops and supplies to and from the Middle-East and India in times of emergency. It would protect and be protected by the air line above—together they would forge new 'overland' links of unprecedented importance for the system of imperial communications.[45]

The plan for a railway from Haifa to Baghdad was therefore still current, even though it had proved necessary to abandon hopes of creating a direct overland connection with India via Persia.

After the train and the car, the aeroplane was Teague-Jones's next venture, from which he filmed in the manner of Antoine Poidebard, the celebrated French Jesuit archaeologist and airman. In one of his films, he can be seen embarking on board the Karachi–Baghdad flight when Imperial Airways brought this route into service, wearing his inevitable pith helmet. From the plane he filmed the coastline of the Persian Gulf, the landing in Mesopotamia, the territory of Iraq, recording the geography of the landscape as seen from the air. As a passenger on the Karachi to Cairo flight via Baghdad on 22 April 1930, Teague-Jones photographed the de Havilland 66—the famous Hercules—refuelling in the middle of the desert: the plane is Imperial Airways' *City of Tehran*. The Karachi to Cairo route had been brought into service in January 1927 to carry passengers, freight and mail. The Hercules had been specially ordered by Imperial Airways for its ability to do long hauls in remote regions, where some of the intermediate stopping places were particularly problematic. These were the stops which Teague-Jones photographed, sighting his camera on the Hercules, the Bedouin and the cans of aircraft fuel—a scene familiar to readers of *Tintin and the Land of Black Gold*. The flights belong to the heroic age of aviation; to help the pilots navigate, a furrow several hundred kilometres long had been dug across the Syrian Desert. It was obviously necessary to make several stops, and the route from Karachi to Cairo that Teague-Jones took on a number of occasions ran through Gwadar, Jask on the Gulf of Oman, Lingeh and Bushire as far as Bassora, then due north to Baghdad before tackling the Syrian Desert in the west, with a stop at Rutba. The plane then went on to Gaza, Alexandria and finally Cairo. How often did Teague-Jones do this journey? Was he personally involved in the setting up of this air link, with its staging-posts clearly situated for strategic reasons? It is reasonable to think so, especially since he wrote a note about air connections in India: he reported on his experiences as a passenger on the Karachi to Cairo line, and offered some criticisms. The pilots are certainly experienced, he writes, but there were not enough of them. Similarly, the nine Hercules belonging to Imperial Airways were not enough for the fleet. He also deals with the question of the stops in Persia at Bushire, Lingeh and Jask, underlining the importance of appointing managers who speak Persian, 'as the Persians are very sensitive'. The quarantine rules should be revised, he concludes, mentioning the case of a passenger arriving from India en route for Cairo and held against his will for five days at Alexandria.[46]

On board these great liners of the sky, in the course of many journeys following the inauguration of the Karachi–Cairo and the Karachi–London flight which came into service shortly afterwards on 30 March 1929, Teague-Jones had the leisure to make some new acquaintances. A Hercules could only carry seven passengers, and the Karachi–London flight took seven days. It was under these circumstances that he met a young Indian called Abdul Ghani in a memorable encounter which he recorded many years later:

I met the young Indian Abdul Ghani in an aeroplane. It was one of the very early flights of Imperial Airways from India to England, and we had both embarked at Karachi, which was then the terminal point in the East. We sat in neighbouring seats and after the first few minutes of strangeness, for those long distance flights were still a novelty to most people, we got into conversation.

Abdul Ghani came of a wealthy Multani merchant family, and he spoke good English. He had graduated at Aligarh university and had recently joined his father's family business. This was his second visit to England and he told me he had also been once to East Africa where his father had relatives in Kenya. He said he was planning to try to extend their business to that territory.

Somehow the conversation turned on the 'Dominion Status' for India, a subject which was prominently in the news at that time, and the Indian press was full of it.

Abdul Ghani surprised me by condemning those Indians who were clamouring for complete independence for India. 'They are damn fools' he said 'and don't know what they are talking about. A lot of them,' he went on, 'particularly the Hindus, are dazzled by the idea of Indian sovereignty. They think that under a Hindu Raj they [could] be prime ministers or governors [or] senior officials. But not me. I'd settle for dominion status every time'.

Curious to follow his reasoning, I asked him to explain.

'Look he said, it's really quite simple. It's because of this'. He slipped his hand into his breast pocket and pulled out a British passport. He patted it affectionately. 'With this little blue book' he said, 'I can travel anywhere in the world, and I am protected and respected. Do you think that I'd swap that for Hindu Raj passport. Never!'

'But what about Dominion Status?' I asked.

'Ah that! Well, it's like this. D'you mind if I talk frankly?' He looked at me in a rather uncertain manner.

'Of course not. Go right ahead'.

'Well, then, you see, if India has dominion status, it means that we Indians are accepted as members of the British family circle as it were. We would all have equal rights within the family'. He paused and threw me side glance.

'Yes I said, go on'.

'So that, supposing, I wanted to go and establish myself in Kenya, or anywhere else, even in England itself, I would have just as much right and just the same opportunities and facilities as, well, as the British themselves'. He paused and with another glance as though to see how I was taking it, he continued. 'Well, if we have equal rights and facilities with you white people, don't you see that we will have tremendous advantages over you?'

'You mean in competition and so forth?'

'Of course, for the simple reason that our standard of living is so much lower than yours. We can undersell you and under-live you. Remember what Kipling said: 'the odds are on the cheaper man'. Well, we are the cheaper men, and given equal conditions and equal opportunities, and dominion status would give us those, we would beat you white people every time'.

'You really think so?' I said.

'I'm sure of it' he replied. 'Take East Africa—Kenya for example, where I want to set up in trade. My family have plenty of capital. What's to prevent our setting up in competition with the big European companies, the big trading agencies, the estate agencies, the department stores, shipping and the hotels. Apart from a paler skin, what has the white man got that we don't have? or that we wouldn't have if we were granted dominion status. Why we'd even compete with you and beat you in your own country. So you see why it would never pay us to have a completely independent India, with our own flag and our own passport.

We would be outside the family, and would have none of those privileges we need to enable us to compete on an equal footing'.

'On an equal footing?' I queried, and he sensed the sarcasm of my voice.

'Well, you know what I mean'.

I did not know exactly what he meant, but from that moment I found myself an ardent champion of complete Indian independence.

I did not maintain contact with Abdul Ghani, though our conversation remained vividly in my memory. The years went by. The British gave up India, handed it over as a flourishing concern, on a silver platter, as it were. The greater part of Moslem India broke away and called itself Pakistan. Talk of dominion status was a thing of the past. Both countries acquired their independence, but both of them elected to remain into the British Commonwealth. Very naturally, since by so doing they would enjoy the best of both worlds. As members of the British Commonwealth Club, they would remain within the family, and would thus be able to compete with the white man on his own ground and with the odds, as Abdul Ghani had said, very heavily in their own favour.

I have seen Abdul Ghani only once since our first meeting, and that was in New York just after World War II. He then introduced himself as a member of a syndicate of Pakistan concerns operating in East Africa, and he showed me a long list of enterprises controlled by them. It was an astonishing list. It included a number of well-known Kenya hotels which had originally belonged to Europeans but had since been acquired by Pakistanis, likewise coffee and sisal plantations, as well as a variety of prominent trading concerns.

Abdul Ghani and his friends and relatives had certainly made the most of their opportunity. As he himself had predicted, it seemed that the white man in open competition with him did not stand a chance. The odds were clearly on the cheaper man.[47]

This fragment of dialogue between the colonial master and the colonised subject has the evocative power of V.S. Naipaul, heralding the period of decolonisation and end of empire which Teague-Jones found so painful. It was during the flight over the Persian Gulf in 1930 that, thanks to Abdul Ghani, he was forewarned of the future that lay ahead.

A season in Tibet

Among the collection of films there is an entire reel devoted to Tibet, which reveals that Teague-Jones had followed another of the legendary roads that lead from India to the heart of the Eurasian continent. His visit to Tibet is slightly surprising, given the small number of travellers who were allowed entry, even in the twenties and thirties, the halcyon years for Anglo-Tibetan relations. Teague-Jones's film probably dates from 1935,[48] the time of Williamson's and Gould's visits to Lhasa. There are no images of the forbidden capital, either because he was not allowed to film there, or, more likely, because he did not go there. The film begins with a series of shots of the caravan route along the River Tista, leading to Tibet via the Chumbi Valley in the Kingdom of Sikkim, and to the Tibetan trading town of Yatung. This road, studded with checkpoints and Anglo-Indian stores all the way to Gyantse, was one of the main access routes to Lhasa from the little kingdom of Sikkim; its maharajah, under British oversight, watched over and regulated the Anglo-Indian trade route under the terms of the Anglo-Chinese Convention of 1890 between Sikkim and Tibet. As was his wont, Teague-Jones filmed the caravan: mules laden with crates of luxury toilet soap, toiling through the snow up the looping track in a countryside typical of this part of the Himalayas. Although the road is furnished at regular intervals with shelters for travellers,[49] it is long and difficult, climbing by slow degrees up the hills that lead to the roof of the world, to the rhythm of the panting men and mules.

The average time to cover the 175 miles from Gangtok in Sikkim to Gyantse in Tibet was eleven days, but Teague-Jones's cine-camera, no doubt for reasons of economy, does not linger on the scene. The next shots are of the slopes of Mount Chomolhari rising above the plain of Phari, the first town worthy of the name, not far from the frontier with Sikkim. The town of Gyantse, where there was a substantial Anglo-Indian trading post, can easily be identified by its walls and its famous monument with a multiplicity of chapels, the Kumbum chorten. Teague-Jones's journey in Tibet apparently ended here. It followed in the steps of Alexandra David-Néel—but without the mystical revelations—and of a few other European travellers. One can identify without much difficulty monuments photographed by others, such as the red 'Tara' near Gyantse, the sculpture of a red Buddha commissioned by a grateful man after his rescue from brigands. It is an exotic Tibet, where Teague-Jones comes across women in Tibetan costume happy to be filmed, and young children, shockingly dirty to English eyes, playing without a care in a Gyantse street less than a metre away from the worm-eaten corpse of a dog. The film ends with shots of a monastery where Teague-Jones witnessed what he thought was a 'Devil dance'. In any case, that is how he labelled the reel. The monastery, which belonged to the Gelugpa spiritual tradition which had been dominant in Tibet since 1642, may not have been in Gyantse. The poverty is striking; rickety doors and staircases, the monks' thread-bare robes, drums with holes in, all are to be seen in the few shots of the dance of 'the black hat'. The dance, in which the four kings who guard the four corners of the compass take part, was a ceremony which normally lasted several hours. Teague-Jones only captured a few minutes of it during what seems to have been the end of this voyage to Tibet.

Once again, it is impossible to identify what political or commercial reasons may have lain behind Teague-Jones's visit to Tibet. At the Anglo-Indian trading-post of Gyantse, his camera lingers on the unloading of packages and crates, the contents of which are unclear. They may have been arms, since the British did occasionally send arms to Tibet, but they could have been any other kind of Anglo-Indian imports. The only Tibetan export was wool, and since 1929 the country had been dependent on India for its supply of currency. Teague-Jones's presence at Gyantse, an important cultural, political and commercial crossroads, can be explained by a conjunction of political, strategic and commercial considerations. Gyantse was a through-route for wool from the neighbouring locality of Gyangro, wood from the frontier region of Bhutan and merchandise from Nepal transported over the Himalayan passes and the sacred road from Sakya to Lhasa. Since Younghusband's expedition to Tibet in 1904, Tibet was one of the key pieces in the variable geometry of the Great Game, in which the opposing players, depending on the political conjuncture, were Britain, China and Russia. At the instigation of the Indian viceroy, Lord Curzon, the British govern-ment of India was attempting to establish a position in Tibet, within whose territory, lying beyond the Himalayan kingdoms, the line of the northern frontier of British India was still uncertain. It had only been established for a few sections defined in the Anglo-Chinese Convention of 1890 relating to the frontier between Sikkim and Tibet, and by the 1914 Simla Convention which established several hundred kilometres of frontier between the east of Bhutan and Burma in the form of the McMahon Line.

At the time of Teague-Jones's visit, Anglo-Chinese rivalry in Tibet was at its peak. On the death of the thirteenth Dalai Lama in December 1933, a Chinese mission had been sent to Lhasa, to which the mission by Williamson and Gould in 1935 was a response. The absence of any reference to Teague-Jones's visit (obviously as Ronald Sinclair), even though his admittance to the country was officially approved by the British authorities, points to a clearly defined mission in the context of Anglo-Chinese rivalry, before China's attention had been deflected from Tibet by war with Japan in 1937. The strict controls and censorship exercised by the government of British India over the admission of travellers to Tibet suggest an informal mission under the auspices of the IPI, which may have been entrusted to Teague-Jones in collaboration with Vivian Gabriel. A mission of this kind would have been a comple-ment to the missions of Williamson and Gould. It would fit with the interventionist stance of the British Indian Foreign Office, which with the active encouragement of

Olaf Caroe was in favour of establishing a British mission in Lhasa, and consolidating India's strategic frontier by means of the Himalayan buffer states, particularly where the McMahon Line ran through the sector of Assam. In the last years of the British Empire, the Caroe doctrine reflected the views of the British government of India and by extension those of its secret services, but not those of the authorities in London. Teague-Jones, who considered the two variants of the Silk Road—north or south of the Takla Makan, through the Tien Shan mountains or along the edge of the Tibetan plateau—to constitute the world's most important commercial and strategic axis, could not have travelled in Tibet without reflecting on these great geostrategic dreams.

During the Second World War[50] the British in fact succeeded in opening several supply routes to China, one across Tibet and another across Soviet Central Asia. During the summer of 1942, one of the supply routes from British India to China passed through Baluchistan, Iran, Turkmenistan and Kazakhstan before finally reaching Xinjiang. A combination of road and rail gave the British a potential capacity to despatch 2,000 tons of supplies per month. It reinstated, in the context of the Grand Alliance, the strategic value of the Transcaspian Railway line. The military imperatives of the Second World War and the Japanese threat thus endow Teague-Jones's tribulations from Turkmenistan to Baluchistan and from India to Tibet with a degree of retrospective coherence. This is where the Great Game of the twentieth and twenty-first centuries is actually taking place. For, still today:

Tibet lies at the heart of that field, where the spheres of influence of China, India, Pakistan, Russia and its former Central Asian Republics, Pakistan, Iran, Iraq, even Myanmar (Burma), and the United States (whose presence here would certainly have astounded Younghusband and Curzon and probably startled Mackinder as well). Whatever it was in Kipling's day, the 'Great Game' has become a mass sport with a huge following.[51]

8

RONALD SINCLAIR IN AMERICA (1941–60)

In Teague-Jones's film archive there are a few traces—some short clips of colonial Morocco, the Straits of Gibraltar and a crossing of the Atlantic in heavy weather—of his sojourn on the other side of the Atlantic from 1941 onwards. A strong swell drew Teague-Jones on to the deserted deck, washed at short intervals by the breaking sea. Braced against the spray, his spirits raised by the raging elements and his eye on the log, he made his ocean crossing as the first phase of the Battle of the Atlantic was at its height. Riding the long swell, the ship headed for America and New York at full speed. As he watched the stormy horizon and the turbulent waves, Teague-Jones was hardly bothered by the possible appearance of a German submarine. At the age of fifty-two the sleeping agent was resuming an official position in the new organisation responsible for setting up an Anglo-American intelligence system. He was full of private delight that the war had restored him, like so many other men, to a job where he could be of immediate use. Already he could see the skyscrapers sprouting on the horizon. New York was the beginning of a new chapter in Teague-Jones's life. Friends in great numbers, receptions, cocktail parties and dinners, a social life charged with the energies of a unique world metropolis, all of these were the pleasures which New York had to offer to 'Ronald Sinclair, British Consul'. But besides this job he had another official mission, one which went to the heart of the Anglo-American relationship at a crucial time when, against a background of the great dismantling of colonialism, power at world level was in the process of passing from one state to another.

While the secret services of the government of India had stopped paying some of their best agents after the First World War, Teague-Jones was able to resume an official position because the Second World War had provided an opportunity to re-employ them and to pay them out of other than private back-door funds. As consul at New York in 1944, he was responsible for 'Indian, Jewish and Communist matters' and for attending to 'the growing number of applications from ex-service men for

205

assistance of one kind and another'.[1] Paid by the government of India, he remained, under cover of consular activities, a political agent whose primary task was to keep an eye on changes in American perceptions of the Indian problem, a matter of ever more burning interest in the context of the war. The British consulate in New York occupied an exceptional place in the American political scene, as an office which combined orthodox consular activity with political duties. As the consul general himself wrote in 1946, it was a useful and indeed essential observation post due to the fact that New York was the financial capital of America, was the biggest city on the continent, 'contains national groups drawn from almost all countries of the world', and was the seat of the United Nations. New York was also 'the principal point of entry for visiting politicians and eminent men of all nationalities and interests who use this city as a sounding board for their views and it is an important Trades Union centre; and the effect of New York politics on national politics cannot be ignored'.[2]

What was true of the importance of the New York consulate as a privileged observation post for British diplomacy was equally the case for the intelligence system set up during the Second World War. Teague-Jones's presence in New York in 1941 was in fact directly linked to the creation of British Security Coordination (BSC). BSC was an intelligence organisation located in the heart of Manhattan, on floors 36–8 of the Rockefeller Center, which coordinated the activities of MI6, the Political Warfare Executive and the Special Operations Executive. Under the direction of William Stephenson, the BSC was supposed to provide liaison with the American and Canadian authorities—including the FBI—and to set up an Anglo-American intelligence system, the need for which was deemed vital in the context of the Second World War. The identity of the deputy director of BSC—an Australian-born intelligence officer—is sufficient to explain Teague-Jones's presence in this outfit: he was Charles Howard ('Dick') Ellis, an old friend of Teague-Jones from the days of the 'Transcaspian episode'. The friendship was made in 1918 in the area between Ashkhabad and Meshed, where Malleson's mission, to which Ellis was directly answerable, was based. In the sixties, well after the Second World War, when Ellis's book on the Transcaspian episode appeared, the two men were still exchanging letters replete with political and strategic matters relating to Iran and Central Asia. For example, the publication of a book by Lev Mirosnikov, the Soviet historian, on British expansion in Iran between 1914 and 1920, stimulated an exchange of well-informed views between them. As both men were fluent in Russian, they used Russian to write about confidential topics in their letters. And after Ellis's death in 1975, Teague-Jones was to stay in contact with his son Peter (Olik) in Canada and his daughter Ann Salwey, children of two different marriages. It is understandable that Ellis, newly recruited by William Stephenson in 1941 and a senior officer in SIS, should have thought of asking for Teague-Jones, his colleague, accomplice and friend. The two men were therefore reunited in New York before the United States entered the war.

RONALD SINCLAIR IN AMERICA (1941–60)

British Security Coordination: at the heart of Anglo-American relations during the Second World War

Teague-Jones's trajectory from India to America might seem atypical and exceptional. In reality, it is largely representative of what Nigel West[3] describes as the 'Indian policeman syndrome'. Many colonial policemen were employed during the Second World War by the British security services:

and more than a few of them came from India, but those aware of the labyrinthine qualities of Indian politics will not belittle the achievements of the Indian police, surrounded as they were by plots, intrigues and disturbances. The British-controlled intelligence system in the sub-continent is even today held up by some of those qualified to judge as an enviable model of an intelligence-gathering organisation.

Rockefeller Center, 38th Floor, Room 3801

Gathering the British intelligence elite together in New York was the initial purpose of British Security Coordination, which was set up in May/June 1940 with Churchill's backing. An intelligence and propaganda service, BSC was placed under the direction of William Stephenson (1896–1989), a talented Canadian industrialist, who had made a fortune between the two wars in a great variety of sectors from real estate to aeronautics, steel, radio, gramophones and cars. With his strong links to industry, the Canadian millionaire had contributed to the British war effort in 1939. In response to this, Churchill had sent Stephenson to New York to set up a secret spy network in the United States, at that point a neutral in the European conflict, with the whole western hemisphere as its proposed scope. Under his cover of official in charge of British passports, Stephenson had installed a branch of SIS in the well-known Rockefeller Center in midtown Manhattan, and given it the name of British Security Coordination. It coordinated action by the different services—MI5, SIS and SOE—across the entire American continent, and provided the interface with American intelligence. At a time when the United States was still neutral, the successful propaganda campaign against the isolationists—the America First Committee in particular—numbered among BSC's first achievements. Stephenson's other collaborators in New York included Hamish Mitchell, also a senior officer in SIS, whose early responsibilities involved protecting equipment bought by the British from German sabotage. According to Nigel West he had sought unsuccessfully to deepen relationships with the FBI and the State Department. BSC's activities were, therefore, directed by three men: William Stephenson, Charles H. Ellis and Hamish Mitchell.

A supposedly unexpurgated account of BSC, published in 1999 with a preface by Nigel West, which William Stephenson's colleagues produced at the end of the Second World War at his behest, gives a general idea of the multiplicity of its activities. In a short preamble published in New York in 1945, Stephenson presents 'this record of lessons learned and of methods evolved under the impetus of war'.[4]

Without the slightest attempt to sensationalise, he states that the report is a contribution to the maintenance and long-term continuance of such a 'coordinated' service. It demonstrates above all, he writes, that:

during the period under review, an organization in the Western Hemisphere restricted in its authority to collecting intelligence by established means would have been altogether inadequate and that the success of secret activities was primarily dependent upon the coordination of a number of functions falling within the jurisdiction of separate government departments in London. It was only as a result of such coordination that BSC had the necessary elasticity to meet the urgent demands of the situation and to adapt itself readily to swiftly changing needs. In referring to it, one feels impelled to make specific mention of the close cooperation afforded BSC by HM Embassy in Washington—without which much that was achieved could not have been. Lord Lothian's intimate concern in the early days proved invaluable; and so, too, did the unfailing support subsequently given by Lord Halifax. The conception of coordinated operations in the field of secret activities, which BSC originally exemplified, was the basis upon which the Americans built, with astonishing speed, their own highly successful wartime Intelligence Service. It is, perhaps, not going too far to suggest that this conception may properly be regarded as essential to the maintenance of worldwide vigilance and national security in the critical years ahead.[5]

Euphemism is one of the characteristics of the language of intelligence, as Stephenson's words demonstrate, since in reality the British services took a rather condescending view of reports from the OSS (Office of Strategic Services), the central point of American intelligence and forerunner of the CIA. Furthermore, the BSC report depicts the early OSS—it was set up in 1941 by 'Wild Bill' Donovan—as a rag-bag made up of a hundred or so middle-aged university graduates, specialists in economics, anthropology and a number of other disciplines, led by a dozen scarcely younger bookworms. The reports produced by OSS during the war, notably on the Middle East, India and the colonial question, were in fact a source of consternation to British intelligence authorities because of their amateurism and elementary character. This simple fact throws a light on the ambivalence of Anglo-American relations in the intelligence field.

It is not easy to identify Teague-Jones's exact contribution to BSC's innumerable activities during the Second World War. Before Pearl Harbour, intelligence and counter-propaganda against the Axis and isolationist circles had been a central focus for BSC. It had in particular mounted a very active campaign against the traffic in German products—for example chemicals produced by IG Farben or BASF and camouflaged as the products of Swiss or Swedish industry—and kept active surveillance on the many German agents distributed across the American continent. Teague-Jones, a German speaker and married to a German, may have been given this kind of mission, particularly since he went to Panama on one unidentifiable occasion. Whatever the case, a short sequence in one of his films provides evidence of his fascination with the system of locks on the Panama Canal. At about the same time—it is unclear whether this was before or after Pearl Harbour—he went to the Caribbean for reasons which, in the context of the war, cannot have been purely those of tourism. These few traces of Teague-Jones's visits to Central America and the Caribbean fit in any case with the priorities fixed by Stephenson in 1942: to combat Axis attempts at subversion in Latin America, and any possible German and, especially, Japanese invasion. BSC's report states that, far from diminishing, the possibility of a German invasion had actually increased:

for the Germans now had the active support of the Japanese, who, during the first four months of 1942, were spreading with terrifying speed and competence over the debris of three empires in the Far East. The Americans learned that Japanese ships were cruising off the vulnerable coast of western South America.

The activities of the 'strategically disposed and militarily organized' Japanese communities in Brazil, the travels of Japanese officers disguised as merchants or household servants, and especially the rather too well-equipped Japanese scientific expeditions to the most remote areas of Latin America were therefore placed under surveillance by the BSC network of agents.

While Teague-Jones's papers provide no support for the hypothesis of his direct involvement in the questions of the long- or near-range threat from Japan to the American continent, his visits to Burma, Singapore and Bangkok—evidenced by his films, but again difficult to date precisely—may be in some way connected with the establishment of the 'Asian Co-prosperity Sphere' announced in 1940 by the Japanese foreign minister, Matsuoka. The fall of Singapore (15 February 1942), shortly followed by the Japanese capture of Rangoon, was a terrible blow to the prestige of the British Empire, raising the possibility of an imminent collapse of British rule in India, and throwing the Japanese threat in the Indian Ocean into sharper relief. The Indian question, which from then on was to be Teague-Jones's main concern in the United States, was set in this context, and weighed heavily not only on British attitudes to supporters of Indian independence, but also on Anglo-American relations. Such questions, with worldwide implications, preoccupied the agents of BSC high up in the Rockefeller Center skyscraper. In the second part of his novel,[6] *Khyber Blood-Feud*, Teague-Jones describes a meeting in New Delhi between 'Jim Allenby', a US Army captain, and 'General Fraser', a senior officer in British intelligence, complementary characters in this disguised autobiography. Teague-Jones has 'General Fraser' address the following remarks to his young hero:

'Well, when this second war started, it found us, as usual, quite unprepared for any big scale emergency. When the Japs came in, and we lost Singapore and Burma, almost anything might have happened there on the Border. But it didn't, thanks very largely to the common sense of the tribesmen.'

Jim nodded again. 'It must have been touch and go sometimes, wasn't it?'

'Yes, it certainly was. But now the tide has definitely turned, and things are much better than they were. Still, we're not out of the wood yet; there are plenty of problems still to be tackled, and, as soon as one is solved, others seem to crop up'.

'I guess, that's how it always is', Jim said.

'The Japs are gone, thank goodness, but the Germans are still up there in Kabul, and just recently we came across fresh signs of their activity'.

Jim sat silent, with a look of concentrated attention on his face. General Fraser sipped his liqueur, put down the glass thoughtfully, then continued in a more serious tone.

'We're convinced the Germans have some new game on because our people recently intercepted and deciphered a secret enemy message. From this we learned that they were sending out a man whom they called Haji Usman. And from the wording of the message it was quite clear that this Haji Usman is an important agent on his way out to the Middle-East and India'.

The paternal figure of the old general brought out of retirement and put to work again, initiating the young American in the mysteries of the new Great Game, is not a bad symbol of the master–pupil relationship between the British and the Americans during the Second World War. But it appears that when he arrived in the United States in 1941, Teague-Jones was at first actively involved in the resolution of a colonial problem which closely affected Anglo-American relations and the strategic imperatives of the Battle of the Atlantic: the problem of the Bermudas.

June 1941: an emergency mission to Bermuda

The Bermudas archipelago in the North Atlantic, lying relatively close to American territory—1,030 kilometres away from North Carolina—is sometimes called 'the Gibraltar of the West' in reference to its strategic position controlling access to the United States and to the Caribbean. A Somers Isles Company colony at the beginning of the seventeenth century, a Royal Navy base in the aftermath of the American Revolution and the second war of independence in 1812, out of which the British planned their attacks on Washington DC and Chesapeake, the British colony of Bermuda had in the nineteenth century become the North American base for the Royal Navy. The two world wars allowed the Allies to test the strategic worth of Bermuda as a marshalling depot for the transatlantic convoys and, during the Second World War, as a naval and air base. In May 1940 the United States demanded the right from Britain to establish military bases there: a request which irritated Churchill, who was determined to make no unilateral concessions so long as the United States remained neutral. But the Battle of the Atlantic was raging. The submarine war was inflicting ever more serious losses on British shipping, while the destruction of the cruisers *Prince of Wales* and *Hood* in the spring of 1941 weighed heavily on Churchill and on British public opinion generally. The prestige of Great Britain suffered badly in that month of May 1941, when 'the panting British asked themselves whether they were losing their mastery of the seas'.[7]

For the British and Americans the setting was now propitious for a settling of the old argument. While as early as September 1940 an agreement had provided the United States with the right to establish bases in Bermuda, in March 1941 the Americans obtained the right to establish naval and air bases. The agreement of

RONALD SINCLAIR IN AMERICA (1941–60)

27 March 1941 states that the mission of Bermuda Base Command is to defend American military and naval installations in Bermuda, to use all means within its capacity to destroy hostile forces at sea or in the air, to serve the navy and to cooperate with local British defence forces.[8] When Teague-Jones visited Bermuda in June 1941, the construction of two American bases was under way. The bases, which were due to be completed in 1942, occupied almost 6 square kilometres of land and polder at Fort Bell on St David Island and at Kingley Field on Long Bird Island. From landing strips for the heaviest bombers, to houses for the inhabitants and batteries for coastal defence, the construction of the bases was an urgent undertaking. In this year of 1941, a turning-point in the war—in June the Germans attacked the USSR, and in December the Japanese attacked the American base at Pearl Harbour— Bermuda's strategic value was incalculable. Far enough away from the US coast, Bermuda enabled long-range air patrols over the Atlantic Ocean. At the same time the islands were near enough to link up with naval or air coastal patrols:

Bermuda's location makes it a key point in the communications of the Northern Atlantic. Under United States control, it provides a valuable location for Naval Operating Base and for air operations against hostile air or surface forces in the Western Atlantic. If this island were to pass into hands of hostile forces, it would become an ideal location from which to conduct submarine and air operations against trans-Atlantic communications and against the coast of the United States. At the present time, because of the strength of British and American Naval forces in the Atlantic, the local defensive forces in Bermuda need to be only strong enough to protect against hostile raids by sea and air.[9]

Such, in broad outline, was the strategic function of Bermuda at the end of June 1941 when Teague-Jones arrived in the archipelago. With its idyllic beaches of pink sand, clear turquoise coral seas, palm-trees stirring in the light breeze, there was nothing in this little island paradise to remind one of the tumult of war. Yet a few days previously something momentous had happened: on 22 June the German Army had invaded the Soviet Union.

Despatched by BSC to examine questions relating to security and intelligence in Bermuda, Teague-Jones was confronted by problems on the local political scene, since the colonial authorities resented the March 1941 agreement on the establishment of American bases as an affront to their 'sovereignty'. The local authorities, under the direction of the governor, Sir Denis Bernard, openly expressed their lack of enthusiasm, not to say outright hostility, and were practising a policy of systematic obstruction, arguing that the agreement of 27 March 1941 was only an agreement and not a treaty. In these circumstances the measures stipulated by the agreement should, according to them, be subject to local legislation. Furthermore, the June 1941 contract for the granting of American military bases in Bermuda also provided for the establishment of a submarine base on Ordnance Island. It was one of many other sources of tension, such as the question of the payment of customs duties and local taxes, which set the island authorities against both the Americans and the British authorities, who were accused of having sacrificed the traditional autonomy of the islands in the name of higher interests. For Teague-Jones, whose main focus was the intelligence system, the task was a test of Anglo-American relations and involved a diplomatic mission to the local authorities:

Steeped in the tradition of generations of Colonial administration based on a high degree of self-government, Bermuda is now finding herself faced with new and wider problems forced upon her by events and changes in the outside world around her, and for which there is no established precedent. As a result of these changes she is finding herself called upon to modify and to a certain extent subordinate her own local interests to those of the greater imperial structure of which the island forms an integral and essential strategic part.[10]

During the week of his mission, from 23 to 29 June, Teague-Jones met the different British political and military representatives, including the head of Imperial Censorship, and of course his excellency the governor. On the American side he had very cordial meetings with Captain Jules James of the US Navy, in charge of the American naval base, the American officer responsible for naval intelligence, and other officers in the American Navy. Having been given the task of assessing the intelligence system in Bermuda, Teague-Jones first had to confront local tensions, which he describes in a short note addressed to 'Director, Security Co-ordination', who could only be either William Stephenson or Charles H. Ellis:

One of the strongest impressions gained during my recent visit to Bermuda was the evident lack of knowledge and understanding of what was going on in the outside world. By this I mean knowledge of those matters which must eventually exert an indirect if not a direct influence upon the local affairs of the Colony. Thus, for example, on the all important question of Anglo-American relations, I found a disturbing lack of comprehension of the scope and significance of these relations, even in the highest official circles. I found that I was accorded an interested hearing when I spoke about matters on which one would have expected one's hearers to have been already well informed.[11]

The political situation naturally affected the intelligence system set up by BSC, in which Bermuda was an essential link. In respect of counter-espionage, Bermuda was one of the most important censorship stations in the western hemisphere: every year tons of mail were examined there so as to extract information which was often of importance. According to the BSC report,[12] Imperial Censorship, which passed on much of the harvested information to the FBI, was admired by the FBI for its Bermuda laboratory, which had specialised techniques for reading invisible inks.

Teague-Jones was able to visit the different departments of the Imperial Censorship service, which was divided into three main branches. While it was 'officially' concerned with the censorship of mail in transit, Imperial Censorship also housed a branch of the secret services. Travellers Censorship was covered at length in Teague-Jones's report to his superiors at BSC, since its operations were suffering from interference from the local authorities. This service, whose duties were to observe and question transatlantic travellers, by sea or by air:

is what may be described as an 'unorthodox' branch of the Department, whose functions have been 'loaned', as it were, to the Security and Intelligence Services, and who by the very nature of those functions are brought into direct contact with and in certain respects come under the control of the local administrative authorities. It is as a result of these points of contact with the Colonial Government that certain friction had arisen which is not only very seriously hampering the efficient working of the Department, but is inducing in the Executive Staff a most deplorable mental state of discouragement and dissatisfaction. It is essential that this state of affairs should be remedied without delay, and to seek a prompt and practical solution to the problem has been my first task.[13]

In a word, the fact that the governor of Bermuda, Sir Denis Bernard, had official responsibility for routine or exceptional surveillance of passengers was damaging the work done by the Censorship officers. His excellency delegated his responsibilities to the colonial secretary, Major Eric Dutton, whose subordinate was A.R. Spurling, in charge of Customs and the Extra Revenue Office. Holding the right to decide whether or not the censors should or should not interrogate such or such a passenger, 'in his own substantive capacity as Extra Revenue Officer, whatever that may imply, Mr Spurling possesses many sterling qualities. He is reputed to be active and pains-taking with an excellent record behind him', but on all the evidence he was not up to the job. Unable to settle legal disputes without referring personally to the colonial secretary, he wasted a great deal of the Censorship officers' time, imposing madden-ing delays: transatlantic vessels normally stopped at Grassy Bay, in fine weather forty-five minutes away from the colonial secretary's office at Hamilton. It was even more of a nuisance when the ship stopped at Murray's Anchorage, an hour and a half from the shore, which meant that it took almost three hours for Spurling to go away and return with his decision. Spurling was easily impressed by the immunity enjoyed by the holders of diplomatic passports: to the great annoyance of the Censor officers, who took it as a slight on their professional prestige, he allowed their personal effects to be spared any searches, and ordered that they were not to be questioned. 'Thus, many opportunities of interrogating knowledgeable travellers with possibilities of acquiring valuable information have been lost merely because Mr Spurling did not approve of the passengers being interviewed.'[14] Conversely, Spurling subjected important passengers to inconsiderate treatment on a number of occasions, which were immediately picked up by the American press. Spurling aside, the whole secu-rity system set-up in Bermuda was suffering from these inefficiencies. Even though the colonial secretary claims that he too was unhappy with Spurling's behaviour, Teague-Jones's proposal was not to replace him, but to nominate:

a fully qualified Security Officer possessing in addition to security experience, the necessary tact and understanding to handle high level international passenger traffic, and the requisite knowledge and status to give prompt decisions in all matters affecting the handling of such traffic without reference to either the Colonial Secretary or to the Governor.[15]

Another local difficulty was that the presence of Hamish Mitchell, BSC's emissary in disguise to Bermuda, visibly discomforted the colonial secretary, Major Eric Dutton, and also to a degree his excellency the governor, who not only refused to meet him, but was reluctant 'to recognise the latter's position and functions as a responsible member of an Imperial Security organisation'. Teague-Jones, who had been given the job of sorting out this problem, therefore had to make enquiries among the different authorities in Bermuda, from officers in the Armed Forces to those in the civil administration and to the most prominent members of the colony's business community. From these enquiries it emerged that there was no particular reason for the colonial secretary's hostile attitude other than the fact, of some importance, that Hamish Mitchell was an American whose true job, that of a senior agent in BSC, could not be acknowledged because it had not been revealed. According to Teague-Jones, the man was generally popular in island circles, well regarded by the officers of the different services with whom he was in daily contact, and also of course in American circles:

He is regarded for what he is—a reputable and respected resident of the Colony, and that while he may not be and doubtless is not accepted as one those true-blood ancient families who point with pride to generations of ancestors born and bred in the Empire's oldest colony, … he is generally popular and welcomed in the principal social circles.[16]

No doubt local officials did not recognise Hamish Mitchell's rightful status because they had been left in ignorance of the exact nature of his job. To put an end to these misunderstandings, Teague-Jones suggests that the nature of his true mission should be revealed to the local authorities. Their lack of understanding:

is the inevitable result of the policy hitherto pursued of veiling the activities and even the name of the organisation in secrecy. While there have been good reasons for this in the past, and while it may not be the right moment to emerge from cover in the United States, it does seem desirable that something should be done to clarify the nature and functions of the organisation in so far as the British colonies in the Western Hemisphere are concerned. By this I do not suggest that we should 'sound the trumpet and beat the drum', but I do feel that a greater degree of frankness and the taking more into our confidence of responsible official circles capable of according useful collaboration, would undoubtedly result in a greater measure of reciprocity to our general advantage. In the case of Bermuda for instance, it would, I feel, strengthen the position of Hamish Mitchell and with him the position of Security Coordination, if he could be openly acclaimed as representative of that organisation instead of screening himself under the cloak of Censorship.[17]

For Teague-Jones it was even more necessary to disclose the true nature of BSC to the local authorities because it would enable direct cooperation with the Americans. As for security in Bermuda, which was in the process of becoming a crucial military and strategic base in the Battle of the Atlantic, the question was one which the local authorities were scarcely aware of in June 1941, at a time when thousands of foreign workers were arriving to work on the building-sites for the bases. Dragged from its peace and calm, not to say torpor, the colony of Bermuda was late in coming to terms with the scale of the global challenges which were now concentrated on its tiny island territory. Besides the need to appoint an officer from MI5 with special responsibility for local security, his excellency the governor and his administration had to be convinced of the need to adopt a friendlier attitude towards the American authorities. To these ends Teague-Jones, who was a friend of America for pragmatic but also for genuinely sympathetic reasons, recommended drastic measures. That the Americans should be regarded as foreign intruders come to trouble the peaceful existence of Bermudans—in October 1941 the American garrison in Bermuda numbered 3,695 men—was particularly intolerable in that the Americans, who were still neutrals, had come to help the British in one of the most critical moments of the war. Bermuda was a forerunner of later ambiguities in Anglo-American relations over the future of the British Empire. But for the time being, in June 1941:

the real problem is clearly psychological, and in fact resolves itself into the inability of the Colonial Government, from His Excellency downwards, to readjust their mental outlook to a radically changed order of things, for which they have neither precedent nor power of adaptability ... Such an attitude must inevitably induce in the other side the very reaction we are so anxious to avoid. The Americans, who at first were very unwilling to accord any assistance, have now been won over to complete collaboration, and in this spirit they have come forward with enthusiasm, expecting an even greater degree of willing cooperation from the British. They have been amazed to meet with the very opposite of this.[18]

Teague-Jones saw this attitude as reprehensible, since it could weigh the scales against the US entry into the war, which was the BSC's priority now that the terms of a close collaboration between the British and American secret services had been settled. For all these reasons the appointment of an agent to coordinate security in Bermuda seemed desirable, inasmuch as he would keep a watch on security in the islands, but also operate as a safety valve for Anglo-American relations, bypassing the long and complex diplomatic route.

However, Teague-Jones's proposal to appoint a local security officer for Bermuda directly seconded from MI5, in addition to Hamish Mitchell from BSC, met with objections. A certain Colonel Stratton argued that such a security officer 'ought to have a position corresponding to a SCO in a British port, and that just as the SCO is subordinate to and responsible to MI5 so the Security Officer in Bermuda ought to be directly under the orders of Security Coordination in New York'. For his part, Major Maude, on a visit to Bermuda from London, favoured the appointment of a single officer, whose status should be that of a regional security officer in England.[19] These purely administrative and technical issues are of no great interest—they merely serve to demonstrate that the work of a secret agent, whose work is subterranean and unofficial, is constantly up against red tape, no doubt made worse by personal rivalries. In this 'Bermuda impasse' Teague-Jones was looking for a workable solution which would smooth over the difficulties: rather than sack the governor of Bermuda, London would do better to spell out some clear policy directions:

It is my belief that if this action were taken from Whitehall, it would not be difficult even for myself on my next visit to Bermuda to induce His Excellency to a adopt a more rational and friendly attitude towards both the Americans and also towards those aspects of the security question which have hitherto not been regarded with favour by him. I venture to suggest this, in the light of my recent talk with His Excellency, whom I found extremely reasonable and open to conviction. I also believe that with a similar approach I might succeed in inducing in the Colonial Secretary a much better spirit of collaboration than he has so far displayed. It is my suggestion that in his case I be afforded an opportunity of trying to bring about improved relations before more drastic remedies are considered. It is in effect my suggestion that we aim at securing the smooth running of the existing machinery before proceeding to scrap and reconstruct.[20]

Here Teague-Jones again displays the pragmatism and understanding of psychology of which he had given proof in other circumstances. Teague-Jones's mission of conciliation to Bermuda was to help him to deal with analogous situations in Latin America and the Caribbean.

Major Sinclair, BSC Coordination officer

The Bermuda file in the Imperial War Museum archives, containing notes, correspondence and longhand drafts, is indisputable evidence of Teague-Jones's membership of BSC during the Second World War. The fact that these papers were not destroyed as in principle they should have been shows that Teague-Jones was determined to leave some relics of a mission of which he was rather proud. Perhaps it was a sin of pride on the part of an agent in the shadows who would have liked in the twilight of his life to have some recognition of his achievements. It was due to his intervention, after all, that the situation in the Caribbean seems to have improved after July 1941. As BSC coordination officer for Bermuda and the Caribbean, his principal duties were to maintain effective and cordial relations between the governors, their colonial secretaries and the representatives of BSC. Bermuda was the ground for a successful experiment in conciliation which Teague-Jones was to apply with tact and firmness in other British colonies in the Americas, thus ensuring that questions of security in the Caribbean were not immediately passed to the Royal Navy.[21] A comparable mission would later take him to British Honduras, where a similar conflict had broken out between the governor of Belize and the American naval and military authorities in the Panama Canal Zone. He was to give a short account of this many years later to an official in the Protocol Department at the Foreign Office:

The Americans had become genuinely alarmed by the heavy loss of shipping by enemy action in the approaches of Panama Canal. They had convinced themselves that enemy submarines were habitually refuelling in British Honduran waters and that the Governor was not taking sufficient preventive action. I had to go down and investigate the matter, and after exhaustive enquiries in British Honduras, the Canal Zone and Mexico, I was able to show conclusively and report to Washington that the American charges were without foundation.[22]

Similarly, at the end of July 1941, Teague-Jones's duties included dealing with communication routes between the United States and the American bases on Jamaica, Trinidad and Antigua. On the morning of 29 July 1941 he, together with a man named Des Graz and a Captain Hyde, met the New York head of Pan American

Airways to discuss the subject of the overly brief stop at Kingston, Jamaica, of the flight from Miami to Barranquilla, Colombia. BSC would have liked the stop to last for forty minutes, which would double the time available for checking the transit passengers at Kingston. The request was made in the context of the surveillance of Axis activities in Central and South America, and of the duty to provide security for the American bases in the Caribbean. A sketch-plan attached to the report shows that the four men also discussed routes and stops for possible transatlantic air links, the first running from New York to Bermuda, the Azores, Lisbon, Sierra Leone, Belem and Port of Spain, the second running from Miami to Monrovia (Liberia) via Natal, passing close to Cape Saõ Roque at the western extremity of Brazil. That these different possibilities for air routes should have been raised is a sign of BSC and FBI concerns; they saw the air link between Rome and Brazil provided by the Italian company LATI (Linie Aeree Transcontinentali Italiane) as a very dangerous propaganda channel for the Axis in the Americas.

His journeys increasing in frequency, Teague-Jones spent three days from 12 to 15 August 1941 at Trinidad, where there was an American base that was part of Caribbean Defence Command. He disembarked at Port of Spain in the company of Brigadier Craig: the place was swarming with Anglo-American agents, and the short stay in Trinidad became a summit conference:

In addition to meeting Major Wren,[23] we were fortunate in that our visit coincided with the arrival of Cmdr Furse, R.N., as also of Mr Anderson from the Consulate in Caracas, who is a Reporting Officer in the SO (I) organisation. This gave us an opportunity of discussing in detail the future basis of cooperation between the Naval Intelligence in the Caribbean, and Security Coordination in that area, and on the adjacent mainland. This question has been dealt with in a separate report. Before our departure Sir Connup Guthrie also arrived in Trinidad accompanied by Mr. Karri Davies, and we were therefore able to discuss with him the prospects of establishing in South America a system of Security Control Officers on a parallel to that already in operation in the ports of [the] USA.[24]

In the course of 1941 there were therefore the beginnings of an Anglo-American relationship which was obviously highly complementary but also highly ambiguous in nature. Teague-Jones's mission of conciliation and persuasion to the colonial authorities in the British territories with American bases took place at a moment of transition in the Second World War, when a British Empire in decline was facing the rising power of American imperialism. Had Rear-Admiral Alfred Mahan not recommended in his well-known work *The Influence of Sea Power upon History* (1890) that the United States should establish not colonies, but naval bases along the line of the main trade routes? The micro-conflicts on the islands with which Teague-Jones was occupied during 1941, all of them in British colonies harbouring American bases, appeared to presage future difficulties in Anglo-American relations, notably over the question of India.

The Anglo-American relationship and the test of India

Having spent the best part of the summer of 1941 dealing with questions of security linked to the Battle of the Atlantic, Teague-Jones returned to New York and his coordination mission at BSC. His preferred field was henceforth to be India, Palestine, Zionism and Communism, all issues of the day, and the sources of constant friction during the Second World War between progressive American circles and the British authorities. At the end of 1941, with both the USSR and the United States on his side, Churchill could feel capable of winning the war, even if in Asia the fall of Singapore (15 February 1942) was a decisive moment for the British in India. For the first time an Asian army had beaten the British. The political consequences of this defeat were not slow to make themselves felt. In the Indian subcontinent the hitherto passive opposition of the Congress party to British rule became more open and opposition mounted in pro-Indian circles in the United States. The issues raised by the Indian question, as seen from Teague-Jones's observation post in the United States, were both to do with colonialism, which was instinctively objectionable to the Americans, and with the express desire of both the British Labour Party and the Americans to win the support of the Indian people for the Allied cause in the world struggle.

The IPI: from imperial security to Anglo-American collaboration

In the face of rumours of an imminent collapse of British rule in India and the reality of the Japanese threat in the Indian Ocean, Churchill was constrained to make a conciliatory gesture in respect of the Indian question. The Cripps mission, described by Patrick French[25] as the 'non-event of 1942', was indeed a political gesture as ostentatious as it was ineffectual. Sir Stafford Cripps, a left-wing Labour politician who had gained recent prestige as British ambassador in Moscow at the time of the German invasion, and was a personal friend of many members of the Congress party, was despatched without delay on a mission destined to failure. The proposal to promote India to the status of dominion after the war, which was supposed to embody the new face of a Britain open to compromise and which Gandhi described as 'a post-dated cheque drawn on a crashing bank', was not really new. However, the Cripps plan specified a cumbersome institutional process and implied that the Muslim provinces would be free to choose to maintain their current status.[26] To Churchill's great relief, the plan was rejected by the Congress party on 10 April 1942, despite Nehru's support for it. Yet it nonetheless set in motion the movement which was to lead to independence and the partition of India. In the course of a press conference in March 1942, Cripps had referred indirectly to the possibility of autonomy for provinces which might remain outside India, which aroused anxiety among leaders of the Congress party who were facing Muslim separatism and the prospect of a balkanisation of the subcontinent. On the other hand Cripps had formulated proposals during his mission which went well beyond London's original intentions.

His promise, for example, of an Indianisation of the administration in the dominion—only interior and defence policy would have remained in British hands—had not received Churchill's backing, which explains the latter's undisguised satisfaction when he received the news of the setback to Cripps' mission.

It was, however, the last chance for a compromise: the failure of Cripps' mission led to a hardening of the Congress party's position, to a strengthening of Gandhi's determination and to the famous 'Quit India' resolution of 14 July 1942, in which the Congress party demanded immediate independence and refused all military cooperation, without however refusing at the same time to support Allied forces in the face of the Japanese threat. The Quit India campaign, which was felt by the British as a real declaration of war, unleashed a wave of arrests on 9 August 1942 in the course of which the intransigent viceroy, Linlithgow, had most of the leaders of Congress, including Gandhi and Nehru, put under arrest. The popular reaction quickly flared up in the following weeks with riots, strikes and acts of sabotage, at a cost of almost 1,000 deaths and 92,000 arrests.[27] But the improvement in the military situation, the halting of the Japanese offensive—despite the fact that the Indian National Army under the nationalist dissident Subhas Chandra Bose had offered its services to Japan in return for a promise of independence—and the abstention of the Muslim population allowed the British to regain partial control. Although the situation was further compounded by the terrible Bengal famine of 1943, which resulted in more than 1 million deaths and in clashes between Hindus and Muslims, the British authorities were thus able to requisition supplies and to raise further troop levies in a climate of relative calm. Now deprived of its leaders, the Congress party subsided for the time being, while with tacit British approval Jinnah's Muslim League strengthened its stance, although it remained undecided about proposals for the future. In March 1940 the League had adopted the 'Pakistan Resolution' at Lahore, which envisaged the creation of an independent Pakistani state, the territory of which it was careful not to define. A secret memorandum on the subject written in February 1941, entitled 'What is Pakistan?', demonstrated how difficult it still was to draw the frontiers of this future Muslim state.[28]

In this context it is worth exploring the mountain of files constituted by the archives of the IPI, to which Teague-Jones remained attached during the Second World War. The structure of the service, which had originally been part of the India Office with John Wallinger as its director, had evolved considerably since the time when he had first joined. From 1924 onwards the service was partly answerable to MI5, and it had also been given a new director in April 1926. At the time Philip Vickery, with whom Teague-Jones was to keep in touch until Vickery's death in 1987, was on his way back from a mission to the United States. There he had been dealing with, among other questions, the Ghadr (Revolt) movement, a revolutionary nationalist movement headed by Lala Har Dayal, who had built his network from among the Indian community of Portland, Oregon, and had won the support of immigrants from the Punjab settled on the west coast of the United States. Surveillance by IPI agents of the Ghadr movement in the United States and Canada continued until 1944, as the IPI archives held in the British Library show. The IPI, which was originally an imperial intelligence service fighting anti-imperialist subversion on Indian soil, rapidly became an intelligence organisation with long tentacles, working closely with MI5 and the Secret Intelligence Service (SIS):

Vickery's network was highly secret. Its existence was never acknowledged officially, and its contact with the outside world was always through indirect channels. All dealings with India went via the Director of the Intelligence Bureau in New Delhi, and IPI's communication with the India Office was routed through a single senior civil servant, usually one of the two assistant under-secretaries of state. This meant that even in the upper echelons of the Government of India, only a handful of people were aware of IPI's function or the real nature of its operations. For most officials it was simply an acronym for an anonymous organization about which they knew very little.[29]

IPI was therefore expected to take an interest in every matter, whether close to home or further afield, that bore on the security of British India: Russian, German or Japanese penetration, subversive communist activity, the Khilafat movement for the restoration of the Muslim Caliphate which had been abolished with the departure of the last Ottoman sultan, anti-British propaganda by the Congress party and so on and so forth. In the early 1920s the IPI began to compile files on Indian associations in the United States which took part in propagating nationalist ideas. It was in this area that IPI, no doubt through the agency of BSC in New York, sought to establish cooperation with the American services—OSS and the FBI—during the Second World War. Soviet activities and the threat of a communist conspiracy were among the other topics of concern in the IPI files. The safety of British India implied surveillance of Russian activities in Persia, Afghanistan and Azerbaijan. In March 1924 a secret Soviet mission headed by V.N. Lossev[30] arrived in northern India. The mission's report, which Lossev sent to his superiors in the Red Army and to the eastern department of the Comintern, was intercepted and copied by IPI, which enabled them to learn the objectives of the mission. The Red Army officer, seconded from the Turkestan front and accompanied by 'Comrade Bashli', had been ordered to make a study of the regions on 'the eastern frontiers of the USSR'. The first objective of the mission was to establish four 'intelligence districts', at Chitral and Peshawar among other places, in the region between the Pamirs and Quetta. The handling of the Lossev memorandum, which was translated into English, authenticated and commented on in detail, demonstrates the calm and professionalism of IPI officials, who were under no illusions about the efficacy of the Soviet services. Checks carried out on the 'facts' in the Lossev memorandum accordingly showed that the persons, places and associations mentioned in it did not exist. According to David Petrie, DIB's head during the 1920s, who wrote more than six pages of hilarious comment with the virtuoso skills of a master of 'internal analysis', the Lossev report was both authentic and perfectly harmless:

I myself incline to the view that Lossev, utilising his previous knowledge of India and maintaining possibly a not unintelligent interest in present-day happenings, really composed his

Diary at some spot a comfortable distance away from the Indian frontier; or, that, in the alternative, if he did come to India, he merely compiled a plausible and readable account of his doings which has little or no foundation in fact. It seems to have been another case of the story-teller being driven to invent the necessary 'corroborative details' to help out the 'bald and unconvincing narrative'. Whichever of these points of view one may select, the fact remains that Lossev undoubtedly practised deceit on his employers—it is simply a question of degree. But I do not believe that if ever he came to this country he ever did any serious work, or that he successfully established any associations or connections that need cause us a moment's uneasiness.[31]

By contrast, the activities of VOKS (Society for the Promotion of Foreign Cultural Relations), a Soviet propaganda organisation over which Olga Kameneva presided, were to be of greater concern to David Petrie because of the 'vast machinery of propaganda directed from Moscow'.[32] The IPI and its network of agents watched, infiltrated and maintained surveillance on individuals, associations, movements and parties throughout the subcontinent. It carried out its mission as an imperial secret service with a high degree of professionalism and enthusiasm and without a plethora of staff. Despite a limited budget and with a relatively small number of highly qualified officials who could draw on their own contacts, IPI was not merely an underground organisation persecuting the resurgent forces of national liberation in India, as post-colonial historiography tends to portray it.

During the Second World War IPI also brought together an unrivalled group of experts on India who were close observers of the development of Anglo-American collaboration. There is no doubt that Teague-Jones, like his colleagues in IPI, responded with incredulity to the mediocre work of OSS. In 1943 three OSS reports, on the creation of Pakistan, on Western India and on North East India, were sent to the Foreign Office from Washington by David Bowes-Lyon. The three reports supplied by the 'Research and Analysis' branch of OSS were greeted by the staff of IPI with no more than amused condescension. The reports were full of factual errors and poor judgement, and were considered a 'pathetic' waste of their authors' time. In the words of an IPI report:

OSS is a very peculiar body in its functions, and it is, of course, for consideration whether these reports need be taken very seriously, or whether information made available by British official channels will not be eyed with suspicion. The very fact that 'research' is necessary on what any British official could tell them in five minutes, suggests a certain perversity of approach.[33]

The ignorance and amateurism manifested by OSS in its early days naturally raises the question of the nature of 'collaboration' between the British and American intelligence services during the Second World War. In New York, Teague-Jones was well placed to judge how much the American attitude to the new process of decolonisation in India owed to ignorance of realities on the subcontinent, and how much to a messianic approach to democracy.

The India League of America: the rising power of a pressure group

Teague-Jones, alias Sinclair, consul in New York from July 1944 to 1950, was tirelessly active during the Second World War, combining underground policy activities with normal commercial consular work. In a letter written to the Foreign Office several years later soliciting the award of a CMG for himself, Teague-Jones recalls that:

a particularly onerous and time consuming duty during the war-years was responsibility for the welfare of Indian seamen stranded in New York. At times we had over four hundred of these people on our hands, and the problems of their housing, feeding, hospitalisation and welfare all fell upon myself. The wholesale provisioning of several hundred Asians, comprising both Hindus and Moslems, with their widely differing requirements respecting the food they were permitted or were not permitted to eat created problems quite unprecedented in the United States. These resulted not infrequently in complications with the American health authorities, and the resultant complaints were a constant headache.[34]

In parallel with his humanitarian work, Teague-Jones devoted himself to an in-depth investigation of circles in the United States which favoured the independence of India, and wrote a number of reports on the India League of America, traces of which can be found in the IPI archives. It is true that these reports are unsigned, but Teague-Jones kept in his personal files a letter from the India Office in London dated 21 December 1944. The letter concerns the thanks expressed by the DIB in New Delhi for the:

very useful reports which you have been sending recently on the affairs and activities of the India League of America. In particular the DIB has cited the last report received by him, via your report date 16th October 1944 entitled 'America and the India question, some current trends'. The DIB adds that he is showing copies of this report to Departments of the Government of India who are most concerned with the problem.[35]

In light of the letter Teague-Jones can be credited as the author of at least some of the reports on the activities of the League. Held in the IPI archives, these mostly date from the end of 1944, but appear while the League was under active surveillance, from January 1943 to April 1945. Its origins were in fact in London, where Krishna Menon, a prominent leader and far-left activist, close to Nehru and roving ambassador for the Congress party in Europe, directed the India League of London. According to IPI agents, at the end of 1943 Menon had been in contact with K.C. Mahindra, head of the Indian Supply Mission in Washington, to whom he had passed material capable of promoting the Congress party's interests in the United States. Described as 'very capable', K.C. Mahindra was a temporary war-time civil servant. An IPI official notes about him that 'he regards himself, probably quite sincerely, as owing loyalty to Government only in so far as it is an Indian Government and not to the British element in it'[36] and that this quite widely shared distinction between the two 'has both its dangerous and its less dangerous sides'.

As the almost complete series of reports on the India League of America in IPI's archives is unsigned, only some of them, dating from the autumn and the winter of

1944, are definitely attributable to Teague-Jones. An early report on the India League of America from the spring of 1943 is attributed to 'Major Shah', recently returned from the United States. According to the historian John Brobst this could be A.S.B. Shah of the Indian Political Service—subsequently a high-ranking security officer in the Pakistani services—whom Teague-Jones would inevitably have encountered during this period. 'Major Shah's' report[37] was submitted to Olaf Caroe,[38] former commissioner in Baluchistan, secretary of state for foreign affairs in the government of India since 1939 and founder in 1942 of the VSG (Viceroy's Study Group). This working group, bringing together senior officials and officers from the Indian Civil Service and the Indian Army, where A.S.B. Shah had made his presence felt as one of Caroe's closest confidants, was given the task of thinking about the main lines to follow in planning the post-war future of India. Caroe—whose geo-strategic insights were subsequently credited with inspiring American policy in South East Asia—was convinced that the Great Game would continue after British withdrawal from India, and that the security of all the countries of the Asian rim-land, from the Persian Gulf to Indochina, constituted one and the same strategic problem. The emergence of American policy towards the Indian subcontinent was a subject of major interest to him, particularly since Major Shah's report explained its internal origins.

The paper clashed with the general view in other BSC reports that the India League of America was in decline in 1943, and that it was no longer capable of influencing Indo-American relations, or even acting as an effective propaganda outlet for Congress party nationalism via its spokesmen, such as, in particular, the charismatic Sikh merchant Sirdar Jagjit Singh. With its direct language and concrete examples, this extremely interesting and politically incorrect document formed the basis for Teague-Jones's enquiry into the India League of America. He underlines the structural point that the make-up of the India League as a group with influence implies a policy of proximity to Jewish American circles. From the British point of view this community of interest was the more to be feared since it existed at the point where the Indian question and the thorny question of Palestine overlapped. According to Major Shah's report:

the activities of the India League may be described as wide spread and all embracing. It has chalked out for itself a comprehensive programme covering the treatment of such vital questions as India's war effort, India's place in the strategy of the United Nations and her political, constitutional, social, economic and industrial future. As a short term policy the League has aligned itself with anti-British forces in America who have taken upon themselves the task of creating isolationist tendencies in the country and making the President's position difficult. Ostensibly it has joined forces with those elements in the polity of the United States, whose sympathies are with China, India and countries under colonial administration. Some of the vague and emotional outcries which are now-a-days so much in fashion in the USA e.g. the Atlantic Charter and the principles of Four Freedoms give the India League a good lever for achieving its own ends. Secretly it has succeeded in coming to an understanding with the Pacifists, Communists, Capitalists and the Jewish groups in America. With the help of these groups it has secured for itself a place in the 'front-page' publicity. Before the war it had plenty of material to publicise but no nation wide audience to reach. The America First Committee had a nation wide organisation and was willing to use Indian propaganda against Great Britain. Thus, they both fitted into each other's schemes admirably. Pearl Harbour gave both these organisations a terrible set back. The America First Committee went underground and the India League became a suspect organisation. The League managed however, to survive this shock by revising its policy and giving a new orientation to its movement. It began by attacking Nazism and Fascism, and embarked upon a virulent anti-Japanese campaign and flung itself whole-heartedly in support of the United Nations war effort. Gradually it reappeared on the American scene as a champion of India's war effort and is now engaged in convincing the American Government and people that India's resources cannot be brought into full play against the Japanese unless she has a popular Government at the helm of her affairs. This line of policy fits in completely with the importance that an average American attaches to the use of India's soil for (a) supply of war material to China and (b) as a base for attacking the Japanese forces in Burma … The Jewish organisations in America offer a fertile field for propaganda and the India League uses them for building up pro-congress sentiments in the country. Jews occupy an influential position in America. The Presidents of the two leading radio networks, *National Broadcasting Company* and *Columbia Broadcasting Company* are Jews. The *New York Times, Asia, Time, Life and Fortune, Nation, Amerasia, Atlantic Monthly, Harper* etc. which devote quite a considerable space to the Indian situation are either owned by Jews or controlled by them. American newspapers draw a major portion of their revenues by advertisements. Most of them yield to any propaganda by Jews who entrust the work of retail advertisements of their stores to newspapers favourably disposed to the Jewish cause. Many of the President's advisers are Jews. Among Secretaries of the Government, Judges of the Supreme Court and those connected with War Production Board, Post War Planning, there are some well known Jews who have been quite outspoken in their sympathies for the Zionist movement in Palestine. Most of the Indian trade i.e. the imports of articles from India to America—jute, goatskin, wool, mica and shellac is handled in America by Jews. The representatives in America of Birla and other Indian industrialists such as Simon Swirling (who has since come to India on the staff of Mr Philipps after entrusting the work of the Agency to his own brother under a different name) also help to establish business contacts between Sirdar J.J. Singh's friends (who are Jewish merchants) and the Indian merchants. These contacts also offer a useful medium for keeping in touch with the political movements in India and the passing of funds between India and America.[39]

Far from being in decline, the India League was redoubling its activities by 'Americanising' itself (i.e. integrating fully into US politics). In September 1944 the president of the League, J.J. Singh—a Congress party member, he had set up as a dealer in Indian art in Manhattan in 1940—had shrewdly declared that his organisation was essentially an American organisation, and that his objective was to make India 'the test-case for Allied war aims'.[40] According to Teague-Jones's reports from New York, the India League had indeed become an American organisation working for American interests. Having made a complete break with Anup Singh—an intellectual and activist in the Indian cause in the United States—who had joined the ranks of the National Committee for India's Freedom, founded in Washington in October 1943, J.J. Singh, and the secretary of the India League, H.K. Rakhit, were there only to provide a guarantee of Indian authenticity for a purely American propaganda organisation. The publication of the monthly *India Today* and the nomination of Pearl Buck, who had recently been awarded the Nobel Prize, as honorary president of the League in 1944, were evidence of this stance, which introduced a discordant, not to say frankly troublesome note, into the relationship between the British and the Americans:

For some time we have observed the aggressive tactics of J.J. Singh who appeared to be acting more and more independently of his Indian colleagues in the League. One gained the impression that he was busy building up a reputation for himself as the outstanding champion of nationalist India with an eye to standing well with the Congress Party, should the latter eventually emerge the dominating factor in an independent India. Now, however, we have to revise somewhat our attitude towards Singh if it is really a fact that he is only a figurehead in the League set-up. This would mean that instead of the initiative being taken by J.J. Singh, and the latter looking for support to his American friends, it is the Americans who are themselves stage-managing the show, with Singh in the role of the principal actor. This immediately places the India League in a totally different light, and vests its activities with an importance we had hitherto not attached to them. Obviously it [is] one thing for a lime-light loving shopkeeper like Singh to distribute a few thousand reprints of anti-British press articles, with the financial assistance of a few friends, but it is a very different matter when the American friends do it on their own initiative, and do it on a large scale ... In short, the India League is now one of the many American political pressure groups in this country, aiming at influencing American present and post war policy—in this case foreign policy—in relation to Britain and Britain's post war relations with India ... It is becoming very evident that in this growing American insistence on complete and immediate independence for India there are interests actively at work which are certainly not motivated by mere sentiment or by sympathy for the downtrodden masses of India. One of the most immediate aims of this pressure group is to influence President Roosevelt to make renewed representations if not actual demands for complete Indian independence to Prime Minister Churchill during the present conference in Quebec.[41]

It seems that Teague-Jones began to follow the development of the India League in 1942, but it is above all from the autumn of 1944 that his investigations, bearing as much on American political attitudes as on the Indian independence movement, became systematic. From 1943 on, the existing links or the convergence of interests between Zionist circles and the India League had become apparent. The coinciding of problems in India and in Palestine was to be mentioned in later reports, eliciting an ironic comment from an IPI agent who notes with some satisfaction that the new stance will at least have the beneficial effect of putting an end to Congress party support for the Khilafat movement. Teague-Jones immersed himself in New York society and continued his inquiries. He reports that an acquaintance who had called casually at the India League office in the role of a journalist was told by an American secretary working there that the League was completely separate from the national committee in Washington and 'was today essentially an American organization functioning primarily in American interests'. He pondered on the financing of the

League, carried out or caused an enquiry to be carried out into J.J. Singh's bank accounts and cheque-books, and commented disbelievingly on a report cobbled together by the FBI on the financing of the India League, probably produced within the 'co-ordination' framework set up by BSC. Although a field project, his enquiry did not prevent him from identifying the principal ways in which the Indian question was being used as an instrument within American politics.

According to his analysis, the cause of Indian independence mobilised the most diverse political and interest groups in the United States. He identified three main strands. First, there were the old isolationists of the America First Committee, many of whom were anti-British by principle and tradition: Republicans, American imperialists, representatives of big business and those who were hostile to the New Deal and to Roosevelt were part of an anti-British and pro-Indian current of opinion. A second strand was made up of liberals, pacifists of all backgrounds including the religious, idealistic opponents of British imperialism. Finally, a third strand was composed of communists and fellow-travellers, a minoritarian but dogmatic current of opinion. However, his attention was principally focused on business circles: big business, the great industrialists, high finance circles, hostile to Roosevelt since the New Deal and haunted by the fear of a collapse and a return of unemployment, were looking anxiously at the prospect of the end of the war. For Teague-Jones, it was obvious that these circles saw the fostering of overseas trade and the conquest of new markets as their post-war life-raft. India, along with Russia and China, was one of these potential markets, hence the interest of American industrialists in the cause of Indian independence:

American industry … must force its way into India. Here it will find itself in direct competition with and opposed by firmly established British vested interests. In open competition with these, the Americans feel they would never stand a chance, and therefore their only hope is to get these British interests ousted by political pressure. They believe this can best be done by supporting the Indian Nationalist cause, and their sympathies are therefore wholeheartedly with that cause.[42]

Now familiarised with American politics, Teague-Jones drew an unflattering portrait of two members of the US Congress, Mundt from South Dakota and Langer from North Dakota, who had been won to the cause of the India League:

In the first place, both these men are understood to be of Swedish stock, which implies an absence of any feeling of sympathy with Great Britain based on blood or tradition. They are described as typical representatives of the Middle West, very ignorant of anything beyond purely local conditions and issues, extremely gullible, with the parochial smugness and rough aggressiveness which goes with that type of ignorance. Their constituents are, in the mass, equally ignorant, with a traditional anti-British bias. Anything savouring of 'imperialism' is anathema to them. These factors taken together make them particularly receptive to almost any form of anti-British propaganda. In politics Republican, and by inclination isolationist, Middle Westerners regard British imperialism as a malignant power for evil—which as much as anything, and more than most things, has brought about the present war, and which, if

226

persisted in, will assuredly bring about further wars. India they have come to regard as the potential cause of future unrest in Asia which will involve the United States and prevent her from enjoying the peace and prosperity to which, as God's own country, she, more than any other nation, claims to be entitled.[43]

Teague-Jones could not have expressed his irritation with American perceptions of the India problem more clearly, particularly as the public side of his official work obliged him to get down into the arena and confront objections and questions from Americans in New York society from a whole range of backgrounds.

Counter-propaganda in the land of democracy

In the autumn of 1944, Teague-Jones annexed to one of his reports on the India League a list of 'attack points' used by the anti-British campaign in the United States. 'Here' he writes, 'is a list of the more popular accusations, arguments or demands that have been publicised, broadcast, preached and shouted at the street corners during the course of the past four years.' From 1944 onwards his duties as consul and his speaking abilities obliged him to give regular lectures and seminars and to reach out to the American public—a public which Teague-Jones found to be generally ignorant and exasperatingly willing to believe the commonplaces of anti-British propaganda. Here is a collection of the expressions falling from American lips before the US entry into the war: 'This is Britain's war, not India's. India was pushed into it without her consent'; 'How can India be expected to fight, when she was not consulted in declaring war'; 'In Asia the war is being fought to perpetuate the British Empire'; and 'Britain has no intention of granting India independence.' After Pearl Harbour and the US entry into the war, Teague-Jones notes a rehash of these arguments: 'Britain refuses to apply the Atlantic Charter to India'; 'Churchill has declared he will not liquidate the British Empire'; 'India would be capable of a much greater war effort if independent'; 'Burma and Malaya were lost because the native population had nothing to fight for'; 'The American war effort in Asia is being frustrated because the British will not give India facilities to put out a maximum effort', and so on. The arguments, which centred on American intervention, such as 'American boys' lives are being thrown away because the Indians are unable to contribute their maximum war effort' or 'Britain freezes India's credits to prevent her developing trade with the United States', were replaced after the Japanese had begun to retreat by a bipolar vision of the post-war world. 'The United Nations will undoubtedly beat Japan, but the failure to give India independence now will leave behind a legacy of hatred that will sow the seeds of the next war between the East and the West.'[44]

Was the cause of the fracture between East and West to be the decolonisation of the subcontinent? It is interesting to note this 'premonition' since, within the framework of the Grand Alliance, the decolonisation of India had the tactical advantage of creating a degree of common ground between the Americans and the Soviets. The theme of the East–West break also confirmed the link between the India League and the East and West Association. This Association, alongside the journal *Asia*, made a logistical and financial contribution to the India League. The latter was also very active on the humanitarian front. The terrible Bengal famine in 1943 had pushed the India League into a campaign of systematic denigration of the British government: a heavily publicised humanitarian effort was soon launched from the United States by J.J. Singh, in collaboration with Richard J. Walsh. Encouraged by this success and thanks to intensive lobbying, J.J. Singh succeeded in winning the support of Mundt, the Republican member of Congress for South Dakota, at the time of the UNRRA (United Nations Relief and Rehabilitation Administration) conference in Atlantic City. Mundt was persuaded to put forward an amendment to legislation relating to UNRRA then under discussion in the Chamber of Deputies, which would extend the field of humanitarian assistance not just to territories liberated from enemy occupation, but to all territories deemed to be strategically important for the conduct of the war, whether they had been occupied or not. To the great displeasure of the British, India was implicitly covered by the Mundt amendment which, despite steady opposition from the British delegates at the Atlanta conference, was endorsed by the House of Representatives and then by the Senate.

In addition to the terrain—a minefield for the British—of American institutions, Teague-Jones was horrified to note the emergence of a kind of political theatre in which the theme of Indian independence was mixed with the denunciation of British tyranny. In January 1945 he attended a gala dinner for 'India Independence Day', a prime example of its kind, where some 900 people had gathered to meet in the presence of Vijaya Lakshmi Pandit, Nehru's sister, who was to embark a few years later on a diplomatic career, becoming from 1947 to 1949 Indian ambassador to the USSR. Mrs Pandit had a pleasant personality, well suited to creating a favourable impression and playing on American emotions:

The speaker stressed the fact that she was not anti-British, and that, indeed, she had many British friends. The conflict between Britain and India was not a conflict between their respective peoples; it was a conflict of policy; they were fighting the policy of the British Government. She repeated the well worn statement that the Indian people were prevented from pulling their weight in the war effort, and took the line that it was quite wrong ... and indeed it was a disgraceful state of affairs that American soldiers had to risk their lives and undergo hardships to fight the would-be invaders of India, when there were millions of Indians who, in a free India, should and would have taken the place of those American troops. There was nothing really objectionable in the speech. Only once did the speaker appear to get a little excited when she referred to the Declaration of Independence. Americans were tremendously and rightly proud of their Declaration of Independence, she said, but when Indians tried to read theirs they were put in jail.[45]

While the sincerity of Mrs Pandit's arguments elicited these relatively favourable comments from Teague-Jones, it was quite otherwise with the other speakers and organisers of this politico-fashionable 'event', at which there appeared, along with J.J. Singh, William Shirer, Lin Yutang and above all Pearl Buck, who did not fail to compare the far-reaching importance of Indian independence with that, two decades earlier, of the birth of the USSR. The presence of Elsa Maxwell, a key member of

New York society, organiser of soirees and receptions for prominent personalities of the day, is an indicator that this was a publicity event. This formidable, dumpy, wise-cracking little woman:

admittedly knows nothing about India but this does not deter her from getting up and talking at considerable length and with considerable fluency on the subject of castes, customs and religious sects in India. She cited facts and figures with a glibness which suggested that she had been learning by heart passages of the Encyclopaedia Britannica. She held the stage for a full half hour, gave herself the full measure of publicity which to her is the breath of life, and then sat down with an obvious feeling of having 'done her stuff' well.[46]

Teague-Jones, reduced to his normal status of observer, nonetheless draws attention to the intelligence and effectiveness of some of the arguments that were advanced. The comparison of the Declaration of American Independence with its Indian equivalent, with relevant quotations in support, the Congress party's disapproval of a British foreign policy which from Munich to the Anglo-Italian agreement had consistently undermined democracy and collective security, seem to him serious, indeed dangerous arguments. The India question, in the American political context, also benefited from the vagueness of the word 'Congress', interpreted in the United States in its American sense 'and in a complete misapprehension as to its actual application in India'.

All this was obviously of no help with the counter-propaganda job which Teague-Jones was supposed to be carrying out in New York. As consul, he had to confront the twin opposition of the India League and of pro-Zionist circles who were exasperated by the establishment of quotas for Jewish immigration into Palestine in 1939. Some political personalities on the New York scene, such as Clare Booth Luce from the Republican Party, as well as a writer, an assistant editor of *Vanity Fair*, a reporter for *Life Magazine* and a Member of Congress, were surfing on the wave of anti-British feeling for their own personal reasons. Others, like the Jewish attorney Emmanuel Celler, Democrat Member of Congress, who had become prominent in 1924 for his vigorous opposition to the Johnson quotas on immigration, were using the rapprochement with the India League as a springboard for the Zionist cause and their personal reputations. It was not so much a lobby group as a network that was taking shape, woven thread by thread between Zionists and Indian nationalists. Taraknath Das, an intellectual active in the Indian cause who had been a refugee in the United States since 1906, and corresponded quite extensively with Supreme Court Judge Felix Frankfurter in 1942–3, seems to have played the role of intermediary between Indian and Zionist circles. Teague-Jones recalls that:

in the case of the Zionists, the Consulate offices became the target of frequent picketing by pro-Zionist and other unfriendly elements. On one occasion our offices were forcibly occupied by a crowd of militant Zionists, mainly students, and the Consul-General and myself were surrounded and compelled to listen to insults and anti-British slogans for over an hour until the police dispersed the crowd. The Indians were less overtly militant, for they were, of course, much less numerous, but they were active in organising lectures and press propaganda. It became my duty to counteract these hostile activities by lecturing and giving talks in schools, colleges, clubs and other social institutions such as Rotarians, Lions etc, in which I explained the true facts of the situation and H.M.G.'s policy in both Palestine and India.[47]

And indeed on many occasions Teague-Jones showed himself to be a persuasive and charismatic lecturer, able to captivate an audience, as Mary Dutton, the director of the Scudder Colvell School for Spanish-speaking students, wrote admiringly after his visit in February 1945. Teague-Jones talked for two hours without a single note about the geography, history, economy and politics of India, with sincerity, elegance and 'a great sense of humour'.

But these occasions were not always a success. At the instigation of the British War Relief Society, Teague-Jones was required to explain the British point of view on India not only to New York pupils but also to their teachers. One evening in March he faced a roomful of primary schoolteachers in Brooklyn from different schools all over the New York region. With a few exceptions the intellectual level of those present seemed rather mediocre, but Teague-Jones mentions the generally friendly and attentive reception given to his lecture, yet again, on the Indian question. One of the teachers, a recruit to the India cause and citing Mrs Pandit as an absolute authority, bombarded the speaker with interjections that were as absurd as they were peremptory:

'Well, I think the British have made a very poor show in India ... Mrs Pandit says this or that, and I would rather believe Mrs Pandit than an Englishman' ... 'The British are to blame for the low percentage of literacy in India. Why have they not done more in the way of free education? Why don't they spend more money on education? Admitting that India does not pay taxes to Britain, and the taxes are imposed—as we are told—by Indian provincial governments—it is the British Government, in the person of the Viceroy, who controls the expenditure of the Indian taxpayers' money. The Indian themselves do not control it. (This is so, because Mrs Pandit says it is!). And who pays the Viceroys' fabulous salary anyway? Isn't it disgraceful that a British official should draw all the salary while millions are starving!' (We sensed the lady was a Communist). Then came the old favourite. 'All this talk of Hindu–Moslem hostility is British propaganda. If the British would only leave India, the two communities would live as happily together as, say, the Jews and Catholics in New York'. (Mrs Pandit again) etc, etc.[48]

In the battle of humanitarian arguments, Teague-Jones, who one senses was now weary of New York, could only resort to humour as his ultimate weapon: his own dignity and that of his country were at stake. But by 1945 the general trends in politics were inescapable: decline of British power, inevitable independence for India, the unresolved question of Partition and how to introduce it, the closing stages in this planetary game coincided with those of his professional career.

The transfer of power

The elegant British consul whose face is reflected in the heavy mirror during an official dinner for representatives of American and British companies stands out as the most distinguished and alert-looking man in the room. The photograph, taken in May 1950, was sent to him by Constance Calenberg, with whom Teague-Jones seems to have been on relatively intimate terms. 'My dear Four Star General', she writes with admiring irony. Constance Calenberg was a colourful character, author of religious poems like 'The Thirst' published in the magazine *Our Hope* in 1949, which ends 'My thirst, assuaged forever at that fountain, Has found the potion sweet of Jesus' love!' She was later to work in the office of the head of Protocol in the State Department, which may explain the official circumstances of her encounter with Teague-Jones. The latter, who since May 1949 had been in charge of the commercial department at the British consulate in New York, then headed by Francis Evans, was responsible for helping British businesses to penetrate the American market. His role was to welcome representatives of British firms who had come to visit American factories and to introduce them into committees set up jointly with representatives of the American economic administration. Among his successes in this field, Teague-Jones was proud of having defended British prestige in the bidding process for building materials to be used in constructing the new United Nations building. Against vigorous American competition, Teague-Jones succeeded in securing an important contract for British firms producing Portland stone. For the consul this modest success symbolised the permanence of British prestige in the post-war concert of nations. But the United Nations also provided the context for the consul's continuing functions as intelligence agent.

The other side of the mirror

In Teague-Jones's archives there are four pages of manuscript notes, scribbled in haste on the back of some lecture notes, which have escaped the archivist's eye. One only has to turn the file over to read the fragments of a story which is worthy of John le Carré. In it Teague-Jones recounts for the benefit of an unknown recipient his meeting with a Soviet agent in New York, leading to a friendship maintained for several subsequent years. The heavily corrected draft of a note was perhaps addressed to his friend Charles H. Ellis, his closest colleague where Russia was concerned. The fragment, which conjures up the conversations and psychology of the protagonists, is interesting even if it is hard to decrypt the precise meaning of the episode:

Ivan Petrovitch Illyushi is not his real name but is sufficiently Russian to serve the purpose. He was already a student [or] only a later school boy when the October Revolution broke out and caught him in Petrograd. His parents[,] both of good [upper-classes] families, fell victims to the Red Terror, and the fate of his younger sister who was at a girl's preparation school in Moscow was never known. [I mention] these latter details just [to show] that Vanya could be expected to retain some more or less vivid recollections of his boyhood, the Tsarist regime as well as of the tragic events of the Revolution. Which probably explains why after nearly forty years of life in Soviet Russia, Vanya is better [at assessing] comparative values than the great majority of his fellow compatriots who were either born under the Soviet system or were too young at the time of the Revolution to have any recollection of the [circumstances and way of life] which preceded it.

MOST SECRET AGENT OF EMPIRE

Vanya is at present living in England. I first met Vanya in New York where he was connected in some rather vaguely defined capacity or other with the Soviet U.N. Delegation. The first time we met … was at a cocktail party and he was very nervous. There were a company of Soviet officials present and although our conversation was of the most innocent nature, and very limited, seeing that Vanya's English was not very fluent and I thought it better not to disclose any knowledge of Russian, other than *da* and *nyet* and *nichevo*, Vanya kept glances of anxiety in the direction of his colleagues and they seemed to be [more or less] keeping an eye on him.

Gradually as we met at other parties, Vanya began to show less nervousness, and when there was no other Soviet official present, his behaviour became completely different and ended almost normal. It was on one of these occasions—we had met a number of times—that I admitted to a knowledge of Russian. I was prepared to see Vanya shut up like a clam but the contrary happened and for the first time we began to discuss questions of real interest. Actually, there was not so much discussion as questions and answers … His desire for information was exhaustive. If the questions had not been so intelligent, they might here reflected the insatiable curiosity of a dilettante. I was about to learn good deal of information about Soviet Russia, get a few new angles on current life in Soviet Russia. When Vanya's tour in the States was up [and] he returned to Russia. He never said anything [and] definitely I had the impression that he was sorry to go back. I wondered if we would meet again. Certainly he said only one time you must come and visit Moscow. Then I will show you round.

We did meet again—just a few months ago—but not in Moscow this time in London. Vanya was now a counsellor in the Soviet Embassy, I did not care to embarrass him by asking him the exact nature of his duties but he said he was a Communist counsellor. From what he told me, the fact was a perfectly genuine one. We met the first time at a small party and Vanya was the only Russian there. His manner was much more free and easy than when I had known him in New York and his English too was much more fluent. So I thought but remembered that Russians are generally very good linguists.

After that Vanya lunched with me at my club and one occasion dined at my club and I attended several minor social functions at the Soviet Embassy. By this time, there was no little restraint left between us, and we chatted and in frankness [discussed] many questions which I could not have dared to mention in the earlier days.

Apart from the noticeable lack of restraint and that absence of that furtive [look] of fear and suspicion which Vanya would frequently show in the New York days [when] Vanya used to glance around and behind him; there was something almost exuberant about the man.

I felt this so strongly one day that on coffee in the smoking room after lunch I said to him:

'You know Vanya, you seem to be really proud of being Russian.'

… He paused in the act of raising his coffee to his lips, and a look of surprise flashed into his eyes. 'Of course, he said, of course I'm proud of being Russian, Why shouldn't I be?'

I hurriedly agreed with him that it was natural that he should be proud of being what he was, and the good humoured twinkle came back into his eyes.

'Oh, I know what you are thinking' he said, 'but you must admit that Soviet Russia really has much to be proud about.'

'Well Sputnik of course!' I began rather grudgingly.

'That of course, but I was thinking more in terms of our giant hydroelectric plants and industrial development generally.'

'Yes', I said, 'I understand your people have made tremendous progress in that field.'

'But that is only one field', he said. 'You have no idea of the tremendous scale on which we are opening up in Siberia for instance and the Arctic regions.'

'Tell me frankly', I asked. 'Do you yourself really believe all this talk by Khrushchev and others that Russia will outstrip America, Britain and the rest of the world in industrial production within a few years?'

Vanya laughed.

'I was never much good at statistics and of course a lot of things that are said by the government is no doubt propaganda but …'[49]

Teague-Jones's manuscript ends here. It is not known what sort of information—detailed or wider-reaching—'Vanya' was able to impart, nor what motivated Teague-Jones, as he attentively observed the changes in the psychology of his prey. 'Vanya's' psychological strength was being tested, maybe with the objective of turning him into a double agent. Personal reasons, with regard to his past in Russia, must also enter into the reckoning. Khrushchev, de-Stalinisation and the thaw did not alter the fact that Teague-Jones was still considered guilty by the Soviet regime of the murder of the twenty-six commissars. Making contact with Soviet circles, beguiling and gaining the confidence of a second-tier official at the embassy who held some kind of intelligence responsibilities, the 'Vanya' episode is mainly interesting for the light it sheds on Teague-Jones's approach, techniques and professionalism. The sadly fragmentary account leaves it to the reader to imagine what followed next.

'Sahib! Sahib!'

While it is not hard to guess at the feelings of pragmatic resignation which Teague-Jones must have experienced during the onward march to independence in 1947, there is no working journal for this period in his personal archives. British and 'imperial' at heart, Teague-Jones had like most of his contemporaries been convinced for a long time that the independence of India was inevitable. As a man whose basic training was in the Punjab and who was used to working with Muslim populations considered to be loyal to British rule, his views on partition were not crystal-clear. It is known that two decades earlier he was a partisan of a 'Muslim policy' in Central Asia, of which Great Britain might be able to take advantage in the context of the new Great Game. But was he in favour of the strategy of 'Divide and Rule', which consisted in encouraging Muslim separatism so as to weaken India and manipulate those interests which were essential for the perpetuation of British power? In this respect his view seems as ambivalent as that of his contemporaries. It was influenced by the long-standing colonial policy of division which had begun in 1909 with the creation of separate electorates and continued during the Second World War with the de facto alliance of Jinnah's Muslim League and the colonial power.[50] On the other hand, partition did not figure among the prospective aims of the post-war British leadership, especially Attlee, and was seen as a development which would objectively weaken the subcontinent, likely to encourage Soviet penetration at a time when the wartime Grand Alliance was collapsing during the Iranian crisis of 1946. With the cold war and the outline of a re-ordering of the Great Game in central and southern Asia, the creation of a separate Muslim state, the future Pakistan, was perceived as a geostrategic development of the first importance. Teague-Jones, who had bulky files on Pakistan and kept up a correspondence with diplomats and different representatives of the state of Pakistan, was convinced of it. Nonetheless, the spectacle as observed from New York of the violence unleashed between Muslims and Hindus—10 to 15 million displaced people, 300,000–500,000 deaths—or between Muslims and Sikhs in the Punjab, was a drama which did not leave him indifferent. One press cartoon among Teague-Jones's many press cuttings sums up his state of mind. The Indian minorities are represented by a woman, horrified by the attack of a bloodthirsty rapist or murderer, who has fled to the door of a British administrator. She is shrieking for help: 'Sahib! Sahib!' But the Englishman is no longer there: his pith helmet is hanging on a hat-peg on the wall, a smoking cigarette is burning away in an ashtray and on the desk, opposite an empty chair, is the letter of renunciation of British sovereignty.

In New York Teague-Jones heard the echoes, from near and far, of the proclamation of the independence of India and Pakistan on 14 and 15 August 1947. So far as his official activities are concerned, the event added another duty to his numerous responsibilities. India and Pakistan did not yet have their own consular facilities: he took care of the transition for both states. However, Indian independence heralded his final retirement, a consequence of a cessation of activities on the part of IPI[51] and the India Office. He received a letter from Sir Paul Patrick at the India Office, dated 14 August 1947, one of the batch sent to all the secret agents of the defunct British Empire in India:

As you no doubt know, the India Office will disappear [on] the 15th [of] August, under the provisions of the India Independence Act. Before this happens, I should like to take this opportunity to thank you personally for the valuable work which you have done during the last few years in connection with Indian affairs in the USA. I understand that your special appointment is likely to terminate towards the end of the year, the diversion of Indian political developments, as we hope, into more peaceful channels having made its further continuance unnecessary. We appreciate the value of the sources of information which you have so skilfully built up and that had the situation in India developed differently these might have proved of continuing value to His Majesty's Government.[52]

In fact IPI ceased to function in August 1947 and its old agents were politely shown the door. One of them, Philip Vickery, the head of IPI, wrote a somewhat bitter note to the India Office in August 1947. Of the same generation as Teague-Jones, a member of IPI since 1915 and director of the intelligence organisation since 1926, Vickery expresses his 'great affection for the India Office'. He says that he is 'as pained to witness its passing as I am to see the partition of the Punjab', while referring in veiled terms to the continuance of the intelligence system after the independence of India.[53] The question was how an organisation capable of supporting the new channels for British influence could be maintained in the subcontinent. Plans had already been prepared in 1946, at the beginning of the process of transfer of power, envisaging the re-employment of Indian agents who could transmit information to Whitehall via MI5. But in the chaos of 1947 and the dissolution of old networks and former loyalties this possible solution, which Vickery had thought up in a hurry, was to have no future, at any rate so far as independent India was concerned.

This was not the case for Pakistan, where the need for experts had apparently led to the enlisting of Teague-Jones's services as soon as the Kashmir question and the first Indo-Pakistani war erupted in 1947–8. Kashmir, a princely state, 75 per cent Muslim but governed by a Hindu maharajah, was invaded in October 1947 by Pathan militiamen from Pakistan with the intention of installing a government of 'Free Kashmir'. In responding to the maharajah's appeal, India stipulated that Kashmir should become part of India after a referendum. The ensuing war of attrition and the settlement of the conflict under UN auspices led the Pakistanis to seek the advice and expertise of former IPI agents. That at least is what is suggested by Teague-Jones's correspondence with Pakistan's ambassador in New York, M.A.H. Ispahani, who, referring to Kashmir, wrote to Teague-Jones thanking him for 'his love and sympathy for the citizens of Pakistan' and assuring him that he 'would always be glad to seek his assistance' when he stood in need of it.[54] On the same subject, Sir Paul Patrick, in a letter of September 1948 replying to Teague-Jones, who had no doubt offered his services without being prompted, also mentioned the possibility of remobilising former agents in the context of Kashmir and the war between India and Pakistan. 'If you were wanted it would of course be by your old colleagues. It would not come my way. But I am passing on your letter to Vickery.'[55] After the Kashmir affair was referred to the UN, Teague-Jones, then in New York, was in a position to play a part in the negotiations during the month of September 1948. They resulted in the agreement for a ceasefire on 1 January 1949 which divided Kashmir into two parts, with India getting Jammu and Kashmir, and Pakistan the territories of Muzaffarabad and Gilgit which went to make up the 'Northern Areas'. Teague-Jones was less optimistic than Sir Paul Patrick about the viability of this agreement. His conviction that the Kashmir question would flare up again was not realised until 1965.

These pointers, taken together, raise questions about the 'transition' of the secret services after the independence of Pakistan, and of the part played in it by former IPI agents, including Teague-Jones among many others. The military intelligence agencies created in Pakistan in 1947, largely inspired by the British model, proved to be particularly badly coordinated during the Indo-Pakistani war. It was an Australian officer of the Indian Army, a wartime member of the Viceroy's Study Group, Major-General R. Cawthorne, a future deputy chief of staff of the Pakistani Army, who in 1948 established the basic organisation for the Inter-Services Intelligence (ISI), the well-known Pakistani intelligence organisation. Very much a product of its colonial heritage, 'a State within the Pakistani State', ISI has since become an organisation operating on almost every front in the global jihad. It is not impossible that in his retirement Teague Jones may have collaborated on this project in its initial stages.

In 1988, a few weeks before his death, Teague-Jones told Val Hennessy, a young English journalist who had come to interview him on the occasion of the publication of his first book, about his love of gardening:

My speciality used to be making tennis courts in India ... I made half a dozen. Used to select a place that was flat, which was more often than not between a Hindu burning ground and a Moslem burying place. Used to play tennis between roast Hindi and putrefying Moslem.[56]

The eccentric old man's casual comment says something about the black humour of the British perspective on the drama of Partition.

Return to the North West Frontier

In the mid-1950s Teague-Jones, now in retirement, decided to leave the hectic pace of New York life, not to return to England, where he had in any case hardly ever lived, but for the charms of a luxurious retreat in Miami, 35 Venetian Way on San Marino island—one of the artificial islands constructed opposite Miami Beach to house expensive residences and marinas, and a decidedly upmarket address, evoking pellucid waters, palm trees, art deco hotels and 1950s architecture. At the time Miami had not yet become a luxury retirement destination for rich Americans, even though Teague Jones and his wife Taddie had every appearance of being a well-off couple leading a conventional life in retirement. During the Second World War his missions to the Caribbean on security matters led him to stop over more than once in Miami. This no doubt accounted for the choice of house, right in the middle of the 'Mecca of hedonism' a few cable-lengths from Cuba. Cuba was where the Castro-led three-year guerrilla war in the Sierra Maestra ended in the overthrow of the Batista regime (1 January 1959) and the flight of more than 250,000 anti-Castro exiles to Miami. At the height of the cold war the Castro revolution on the doorstep of America, backed by the Soviet Union, aroused anxiety and led to the CIA-orchestrated attempt in April 1961 to invade Cuba at the Bay of Pigs. Teague-Jones's presence in Miami, where he stayed until 1960 and made friends with some émigré Cuban families, may have had something to do with these events. Was he not, after all, an expert on communism, capable of spotting a Soviet spy on the loose in the neighbourhood, or assessing the radicalism of the anti-Castro militants in Little Havana whose headquarters were the Restaurant Versailles?

While the United States, its attention riveted on the Cuban Revolution, was implementing the doctrine of containment and roll-back wherever it could, Teague-Jones, always deeply interested in world affairs, was following current events, at present less strife-torn and newsworthy, on the North West Frontier. Why was he still thinking about the arid rocky hills of north-west Pakistan, so distant from the artificial paradise of Florida with its wealthy sun-tanned pensioners? Did the sight of them remind him of the physical and moral nobility of the men of the Frontier? Did he feel nostalgia for his youth in the harsh land which demanded, and produced, warlike men? Whatever the reason, he kept an attentive eye on the news from Pakistan and Afghanistan. He read the newspapers, and with the help of press cuttings, reading records and file cards, created dossiers on Jinnah, on the concept of Pakistan,[57] on its Muslim supporters and opponents, and on attempts at conciliation between Hindus and Muslims, to mention just a few examples. Under the guise of a plain man with an interest in the subject—albeit one who was better informed than most of his contemporaries—he also kept up contacts and even correspondence with a variety of representatives from the Pakistani and Afghan embassies in Washington. He could no longer travel over the ground in person, but he did so in his mind, pondering maps of this pivotal area on the Eurasian continent, which had not yet come to be known to experts by the generic nickname 'Af-Pak'. He was particularly interested in the roads and communication routes, since they were the exact framework for the rules of the new Great Game, in which the Americans had now replaced the British in Afghanistan. While the Russians had built roads in the north and north-west of Afghanistan, the Americans had done the same in the south and south-east.

It was about the road from Kushk to Herat—the gates of Soviet Turkmenistan—at Kandahar that Teague-Jones wrote to the Afghan embassy in Washington. At Kandahar the Americans had started to build a new airport, reacting to the Soviet initiative to modernise the one at Kabul. In fact since the mid-1950s the whole region had become an active front for Soviet expansion. The cold war and the confrontation between the two opposing powers had assumed an old shape as the Great Game in Central Asia. In Afghanistan, Mohammed Daoud, King Zafir Shah's prime minister, who had been in power since 1953, was leaning increasingly towards the Soviets. The southern frontier, never clearly defined, between Afghanistan and Pakistan, Muslim states positioned on the hinge between the Iranian and Indian worlds, constituted a zone of permanent instability in the notorious North West Frontier, once that of India, now of Pakistan. From 1956 onwards, the USSR had been pursuing a more aggressive policy. A $100 million loan announced by Khrushchev, soon followed by other loans, put Afghanistan in a position of growing financial, economic and political dependence on the USSR. While with Soviet military assistance the Afghan army and air force were equipped with weapons and planes manufactured in the USSR, the Soviets also established a presence in many sectors of the economy. They carried out large infrastructure works, exploited the gas-fields and took part in training the army, the civilian administrators, engineers and technicians.

It was against this background that the Pakhtunistan affair erupted. The affair concerned the territory of the Pushtun, an ethnic group which straddles the frontier and accounts for 45 per cent of the Afghan population and 15 per cent of the Pakistani population. At the end of the 1950s the irredentist claim for the self-determination of Pakhtunistan was an expression of the Afghan government's challenge to the legitimacy of the Durand Line. It aroused the suspicion that it was a manoeuvre by the Soviets—masters of the strategy of using minorities for political ends—with the aim of destabilising Pakistan's north-west frontier. After 1955, the date when Pakistan joined the Baghdad Pact between Iraq, Turkey, Pakistan, Iran, the United States and the United Kingdom, the Soviets had been sending out increasingly frequent signals. The same year Bulganin declared during a visit to Afghanistan that the USSR supported the Pakhtunistan cause. There followed several frontier incidents, and periods in which diplomatic relations between Afghanistan and Pakistan were broken off. But in the spring of 1959, when Teague-Jones began an exchange of letters with S.M. Haq, the press attaché at the Pakistani embassy in Washington, relations between the two countries were going through an improvement. In particular there was an agreement allowing Afghanistan to benefit from duty-free transit of goods via the port of Karachi and Pakistani railways. Teague-Jones commented briefly to his correspondent:

I am very glad to note that the recent exchange of visits by the Head of State of the countries has resulted in a general improvement of relations. Most important of all, it seems to me, is the signing of the Transit Trade Agreement, with which, it is to be hoped, a major cause of irritation will have been removed. Land-locked countries are prone at times to suffer from claustrophobia, and Afghanistan would appear to be no exception. I suspect their northern neighbours have been playing on this, and the drive to open the highway to Kandahar may be in part the result of it. The antidote is certainly the provision of every possible facility for the transiting of goods via Karachi and rail to Afghanistan. I recently had a letter from a correspondent well informed on Soviet economic developments who stressed that the Russians were already delivering trucks and heavy machinery from factories in Czechoslovakia by direct rail to the Afghan frontier. I was unaware of this new Transit Agreement with Pakistan, but I pointed out that while the Russians could undoubtedly undertake such deliveries physically, they could never hope to make them an economic competition with seaborne shipments direct to Karachi and thence by rail to the Afghan border.[58]

The whole Pakhtunistan affair, even if it was only revived sporadically during the second and third Indo-Pakistani wars in 1965 and 1972, manifested 'a design for aggression' on the part of Afghanistan and, behind it, the Soviet Union. Such in any case was Teague-Jones's diagnosis in an unpublished article, the prophetic quality of which is apparent in the light of the most recent events. 'Ominous rumblings are once again making themselves heard on the NW Frontier, where Afghanistan marches with Pakistan', a frontier which was that of the British Raj until 1947, where Teague-Jones's adventurous life had begun before the First World War. In order to contain the endemic restlessness of the tribes in this desolate terrain the British had built:

a formidable system of frontier defence based on permanent garrisons at strategic advance posts linked with military roads and air support. To these were added the natural defences of the country itself, stark rugged mountain ranges, with only here and there a gorge or valley permitting ingress, and the whole constituted a formidable bulwark against local tribal unrest, hostilities with Afghanistan, or, if needs be, a Russian invasion.[59]

In 1947, following independence and Partition, this defence system was trans-ferred to Pakistan, which by virtue of its geographical position had become the sur-veillance bastion for the North West Frontier. As a Muslim state, Pakistan was count-ing not only on gathering in the Muslim populations of the subcontinent, but on benefiting from solid support from the neighbouring Muslim kingdom of Afghanistan. This overreliance on the religious factor led to Pakistani withdrawal of most of the military garrisons installed by the British in the tribal areas, where raids and depredations resumed at a record rate. With his intimate knowledge of the North West Frontier, Teague-Jones was confident that the chronic instability of the area was due above all to economics and not politics. He recalled many discussions on the subject when he was living almost symbiotically alongside Pushtuns with dif-fering tribal loyalties—Afridis, Mohmans, Yusufzais, Mahsuds or Waziris—and always receiving the same response:

Sahib, we do not raid for the fun of the thing. We raid because we have to live. Look at our country! Water is very scarce, but whenever it exists we cultivate what little food we can. But there is never sufficient for us to live on. We bring a few sheep skins and a few loads of fire-wood down to sell in the bazaars, and with the few rupees we get we purchase flour for bread. But it lasts us no time. The Government offers us land in the plains, but we are hill people; the heat down there would kill us. The government understands our position and pays us tribal allowances to compensate us for not raiding, but the yearly allowance only works out at a few annas per individual. Now I ask you Sahib, can a healthy tribesman with a family exist on that? And so we have to raid, just as our fathers raided in their time, and as did their fathers before them, right away back to Iskander Rumi (Alexander the Great).[60]

The Pakistani authorities were aware of this aspect of the problem, which would remain a purely domestic issue were it not for foreign interference which complicated the picture, creating a new situation in comparison with the colonial era. Teague-Jones saw Pakistan as subject to interference from three neighbouring states, Afghanistan, India and Soviet Russia. All three played an active part in the region and, for differing reasons, displayed the same level of hostility towards Pakistan. India's hostility flowed naturally from Partition, perceived as an unnatural act which by the very creation of Pakistan had given birth to a dangerous and unworkable experiment. 'Today', Teague-Jones wrote:

India regards Pakistan as an enemy with a dagger pointed straight at her heart. She is exceed-ingly suspicious of Pakistani intentions, and the possibility of war between the two neigh-bours cannot be excluded. India therefore fears any increment of Pakistan's military strength and protested strongly against America's recent grant of military aid. She very naturally deplores the insecurity of a situation which sees her most vital land defences, including the Khyber Pass, in what she regards as unfriendly hands.[61]

Afghanistan for its part had begun to display an interest in the tribal areas: shortly after the proclamation of Pakistan's independence, the notion of 'Pakhtunistan' emerged as a label for Pushtun territory on both sides of the frontier. The boundaries of this hypothetical Pakhtunistan challenged the very existence of Pakistan—they would comprise not only the tribal areas including Baluchistan, but also the districts of Peshawar, Kohat, Bannu and Dera Ismail Khan, including incidentally the non-Pushtun populations of these areas. The demand for Pakhtunistan was in fact a way of unlocking Afghanistan, by providing it with access to the sea on the Persian Gulf, and to India in the east via the Indus Valley. No one appeared to take this fanciful plan very seriously, given that Pushtun irredentism seemed to have such a flimsy foothold in reality on the ground, even when the Afghan government lent its support to the famous Faqir of Ipi, who was suddenly put forward as the leader of the movement. 'In whose brains did the very idea of Pakhtunistan germinate?' Teague-Jones wondered. Undoubtedly the Afghans. But at the same time it was unlikely that the Afghan government had of its own initiative adopted a strategy based on the minorities on its southern frontier, at a time when its northern frontier with the USSR was under strain from the presence of Turkmen, Uzbek and Tajik trans-frontier minorities. Moreover, the Soviets were keeping up a constant pressure on that frontier, claiming sovereignty over, among other territory, certain strategic islands in the Oxus. All this was modified by the British withdrawal in 1947: Soviet–Afghan relations suddenly became amicable, and contrary to expectation the issue of the Oxus islands was settled in favour of Afghanistan. 'But why this sudden friendship?' an Afghan diplomat friend asked Teague-Jones. 'There must be some catch somewhere!'

Shortly afterwards, Teague-Jones had a private conversation with another well-informed Afghan official:

— 'Thank God, we have at last reached a settlement with the Russians. Now we are in a position to play a strong hand in the East … the British held the Khyber but it never belonged to them. It is ours by right, and we shall take it. But we shall not stop at Jamrood or even Peshawar' he added.

— 'How far will you go?' the writer asked.

— 'To the Indus anyway'

— 'And will you stop there?'

— 'Allah knows. We crossed it before, and after all it is only a river'.

This was before one had heard the name Pakhtunistan, and Afghanistan was at that time in no position to challenge the superior military power of her new Moslem neighbours. The Afghan official was possibly expressing only his own opinion, but in the light of the current official attitude in Kabul his remarks were, to say the least, prophetic.[62]

There was no doubt in Teague-Jones's mind that the Soviets, now influential in Daoud's Afghanistan, were the real instigators of the Pakhtunistan plan, which had been elevated to a national cause. The king himself was calling for the Pushtun tribes on the other side of the Durand Line to revolt, while the Pakistanis had reacted by closing the Khyber to all traffic from Afghanistan. But in the modern era of air transport, the Khyber Pass had lost much of its role as strategic gateway. From Kabul airport one could build an air bridge between Afghanistan and India, while the Soviets had been quick to propose direct supply lines by land:

That the Russians are behind the Afghans and are actively encouraging them to embarrass, threaten and eventually harass Pakistan with tribal unrest and revolt is more than a mere possibility. Soviet Russian long term policy, like that of the Tsarist imperialists before it, has consistently envisaged an advance into India with an outlet on the Indian Ocean as an eventual objective. Today India presents no immediate problem, and her present policy of neutralism is harmless and even beneficial in Soviet eyes. Pakistan on the other hand is not only a formidable barrier blocking the road to Delhi. Her alliance with the Western Democracies puts her definitely in the anti-Soviet camp, and, as the biggest Moslem power in the world today, her attitude both encourages and influences the other Moslem states to follow her example. Therefore Moscow has decided that Pakistan must be weakened, and, if possible, eliminated, and that is briefly the master plot behind the fantastic demand of an independent 'Pakhtunistan'.[63]

Looking back half a century later, Teague-Jones's analysis contained several accurate premonitions, including, above all, that of the Soviet presence in Afghanistan, which was to draw the USSR inexorably into the Afghan mire from 1979 on. The USSR collapsed in 1991, two years after the withdrawal of its troops from Afghanistan. Two decades later the tribal areas, now subjected to 'Talibanisation', are central to world politics. In 2010, Pentagon officials published geological data gathered by Russian mining experts during the occupation of Afghanistan in the 1980s. They showed that the territory of Afghanistan conceals a real treasure-house of minerals—including gold, copper and lithium—which could raise the country to the first rank of world exporters. Such wealth—worth 1,000 billion dollars according to *The New York Times*—would obviously have an important bearing on the future of 'Af-Pak'. Teague-Jones was not therefore wholly wrong when he stressed the primacy of economics in the region. The future will reveal whether the conclusion that he reached at the end of the 1950s was or was not prophetic: '*Pakistan delendus est.*'

EPILOGUE

Yârân chô bettefâq-e didâr konîd
Bayâd ke ze dûst yâd be yâd konîd,
Chûn bâde-ye khôshgovâr noshid beham
Nawbat chô bemâ resîd nekû yâd konîd

Among your friends gathering
The absent remembering
And wine glasses emptying
Have a thought for me then

Written in a fine calligraphic hand, this parody of a Persian quatrain—the poet has allowed himself some spelling licence in order to get his words to fit the tight structure of classical Arab-Persian prosody—is on the last page of Teague-Jones's address book. Whether or not he was the author, the short poem could not be better located in a notebook where many friends, inevitably, were among the list of absentees. In each case Teague-Jones marks their name with a cross and draws a line through it. Sir Francis Evans and Sir Philip Crawford Vickery enjoyed a long life in the notebook, while against the name of Charles Howard Ellis, Teague-Jones cut out and pasted the obituary notice which appeared in the press. '*No flowers, by request.*' Major T.S.W. Jarvis, witness and protagonist in the case of the twenty-six commissars, survived in the notebook for quite a long time; Teague-Jones clearly remembered to send him greetings every year on his birthday. An old address book is certainly not an adequate summary of someone's social life, particularly when its owner is an intelligence agent who has been trained to destroy all traces of his passage. But this intimate relic gives an idea of his social range and suggests the geographical extent of his personal network at a particular moment in his life.

Teague-Jones's circle of acquaintances during the last twenty years of his life reveals his familiarity with smart English society, of the kind he had known in colonial India. Out of professional habit he sometimes wrote a short note on his links with such and such a person, or on the circumstances of a meeting with another. There are many women in the address book, such as Lady Adeline Ampthill, wife of John

Hugo Russell, 3rd Baron Ampthill, about whom nothing is known apart from her address in fashionable Holland Park. Also in the book is the name of Sibyl Hathaway, 21st Dame of Sark, the ruler of the tiny British island of Sark. A remaining 'very good friend from the time of Peshawar' was Kate, Dorothy K. Collings, born Fox-Strangways in 1892 and married to Major Edward Gardiner Collings. In 1914 the young couple were living in Peshawar, a forward post on the North West Frontier, as was Teague-Jones. Kate was twenty-two at the time, and we do not know the nature of her friendship with Teague-Jones. Was it confined to tennis parties in the British cantonment, or did Kate venture with him on to the winding paths of the Khyber Pass? Whatever the case may be, the Collings couple may very well have been the inspiration for the Frasers in the novel *Khyber Blood-Feud*. In real life, Teague-Jones was to become godfather to Kate's son who was born several years later in 1924. Nothing much more is known about this godson, Geoffrey Stephen d'Auvergne Collings, other than Teague-Jones's note of the date of his marriage. Geoffrey's family was struck by tragedy: his elder sister Barbara d'Auvergne Collings's life was brutally cut short in an air accident along with those of her husband and two of her three children. Teague-Jones also seems to have been close to Kate's sister, Marjorie Swift, and made a few notes on the military career of one of her sons. All this suggests a circle of aristocratic friends like those he knew in his adolescence in high society in St Petersburg.

Among other names in the book are those of Mrs Halleck A. Butts, widow of a former American commercial attaché in Tokyo, and Prince Alexander Makinsky, known as 'Shura', a White Russian émigré born in 1902 at Maku in Iran. An American citizen and violently anti-communist, Prince Makinsky was vice-president of the Coca-Cola Export Corporation from 1948 to 1953, at a time when the firm was facing a virulently anti-American campaign led by the French Communist Party. During the cold war, Teague-Jones also corresponded with Sanford Griffith, a New York consultant on questions of frontiers and minorities, a troubled character who apparently joined British intelligence at the end of the 1930s and then gravitated to the Anti-Defamation League, B'nai Brith, the well-known organisation dedicated to the fight against anti-Semitism in the United States. At one time suspected of being a Soviet agent, Sanford Griffith had taken an interest in the late 1950s in French policy in Algeria. Teague-Jones no doubt corresponded with him on issues such as the threat of Soviet expansion in the Middle East and Central Asia in which he still had a great interest in the early 1960s. But the address book with its names and surnames, addresses of oculists and monumental masons, does not shine much of a light on Teague-Jones's close relationships. Family relationships, to the extent they existed at all, were tenuous. Yet on his death it was to one of his distant nieces that he left the substantial sum of £255,551.

Among those friends who had disappeared, Charles H. Ellis occupied a special place. Ellis, whose first wife, Lilia Zelensky, was a White Russian. Ellis, who at the head of BSC during the Second World War, had unmasked a Soviet mole in the American Treasury Department. Ellis, who had ended his career in SIS in a high-level job in the Far East and Singapore. Ellis, in conclusion, who in the 1980s some years after his death was the target of a posthumous attack by the virulent essayist, Chapman Pincher. At the beginning of the 1980s the British secret services were the object of a vicious campaign of disinformation, probably orchestrated by the KGB, the purpose of which was to discredit services already severely damaged by the revelation of double agents such as Philby, MacLean and Blunt. How did Charles H. Ellis's name fall victim to Chapman Pincher's venomous pen, accused of nothing less than spying for Germany and the Soviet Union? It is difficult to get to the bottom of the story, since the author never bothered to cite his sources explicitly, nor even to look at Ellis's book on the Transcaspian episode, despite the light it sheds on his political even-handedness. The scandal, which was taken up widely in the British press in 1982–3, was devastating for Ellis's family and close friends, and aroused the indignation of some of his former colleagues. Teague-Jones, then ninety-two and certainly emotionally affected by the Ellis affair, was unable to contribute publicly to the argument, which would have required him to make a full or partial disclosure of his own identity in circumstances which could not have been more unfavourable. But he certainly sent discreet messages of sympathy to Ellis's children, with whom he had kept in contact. The latter ran up against a wall of silence with the British authorities, who would neither confirm nor deny Ellis's guilt. In accordance with the rule of silence in such matters, Mrs Thatcher would not agree to a departure from the principle of secrecy in defence of 'the national interest', even for Ellis's daughter who beseeched her for the truth 'whatever it might be'. But according to his former colleagues, there was no doubt as to Ellis's loyalty as an agent:

Ellis was privy to 'Ultra' and 'Magic', the greatest intelligence secrets of the war, which were the reading by SIS of all German and Japanese High Command and military radio communications. If Ellis had been working for Germany, he would have told Berlin these vital secrets. But, as Germany never knew that these codes were compromised, it is proof positive that Ellis was loyal to Britain.

Similarly Ellis came into official contact in New York in 1941 with Germany's star spy, the Yugoslav Dusko Popov, who was deceiving the German Abwehr by being actually employed by British MI6. Popov continued to enjoy German Abwehr's confidence to the end of the war, working in Lisbon and London. Again proof that Ellis was no German double agent, or he would have told Germany about Popov.

Sir William Stephenson, wartime chief of Western Hemisphere intelligence, to whom Ellis was deputy, states that Ellis was one of the important architects of the Allied victory and that innuendos against him are unfounded and highly suspect pure KGB disinformation aimed at discrediting the British, American, and Australian intelligence services.[1]

With destinies that crossed, from Iran and Transcaspia at the end of the First World War until New York in the Second World War, Ellis and Teague-Jones also had the common experience, although sixty years apart, of being the target of Soviet propaganda. One could almost write a history of KGB disinformation campaigns based on the affair of the twenty-six commissars and the Ellis affair. Far from being a double agent in the service of Germany or the Soviet Union, Ellis was in fact completely cleared several years later.

In 1988, the year of his death, Teague-Jones finished his novel *Khyber Blood-Feud*, subtitled *A Tale of the Afghan Border*, which remains unpublished. A coded autobiography, the novel's foreword expresses the author's fascination for the world of the Frontier:

This is a story of primitive human passions and emotions; of love, jealousy, and revenge; of all those qualities, good and bad, which go to make that most complex of all elements, the human character. The term 'primitive' is used advisedly because, while all these passions and emotions persist and daily manifest themselves in the most modern conditions of what we are pleased to call our western civilization, the setting of this particular story is the very antithesis of those conditions. For it is centered in one of the most remote, but at the same time one of the most romantic localities of the ancient world, where, at the time of the beginning of this narrative, conditions of human life had not materially changed through many centuries, and the country itself had remained, as it were, an oasis of ancient custom and tradition surrounded by a world of modern machinery and constant change. The scene of our story is the Khyber Pass.

Within the maze of the sun-scorched treeless ranges and ravines which constitute this mountain border-land, there have lived for untold centuries a virile race of tribes-people. These are the Pathans, or the Pakhtoons ... The Khyber hills are inhabited by a people whose social structure is still the patriarchal system of biblical times, where the Mosaic Law 'an eye for an eye; a tooth for a tooth; and a life for a life' is still the basis of summary justice, and where, in consequence, blood-feuds between clan and clan, village and village, and family and family, constitute the leitmotif of every tribesman's existence.[2]

This is not a product of Teague-Jones's imagination, because he did actually take part in the settlement of a blood-debt during his youth on the North West Frontier. If he ever acted as an executioner, it was not in the Turkmen desert, but in the tribal areas of North West India, where the harsh 'Pushtun Way', the notorious *Pushtunwali*, required a murder. The main plot of the novel, set among the Afridi tribe and very close to Teague-Jones's own experiences, is the settlement of a debt of honour. Love is not absent from the wild Frontier country, where a direct approach to a woman is an unlikely venture. The novel is in two parts and relates the saga of two generations of Afridis—a tribe of mountain herdsmen who live from robbery and pillage—involved in the settlement of an old blood-debt. There are also protagonists representing the *feringhis* (the 'Whites') in this Frontier novel, which takes place between the First World War—the period when Teague-Jones was himself a member of the Frontier Constabulary—and the Second World War. The hero, Jim Allenby, son of Sarfraz Khan and an Englishwoman, is fated like Teague-Jones to lose his parents while young, and thus to have an exceptional life. On the death of his father, killed during an ambush fight between the Afridis and a British patrol, Jim Allenby is baptised and put under the protection of Eileen Fraser, the young wife of Major Fraser, an officer in Military Intelligence at Peshawar. The adoption will decide Jim's fate, for he is soon despatched to the United States to be educated far from the harsh tribal law of the Frontier.

EPILOGUE

Fate will also decide on his return: twenty years later Jim Allenby has not, despite his long stay in the United States, forgotten his Pushtun descent. As an officer in the US Army, he is sent to New Delhi at the beginning of the Second World War as part of an Anglo-American mission to India. The mission is not exactly a military one as Major General Neil Fraser, who has been promoted in the intervening twenty years, informs him:

Well, in a very few words, I want you to come and work with me on very much the same sort of problems that your father was occupied with up to his death. I can promise you that it'll be interesting work, in fact, very interesting, but it is not regular soldiering, and for that reason you may wish to consider carefully whether you want to take it up or not.[3]

The job is to pursue an agent sent by the Germans to Afghanistan, a certain Haji Usman. It is not hard to see in him the transposed figure of Wassmuss, and Teague-Jones gives Jim, who becomes Jamal Khan, adventures which strongly resemble his own. Disguised as a man of the Frontier, having perfected his Pushtu—the language which he spoke fluently as a child—he carries out his secret mission, which leads him as far as the tunnels and caves of Waziristan, which have since become so notorious. On the tomb of his parents in the European cemetery in Peshawar, Jim meditates on the destiny which has brought him not only to carry out a political mission but also to redeem his own parents' tragic fate:

'Sarfraz and Margaret Allenby', he read again the wording on the stone. My father was a Moslem who gave up his religion and his traditions to marry a Christian. My mother gave up her culture and the traditions of her white race to marry my father. Now, here am I, their son—an American who, having been taken half way round the world to escape this sort of life, have now, of my own free will, come all the way back to plunge headlong into it again. Or was it my own free will? I begin to wonder ... Or was it really *qismet*, inevitable and irrevocable fate, prescribed by Allah?[4]

The same irrevocable fate had destined Teague-Jones to a long life of travel and adventure, the vicissitudes of which surpassed anything in a work of fiction. Shaped and trained in Waziristan, epicentre of world geopolitics, 'the spy who disappeared' in the turmoil of the affair of the twenty-six commissars, deserved to reappear, so clearly does his destiny as an agent of the British Empire illuminate present developments in the regions between Russia, Central Asia, Transcaucasia, India, Pakistan and the Middle East, the lands of the old, and the new, Great Game.

NOTE ON THE SOURCES

The reader will find the bibliographical references for this work in the footnotes. It has not been possible to trace the holders of the copyright to the two works by Teague-Jones published by Gollancz in London which are extensively quoted in this book. These are *Adventures in Persia*, London: Gollancz, 1988 (ISBN 0–575–04789–5) and *The Spy Who Disappeared: Diary of a Secret Mission to Russian Central Asia*, preface and postscript by Peter Hopkirk, London: Gollancz, 1990 (ISBN 0–575–050807-x).

The following is a brief indication of the archival sources used, all available in London or at Kew.

In the British Library, the different series of archives in India Office Records (L/PS and L/PJ) enable one to locate Reginald Teague-Jones in the institutions and context of his period.

Reginald Teague-Jones's personal archive (Sinclair collection, MSS C 313), containing sixty-six files of documents and photographs, is held in the British Library.

At the Imperial War Museum in London there is a box of archive material relating to Reginald Teague-Jones's missions during the First and Second World Wars. In the present work, this material is referenced as IWM, Sinclair Papers 67/329/1. This collection also includes photographs. Thanks to Matthew Lee, Keeper in the Film Archives Department at the Imperial War Museum, it has been possible to find and make use of Teague-Jones's film material.

Different series in the National Archives at Kew (NA)—Foreign Office (FO), War Office (WO), Board of Trade (WO)—made it possible to do the necessary cross-checking. These sources also contain some important reports from Teague-Jones which relate to the affair of the twenty-six commissars and to Central Asia in general.

Finally, the chapter on Baku and the twenty-six commissars is based on documents held in the archive of the Service historique de l'armée de terre (SHAT) at Vincennes, and in the personal archives of Brian Pearce.

NOTES

INTRODUCTION

1. NA, FO 57/377, Ronald Sinclair to G.G. Collins (Foreign Office), Marbella, 12 May 1973.
2. Walter Benjamin, 'Sur le concept d'histoire', in *Ecrits Français*, Paris: Gallimard, p. 433.
3. He is the translator of Paul Veyne's *Le Pain et le Cirque*, Roland Mousnier's *Les institutions de la France sous la monarchie absolue* and of Marcel Liebman, Maxime Rodinson and even Trotsky.
4. Between Tajikistan, China and today's Pakistan.
5. Brian Pearce, *The Staroselsky Problem 1918–1920: An Episode in British–Russian Relations in Persia*, London: Centre of Near and Middle Eastern Studies SOAS, School of Slavonic and East European Studies, 1994, p. 33.

1. CHILDHOOD IN LIVERPOOL AND ST PETERSBURG

1. See Marie-Louise Karttunen, 'Making a Communal World: English Merchants in Imperial St. Petersburg', Dissertation, University of Helsinki, 2005.
2. Ibid. p. 47.
3. BL, MSS C 313/28, Ronald Sinclair, 'Red Sunday, My Most Impressive Recollection ', in *The Illustrated Weekly of India*, 27 Jan. 1935.
4. See Igor Arkhangelsky, *Annenschule skvoz' tri stoletiya shkola na Kirochnoy, Sobytiya, uchitelya, ucheniki*, St Petersburg: Izd.Zvezda, 2004.
5. Sinclair, 'Red Sunday'.
6. *Les débuts de la première Révolution Russe, Sources et Documents*, Moscow, 1955, pp. 28–31.
7. G.A. Henty, *Saint Bartholomew's Eve: A Tale of the Huguenot Wars*, 1896.
8. Sinclair, 'Red Sunday'.
9. Karttunen, 'Making a Communal World', p. 47.
10. Sinclair, 'Red Sunday'.
11. Ibid.
12. Orlando Figes, *A People's Tragedy: The Russian Revolution, 1891–1924*, London: Jonathan Cape, 1996, p. 176.
13. Ibid.
14. Sinclair, 'Red Sunday'.

15. Ibid.
16. Ibid.
17. Ibid.
18. Figes, *A People's Tragedy*, p. 177.
19. Sinclair, 'Red Sunday'.
20. Ibid.
21. Figes, *A People's Tragedy*, p. 177.
22. Sinclair, 'Red Sunday'.
23. Ibid.
24. Figes, *A People's Tragedy*, p. 180.
25. Ibid. p. 181.
26. Ibid.

2. FROM THE PUNJAB TO THE NORTH WEST FRONTIER: THE MAKING OF A GENTLEMAN OF THE RAJ

1. NA, FO 57/377, self-recommendation for award by Ronald Sinclair.
2. See Terence Creagh Coen, *The Indian Political Service: A Study in Indirect Rule*, London: Chatto and Windus, 1971, p. 177.
3. John S. Galbraith, 'The "Turbulent Frontier" as a Factor of British Expansion', *Comparative Studies in Society and History*, 2, 2 (Jan. 1960), pp. 150–68.
4. See Christopher Alan Bayly, *Empire and Information: Intelligence Gathering and Social Communication in India*, Cambridge: Cambridge University Press, 2000.
5. The Thuggee and Dacoity Department had been set up by the government of India in 1835 under the direction of Colonel William Sleeman. It continued to function until 1904, when it was replaced by the Central Criminal Intelligence Department.
6. Winston S. Churchill, *My Early Life, 1874–1904*, New York: Simon and Schuster, 2010, pp. 104–5. 'The British lines or cantonments are in accordance with invariable practice placed five or six miles from the populous cities they guard; and in the intervening space lie the lines of the Indian regiments. The British troops are housed in large, cool, colonnaded barracks. Here forethought and order have been denied neither time nor space in the laying out of their plans. Splendid roads, endless double avenues of shady trees, abundant supplies of pure water; imposing offices, hospitals and institutions; ample parade-grounds and riding schools characterize these centres of collective life of considerable white communities.'
7. Jacques Pouchepadass, *L'Inde au XXe siècle*, Paris: Presses Universitaires de France, 1975, p. 65.
8. See Dennis Kincaid, *British Social Life in India, 1608–1937*, London: Routledge, 1973 (1st edn 1938). There are some amusing illustrations in this light and humorous book, notably a sketch of a man dreaming of his memories of a duck hunt in India, amid 'mists of nostalgia, recalling only the good things'.
9. See P.E. Razzell, 'Social Origins of Officers in the Indian and British Home Army: 1758–1962', *The British Journal of Sociology*, 14, 3 (Sep. 1963), pp. 248–60.
10. See P.J. Cain and A.G. Hopkins, *British Imperialism: Crisis and Deconstruction, 1914–1990*, London and New York: Longman, 1993, p. 178.
11. Pouchepadass, *L'Inde au XXe siècle*, p. 66.
12. NA, FO, 57/377, self-recommendation for award by Ronald Sinclair.

13. A Cambridge graduate who entered the Indian civil service in 1897, Vivian Gabriel's career began in 1898 in Bengal, followed by Rajputana and Central India, where he was appointed assistant magistrate and collector. After a short posting to the India Office in 1902 as assistant political ADC, then a special secondment to the Coronation Durbar in 1903, he was made undersecretary for foreign affairs, government of India, serving from 1903 to 1907. The high point of British imperial glory, the Delhi Durbar of 1903 was the second celebration in Delhi of the coronation of a British monarch as emperor of India. But contrary to the Proclamation Durbar of 1877, a closed, official ceremony to mark the coronation of Queen Victoria as empress of India, the 1903 Durbar was the occasion for two weeks of imperial festivities. The meticulous organisation demanded by the viceroy, Lord Curzon, required the special secondment of a number of senior officials like Vivian Gabriel. After taking part in the Durbar's elephantine—both literal and figurative—pomp and circumstance, and possibly making the security arrangements for the ceremonies which Edward VII did not attend in person, to Curzon's great disappointment, Vivian Gabriel was appointed resident in Western Rajputana States in 1908. In 1909 he became chief secretary to the commander in chief in the North West Frontier Province, and the following year secretary agent to the governor general of Central India. After a further secondment as secretary to the sumptuous Coronation Durbar of 1911 for King George V and Queen Mary, Vivian Gabriel, who had been sent on special missions to Nepal in 1908 and Libya in 1912, joined the Indian Political Service in 1913. At the beginning of the First World War, Vivian Gabriel left Nagpur in Central India to serve in the military operations branch of the War Office in 1915 as a general staff officer at the head of a British military mission to the Italian Army from 1915 to 1917, and then as liaison officer to the Aegean Squadron in 1917–18; with this background he may very well have been one of the people who installed Teague-Jones in his job. A descendant of one of the oldest families in Gubbio, the Gabrielis, Vivian Gabriel bequeathed a remarkable collection of oriental and Tibetan works of art to the municipal museum of Gubbio.

14. Ariane Audoin-Dubreuil, *La Croisière Jaune sur la route de la soie*, Grenoble: Glénat, 2007, pp. 108–9.

15. Ibid. p. 114.

16. See Caesar E. Farah, 'Smuggling and International Politics in the Red Sea in the Late Ottoman Period', in G. Rex Smith, J.R. Smart and B.R. Pridham (eds), *New Arabian Studies*, vol. 5, Presses de l'université Laval, 2000, pp. 47–66.

17. See Coen, *The Indian Political Service*, pp. 4–5.

18. The Intelligence Bureau bequeathed by the British administration in 1947 to the government of independent India, and to which the IPI was answerable during the colonial era, had been founded by Major General Sir Charles MacGregor, head of intelligence for the British Indian Army at Simla in 1885. In the context of the Great Game at the end of the nineteenth century, the organisation's principal objective at the time was to contain the Russian threat in Afghanistan, and to maintain strategic control over the North West Frontier of British India.

19. BL, IOR, L/PJ/12/776, IPI, situation of Col. Vickery, 1946.

20. BL, IOR, L/PJ/12/780, minute paper, Indian Political Intelligence.

21. BL, IOR, MSS C 313/20, Ronald Sinclair, *Khyber Blood-Feud: A Tale of the Afghan Border*, pp. 144–5.

22. Halford J. Mackinder (1893–1943). After studying physics at Oxford, he taught geography there from 1887 to 1905. From 1903 to 1908 he was also director of the famous London School of Economics. Elected to the House of Commons, he was appointed British high commissioner in Southern Russia (1919–20) after the First World War. After the cessation of foreign intervention, he returned to Great Britain and occupied a number of different senior government posts. Author of many published works, he put forward the concept of 'heartland' in *Britain and the British Seas* (1904) and especially in 'The Geographical Pivot of History', the title of a lecture given at the Royal Geographical Society.

23. Nicholas J. Spykman (1893–1943), one of the fathers of geopolitics in the United States, developed and modified Mackinder's theory in *America's Strategy in World Politics: The United States and the Balance of Power* (1942) and *The Geography of Peace* (1944). For him the 'heartland' (Germany, Russia) is not the real geographical pivot, globally speaking. Instead Spykman identifies the ring of lands surrounding it, the 'rimland' from Western Europe to East Asia, including the Middle East and the subcontinent, as the essential zone in geopolitical terms. This view of geopolitics was to become the basis for the strategy of 'containment' after the Second World War.

24. See *Frontiers and Overseas Expeditions from India*, compiled in the Intelligence Branch Army Headquarters, India, reprint Mittal publications, Delhi, 1983, vol. 1, part 1 'Tribes North of the Kabul River'.

25. George MacMunn, *Turmoil and Tragedy in India 1914 and After*, London: Jarrolds Publishers, 1935, p. 131.

26. About the Durand Line, Teague-Jones notes: 'however, the Durand line was not rigidly based upon exact topographical data and many errors, particularly of an ethnic nature, were committed, whereby the line passed through and separated regions inhabited by one and the same single tribe. There was also frequent confusion owing to different rendering of places [and] names, while it subsequently appeared that some stretches of the line were purely hypothetical and based upon guesswork. Finally, owing to the difficult nature of the terrain, one small section of the frontier remained undemarcated until the conclusion of the Third Afghan War in 1919. Although the Durand Agreement provided for the extension of the sphere of British influence to cover the independent tribal areas, when it came to actual practical working it was found impracticable to carry administration and law enforcement into the interior of a rugged mountainous and hostile territory. It was therefore found convenient to draw an administrative boundary which roughly followed the line of the border foothills and divided the settled British Indian Districts from the mountainous tracts of what was called Independent Tribal Territory.' BL, IOR, MSS Eur C 313/15.

27. BL, IOR, MSS Eur C 313/1.

28. BL, IOR, MSS Eur C 313/15, ff. 11–15. The North-West Frontier.

29. BL, IOR, MSS Eur C 313/1.

30. Ibid.

31. The highest peak in the Suleiman range, the legendary Takht-i-Suleiman is said by some to be 'Solomon's Throne', and in other tales is the spot where Noah's Ark grounded. Its rock wall reminds one of the face of Montagne Sainte-Victoire; believed to be one of the main birthplaces for the Pashtun people, Takht-i-Suleiman is a place of pilgrimage—indeed, there is a 'chapel' near the summit. The first ascent of the summit by Major McIvor and Captain McMahon in 1891 was supposed to be more than a feat of mountain-climb-

ing; it was intended to show the tribes that the British were able to dominate Sherani territory. See the evidence of Captain McMahon, British deputy-commissioner, at the Commission for the Frontier between Afghanistan and Baluchistan, in *Geographical Journal*, 4, 5 (Nov. 1894).

32. BL, IOR, MSS Eur C 313/1.
33. Ibid.
34. Ibid.
35. Ibid.
36. BL, IOR, MSS Eur C 313/15, ff. 11–15. The North-West Frontier.
37. The *chigga* is the name for the pursuit party. These were organised in most villages within the pacified districts. Such villages were obliged by law not only to resist but also to pursue the tribal raiders who threatened them. To this end each village was supplied by the government with rifles and ammunition.
38. 'The weapons of the nineteenth century are in the hands of the savages of the Stone Age', Winston Churchill, in *The Story of the Malakand Field Force: An Episode of the Frontier War*, London: Longmans, 1901 (1st edn 1898), p. 5.
39. Quoted in Coen, *The Indian Political Service*, p. 37.
40. See Major-General J.G. Elliott, *The Frontier, 1839–1947*, London: Cassell, 1968, James W. Spain, *The Pathan Borderland*, The Hague: Mouton, 1963.
41. Spain, *The Pathan Borderland*, p. 152.
42. Churchill, *The Story of the Malakand Field Force*, pp. 3–4. 'Among the wild animals of the region the hunter may pursue the black or brown mountain bear, an occasional leopard, markhor and several varieties of wild goat, sheep and antelope. The smaller quadrupeds include hares and red foxes, not unlike the British breed, only with much brighter coats, and several kind of rats, some of which are very curious and rare. Destitute of beauty but not without use, the scaly ant-eater is frequently seen; but the most common of all the beasts is an odious species of large lizard, nearly three feet long, which resembles a flabby-skinned crocodile and feeds on carrion. Domestic fowls, goats, sheep and oxen, with the inevitable vulture, and an occasional eagle, complete the fauna. Over all is a bright blue sky and powerful sun. Such is the scenery of the theatre of the war.'
43. BL, IOR, MSS Eur C 313/1.
44. BL, IOR, L/PS/10/837, file 3822 (1922), 'The Future of Central Asia: British or Russian Predominance?' 23 Aug. 1922.
45. Churchill, *The Story of the Malakand Field Force*, p. 4.
46. BL, IOR, MSS Eur C 313/1, 31 Mar. 1915.
47. BL, IOR, MSS Eur C 313/1.
48. Quoted by Churchill, *The Story of the Malakand Field Force*.

3. THE PERSIAN GULF AND THE HUNT FOR 'MR WASSMUSS'

1. Justus Perthes Verlag was founded in Gotha (1875). About cartography and nationalism, see Guntram Henrik Herb, *Under the Map of Germany: Nationalism and Propaganda 1918–1945*, London: Routledge, 1997.
2. BL, MSS Eur C 313/3.
3. See Yann Richard, *L'Iran, Naissance d'une république islamique*, Paris: Editions de la Martinière, 2006, p. 141.
4. Sean McMeekin, *The Berlin–Baghdad Express: The Ottoman Empire and Germany's Bid for World Power, 1898–1918*, London: Penguin, 2011.

5. Peter Hopkirk, *Like Hidden Fire: The Plot to Bring Down the British Empire*, New York: Kodansha International, 1994, p. 28.
6. Quoted in Antoine Fleury, *La politique allemande au Moyen-Orient, 1919–1929*, Leiden and Geneva: Institut universitaire des hautes études internationales, 1977, p. 27.
7. Oliver Bast, *Les Allemands en Perse pendant la Première Guerre Mondiale d'après les sources diplomatiques françaises*, Paris: Peeters, 1997.
8. Richard, *L'Iran, Naissance d'une république islamique*, p. 156.
9. Ibid.
10. Christopher Sykes, *Wassmuss: 'The German Lawrence'*, London: Longmans, 1936, pp. 98–9.
11. Ibid. p. 152.
12. Sir Percy Sykes, 'South Persian and the Great War', *The Geographical Journal*, LVIII, 2 (Aug. 1921), p. 104.
13. The South Persia Rifles were, however, largely disbanded in the spring of 1918 following mutinies and defections in the course of which British officers were murdered.
14. John Buchan, *Greenmantle*, Harmondsworth: Penguin Books, 1956, pp. 18–19.
15. Quoted in Bast, *Les Allemands en Perse pendant la Première Guerre Mondiale d'après les sources diplomatiques françaises*, p. 112.
16. Sykes, *Wassmuss: 'The German Lawrence'*, p. 36.
17. Raoul Blanchard, *Géographie Universelle*, sous la direction de P.Vidal de la Blache et L.Gallois, tome 8, *Asie occidentale*, Paris: Colin, 1929, p. 151.
18. Sykes, *Wassmuss: 'The German Lawrence'*, p. 41.
19. BL, IOR, MSS Eur C 313/3.
20. Blanchard, *Géographie Universelle*, p. 151.
21. Imperial War Museum, Major Ronald Sinclair 67/329/1, 'The Story of Missions in Central Asia and Transcaucasia', ff. 569–70.
22. Sykes, *Wassmuss: 'The German Lawrence'*, p. 198.
23. See Brian Pearce, *The Staroselsky Problem 1918–1920: An Episode in British–Russian Relations in Persia*, London: Centre of Near and Middle Eastern Studies SOAS, School of Slavonic and East European Studies, 1994.
24. Reginald Teague-Jones, *The Spy Who Disappeared: Diary of a Secret Mission to Russian Central Asia*, London: Gollancz, 1990, p. 18.
25. Ibid.
26. Ibid. p. 20.
27. Ibid. p. 21.
28. Ibid.
29. Ibid. pp. 21–2.
30. Ibid. p. 22.
31. Ibid. p. 23.
32. C.H. Ellis, *The Transcaspian Episode, 1918–1919*, London: Hutchinson, 1963, p. 23.
33. Ibid. p. 25.
34. Teague-Jones, *The Spy Who Disappeared*, p. 35.
35. Ibid.
36. Ibid. pp. 36–7.
37. Ibid. pp. 37–8.
38. Ibid. pp. 43–4.
39. See Taline Ter Minassian, *Colporteurs du Komintern, L'Union Soviétique et les minorités au Moyen-Orient*, Paris: Presses de Sciences po, 1997.
40. Teague-Jones, *The Spy Who Disappeared*, p. 45.

4. ASHKHABAD AND THE TRANSCASPIAN EPISODE

1. See Roberto Gulbenkian, 'L'habit arménien, laissez-passer oriental pour les missionnaires, marchands et voyageurs européens aux XVIe et XVIIIe siècles', *Revue des Etudes Arméniennes*, 25 (1994–5), pp. 369–88.
2. Reginald Teague-Jones, *The Spy Who Disappeared: Diary of a Secret Mission to Russian Central Asia*, London: Gollancz, 1990, p. 49. The choice of Armenian dress is a reminder of the role of Armenian merchants in the intelligence and spy networks operated by the Portuguese in the sixteenth century, at a time when the latter dominated commercial traffic in the Indian Ocean. See Dejanirah Couto, 'Arméniens et Portugais dans les réseaux d'information de l'océan Indien au XVIe siècle', in Sushil Chaudhury and Kéram Kévonian (eds), *Les Arméniens dans le commerce asiatique au début de l'ère moderne*, Paris: Editions de la MSH, 2007, pp. 171–96.
3. Teague-Jones, *The Spy Who Disappeared*, p. 52.
4. Ibid.
5. Ibid. p. 54.
6. Ibid. p. 57.
7. See Chapter 5.
8. Teague-Jones, *The Spy Who Disappeared*, p. 58.
9. Ibid. pp. 62–3.
10. Ibid. p. 66.
11. Ibid. pp. 68–9.
12. Ibid. p. 75.
13. NA, WO 106/61, 'The Russian Revolution in Transcapia', report written by Captain Reginald Teague-Jones in Ashkhabad, 26 Jan. 1919, transmitted to MI5 on 15 Apr. 1919.
14. Ibid.
15. Ibid.
16. Ibid.
17. Teague-Jones, *The Spy Who Disappeared*, p. 109 onwards.
18. NA, WO 106/61, The Russian Revolution in Transcaspia.
19. Ibid.
20. Teague-Jones, *The Spy Who Disappeared*, pp. 113–14.
21. Ibid. pp. 114–15.
22. Ibid. p. 182.
23. IWM, Sinclair Papers, 67/329/1, Reginald Teague-Jones (Ashkhabad) to Ronald MacDonell (Enzeli), 29 Oct. 1918.
24. Teague-Jones, *The Spy Who Disappeared*, pp. 194–5.
25. IWM, Sinclair Papers, 67/329/1, Reginald Teague-Jones (Ashkhabad) to Ronald MacDonell (Enzeli), 29 Oct. 1918.
26. See Michael Sargent, 'British Military Involvement in Transcaspia (1918–1919)', Caucasus Series 04/02, Defence Academy of the UK, Conflict Studies Research Centre, Apr. 2004, p. 23.
27. Teague-Jones, *The Spy Who Disappeared*, p. 194.
28. IWM, Sinclair Papers, 67/329/1, Reginald Teague-Jones (Ashkhabad) to Redl (Meshed), 15 Oct. 1918.
29. Atyrau, a Kazakh city endowed with an abundance of oil and natural gas, lies on the banks of the Ural River, 30 kilometres from the Caspian shore.

30. IWM, Sinclair Papers, 67/329/1, Reginald Teague-Jones (Ashkhabad) to Col. Fleming (Krasnovodsk), 26 Oct. 1918.
31. Ibid.
32. Teague-Jones, *The Spy Who Disappeared*, p. 152.
33. IWM, Sinclair Papers, 67/329/1, Reginald Teague-Jones (Ashkhabad) to Fleming (Krasnovodsk), 14 Dec. 1918.
34. Teague-Jones, *The Spy Who Disappeared*, p. 154.
35. See Daniel C. Waugh, *Etherton at Kashgar: Rhetoric and Reality in the History of the 'Great Game'*, Seattle: Bactrion Press, 2007.
36. IWM, Sinclair Papers, 67/329/1, Reginald Teague-Jones (Ashkhabad) to Col. Redl (Meshed), 22 Sep. 1918.
37. Ibid.
38. IWM, Sinclair Papers, 67/329/1, Reginald Teague-Jones (Ashkhabad) to Col. Redl (Meshed), 24 Sep. 1918.
39. Ibid.
40. IWM, Sinclair Papers, 67/329/1, Reginald Teague-Jones (Ashkhabad) to Fleming (Krasnovodsk), 22 Oct. 1918.
41. IWM, Sinclair Papers, 67/329/1, Knollys (Kaakhka) to Reginald Teague-Jones (Ashkhabad), 23 Oct. 1918.
42. IWM, Sinclair Papers, 67/329/1, Reginald Teague-Jones (Ashkhabad) to Knollys (Kaakhka), 24 Oct. 1918.
43. Teague-Jones, *The Spy Who Disappeared*, p. 141.
44. IWM, Sinclair Papers, 67/329/1, Reginald Teague-Jones (Ashkhabad) to Knollys (Kaakhka), 24 Oct. 1918.
45. Teague-Jones, *The Spy Who Disappeared*, p. 142.
46. Ibid. p. 182.
47. Ibid. pp. 186–7.
48. Ibid. p. 187.
49. IWM, Sinclair Papers, 67/329/1, Reginald Teague-Jones (Ashkhabad) to Redl (Meshed), 11 Dec. 1918.
50. IWM, Sinclair Papers, 67/329/1, Reginald Teague-Jones (Ashkhabad) to Fleming (Krasnovodsk), 22 Jan. 1919.
51. IWM, Sinclair Papers, 67/329/1, Fleming (Krasnovodsk) to Reginald Teague-Jones (Ashkhabad), 16 Dec. 1918.
52. IWM, Sinclair Papers, 67/329/1, Fleming (Krasnovodsk) to Reginald Teague-Jones (Ashkhabad), 29 Dec. 1918.
53. IWM, Sinclair Papers, 67/329/1, Reginald Teague-Jones (Ashkhabad) to Fleming (Krasnovodsk), 22 Jan. 1919.
54. C.H. Ellis, *The Transcaspian Episode, 1918–1919*, London: Hutchinson, 1963, p. 159.
55. Ibid. p. 25.
56. Teague-Jones, *The Spy Who Disappeared*, p. 78.
57. Ibid. pp. 78–9.
58. Ibid. pp. 154–5.
59. IWM, Sinclair Papers, 67/329/1, Foreign Affairs Minister of Transcaspian Government Zimin to General Malleson, head of British military mission, 22 Dec. 1918.
60. Ibid.
61. Ibid.

62. IWM, Sinclair Papers, 67/329/1, intelligence report, Ashkhabad, 22 Jan. 1919.
63. Teague-Jones, *The Spy Who Disappeared*, pp. 199–200.
64. Ibid. pp. 202–3.

5. THE LEGEND OF THE TWENTY-SIX COMMISSARS: TEAGUE-JONES, HERO OR VILLAIN?

1. Sergeï Esenin, 'Ballad of the 26 Commissars', *Bak.Rab.*, 22 Sep. 1924, n°314.
2. Jules Verne, *Claudius Bombarnac*, Paris: Hetzel, 1892, p. 61.
3. Kurban Saïd, *Ali and Nino*, New York: Pocket Book, 1972, p. 12. See the biography of Kurban Saïd (Lev Nussimbaum) by Tom Reiss, *The Orientalist: Solving the Mystery of a Strange and Dangerous Life*, New York: Random House, 2005.
4. C.H. Ellis, *The Transcaspian Episode, 1918–1919*, London: Hutchinson, 1963, p. 13.
5. Reginald Teague-Jones, *The Spy Who Disappeared: Diary of a Secret Mission to Russian Central Asia in 1918*, London: Gollancz, 1990, p. 99.
6. BL, IOR, MSS C 313/6, f. 69.
7. BL, IOR/L/PS/11/3441, 3578, 3633.
8. BL, IOR, MSS C 313/6, f. 69.
9. SHAT, 7 N 1662. Agreement between the Transcaspian government (Dokof) and the British government (General Malleson), Meshed, 19 Aug. 1918.
10. Teague-Jones, *The Spy Who Disappeared*, pp. 90–1.
11. Ibid. p. 61.
12. They will be remobilised for the defence of Baku during the advance of the Ottoman troops, although 3,000 of them, allied to a Communist artillery unit commanded by Petrov, refuse to support the defence of Baku after the fall of the twenty-six commissars and the installation of the Centro-Caspian Dictatorship.
13. See Nikita Dastakian, *Il venait de la Ville Noire, Souvenirs d'un Arménien du Caucase*, foreword by A. Tèr Minassian, L'Inventaire, CRES, 1998, p. 107.
14. See Serge A. Zenkovsky, *Pan-Turkism and Islam in Russia*, Cambridge, MA: Harvard University Press, 1960.
15. Teague-Jones, *The Spy Who Disappeared*, p. 88.
16. Ibid. p. 94.
17. See *Brat'ia naveki, Dokumenty i materialy ob istoritcheskoj drujbe russkogo i azerbaidjanskogo narodov*, Baku, Az.Gos.Izd., 1987, document no. 235, pp. 327–9.
18. Teague-Jones, *The Spy Who Disappeared*, p. 100.
19. Ibid.
20. On the siege of Baku from General Dunsterville's point of view, see Peter Hopkirk, *Like Hidden Fire: The Plot to Bring Down the British Empire*, New York: Kodansha International, 1994, p. 341 and above all Brian Pearce, 'Dunsterforce and the Defence of Baku, August–September 1918', in *Revolutionary Russia*, 10, 1 (June 1997), pp. 55–71.
21. See *Hayeri godoradznere Bakvi yev Elizabedpoli nahadagnerum 1918–1920*, Yerevan: Hayastani Hanrabedoutian Badmoutian Arkhiv, 2003, pp. 290–301. See the report (in Russian) on the Baku events by the inquiry commission, Tiflis, Apr. 1919, no. 259.
22. SHAT, 7 N 1662, correspondence of Resht French vice-consulate, 7 Oct. 1918.
23. See *Hayeri godoradznere Bakvi yev Elizabedpoli nahadagnerum*, no. 111, p. 118.
24. Ronald Grigor Suny, 'Nationalisms and Social Class in the Russian Revolution: The Cases of Baku and Tiflis', in Ronald Grigor Suny (ed.), *Transcaucasia, Nationalism and Social*

Change: Essays in the History of Armenia, Azerbaijan and Georgia, Ann Arbor: University of Michigan Press, 1983, p. 247.

25. SHAT, 7 N 1662, French consulate in Tauris, in charge of the vice-consulate of Resht, 7 Oct. 1918.

26. Extracts from Shchegoliutin's deposition at the war trial of the Turkfront, in A.S. Bukshpan, *Poslednie dni kommissarov Bakinskoj Kommuny po materialam soudebnykh protsetsov*, Baku: Istpart, 1928, p. 106.

27. See Hopkirk, *Like Hidden Fire*, pp. 366–7. Alexei Dirdikin made no deposition during the judicial process relating to the affair of the twenty-six commissars, and for good reason; his murdered body was found on the day after the events. According to Peter Hopkirk, who does not quote his sources, Dirdikin's evidence was gathered by his family and passed on to the priest officiating at the funeral. The notes made by the priest were apparently rediscovered more than fifty years later.

28. See Mikhail Lifshits, *Kto vinovat 26-ti, S prilojenim dnevnika Funtikova*, Tiflis: Zakniga, 1926.

29. Brian Pearce, 'The 26 Commissars', *Sbornik, Study Group on the Russian Revolution*, nos 6–7, 1981, p. 54.

30. See Anahide Ter Minassian, *La République d'Arménie*, Brussels: Complexe, 2006 (reed), pp. 98–101.

31. It should be remembered that Stepan Shahumian's freedom of initiative was in any case limited by party discipline, which required him to follow Lenin's conciliatory policy towards the Germans. See Brian Pearce, 'The Tragedy of Baku', in *How Haig Saved Lenin*, London: MacMillan, 1987.

32. Anastase Mikoyan (trans. from the French version), *Une Vie de Lutte*, Moscow: Editions du Progrès, 1973, p. 137.

33. Ibid. p. 153.

34. Pearce, 'The 26 Commissars', pp. 54–66.

35. See Brian Pearce, 'A Passage to Krasnovodsk", *Sbornik*, 11 (1985), pp. 131–4.

36. Ibid. p. 134.

37. Mikoyan, *Une Vie de Lutte*, pp. 156–7.

38. Pearce, 'A Passage to Krasnovodsk', p. 134.

39. Mikoyan, *Une Vie de Lutte*, pp. 158–9.

40. Teague-Jones, *The Spy Who Disappeared*, p. 140.

41. BL, IOR, L/MIL/17/552, telegram dated 18 Sep. 1918.

42. BL, IOR, MSS C 313/12, ff. 11–14, 12 Nov. 1922, Card 1846 of 1923.

43. BL, IOR, L/MIL/17/555, telegram dated 23 Sep. 1918.

44. IWM, Major Ronald Sinclair 67/329/1. Political and military correspondence, Transcaspia. Telegram dated 24 Sep. 1918.

45. Clifford Kinvig, *Churchill's Crusade: The British Invasion of Russia, 1918–1920*, London: Hambledon Continuum, 2006.

46. Interview with Ann Randall, Ronald Sinclair's nurse, Englefield Greens, 12 June 2008.

47. Vadim Chaikin, *K istorii Rossiskoj Revoliutsii, Vypusk 1, Kazn' 26 Bakinskikh komissarov*, Moscow: Izd.Z.N.Grjebina, 1922.

48. Brian Pearce Papers, letter from Brian Pearce to Ronald Sinclair, 30 Aug. 1979.

49. Brian Pearce Papers, letter from Ronald Sinclair to Brian Pearce, 20 Nov. 1979.

50. Ibid.

51. On the context of Vadim Chaikin's inquiry and on the accusation, see Brian Pearce's essen-

tial study. Brian Pearce, 'On the Fate of the 26 Commisars', *Sbornik*, 6–7 (1981), pp. 83–95.

52. See Chaikin, *K istorii Rossiskoj Revoliutsii, Vypusk 1, Kazn' 26 Bakinskikh komissarov*, pp. 181–3.

53. Mikoyan, *Une vie de lutte*, p. 176.

54. Quoted by Pearce, 'On the Fate of the 26 Commissars', p. 85.

55. Ibid. p. 86.

56. N.N. Narimanov, *Azerbaidjanskaya bednota*, no. 39, 10 Sep. 1920.

57. The Kaurosta was the Caucasian branch of the Rosta Agency in charge of the agitprop.

58. BL, IOR/L/PS/18/C/203, information on the Baku Conference.

59. *Kommunist*, Baku, 3 Sep. 1920.

60. Quoted in Pearce, 'On the Fate of the 26 Commissars', p. 86.

61. Ibid. p. 87.

62. See A.S. Bukshpan, *Poslednie dni kommissarov Bakinskoj Kommuny po materialam soudebnykh protsetsov*.

63. Ibid. p. 120.

64. Brian Pearce, 'Communication', *Revolutionary Russia*, 3, 1 (Jan. 1990), p. 112.

65. Files no. 74–5. Stenographic report of a broadcast of Radio Yerevan, no mention of date.

66. See *Hayastani Hanrabedutyun*, 13 Jan. 2009. According to the announcement at Baku by the official responsible for the district of Sabahili, Sakhib Alekberov, the removal of the funeral monument would make it possible to build an underground car park. However, the announcement states that the tombs of Nariman Narimanov, Meshati Azizbekov and Rikard Chorkev will be left undisturbed.

67. *Haratch*, 30 Jan. 2009.

68. See V. Tatlin and S. Dymshits-Tolstoaia, 'Memorandum from the Visual Arts Section of the People's Commissariat for Enlightenment to the Soviet of People's Commissars: Project for the Organization of Competitions for Monuments to Distinguished Persons (1918)', introduction by John Bowlt, *Design Issues*, 1, 2 (Autumn 1984), pp. 70–4.

69. Quoted in Pearce, 'On the Fate of the 26 Commissars', p. 89.

70. See Michael G. Smith, 'Cinema for the "Soviet East": National Fact and Revolutionary Fiction in Early Azerbaijani Film', *Slavic Review*, 56, 4 (1997), pp. 645–78.

71. BL, IOR/L/PS/12/4003, Anglo-Soviet Debts and Claims Committee, Shooting of the 26 Baku Commissars.

72. BL, IOR, MSS D 942, Major T.S.W. Jarvis Papers, f. 3.

73. Mikoyan, *Une vie de lutte*, p. 180.

6. THE RETREAT OF THE WHITE ARMIES: FROM CONSTANTINOPLE TO THE CAUCASUS (1919–21)

1. BL, IOR, MSS Eur C 313/12, T.S.W. Jarvis to C.S. Jarvis, Ashkhabad, 2 Feb. 1919. Major C.S. Jarvis, member of the Royal Central Asian Society, Lawrence of Arabia Memorial Medal (1938), died 9 Dec. 1953. See his obituary in *Royal Central Asian Journal*, XLI, part II (Apr. 1954), p. 93.

2. IWM, Sinclair Papers, 67/329/1, 'The Story of Missions in Central Asia and Transcaucasia', ff. 528–9.

3. Ibid. f. 530.

4. See M. Larcher, *La guerre turque dans la guerre mondiale*, Paris: Chiron, Berger-Levrault, 1925, p. 545.

5. See François Georgeon, *Abdulhamid II, le Sultan Calife*, Paris: Fayard, 2003, pp. 127–46.

6. BL, IOR, MSS, C313/14, Reginald Teague-Jones, Notes on Constantinople and the Old Seraglio in 1923, f. 4.

7. Ibid. ff. 4–7. Here are two extracts of this rhyming report:
My Lord/Today I went to see/The Caliph, whose simplicity/Appeared in all things;/nowhere more/Than just inside the great front-door;/No Teshrifatdji blocked the way;/An underling of Adnan Bey,/Short-coated, passed me on to where/Hard by a most impos-ing stair,/ A military ADC/Of obviously low degree,/Not knowing what he had to do,/Wisely did nothing; while a few/Dilapidated servants hung/About the vestibule. A young/But staid lieutenant of Marine/Then flashed upon the giddy scene/And let me upward to a room/Containing two officials whom/I gathered from their own report/To be the Caliph's modest court./There was no obsolete display;/The flunkeys and the coffee-tray/Prescribed by outworn etiquette/Were absent; but a cigarette,/A remnant haply of old stocks,/Was served me in card-board box./Which I had hardly lighted, ere/The Caliph summoned me. I fear/The audience chamber struck a note/A hyper-critic might have thought/Too reminiscent of the age,/Ere Kemal entered on the stage,/When sumptuous Emperors of old/Mis-spent the people's hard-won gold./For instance, I have rarely seen/In any spot where I have been/A sofa quite so large as that/Whereon this simple Caliph sat./Or chairs so formidably gay/As mine and that of Adnan Bey./Not his the fault; if this was so;/Indeed, his person served to show/How insignificant a part/Is played by decora-tive art/In this new Turkey and how much/Is due to Nature's gracious touch./His beard!—/Your Lordship will excuse/A cogent impulse to enthuse!/A beard that proved in every hair/The efficacity of prayer;/A beard that should create a hum/ In all the realms of Beaverdom./So white; so thick; and it appeared/To be centrifugally geared. …/My flow of inspiration flagged,/The more the conversation sagged./A problem then arose. 'Twas this:/How get a Caliph to dismiss/A High Commissioner? One knows/One waits his sig-nal ere one goes./Whereas—I twiddled both my feet;/I dropped my eye-glass; 'Tis a neat/Device I constantly employ/When company begins to cloy./I wore a look of patient pain/As though from tooth-ache.—All in vain!/He made no move, he gave no sign;/Again the initiative was mine./I said, 'Your Majesty, do you/Permit departure'? and withdrew./Time was when I should still have failed/To make my exit unregaled/With cigarettes and tea before/I left the Palace; now no more/Such senseless courtesies delay/The visitor upon his way./Nor do high officers of Court,/Or teshrifatdjis from the Porte,/Squander his pre-cious time of theirs./I was shown rapidly downstairs./Sped like some swiftly falling star/Straight from the Presence to my car/And so to Pera, whence I send/This record home, my Lord; and end,/With truth and great respect from your/Obedient humble servant Hor-/Ace Rumbold, High Commissioner.

8. The Ottoman sultans held the position of caliph. Mustafa Kemal was to abolish the Sultanate in 1922 and the Caliphate on 3 Mar. 1924.

9. Elmer Davis, 'Hives of Russian Refugees, Half-Starved Throngs in Constantinople and Near East Peddling Jewels and Furs for Existence: Will They Go Back?' *New York Times*, 8 Jan. 1922.

10. IWM, Sinclair Papers, 67/329/1. Drawings and caricatures are unattributed.

11. Davis, 'Hives of Russian Refugees'.

12. See M.D. Wrangel, baronne, *Ma vie et ma fuite du 'paradis communiste'*, Lausanne: Bibliothèque universelle, 1922.

13. BL, IOR, MSS C 313/2, extracts from the diaries of Reginald Teague-Jones regarding the operations in Crimea and in Georgia.

14. Ibid. ff. 11–12.

15. See Richard Pipes, 'Les relations diplomatiques du gouvernement de Wrangel en Crimée, 1920', *Cahiers du Monde Russe et Soviétique*, 4, 4 (1963), pp. 401–35.

16. Ibid. p. 403.

17. Ibid. pp. 411–13. Struve to Maklakov, Paris, 8 June 1920.

18. BL, IOR, MSS C313/2, extracts from the diaries of Reginald Teague-Jones regarding the operations in Crimea and Georgia.

19. Ibid.

20. Quoted in Pipes, 'Les relations diplomatiques du gouvernement de Wrangel en Crimée, 1920', p. 433. Wrangel to Struve, *Kornilov* Cruiser, 24 Nov. 1920.

21. Ibid.

22. See Anahide Ter Minassian, 'Indépendance et soviétisation des républiques transcaucasiennes', in *Histoires croisées: Diaspora, Arménie, Transcaucasie, 1890–1990*, preface by Pierre Vidal-Naquet, Marseille: Parenthèses, 1997, pp. 165–74.

23. BL, IOR, MSS C 313/8, the capture of Krasnovodsk (at the beginning of 1920) by the Bolsheviks and the effect of such on the Caucasus, ff. 5–6.

24. Ibid. ff. 6–9. Political parties in the Caucasus.

25. Ibid. ff. 10–12. Bolshevism in the Caucasus.

26. Ibid. ff. 13–15.

27. Quoted in Ter Minassian, A. 'Indépendance et soviétisation des républiques transcaucasiennes', p. 169. An Anglo-Russian trade agreement was signed on 16 Mar. 1921, and although Lloyd-George had pronounced himself in favour of an independent Georgia, which he saw as a 'barrier against Bolshevism', Great Britain would ultimately resume trade talks with Soviet Georgia. See Dennis Ogden, 'Britain and Soviet Georgia, 1921–1922', *Journal of Contemporary History*, 23, 2 (Apr. 1988), pp. 245–58.

28. IWM, Sinclair Papers, 67/329/1, 'The story of missions in Central Asia and Transcaucasia', f. 556.

29. Ibid. f. 563.

30. Ibid. f. 579.

31. See John D. Rose, 'Batum as Domino, 1919–1920: The Defence of India in Transcaucasia', *The International History Review*, 2, 2 (Apr. 1980), pp. 266–87.

32. IWM, Sinclair Papers, 67/329/1, 'The Story of Missions in Central Asia and Transcaucasia', f. 589.

33. Ibid. f. 589.

34. BL, IOR, MSS C 313/8, ff. 26–7. Draft letter to Graves, Batum, 28 Feb. 1921.

35. See Serge Afanasyan, *L'Arménie, l'Azerbaïdjan et la Géorgie de l'indépendance à l'instauration du pouvoir soviétique, 1917–1923*, Paris: L'Harmattan, 1981, p. 187.

36. Revkom is the Soviet Russian acronym for revolutionary committee.

37. BL, IOR, MSS C313/8, f. 24. Situation in the North Caucasus.

38. Ibid. f. 20. General situation in Transcaucasia.

39. Ruben Ter Minassian (1882–1951) a revolutionary and *fedaï* involved in 1906–8 in the self-defence of the Armenian populations in the eastern provinces of the Ottoman Empire, a member of the Bureau of the Revolutionary Armenian Federation, was in charge of the

Armenian troops in the Caucasus from 1917 to 1921. Minister for war in independent Armenia, he was one of the pillars of resistance to the communists in the Zangezur area after Sovietisation. He subsequently emigrated to Persia and thence to Europe.

40. BL, IOR, MSS C 313/8, f. 26. Situation in Armenia.
41. Ibid. ff. 20–3. General situation in Transcaucasia.
42. Ibid.
43. See Richard G. Hovannisian, 'Armenia and the Caucasus in the Genesis of the Soviet–Turkish Entente', *International Journal of Middle-East Studies*, IV (1973), p. 130.
44. IWM, Sinclair Papers, 67/329/1, 'The Story of Missions in Central Asia and Transcaucasia', f. 523.
45. BL, IOR, MSS C 313/8, notes on Turkish forces concentrated on the Georgian and Armenian frontiers from Georgian secret sources, f. 16, 16 Dec. 1920.
46. Ibid. ff. 18–19. Turkish military situation. Information from the Georgian Intelligence Department.
47. BL, IOR, MSS C 313/8, f. 28. Nationalist foreign policy.
48. Meaning in fact autonomy.
49. Ibid. ff. 27–8. The present situation in Ajaristan.
50. BL, IOR, MSS C 313/8, f. 29. The situation in Ajaria, 27 Mar. 1922.
51. Ibid.
52. BL, IOR, L/PS/10/837, file 3822 (1922), Ronald Sinclair, 'The Future of Central Asia, British or Russian Predominance?' 24 July 1922. This report was transmitted to FO 23 Aug. 1922.
53. BL, IOR, L/PS/10/837 file 3822 (1922), 8 Aug. 1922.
54. BL, IOR, L/PS/10/837 file 3822 (1922), 23 Aug. 1922.
55. BL, IOR, L/PS/10/837 file 3822 (1922), 28 Aug. 1922, Sir Arthur Hirtzel to S of S.

7. RONALD SINCLAIR, IMPERIAL TRAVELLER

1. William Engdahl, *A Century of War: Anglo-American Oil Politics and the New World Order*, London: Pluto Press, 2004, p. 8.
2. BL, IOR, L/PJ/12/780, 8 Mar. 1924.
3. Ibid.
4. BL, IOR, L/PJ/12/780, secret report signed M.C.S., 16 Nov. 1921.
5. Reginald Teague-Jones, *Adventures in Persia*, London: Gollancz, 1990, p. 12.
6. Ibid. pp. 69–70.
7. See Geoffrey Jones, LSE, 'The Imperial Bank of Iran and Iranian Economic Development, 1890–1952', *Business and Economic History*, 2nd Series, XVI (1987), pp. 69–80.
8. See Mark Brayshay, Mark Cleary and John Selwood, 'Interlocking Directorships and Trans-National Linkages within the British Empire, 1900–1930', *Area*, 37, 2 (2005), pp. 209–22.
9. See Taline Ter Minassian, *Colporteurs du Komintern, L'Union Soviétique et les minorités au Moyen-Orient*, Paris: Presses de Sciences po, 1997.
10. See Carmen Abou Jaoudé, 'Selim Takla et la fondation du ministère des Affaires étrangères', in Gérard D. Koury (ed.), *Selim Takla 1895–1945, Une contribution à l'indépendance du Liban*, Paris: Karthala, 2004, pp. 359–68.
11. Teague-Jones, *Adventures in Persia*, p. 19.

12. See John M. Munro and Martin Love, 'The Nairn Way', *Saudi Aramco World*, 32, 4 (July–Aug. 1981), and John M. Munro, *The Nairn Way*, New York: Caravan Books of Delmar, 1980.

13. William Holz, 'The Little House on the Desert', *Saudi Aramco World* (Nov.–Dec. 1984), pp. 28–33.

14. NA, AVIA 2/1867, Damascus–Baghdad Air Route: proposals for development by Nairn Eastern Transport Company (1929).

15. Teague-Jones, *Adventures in Persia*, p. 22.

16. Zobeida was also the name of Caliph Harun al Rashid's favourite wife.

17. Ibid. p. 25.

18. Ibid. p. 31.

19. Ibid. pp. 53–4.

20. Ibid. pp. 54–5.

21. Ibid. p. 68.

22. Ibid. pp. 71–2.

23. Ibid. p. 77.

24. Ibid. p. 95.

25. See Ter Minassian, T., *Colporteurs du Komintern, L'Union Soviétique et les minorités*, p. 101 onwards.

26. Ibid. p. 98.

27. Val Hennessy, 'Give the Girl a Vodka', *You*, 23 Oct. 1988, p. 82.

28. See Yann Richard, *L'Iran, Naissance d'une république islamique*, Paris: Editions de la Martinière, 2006, pp. 186–7. For a detailed and nuanced analysis of British involvement in Reza Khan's rise to power, see Michael P. Zirinsky, 'Imperial Power and Dictatorship: Britain and the Rise of Reza Shah, 1921–1926', *International Journal of Middle-East Studies*, 24, 4 (Nov. 1992), pp. 639–63.

29. Teague-Jones, *Adventures in Persia*, p. 113.

30. Ibid. pp. 113–14.

31. Ibid. pp. 115–16.

32. Ibid. p. 131.

33. Ibid. p. 133.

34. The numbers of Armenians deported during the era of Shah Abbas have been variously estimated by historians as ranging from 50,000 to 300,000. See Michel Morineau, 'Questionnaire pour les Arméniens aux XVIIe et XVIIIe siècles. Présence, position et place dans l'oekoumène économique', in Sushil Chaudhury and Kéram Kévonian (eds), *Les Arméniens dans le commerce asiatique au début de l'ère moderne*, Paris: Editions de la MSH, 2007, p. 23.

35. Teague-Jones, *Adventures in Persia*, p. 143.

36. Ibid. p. 162.

37. Ibid. p. 167.

38. NA, BT 196/33, railway construction in Persia.

39. Teague-Jones, *Adventures in Persia*, pp. 190–1.

40. Ibid. p. 201.

41. GRO overseas, Consular Index, Marriage 1931–5, vol. 27, p. 179, Consulate Cairo, Sinclair-Danecker.

42. BL, IOR, MSS C 313/14, f. 161. Notes on Harris B. Ellis, *Heritage of the Desert*.

43. BL, IOR, MSS C 313/54, 'The Fate of the Temple of Philae, An Archaeological Tragedy', signed by Ronald Sinclair, member of the Royal Geographical Society.

44. BL, IOR, MSS C 313/14, ff. 64–5. Substance of a talk at the Rotary Club of Union City, New Jersey.

45. Morton B. Stratton, 'British Railways and Motor Roads in the Middle-East, 1918–1930', *Economic Geography*, 20, 2 (Apr. 1944), p. 116.

46. BL, IOR, MSS C 313/16, f. 81. The air route to India: some experiences and criticisms by a recently arrived passenger.

47. BL, IOR, MSS C 313/16, ff. 68–70.

48. The author is deeply grateful to Laurent Deshayes for his expert knowledge of Tibet and for his detailed and accurate comments. Teague-Jones's film can be seen in relation to the cinematic oeuvre of the period. See Peter H. Hansen, 'The Dancing Lamas of Everest: Cinema, Orientalism and Anglo-Tibetan Relations in the 1920s', *American Historical Review*, 101, 3 (1996), pp. 712–47.

49. See Alex McKay, *Tibet and the British Raj: The Frontier Cadre, 1904–1947*, London: Curzon, 1997, p. 87.

50. See Hsiao-Ting Lin, *Tibet and Nationalist China's Frontier: Intrigues and Ethnopolitics, 1928–1949*, Vancouver, Toronto: UBC Press, 2006, p. 126.

51. Alistair Lamb in his foreword to Julie G. Marshall, *Britain and Tibet 1765–1947: A Select Annotated Bibliography of British Relations with Tibet and the Himalayan States including Nepal, Sikkim and Bhutan*, London: Routledge, 2005, pp. XV–XVI.

8. RONALD SINCLAIR IN AMERICA (1941–60)

1. NA, FO 366/2129. Staff at Her Majesty Consulate-General, New York, British Consulate General, 30 Sep. 1946, Francis E. Evans (British Consul, NY) to M.S. Henderson, FO.

2. Ibid.

3. Nigel West, *MI5, British Security Service Operations 1909–1945*, London: The Bodley Head, 1981, pp. 16–17.

4. William Stephenson, 31 Dec. 1945, foreword to the report of British Security Coordination, see British Security Coordination, *The Secret History of British Intelligence in the Americas, 1940–1945*, introduction by Nigel West, New York: Fromm International, 1999, p. XXI.

5. Ibid. p. 282.

6. BL, IOR, MSS 313/20, *Khyber Blood-Feud*, pp. 137–8.

7. René Girault and Robert Frank, *Turbulente Europe et nouveaux mondes, 1914–1941*, Paris: Masson, 1988, p. 263.

8. NA, WO 32/9590, Leased Bases American order of battle, 1941–2.

9. Ibid.

10. IWM, Sinclair Papers, 67/329/1. Bermuda, p. 1.

11. IWM, 67/329/1, Sinclair papers, Bermuda. Ronald Sinclair to DSC, 29 June 1941.

12. British Security Coordination, *The Secret History of British Intelligence in the Americas*, pp. 354–5.

13. IWM, 67/329/1, Sinclair Papers, Bermuda, p. 2.

14. Ibid. p. 4.

15. Ibid. p. 5.

16. Ibid. pp. 6–7.

17. Ibid. pp. 7–8.

18. Ibid. p. 10.
19. IWM, 67/329/1, Sinclair Papers, Bermuda, 23 June 1941.
20. IWM, 67/329.1, Sinclair Papers, Bermuda, Recommendation, p. 2.
21. IWM, 67/329/1, Sinclair Papers. Role of the Royal Navy in Caribbean Security, New York, 9 July 1941.
22. NA, FCO 57/377. Self-recommendation for award by Ronald Sinclair. Ronald Sinclair to G.G. Collins (Protocol and Conference Department, Foreign Office), 15 Nov. 1972.
23. Walter Wren was one of the founders of BSC.
24. IWM, Sinclair Papers, 67/329/1, Sinclair Papers, Trinidad.
25. See Patrick French, *Liberty or Death: India's Journey to Independence and Division*, London: Harper Collins, 1997, p. 140.
26. See Bernard Droz, *Histoire de la décolonisation au XXe siècle*, Paris: Seuil, 2006, pp. 76–7.
27. Ibid.
28. See French, *Liberty or Death*, p. 132.
29. Ibid. p. 101.
30. BL, IOR, L/PJ/12/251. Soviet espionage in India: report on a secret mission.
31. BL, IOR, L/PJ/12/251, f. 64. Sir David Petrie (DIB) to Major Sir John Wallinger (IPI), Delhi, 11 Feb. 1926.
32. BL, IOR, L/PJ/12/315, File 1332/27. Russian Society for Promotion of Cultural Relations, VOKS in India, 25 Feb. 1929.
33. BL, IOR, L/PJ/12/652, File 1993/42, f. 13. US office of OSS: IPI's views on publications and co-operations with representatives in India, 10 May 1943.
34. NA, FCO 57/377. Self-recommendation for award by Ronald Sinclair. Ronald Sinclair to G.G. Collins, 15 Nov. 1972.
35. BL, IOR, MSS 313/17, f. 4, London, 21 Dec. 1944.
36. BL, IOR, L/PJ/12/487, File 262/35. India League of America, f. 55, 16 Oct. 1943.
37. BL, IOR, L/PJ/12/487, File 262/35, India League of America, f. 66.
38. Olaf Caroe, the author of *Wells of Power*, on the subject of petroleum and the Persian Gulf, of *Soviet Empire* on Stalin's nationalities policy in Central Asia and of a book about the Pathans, is the subject of a book by Peter John Brobst, *The Future of the Great Game: Sir Olaf Caroe, India's Independence and the Defence of Asia*, Akron, OH: The University of Akron Press, 2005.
39. BL, IOR, L/PJ/12/487, File 262/35, India League of America, ff. 67–9.
40. BL, IOR, L/PJ/12/487, File 262/35, f. 177. India League of America, 25 Sep. 1944.
41. BL, IOR, L/PJ/12/487, File 262/35, ff. 180–2, India League of America, 14 Sep. 1944.
42. BL, IOR, L/PJ/12/487, File 262/35, f. 193. Indian League of America, 5 Sep. 1944.
43. BL, IOR, L/PJ/12/487, File 262/35, f. 227. India League of America, the Indian Problem and American Politics, 28 Dec. 1944.
44. BL, IOR, L/PJ/12/487, File 262/35, f. 200.
45. BL, IOR, L/PJ/12/487, File 262/35, f. 234. India League of America. 'India Independence Day' Dinner, 29 Jan. 1945.
46. Ibid.
47. NA, FCO, 57/377, self-recommendation for award by Ronald Sinclair, 9 Oct. 1972.
48. BL, IOR, MSS C 313/19, f. 2. New York schoolteachers and India, 22 Mar. 1945.
49. BL, IOR, MSS 313/16, ff. 28–32. Manuscript on the reverse of a document entitled 'The Lion and the Tiger in India and Persia'.
50. See Droz, *Histoire de la décolonisation au XXe siècle*, p. 132.

51. See French, *Liberty or Death*, p. 339.

52. NA, FCO, 57/377. Paul Patrick (India Office, Whitehall) to Ronald Sinclair, 14 Aug. 1947.

53. See French, *Liberty or Death*, pp. 339–40.

54. BL, MSS C 313/12, f. 20. M.A.H. Ispahani to Ronald Sinclair, New York, 27 Jan. 1948.

55. BL, IOR, MSS C 313/12, f. 23. Paul Patrick to Ronald Sinclair, 25 Sep. 1948.

56. Val Hennessy, 'Give the Girl a Vodka', *You*, 23 Oct. 1988, p. 82.

57. About the parallel and indeed synchronic concepts of Pakistan and Israel as religious nation-states, the reader must refer to Faisal Devji, *Muslim Zion: Pakistan as a Political Idea*, London: Hurst, 2013.

58. BL, MSS C 313/18, f. 47. Ronald Sinclair to S.M. Haq, press attaché at the embassy of Pakistan in Washington, 7 July 1959.

59. BL, IOR, MSS 313/15, ff. 16–25. Ronald Sinclair, 'Pakhtunistan: Design for an Aggression'.

60. Ibid.

61. Ibid.

62. Ibid.

63. Ibid.

EPILOGUE

1. A.M. Ross-Smith, 'A Case for Exoneration', *Daily Telegraph*, 11 Apr. 1983.

2. BL, IOR, MSS C 313/20, Ronald Sinclair, *Khyber Blood-Feud: A Tale of the Afghan Border*, foreword.

3. Ibid. f. 135.

4. Ibid. f. 157.

INDEX

INDEX

INDEX

Cologne, 59; Hanover, 57; navy of, 57; Ohlendorf, 57

Ghadr Revolt: 219; IPI surveillance of, 219–20

Ghani, Abdul: 200

Ghazanfar-es-Saltaneh: Sheikh of Borazjan, 58

Gollancz: personnel of, 3, 5, 175

Gordon, A.: 70, 92

Graz, Des: 216–17

Great Game: 8, 48, 75, 106, 108, 204, 223, 233, 237, 247; Anglo-Russian Convention (1907), 7, 37, 50–1; concept of, 7

Greco-Turkish War (1919–22): 163; Battle of Afion-Karahisar (1922), 164; Battle of Sakaria (1921), 166

Greece: 163; military of, 166

Grey, Colonel: background of, 69

Griffith, Sanford: 244

Gulf of Aden: 33

Gulf of Oman: 33, 61, 199

Gulghandanian, Abraham: head of National Armenian Council, 111

Haines, Captain: 94

Hamun, Lake: 67–8

Haq, S.M.: correspondence of, 238

Harding Stan: 132

Hathaway, Sibyl: 244

Hennessy, Val: 236

Himalayas (mountains): 202–4

Hindu Kush (mountain range): 37, 102

Hinduism: 29, 88, 234

Hirtzel, Sir Arthur: 31, 56, 172; influence of, 168–9

Hitler, Adolf: accession to power (1933), 195

Hovsepiants: 71

Hummet: members of, 153

Hungary: Budapest, 6; Revolution (1956), 6

Hussain, Gulab: 72; background of, 73

Hussain: Sheikh of Kutar, 58

Hussein of Mecca, Sharif: family of, 196

Hyde, Captain: 216–17

Ibn Bassam: 178

Ievlev, Woldmar: 17

IG Farben: 208

Ijenlew, Alexei: 17

Ilintovich, Vladimir: 17

Imperial Airways: 177; plane fleet of, 179, 200

Imperial Bank of Persia: branches of, 54–5, 177, 189; founding of (1889), 176

Imperial War Museum: 2, 123; collections of, 60, 193–4, 216

imperialism: 131; American, 131, 217; British, 6, 106, 116–18, 129, 133, 136, 176, 226, 233; European, 131; French, 118; official, 31; White Russian, 151

India: 8, 34, 37, 39, 50, 56, 59–61, 104, 108, 123–4, 128, 156, 162, 174–5, 193–5, 198, 200, 204, 207–8, 217, 221, 227, 240, 243, 247; Assam, 204; Bengal Famine (1943), 219, 228; Bombay, 175; borders of, 38; British Raj (1858–1947), 2, 5, 20, 28, 34, 36, 48, 170, 203–4, 218, 220, 234, 238; Colony of Aden, 33; Congress, 30; Delhi, 29, 35, 56–7, 65–6, 69, 73; Ferozepur, 30–1; government of, 35, 174, 203, 205–6; Great Rebellion (1857–8), 28; Hindu population of, 29, 219, 234; Independence of (1947), 233–4; Indian Civil Service (ICS), 30–2; Indian Political Service, 28–9, 31–4, 223; military of, 31–3, 41, 50, 68, 70, 81, 88, 98, 101, 235; Muslim population of, 29–30, 170, 219, 234; New Delhi, 27, 209, 222, 247; North West Frontier Province, 3, 7–8, 27, 32–4, 36–41, 44–6, 54, 62, 168, 236, 244, 246–7; Partition (1947), 28, 30, 33–4, 221, 234, 239; Phillaur, 29; Punjab, 28–30, 34; Sikh population of, 29; Simla, 65–7, 72, 123, 163; Waziristan, 3, 39, 42

India League of America: 223, 229; members of, 224–5

India League of London: 222

Indian Congress Party: 218, 224; members of, 222; 'Quit India' campaign, 219

Indian National Army: members of, 219

274